AN ILLUSTRATED GUIDE TO
THE WORLD'S
AIRLINERS

AN ILLUSTRATED GUIDE TO
THE WORLD'S
AIRLINERS

William Green and Gordon Swanborough
Airlines section by John Mowinski

Published by Arco Publishing Inc.
NEW YORK

A Salamander Book

Published by
Arco Publishing, Inc.,
215 Park Avenue South,
New York,
N.Y. 10003,
United States of America.

©1982 by Salamander Books Ltd.
27 Old Gloucester Street,
London WC1N 3AF,
United Kingdom.

All rights reserved.

ISBN 0-668 05612-6

All correspondence concerning the
content of this volume should be
addressed to Salamander Books Ltd.

This book may not be sold
outside the USA and Canada.

Contents

Credits

Authors: William Green and Gordon Swanborough are highly respected authorities on world aviation; they produce the monthly *Air International*, and have published a number of books under joint authorship. John Mowinski is a contributor to many well-known aviation journals in the United Kingdom. He currently works for British Aerospace in Kingston-upon-Thames.

Editor: Philip de Ste. Croix
Designer: Nick Buzzard

Three-view drawings:
© Pilot Press Ltd.
Color profiles:
© Salamander Books Ltd.
Photographs: The publishers wish to thank all the official international governmental archives, aircraft manufacturers and private collections who have supplied photographs for this book.

Printed in Belgium by Henri Proost et Cie.

Introduction

After a lengthy post-war period of rapid expansion and vigorous growth, the world airline industry suffered something of a set-back at the beginning of the present decade. While the underlying trend continued to be upwards, and forecasts of growth up to the end of the century were still bullish, the worldwide recession of the early 'eighties had its inevitable impact, especially as it came at the very moment that the airlines were engaged in fare-cutting battles to remain competitive and woo new business.

As a consequence of these two developments, many airlines—among them some of the longest-established and best-known major operators—were in serious financial difficulties by 1982. Mergers and bankruptcies increased sharply and the inevitable consequence was that the aircraft manufacturers in turn found their markets drying up, at least temporarily. Sharp reductions in production rates became the order of the day, and for Lockheed the cut-back made continued manufacture of the TriStar so uneconomic that it was taken off the market completely, leaving the company to absorb a large loss on the programme.

As it takes anything up to 10 years to bring a new transport aircraft from concept to revenue service, the manufacturing industry was still busily engaged, when this book was compiled, in

promoting, producing and trying to sell an extensive range of airliners that for the most part had been conceived during the 'seventies while the market was still burgeoning. All are described and illustrated, from the mighty Boeing 747 down to the third-level and commuter airliners that have played an important role in bringing air travel to smaller communities and developing nations. Among the types included, many already have a secure place in the history of air transport; others have yet to prove themselves and some, indeed, may never proceed into production.

Collectively, however, these airliners represent the finest products of one of the 20th century's most technologically advanced industries. For many years, leadership of that design and industrial activity has tended to be centred upon the US West Coast, where Boeing, McDonnell Douglas and Lockheed have made up the Big Three of jet airliner manufacturers. Increasingly, that leadership has been challenged from Europe, and the success of Airbus Industrie is apparent in this book. In more specialised fields, companies in Brazil, Canada and Australia, as well as Europe, can also claim their successes. For the air traveller, getting from A to B may have become so routine as to be boring, but producing the aircraft in which he travels is no less exciting or challenging than it has ever been.

Aérospatiale Caravelle
France

Power Plant: Two 12,600lb st (5725kgp) Rolls-Royce Avon 532R or 533R turbojets.
Performance: Max cruising speed at 25,000ft (7620m), 525mph (845km/h); best economy cruise, 488mph (785km/h); range with max payload typical reserves, 1,430mls (2300km).
Weights: Basic operating 63,175lb (28,655kg); max payload, 18,080lb (8200kg); max take-off, 110,230lb (50,000kg).
Dimensions: Span, 112ft 6in (34·30m); length, 105ft 0in (32·01m); height, 28ft 7in (8·72m); wing area, 1,579sq ft (146·7m²).

The origins of the Caravelle, which was the world's first short-to-medium range transport designed to be powered by turbojet engines, lay in a specification drawn up in 1951 by the French government civil aviation agency, SGACC. The purpose of the specification was to encourage the development in France of a commercial aircraft having export appeal and matching in technical excellence the new generation of post-war airliners that was emerging in the USA and the UK. Since the types of jet airliner already then being developed were for use over medium-to-long ranges, the SGACC decided to focus the attention of the French industry on a medium-to-short range aircraft, and the specification issued on 6 November 1951 suggested a payload of 6–7 tonnes to be carried over a range of 1,000–1,200mls (1930km) at an average speed of more than 380mph (700km/h).

From numerous projects submitted, the SGACC eventually selected – in September 1952 – the X210 design by the state-owned SNCASE company (later merged with SNCASO to form Sud Aviation, and then with Nord to form Aérospatiale). This was at first proposed with three locally-developed Atar turbojets grouped in and on the rear fuselage, but the Rolls-Royce Avon was chosen as being more reliable for early operation and as this offered considerably more power, only two were required, giving the Caravelle its unique (at the time of introduction) rear-engined layout. The

Right: An Air France Caravelle III surrounded by some of the typical ground service vehicles that attend each airport arrival. Air France put the Caravelle into service in May 1959 and purchased a total of 46 out of the overall production total of 280, but retired the last of the type on 28 March 1981, at the conclusion of a service from Amsterdam to Paris. At that time, Caravelles had totalled some 7 million flight hours in world-wide service, and more than 150 were still in service.

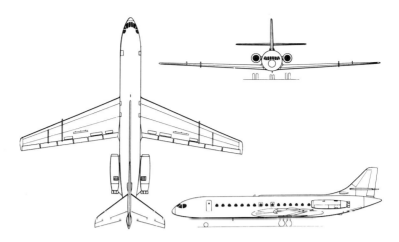

*Above: Three-view of the Aérospatiale Caravelle VI-R, the suffix
indicating the use of thrust reversers on the Avon engines.*

aerodynamic disadvantages of T-tail arrangements were avoided by locating
the tailplane just above the fuselage, and the wing was given modest
sweepback. A seating capacity of 52 was projected at this early stage, with
five-abreast seating.

Design and construction of the SNCASE transport was wholly financed
by the French government, a contract being placed on 3 January 1953 for
two flying prototypes and two structural test airframes. The designation
became SE210 and the name Caravelle was adopted in due course. First
flights were made by the two prototypes on 25 May 1955 and 6 May 1956
respectively, both having Avon RA.26 engines compared with the Avon
RA.29 intended for production models. Meanwhile, the order book had
been opened with a contract from Air France for 12 placed on 16 November
1955, and other European operators were beginning to join the queue. ▶

French certification of the Caravelle was obtained on 2 April 1958 (followed by US type approval six days later) and the first production Caravelle I flew on 18 May 1958. Deliveries to Air France began on 19 March 1959 and the first regular service was operated by the national airline on 6 May 1959, while SAS became the first to use an exported Caravelle, on 15 May. The Caravelle Is had Avon RA.29 Mk 522 engines and differed from the prototype in that the fuselage was lengthened by 4ft 7½in (1·5m) and a long extension of the dorsal fin along the top of the fuselage housed communications antennae. Various layouts were evolved, for up to a maximum of 99 passengers, 64 being a more typical figure in mixed-class arrangements. Twenty Caravelle Is were followed by 12 Caravelle IAs (the first of which flew on 11 February 1960) which had RA.29/1 Mk 526 engines, and all these early aircraft were later uprated to Caravelle IIIs with RA.29/3 Mk 527 engines, permitting the use of higher operating weights and cruising speeds. In addition, 78 Caravelle IIIs were built as such, the first flight being made on 30 December 1959.

Caravelle designations were linked at this stage with the engine designations, so that the next to appear, based on the Avon RA.29/6 Mk 531, was the Caravelle VI, again with a step-up in weights and performance, but no change of dimensions. The first Caravelle VI (the Mk III prototype converted) flew on 10 September 1960, and Sabena was the first to operate this variant, starting on 18 February 1961. A significant order for 20 Caravelles placed by United Airlines in February 1960 led to the development of the Caravelle VI-R, which had Avon 532R or 533R engines with thrust reversers and certain other features to meet US requirements, including additional wing spoilers and more powerful brakes. The first VI-R flew on 6 February 1961 and deliveries to United began in June, the first service being flown on 14 July. The designation Caravelle VI-N was then adopted to distinguish the earlier standard of aircraft without thrust reversers, production of the VI-N totalling 53 and of the VI-R, 56, this completing production of Avon-engined versions of the airliner.

The use of alternative power plants was studied by Sud Aviation for some time, and during 1960 a Caravelle III was sold to General Electric and fitted in the USA with CJ805-23C turbofans. First flown on 29 December 1960, it was known as the Caravelle VII. The same engines were specified for the projected Caravelle 10, which would have had a 3ft 4in (1-m) fuselage extension, and for the Caravelle 10A (also known as the Caravelle Horizon and then as the Caravelle Super A) which was intended specifically to meet TWA requirements, having a wing root leading edge extension, raised window line, double-slotted flaps and fin/tailplane acorn fairing. TWA ordered 20 in 1961 but cancelled in 1962 and only a prototype was flown,

on 31 August 1962. In parallel, Sud developed the Caravelle 10B (later, Super B or just Super Caravelle) with 14,000lb st (6350kgp) Pratt & Whitney JT8D-1 turbofans. A prototype flew on 3 March 1964 and production of this variant totalled 22, the first of which entered service with Finnair on 16 August 1964. This had a gross weight of 114,640lb (52,000kg), but Sterling Airways introduced the Super B at a weight of 119,050lb (54,000kg) on 23 February 1968 and the final examples, also for Sterling, had a max take-off weight of 123,460lb (56,000kg). Seating arrangements in the Super B provided for 68 to 105 passengers.

Use of the JT8D-7 engines in what was basically the Caravelle VI airframe, with Sud-designed cascade thrust reversers, led to the introduction of the Caravelle 10R, first flown on 18 January 1965. While passenger capacity remained unchanged, the payload/range and speed performance was improved; 20 were built, the first operator being Royal Jordanian Airlines (Alia) on 31 July 1965. Closely related to the 10R, the Caravelle 11R was developed for mixed passenger/cargo operations, having a large side-loading freight door and a movable bulkhead to separate freight and passenger compartments. The fuselage was lengthened, compared with the 10R, by 3ft 0½in (0·93m). First flight of the prototype was made on 21 April 1967 and the first of six entered service on 22 September 1967, the only operators being Air Afrique, Air Congo and Transeuropa.

As the final Caravelle variant, Sud produced the Caravelle 12, a stretched-fuselage version of the Super B, lengthened by 10ft 7in (3·21m) and with structural reinforcement to permit operation at weights up to 127,870lb (58,000kg), the highest for any Caravelle version. The engines were 14,500lb st (6577kgp) JT8D-9 turbofans and the maximum seating was for 140 passengers in a high-density arrangement. The Caravelle 12 was developed primarily for the IT operations of Sterling Airways, which acquired seven, the first flight being made on 29 October 1970. In addition, Air Inter bought five Caravelle 12s, delivery of the last of these in 1972 bringing production of the type to a close at a grand total of 282, of which three were unsold prototypes.

The major users of the Caravelle were Air France, which acquired 46 in all, SAS and Alitalia with 21 each, United and Sterling with 20 apiece, Iberia with 19, Air Inter with 14 and Finnair with 12. Although the Caravelle had been displaced by larger and newer types on most primary routes by the mid'seventies, it remained in service in substantial numbers in the early 'eighties on secondary routes and for charter flights.

Below: Air Inter, providing domestic air services in France, was flying 23 Caravelles in 1982, including 12 of these Super Caravelle 12s.

Aérospatiale Corvette
France

Power Plant: Two 2,310lb st (1048kgp) Pratt & Whitney (UACL) JT15D-4 turbofans.

Performance: Max cruising speed, 495mph (796km/h) at 30,000ft (9144m); best economy cruise, 391mph (630km/h) at 36,100ft (11,000m); initial rate of climb, 3,000ft/min (15·25m/sec); service ceiling, 38,000ft (11,580m); range with max payload, 1,022mls (1645km); range with max fuel (including tip tanks), 1,670mls (2690km).

Weights: Empty equipped, 7,985lb (3622kg); max payload, 2,248lb (1020kg); max take-off, 13,450lb (6100kg).

Dimensions: Span, 42ft 0in (12·80m); span (over tip tanks), 43ft 5¼in (13·24m); length, 45ft 4in (13·82m); height, 13ft 10in (4·23m); wing area, 236·8sq ft (22·00m²).

Among the smallest jet aircraft developed with third-level airline operations in view, the Corvette was also marketed as an executive jet, and was evolved especially to meet North American requirements. It originated shortly before the Sud-Nord merger into Aérospatiale, initially as a joint project between the two State-owned companies – hence the original SN600 designation. The prototype flew on 16 July 1970 but was lost during flight development, small changes being made in the SN601 second and third prototypes flown on 20 December 1972 and 7 March 1973 respectively. The first full production standard aircraft flew on 9 November 1973 and French certification was achieved on 28 May 1974.

Production deliveries were delayed by a protracted strike at UACL, Canadian source of the JT15D turbofan engines, but Air Alpes, a French local service airline, had two in service by September 1974, one of these being in full Air France livery for operation on the Lyons–Brussels route while the other operated on Air Alpes' own routes out of Paris and was joined by two more early in 1975. The Corvette 100, as the initial production version was known, had a crew of two and up to 12 individual passenger seats in two rows, and could be fitted with wing-tip tanks to extend range. The Corvette 200 was projected to have the fuselage lengthened by 6ft 7in (2·0m) to accommodate up to 18 passengers but this did not proceed beyond the design stage, and production of the Corvette 100 ended in 1977 at a total of 40. Several Corvettes were in service in Europe and North Africa in the early 'eighties for scheduled airline operation, others being used for air taxi, charter and business flying.

Right: Dual markings on this Corvette indicate that it was owned – at the time the photograph was taken – by Air Alpes but was being operated on local routes on behalf of Air France. Such arrangements between operators are frequently made to permit the use of the most suitable equipment for particular routes at particular times of the year.

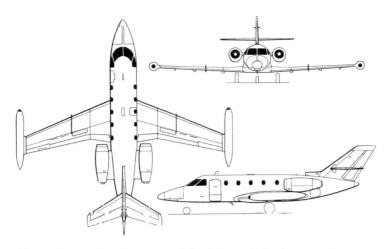

Above: Three-view drawing of the Aérospatiale Corvette short-haul airliner, production of which ended after 40 had been built.

Below: The Corvette in Air Alsace markings, with optional wing tip tanks fitted. Seating 12, the Corvette proved a little too small for the market it was designed to fulfill.

Aérospatiale (Nord) 262 Frégate and Mohawk 298
France

Power Plant: Two 1,145ehp Turboméca Bastan VII turboprops.
Performance (N 262A): Max speed, 239mph (385km/h); typical cruising speed, 233mph (375km/h); initial rate of climb, 1,200ft/min (6·1m/sec); service ceiling, 23,500ft (7160m); range with max payload, 605mls (975km); range with max fuel, 1,095mls (1760km).
Weights: (N 262A): Basic operating weight, 15,496lb (7029kg); max payload, 7,209lb (3270kg); max take-off weight, 23,370lb (10,600kg); max landing, 22,710lb (10,300kg).
Dimensions: Span: (N 262A): 71ft 10in (21·90m); (Fregate), 74ft 1¾in (22·60m); length, 63ft 3in (19·28m); height, 20ft 4in (6·20m); wing area (N 262A), 592sq ft (55.0m²); (Fregate), 601sq ft (55·79m²).

Sometimes referred to as the Aérospatiale Frégate but in fact better known as the Nord 262, this commuter transport had its origins in a design by the well-known French engineer Max Holste. His company, Avions Max Holste, built a prototype known as the MH-250, with Pratt & Whitney Wasp piston radial engines, as a small utility transport, and followed this with a second prototype, the MH-260, in which Turboméca Bastan turboprops were substituted for the Wasps. First flight dates for these two prototypes were 20 May 1959 and 29 July 1960 respectively. Nord Aviation (state owned and subsequently merged with Sud to form Aérospatiale) participated in production of a batch of 10 MH-260s, which were operated by

Below: One of the Nord 262s converted in the USA to Mohawk 298 standard for operation on the Allegheny Commuter network.

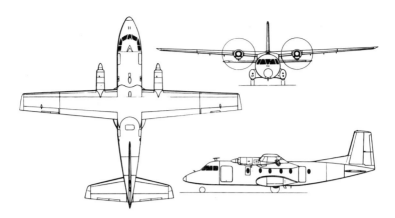

**Above: The Aérospatiale (Nord) N.262C Frégate, with Turboméca
Bastan engines, showing the extended wing-tips of this version.**

Widerøe Flyveselskap and Air Inter, and at the same time undertook development of the improved Nord 262, with a pressurized, circular-section fuselage replacing the square-section unpressurized fuselage of the MH-260.

With seating for 24–26 passengers in typical airline layouts, arranged three-abreast, the Nord 262 was aimed at the regional or third-level operator with only short sectors (up to about 600mls/970km) to serve. The prototype first flew on 24 December 1962 and was joined by three pre-production Nord 262s in certification flying, these being constructed at Châtillon-sous-Bagneux and assembled for flight testing at Melun-Villaroche. French certification was awarded on 16 July 1964, by which time the first production aircraft was ready to enter service with Air Inter, having made its first flight on 8 July 1964. Further small improvements established the full production standard with effect from the fifth airframe, the first four being designated Nord 262Bs and the main production run of 67 aircraft that followed being Nord 262As. The A model first flew early in 1965, was certificated in March and entered service in August. All production aircraft were constructed and flown at Bourges.

An early customer for the Nord 262A was Lake Central in the US, which purchased a fleet of 12 for a commuter-type operation typical of that for which the aircraft had been designed. After Lake Central had been acquired by Allegheny Airlines, the Nord 262s continued in service in the latter's colours, and in 1974 the airline embarked on a programme to fit 1,180shp Pratt & Whitney PT6A-45 turboprops in place of Bastans in nine aircraft still in the company's service. The conversion work was undertaken by Mohawk Air Services and the modified aircraft were to become known as Mohawk 298s, taking the number from FAR 298, the airworthiness regulation covering third-level operations in the USA. The first flight of a converted example was made on 7 January 1975 and after FAA certification on 19 October 1976 the Mohawk 298 entered service on the Allegheny commuter network early in 1977.

After the Nord/Sud merger into Aérospatiale, a version of the 262 with 1,145ehp Bastan VII engines in place of 1,080ehp Bastan VICs was developed, this new model also featuring wing-tips of revised design that added 2ft 3¾in (0·70m) to the overall span. First flown in July 1968, this N.262C version was named Frégate, its military equivalent being the N.262D. Certification was obtained on 24 December 1970, but the only major order for the improved Frégate came from the French Armée de l'Air, which bought 18 to join six Nord 262As acquired earlier. The Aéronavale had also bought 15 Nord 262As. Other sales were mostly in twos and threes to airlines in Europe, North Africa and Asia.

Aérospatiale/Aeritalia ATR 42
International

Power Plant: Two Pratt & Whitney Canada PW100/2 turboprops each rated at 2,000shp for take-off.

Performance: Max cruising speed, 319mph (513km/h); initial rate of climb, 1,860ft/min (9·45m/sec); operating ceiling 25,000ft (7620m); range with 42 passengers and typical reserves, 840mls (1350km).

Weights: Manufacturers weight empty, 18,340lb (8319kg); operating weight empty, 20,500lb (9296kg); max zero fuel weight, 31,100lb (14,105kg); fuel load, 9,910lb (4500kg); max take-off weight, 32,440lb (14,715kg); max landing weight, 31,790lb (14,420kg).

Dimensions: Span, 80ft 7in (24·57m); length 73ft 10in (22·50m); height 24ft 9in (7·55m); wing area, 586·65sqft (54·5m²).

Agreement was reached on 29 October 1981 by the management bodies of Aérospatiale in France and Aeritalia in Italy to proceed with full-scale development of a new regional transport, the ATR 42, following the preliminary accord reached by the two companies in July 1980 for a joint study. Previously, both companies had their own project designs for aircraft in this category, respectively known as the AS 35 and the AIT 320.

As launched, the ATR 42 is a conventional high wing monoplane, with main undercarriage units housed in fuselage-side blisters and the tailplane mounted high on the fin (but not quite as a "T"). The aircraft has been sized for a basic 42-seat layout, four-abreast at a 32in (81cm) pitch; this allows a maximum of 49 seats at 30in (76cm) pitch but there is a project for a stretched ATR 42-200 with a basic layout for 60 passengers. Market studies conducted during the design definition phase showed a potential need for 2,090 civil aircraft in the 30/49-seat category, and another 1,670 in the 50/70-seat class in the period up to year 2000. Assuming that the ATR 42 could claim 17–24 per cent of this market, sales of 380–515 of the basic variant were anticipated by the manufacturers, plus 260–385 examples of the stretched ATR 42-200.

To these totals could be added about 30 of the basic model for military use, plus 140–180 if a cargo variant is developed, with rear-loading ramps for military and civil needs. Thus, total sales of between 810 and 1,110 ATR 42s were foreseen, although the financial estimates were based on the sale

Right: An impression of the Aérospatiale/Aeritalia ATR 42 regional transport is given by this model photograph, showing the configuration that had been adopted at the time the programme was launched towards the end of 1981. To fly for the first time in the summer of 1984, the ATR 42 represents a fusing of independent but similar design projects begun in the mid-seventies.

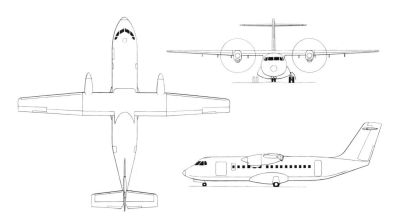

Above: The Aérospatiale/Aeritalia ATR 42 regional transport, showing its conventional high-wing layout with a T-tail arrangement.

of 450 basic and 300 stretched aircraft. At the time of the programme launch some 33 companies had shown a positive interest in the ATR 42 and 14 of these had paid deposits on conditional orders for 50 aircraft, with another six on option, the majority of these initial customers being in North and Central America.

The joint agreement provided for launching costs and manufacturing to be split equally between France and Italy, although provision was made for other partners to join Aérospatiale and Aeritalia in due course. While Aeritalia was building the fuselage and tail unit of the ATR 42, Aérospatiale was responsible for the wing, power plant, flight deck and — for all civil aircraft — final assembly and flight testing at Toulouse. A second final assembly line may be established in due course by Aeritalia in Naples, exclusively to handle the military and commercial cargo variants.

The Pratt & Whitney PW100 turboprop selected to power the ATR 42 is a developed version that will offer a maximum take-off power of 2,000shp — some 6·5 per cent more than the PW1120 specified for the de Havilland Canada Dash 8. Flight testing of the ATR 42 itself is to begin in August 1984, with the second example flying in October, and certification expected in the third quarter of 1985, with deliveries starting in December of that year.

Aérospatiale/BAC Concorde
International

Power Plant: Four 38,050lb st (17,260kgp) Rolls-Royce/SNECMA Olympus 593 Mk 610 turbojets with silencers and reversers.
Performance: Max cruising speed, 1,450mph (2333km/h) at 54,500ft (16,600m); best range cruise, Mach = 2·05; service ceiling about 60,000ft (18,288m); range with max payload, 3,050mls (4900km); range with max fuel, 4,490mls (7215km).
Weights: Basic operating, 170,000lb (77,110kg); typical payload, 25,000lb (11,340kg); max take-off, 400,000lb (181,400kg); max landing, 240,000lb (108,860kg).
Dimensions: Span, 84ft 0in (25·60m); length, 203ft 11½in (62·17m); height, 40ft 0in (12·19m); wing area, 3,856sq ft (358·25m²).

Although the Tupolev Tu-144 was first to fly and first to reach supersonic speed during its flight test programme, the Concorde was the world's first supersonic airliner to enter regular service carrying revenue passengers. When that milestone was reached early in 1976, just over 20 years had elapsed since the first steps were taken in Britain that were to lead to development of an SST (supersonic transport) and the creation of an Anglo-French programme to build and test such an aircraft.

Preliminary design work undertaken by British companies and government agencies in 1955 led to the setting up in 1956 of a Supersonic Transport Aircraft Committee (STAC) to study the feasibility of an SST. Among the specific project studies looked at by STAC was the Bristol Type 198 — a design number covering several different aircraft configurations of which the most favoured came to be a slender delta-winged layout with eight engines and able to operate across the North Atlantic at Mach = 2·0. Through a process of continuous refinement, this evolved into the smaller Bristol 223, with four engines and 110 seats for London—New York operation.

While this work went on in Britain, a similar process was under way in France, leading by 1961 to evolution of a project called the Super Caravelle that was strikingly similar to the Bristol 223. This similarity of project and objective facilitated a merging of the designs, at government behest, and a protocol of agreement was signed between Britain and France on 29 November 1962, since which time Concorde has been a joint project, costs

Right: Concorde 206, registered G-BOAA, was the second example to join British Airways and is seen here in the climb to cruising altitude, with the nose raised. Seven Concordes were serving with British Airways in 1982 and seven with Air France, but both airlines had ceased, on economic grounds, operating Concordes on all but the North Atlantic routes to New York, Washington and Mexico City.

18

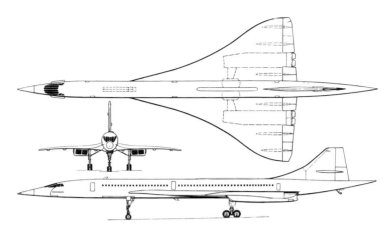

***Above:** Three-view of the Aérospatiale/BAC Concorde in its final production configuration; the prototypes had a shorter fuselage.*

and work being equally shared. Principal airframe companies were BAC (which had absorbed Bristol) and Aérospatiale (incorporating Sud) and the engine companies were Rolls-Royce (which had meanwhile acquired the Bristol Siddeley engine company in which Concorde's Olympus engines originated) and SNECMA.

The Concorde programme was handled in a number of stages, embracing the construction and testing of two prototypes, known as Concorde 001 and Concorde 002; two pre-production aircraft, originally known as Concorde 01 and 02 and subsequently as Concorde 101 and 102; and a production sequence commencing with Concorde 201. Production of an initial batch of 16 aircraft was authorized by the two governments and production of major airframe and engine components was divided between companies in Britain and France without duplication. Separate final assembly lines were set up at Toulouse and Filton, alternate aircraft being assembled in Britain and France.

Concorde 001 made its first flight from Toulouse on 2 March 1969, its first supersonic flight on 1 October 1969 and the first excursion to Mach = 2 ►

on 4 November 1970 (on its 102nd flight). Concorde 002 joined the programme from Filton on 9 April 1969 and these two aircraft built up hours and experience steadily throughout 1970, 1971, 1972 and 1973. With a design gross weight of 326,000lb (148,000kg); these prototypes were slightly smaller than the production standard, which introduced lengthened front and rear fuselages, revised nose visors, changes to the wing geometry and uprated engines.

These new features appeared progressively on Concorde 101, first flown from Toulouse on 17 December 1971, and Concorde 102, flown from Filton on 10 January 1973. Design gross weight was 385,000lb (174,640kg) and versions of the Olympus 593 engine fitted were rated at 38,050lb st (17,260kgp) compared with the 38,285lb st (14,890kgp) at which the prototypes had begun. Production aircraft, represented by Concorde 201 flown from Toulouse on 6 December 1973 and Concorde 202 flown from Filton on 13 February 1974, have Olympus 593 Mk 610 engines and 400,000 lb (181,400kg) gross weight. The cabin permits 128 passengers to be carried in a 2+1 arrangement, or up to 144 in high density layouts.

Concordes 203 and 204 flew on 31 January and 27 February 1975 respectively and were extensively used for development flying and route-proving, leading to the certification of the Concorde for full passenger-carrying operation on 13 October 1975 (in France) and 5 December 1975

Below: One of the Air France fleet of Concordes climbs away from the runway at the final assembly centre at Toulouse.

(in the UK). Concordes 205 and 206 flew on 25 October and 5 November 1975 and were used to inaugurate SST scheduled services on 21 January 1976, by British Airways from London to Bahrein and by Air France from Paris to Dakar and Rio de Janeiro. Operations from London and Paris across the North Atlantic to Washington (Dulles) began on 24 May 1976, and on the important routes to New York from Paris and London in December 1977. In the same month, a joint British Airways/Singapore Airlines service from London to Singapore via Bahrein was also launched, but was not establshed on a regular basis until early 1979. This service was suspended in 1980.

The last two Concordes made their first flights on 26 December 1978 (No 215 in France) and 20 April 1979 (No 216 in Britain) and were eventually to be taken into the Air France and British Airways fleets respectively. On 12 January 1979, Braniff began operating Concordes between Washington and Dallas/Fort Worth, leasing aircraft time from Air France and British Airways at the end of transatlantic services into Washington and using its own crews for the subsonic overland flights. Braniff was forced to terminate this arrangement in June 1980, however, as an economy measure; this left Concordes operating only on the BA routes from London to New York and Washington, and the Air France routes from Paris to those two cities and to Rio de Janeiro.

Below: Viewed through the heat haze on the runway, a Concorde prepares for take-off, its nose drooped to improve the pilots' view.

Below: Concorde 206 G-BOAA in the livery in which it entered service with British Airways.
Left: Concorde 205 F-BFVA in Air France colours.

F-BVFA

G-BOAA

Ahrens AR 404
International

Power Plant: Four 420shp Allison 250-B17C turboprops.
Performance: Cruising speed, 201mph (324km/h) at 800ft (244m) on max continuous power; initial rate of climb 1,200ft/min (6·5m/sec); service ceiling 18,000ft (5486m); range, 850naut mls (1574km) with standard tankage, 1,200naut mls (2223km) with max fuel.
Weights: Empty, 9,980lb (4527kg); max payload, 8,520lb (3865kg); payload with full standard fuel and two crew, 4,325lb (1962kg); max take-off weight, 18,500lb (8390kg).
Dimensions: Span, 66ft 0in (20·12m); length, 54ft 9in (16·69m); height, 19ft 0in (5·79m); gross wing area, 422sq ft (39·20m²).

The AR 404 design originated during 1976 when Ahrens Aircraft Corp in California constructed a prototype, the first flight of which was made on 1 December 1976 at Oxnard. Powered by four Allison 250B-17B turboprops, the AR 404 was designed to meet the needs of developing countries for a simple, rugged cargo or passenger transport, suitable for military or civil use. The backing of the government of Puerto Rico was obtained by Ahrens for production of the AR 404 and facilities were made available at the former USAF Ramey AFB. The prototype was moved to Ramey for flight development, in the course of which (after the first six flights) it was fitted with a hydraulically retractable undercarriage.

A pre-production prototype, assembled in Puerto Rico, first flew on 26 October 1979. After a relatively short test programme, this aircraft was grounded while the full production configuration was established. With modifications, it flew again on 23 September 1981. Basic features of the design include the square-section fuselage, and the cantilever wing with a parallel chord over its 66ft (20·12m) span. The pre-production prototype introduced a lengthened fuselage with more closely-pitched windows, offering a cabin length of 28ft 0in (8·53m) of constant cross-section,

Right: Seen here on a test flight towards the end of 1981, this is the second prototype of the Ahrens AR 404 utility transport after it had been modified to represent the production configuration. A second similar example of the production model joined the flight test programme at the end of 1981, and these two aircraft were being used during 1982 to obtain FAA certification. Production of this simple but rugged transport was being backed by the government of Puerto Rico.

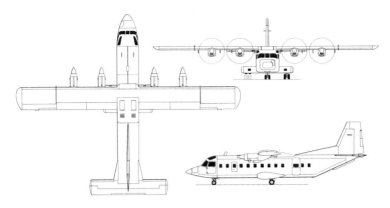

Above: This three-view drawing shows the Ahrens AR 404 in its production form, with a longer fuselage than originally planned.

behind which is a two-position loading ramp that is air-openable for paradropping of personnel or supplies. Since this second aircraft began flight testing, it has been given a larger dorsal fin, the chord of the vertical fin has been increased at the leading edge, strakes have been added between the tailplane leading edge and the fuselage side, and the nose cone has been lengthened to provide increased baggage storage, thus giving more cabin volume for passengers or freight. The AR 404 has a non-pressurized fuselage that allows for containerized cargo up to LD3 container size, or two-and-one passenger seating for up to 30 passengers with an aisle width of 15in (38cm). A fold-up seat design allows for quick convertibility.

Certification of the AR 404 to FAR Part 25 was expected in the third quarter of 1982. The company had declined to take deposits on production line positions until performance guarantees could be given, but by late 1981 letters of intent had been accepted in respect of more than 100 aircraft, for which nominal line or delivery positions have been allocated.

Airbus A300
International

The following specification refers to the A300B4-200:

Power Plant: Two General Electric CF6-50C2 turbofans rated at 52,500lb st (23,815kgp) or Pratt & Whitney JT9D-59A1 turbofans rated at 53,000lb st (24,040kgp).

Performance: Maximum operating speed (VMO) 345 knots (639km/h) CAS, MMO = 0·82; max cruising speed, 552mph (889km/h) at 31,000ft (9450m); long-range cruise 531mph (854km/h) at 33,000ft (10,060m); still-air range with max payload, 1,950mls (3140km); range with max fuel, 3,400mls (5470km).

Weights: Typical operating weight empty, 194,520lb (88,200kg); max structural payload, 78,900lb (35,800kg); max usable fuel, 108,030lb (49,000kg); max take-off weight, 347,230lb (157,500kg); max landing weight, 295,420lb (134,000kg); max zero fuel weight, 273,370lb (124,000kg).

Dimensions: Span, 147ft 1in (44·84m); length, 175ft 11in (53·62m); height 54ft 2in (16·53m); wing area, 2,800sq ft (260m²).

Entering service with Air France on 23 May 1974, the A300 was the fourth of the "wide-body" airliners to become operational, and the first of the type to be produced in Europe. It was also the first product of a truly international programme of development and production to reach commercial service, all previous international programmes having related to military aircraft.

In typical European layouts, the A300 carries 281 passengers eight-abreast (with two aisles); a mixed-class configuration carries 32 first-class passengers six-abreast and 160—200 tourist-class, while a high-density layout for Inclusive Tour operators will accommodate 345 nine-abreast. It was designed primarily for short-to-medium ranges but several possible variations of the basic design were planned from an early stage, to provide more range or greater passenger capacity in various combinations.

The Airbus project began during 1965 as an Anglo-French initiative to develop a large capacity transport for BEA and Air France; at about the same time, a group of German manufacturers combined (as Arge Airbus) to study a similar project for Lufthansa. These activities were brought together during 1967 and the three respective governments signed a Memorandum of Understanding on 26 September 1967 to cover the evolution of an Airbus-type aircraft. It was agreed that France would have design leadership and that Rolls-Royce RB.207 engines would be used; the aircraft was to be known as the A300 and the next phase of development was to be approved by the government steering committee only if orders for 75 aircraft could be foreseen. Nominated airframe contractors were Sud (later Aérospatiale), Hawker Siddeley and the German Airbus group.

By the end of 1968, the A300 was defined as an aircraft carrying up to 306 passengers in tourist-class arrangements, with a gross weight of 330,000lb (149,700kg) and powered by two 50,000lb st (22,680kgp) RB.207s. This project looked rather unattractive against the DC-10 and L.1011 TriStar which were close to being launched in the USA, and the smaller A300B proposal emerged in December 1968 with 252 passengers, a gross weight of 275,500lb (125,000kg) and British or US engines in the 45,000—50,000lb st ▶

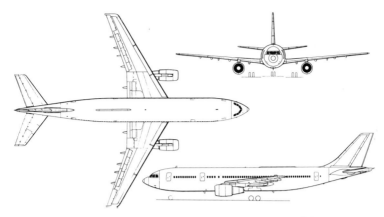

Above: The three-view depicts the A300B2; the A300B4 is dimensionally similar but carries more fuel. Larger and smaller variants have been projected.

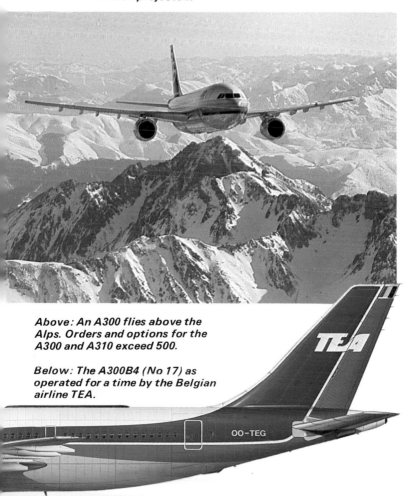

Above: An A300 flies above the Alps. Orders and options for the A300 and A310 exceed 500.

Below: The A300B4 (No 17) as operated for a time by the Belgian airline TEA.

OO-TEG

(20,410–22,680kgp) bracket. In the absence of firm airline orders, the UK government withdrew from the Airbus consortium in March 1969 but Hawker Siddeley remained in as a full risk-sharing partner, having responsibility for design and construction of the wing. France and Germany confirmed their intention to go ahead on 29 May 1969, and small shares in the programme were subsequently acquired by Spain and the Netherlands.

The final assembly line for the Airbus was set up at Toulouse, in Aérospatiale facilities, and an Aero Spacelines Guppy outsize transport was acquired to ferry components from the UK and Germany to this production centre. Basis for development was the A300B, to be powered by General Electric CF6-50A turbofans, and a series of variants from B1 to B11 had been identified up to the end of 1974. The designation reverted to A300 in 1974.

The first two examples built, making their first flights on 28 October 1972 and 5 February 1973 respectively, were to A300B1 standard as originally defined, but for production the fuselage was stretched by 8ft 9in (2·65m) and gross weight went up to 302,000lb (136,985kg). This was the A300B2, first flown on 28 June 1973 and granted French and German C of A on 15 March 1974, followed by US certification on 30 May and approval for Cat III operations on 30 September.

The second major Airbus variant was the A300B4, dimensionally similar to the B2 but with more fuel for increased range. Operating at a higher gross weight, this required the extra power of CF6-50C engines, first flown in a B2 (aircraft No 8) and then in the first B4 (aircraft No 9), these two aircraft making their first flights on 2 October 1974 and 26 December 1974, respectively. Air France became the first operator of the Airbus when it put A300B2s into service on 23 May 1974. Late in 1978, the British government concluded negotiations with France and Germany providing for British Aerospace to become a full risk-sharing partner in Airbus Industrie, with effect from 1 January 1979, since which time Britain's share has been 20 per cent of both the A300 and the new A310 (separately described).

With production of the A300B2 and B4 firmly established, further variants have been developed in response to market requirements, this also leading to a new series of designations. While early A300s were powered by the 49,000lb st (22,226kgp) CF6-50A, the 51,000lb st (23,133kgp) CF6-50C later became standard, with the more powerful CF6-50C2 (as indicated in the specification above) also available, this engine being first flown in an A300B2 demonstrator on 10 May 1978. A

Above: Air France was the first airline to operate the Airbus and now has a mixed fleet of A300B2s (illustrated) and A300B4s.

further engine option became available in 1978 when SAS ordered A300B2s with 53,000lb st (24,040kgp) Pratt & Whitney JT9D-59A1s. These engines first flew in the A300 on 28 April 1979 and 54,000lb st (24,500kgp) J19D-59Bs were also offered.

Numerical suffixes were introduced by Airbus Industrie to distinguish major versions of each series: the A300B2-100 is the basic model of the B2, and the -200 (originally B2K) has Krueger flaps on the wing root leading edges to improve the "hot and high" performance. The A300B4-100 is the basic long-range model at the weight quoted in the above specification while the B4-200 has a gross weight of 363,800lb (165,000kg) and optional extra tankage in the rear cargo hold. A mixed-traffic version, the A300C4, has a side-loading cargo door and was first flown towards the end of 1979.

During 1981, the first orders were placed for the A300 600, with deliveries (to Saudia) to start in the spring of 1984. The -600 is dimensionally the same as the B2 and B4 versions, but it incorporates the rear fuselage designed for the A310, permitting two additional seat rows in the cabin, together with many other new features designed for the A310, including a new Garrett APU, the advanced forward-facing crew cockpit or FFCC (first flown in an A300B4-200 for Garuda on 6 October 1981) and a choice of new-generation engines. These can include the 56,000lb st (25,400kgp) JT9D-7R4H and the 59,000lb st (26,762kgp) CF6-80C1, as well as versions of the Rolls-Royce RB.211-524. Weights up to 374,785lb (170,000kg) have been projected for versions of the A300-600.

By the end of 1981, the Airbus order book had just passed the 500 mark, counting firm orders and options for the A300 and the A310. Of this total, 255 orders and 62 options were for variants of the A300; deliveries by the year-end totalled 155. Of the future variants originally projected as the A300B5 to B11, the B10 had become the A310; the B designations have subsequently been dropped in favour of two new series, SA for single-aisle types, leading to the A320, separately described, and TA for the twin-aisle types, of which the most significant in 1981 were the TA9, TA11, and TA12, all of which were aimed at airline requirements for long-range and very-long-range transports.

Airbus A310
International

The following specification refers to the A310-200:

Power Plant: Two General Electric CF6-80A1 or Pratt & Whitney JT9D-7R4D1 turbofans of 48,000lb st (21,800kgp) each or CF6-80A3 or JT9D-7R4E1 turbofans of 50,000lb st (22,680kgp) each.

Performance: Design speed (VMO) 414mph (667km/h) and (MMO) 0·84; max cruising speed, 562mph (904km/h) at 33,000ft (10,060km); long-range cruise, 515mph (828km/h) at 37,000ft (11,277m); range with 214 passengers (basic aircraft) 3,740mls (6020km)

Weights: Operating weight empty, 169,500lb (76,870kg); max payload, 69,700lb (31,610kg); max take-off, 291,060lb (132,000kg); max landing 261,250lb (118,500kg); max zero fuel, 239,250lb (108,500kg).

Dimensions: Span, 144ft 0in (43·90m); length 153ft 1in (46·66m); height, 51ft 10in (15·80m); wing area, 2,357sq ft (219·0m²).

In July 1978, Airbus Industrie gained the backing of the French and German governments to launch a derivative of the A300 with a shorter fuselage and a new wing. Projected since 1974 as the A300B10, this new version was redesignated A310 and at the time of its launch it had the backing of several major airlines — notably Swissair and Lufthansa.

Final definition of the A310, during the closing months of 1978, established a fuselage that was shorter than that of the A300 by 13 standard frame sections, but with a redesign of the new fuselage contours which meant that only 11 seat rows were eliminated rather than 13. This provided for a maximum of 255 seats in a high-density arrangement, or 214 in a typical mixed-class layout with 18 seats six-abreast and 196 eight-abreast. During this period of final definition, Britain again became a full risk-sharing partner in the Airbus consortium, and British Aerospace was nominated to design, develop and manufacture the wings of the A310. This is a further evolution of the A300 wing, for which Hawker Siddeley (now part of British Aerospace) had been responsible, and features double-slotted Fowler flaps on the trailing edge and full-span leading-edge slats. Roll control is by a combination of spoilers and inboard ailerons; there are no low-speed ailerons on the outer portions of the wing.

The A310 also has a smaller tailplane, revised main landing gear and new engine pylons. A range of engine options was offered by Airbus, including versions of the Pratt & Whitney JT9D, General Electric CF6 and Rolls-Royce RB.211, and short- and medium-range versions of the A310 were proposed (as the -100 and -200 respectively). However, the -100

Right: The A310 was launched in July 1978 as a junior partner for the A300, featuring a new wing and fuselage of the same cross section and construction but slightly reduced length. Like the A300, the A310 is offered, and has been ordered, with both Pratt & Whitney and General Electric CF6 engines. The first A310 (illustrated) was rolled out at Toulouse on 16 February 1982.

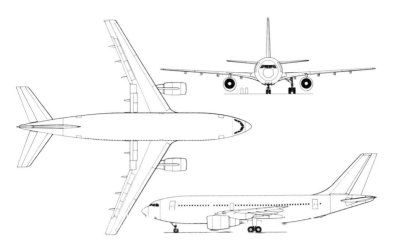

Above: The line drawing depicts the A310 in the form in which it was launched in 1978 as the second member of the Airbus family.

was subsequently dropped and the A310-300 was offered as a longer-range alternative to the basic A310-200. The two versions have identical overall dimensions and fuel capacity but differ in operating weights and therefore in the distance over which maximum payload can be carried. Maximum take-off weight of the basic A310-200 is as quoted above; that of the A310-300 is 305,500lb (138,500kg) while a further option at 319,700lb (145,000kg) is also planned.

The first firm order for A310s was confirmed by Swissair on 14 March 1979, when it contracted with Airbus for 10 aircraft and took options on 10 more. Swissair subsequently specified JT9D /R4 engines (several models of which are now on offer for the A310, at thrusts to match the various weight options). The next two customers — Lufthansa and KLM — both specified General Electric CF6-80A engines, however, and development of the A310 with these alternative power plants then proceeded in parallel. The first two A310s, Nos 162 and 172 in the overall Airbus sequence, were both in Swissair configuration, the third (No 191) was the first with CF6-80As (for Lufthansa); the fourth (No 201) was also for Lufthansa and the fifth (No 217) for Swissair. From the sixth A310 (No 224) final assembly was to be integrated with that of the A300. The first A310 was scheduled to fly at the end of March 1982 and 88 A310s were on order by the end of 1981, with 90 more on option.

Airbus A320
International

Power Plant: Two advanced technology turbofans of about 25,000 lb st (11,340kgp) each.

Performance: Typical cruising speed, 450kt (832km/h) at 35,000ft (10,670m) (Mach = 0·78); range with max payload (-100), 1,370naut mls (2538km); range with max payload (-200), 1,250naut mls (2315km); range with 154 passengers (-100), 1,910naut mls (3538km); range with 172 passengers (-200), 2,000naut mls (3700km); all ranges based on ISA no wind condition with 45-min continued cruise and 200naut mls (320km) diversion.

Weights (-100): OWE, 86,530lb (39,250kg); max weight-limited payload, 40,476lb (18,360kg); max fuel, 28,440lb (12,900kg); max take-off weight, 145,500lb (66,000kg); max landing weight 135,500lb (61,450kg); max zero fuel weight, 127,000lb (57,600kg).

(-200): OWE, 87,410lb (39,650kg); max weight-limited payload 42,815lb (19,420kg); max fuel, 41,446lb (18,800kg); max take-off weight, 158,510lb (71,900kg); max landing weight, 138,650lb (62,880kg); zero fuel weight, 130,245lb (59,080kg).

Dimensions: Span, 113ft 1½in (34·48m); length overall 122ft 7¼in (37·41m); height 38ft 7in (11·78m); wing area, 1,354sq ft (125·8m²); sweepback, 25 deg at quarter chord; aspect ratio 9·5:1.

Air France announced on 6 June 1981 that it had signed a preliminary contract with Airbus Industrie in respect of 50 A320 short/medium-range 150-seat transports, for delivery from 1986. Two days previously, Airbus had announced the "industrial launching" of the new project, third in the product line offered by the international consortium. The period of the Paris Air Show 1981 thus saw the seal of success placed upon a prolonged effort by Airbus to launch a new "150-seat twin" ahead of the potential competition, although the way in which development was to be financed, and work shared, between the partners had still to be agreed, and had not been settled up to the end of 1981. Announcing the Air France contract, which was for 25 aircraft with 25 more on option, Airbus Industrie stated that "the A320 will be produced by the present Airbus Industrie partners, Aérospatiale, Deutsche Airbus (MBB and VFW), British Aerospace and CASA, with the possible participation of other manufacturers".

The A320 was at first planned in two variants, the 130-seat -100 and 160-seat -200, these having been known in the earlier stages of development as the SA-1 and SA-2 respectively (SA indicating that they were designed for single-aisle cabin layout, compared with the twin-aisle A300, A310 and other future projects derived therefrom). In principle, the Air France contract was to cover 16 A320-100s and 34 A320-200s; the two types having identical airframes except for the fuselage lengths of 118ft 3in (36·04m) and 128ft 9in (39·24m) respectively. As design definition continued during 1981, this plan was abandoned and a single fuselage length was adopted as indicated above. The -100 and -200 designations continued in use, however, to distinguish "light" and "heavy" variants, the latter having increased fuel capacity in a centre section tank and therefore a greater range.

Based on its studies of the likely market for a 150-seat twin, and intensive discussions with airlines throughout the world, Airbus Industrie reached the conclusion that its SA-1/SA-2 proposals were generally correct in performance terms; the customers showed a strong preference for an all-new design while recognising the value of the maximum practical commonality with the A310, and also stressed fuel saving as the single most important economic parameter.

Experience with the A300 was to be used in the A320 in respect of such

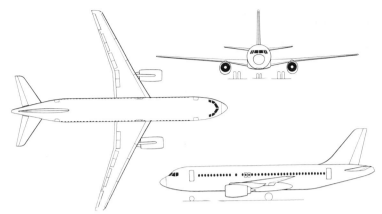

Above: This three-view shows the A320 as planned early in 1982. Earlier plans to offer two fuselage lengths had been dropped.

Below: A model of the A320 serves to show the family likeness between this project and the much larger A300 and A310.

features as low-bleed air conditioning, electrical signalling for improved engine control and monitoring, CRT displays and digital equipment on the flight deck and advanced composite materials in the structure. The flight deck, designed for two crew operation, was based on A310 experience, and systems also have A310 commonality. The wing design was new but based on research conducted in respect of the A310 using the most advanced aerodynamics to reduce fuel burn. It was being designed to have a simple but efficient high-lift system and provision for active controls to be introduced later. The tailplane also features active control stability.

The A320 requires two engines of approximately 25,000lb st (11,340kgp), and the three major engine manufacturers were all defining their positions in respect of the A320 market. As 1981 ended, Rolls-Royce appeared to have a lead through its development of the RJ500 jointly with Japan Aero Engines, the RJ500-35 being of the required thrust and expected to run in 1983, for certification early in 1986. The General Electric/SNECMA partnership, CFM International, adopted the designation CFM56-2000 for its projected derivative in this class, but a joint approach by R-R, JAE, GE and SNECMA remained an alternative possibility. Pratt & Whitney was proposing the PW-2025 as a further variant in its family of related designs derived from what was the JT10D.

Antonov An-14 and An-28
Soviet Union

The following data is for the An-28:

Power Plant: Two 970shp Glushenkov TVD-10B turboprops.

Performance: Max cruising speed, 217mph (350km/h); initial rate of climb, 2,360ft/min (12·0m/sec); single-engined climb rate, 785ft/min (4·0m/sec); range with max payload, 317mls (510km); range with max fuel, 805mls (1300km).

Weights: Empty weight, about 7,716lb (3500kg); max payload, 3,415lb (1550kg); max take-off weight, 13,450lb (6100kg).

Dimensions: Span, 72ft 7in (21·99m); length, 42ft 7in (12·98m); height, 15ft 1in (4·60m); wing area, 427·5sq ft (39·72m²).

Developed to meet an Aeroflot requirement for a small utility transport offering a higher performance and standard of comfort than the general-purpose An-2 but with comparable short take-off and landing characteristics, the An-14 *Pchelka* (Little Bee) was flown for the first time on 15 March 1958 but suffered extremely protracted development. Series manufacture did not begin until 1965, and the definitive production model bore little similarity to the prototypes. Several hundred examples of the An-14 were built, primarily for use by Aeroflot, versions including a five-seat executive transport, a light freighter, geological survey and photographic models, and an ambulance capable of accommodating six casualty stretchers and a medical attendant.

A braced high-wing monoplane with an all-metal semi-monocoque pod-and-boom fuselage and two-spar wing carrying full-span leading-edge slats and double-slotted trailing-edge flaps, the An-14 was intended for single-pilot operation.

Essentially a scaled-up, turboprop-powered derivative of the An-14, the An-28 was flown in prototype form for the first time in September 1969, but also suffered a protracted gestation, State trials not being completed until the summer of 1972 and the definitive model not appearing until early 1974 when it was publicly displayed at Sheremetyevo International Airport, Moscow.

Initially referred to as the An-14M, the An-28 retains little more than a similarity of basic configuration to the An-14 and possesses twice the capacity. During the course of development, progressive changes were made to the wing and its high-lift devices, to the tail assembly and to the

Below: The Antonov An-14 has become widely used in the light utility role in the Soviet bloc countries; this one serves in Bulgaria.

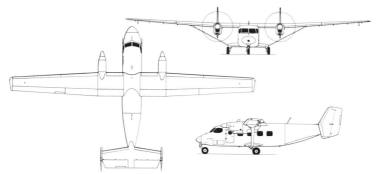

Above: Three-view drawing of the Antonov An-28, a progressive development of the An-14, with turboprops and a new fuselage.

stub wings carrying the main units of the non-retractable levered-suspension undercarriage. Originally, all three members of the undercarriage were retractable, the main members retracting into fairings at the base of the fuselage and the nosewheel retracting aft into the fuselage nose, but all examples of the An-28 subsequent to the first aeroplane have featured fixed landing gear.

Features shared by the An-14 include hinged wing trailing edges comprising double-slotted flaps extending to the wingtips and incorporating single-slotted ailerons, and wide-tread low-pressure balloon tyres to permit operation of the aircraft at its normal loaded weight from unimproved strips of 600–650 yards (550–600m) length. The passenger cabin has up to 17 seats three-abreast (two to starboard and one to port), the seats folding back against the walls when the aircraft is operated in the freighter or mixed passenger/cargo rôles. Access to the main cabin is provided by clamshell-type doors under the upswept rear fuselage.

The prototype of the An-28* and the first pre-production example were powered by 810shp Isotov TVD-850 turboprops, but the latter was re-engined in April 1975 with 960shp Glushenkov TVD-10 engines and these were subsequently confirmed for use in production models. After the An-28 had been selected for large scale production in 1978, manufacture was entrusted to the PZL-Mielec factory in Poland, from which deliveries were expected to begin in 1982, initially to meet Aeroflot's needs for a replacement for the An-2 biplane. A production rate of 200 a year was expected to be achieved by 1983.

Below: An early example of the Antonov An-28, large-scale production of which was getting under way in Poland during 1982.

Antonov An-24, An-26, An-30, An-32
Soviet Union

The following specification relates to the An-24V *Seriiny II:*

Power Plant: Two 2,500ehp Ivchenko AI-24 *Seriiny II* turboprops.

Performance: Max cruise, 310mph (498km/h); best-range cruise, 280mph (450km/h) at 19,700ft (6000m); initial climb, 1,515ft/min (7·7m/sec); service ceiling, 27,560ft (8400m); range (max payload and reserves), 341mls (550km), (max fuel and 45 min reserves), 1,490mls (2400km).

Weights: Empty, 29,320lb (13,300kg); max take-off, 46,300lb (21,000kg).

Dimensions: Span, 95ft 9½in (29·20m); length, 77ft 2½in (23·53m); height, 27ft 3½in (8·32m); wing area, 807·1sq ft (74·98m²).

Among the most widely used and most-exported of Soviet commercial transports, having been in continuous production for some 15 years with more than 1,000 delivered in a variety of versions, the An-24 short-range transport is numerically the most important airliner in the Aeroflot inventory, in which it has succeeded the piston-engined Ilyushin Il-14.

Flown for the first time in April 1960, the An-24 was intended originally to accommodate 32—40 passengers but during the course of prototype construction a change in the Aeroflot requirement resulted in the aircraft being developed as a 44-seater. A second prototype and five pre-production aircraft, including two for static and fatigue testing, were employed for manufacturer's and State trials, and Aeroflot inaugurated services with the An-24 over the routes between Moscow, Voronezh and Saratov in September 1963. The initial production 44-seater was supplanted at an early stage by the 50-seat An-24V which gave place in turn, in 1968, to the An-24V *Seriiny II* embodying various refinements including an extended centre section chord with enlarged flaps, increasing gross wing area to 807·1sq ft (74·98m²) from 779·9sq ft (72·46m²). This version also used AI-24 *Seriiny II* turboprops, which, having water injection and a similar rating to the initial AI-24 engines, could be replaced by 2,820ehp AI-24T turboprops to meet specific hot-and-high operating requirements. The *Seriiny II* aircraft had a normal flight crew of three and standard accommodation for 50 passengers in one-class four-abreast seating, but various optional mixed passenger/freight and convertible cargo/passenger arrangements were offered.

Specialized freighters generally similar to the An-24V *Seriiny II* are the An-24T and An-24RT, the latter having a Tumansky RU-19-300 auxiliary turbojet of 1,984lb (900kg) thrust in the starboard engine nacelle for use under hot-and-high conditions, permitting take-off with full payload from airfields at altitudes up to 9,840ft (3000m) above sea level and in temperatures up to ISA+30°C. Both models had provision for five crew members and the normal passenger door at the rear of the cabin deleted and replaced by a ventral freight door which hinged upward and aft for cargo loading. A 3,300lb (1500kg) capacity electric winch was fitted to hoist cargo through the ventral door and an electrically- or manually-operated 9,920lb (4500kg) capacity conveyor was installed in the cabin floor. The An-24RV was similar to the *Seriiny II* passenger transport apart from having a similar auxiliary turbojet to that installed in the An-24RT.

A further specialized version was the An-24P (*Protivopozharny* or, simply, *Pozharny*) intended for fighting forest fires. First tested in October 1971, the An-24P carried parachutists and fire-fighting equipment which could be dropped in the vicinity of a fire.

Derived from the An-24RT and intended for both military and civil applications, the An-26 was evolved during the late 'sixties with production deliveries commencing in 1969. Its principal new feature was a redesigned rear fuselage of "beaver-tail" configuration incorporating a two-position door which could be lowered to form a conventional ramp for the loading of

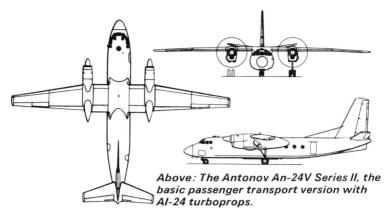

Above: The Antonov An-24V Series II, the basic passenger transport version with AI-24 turboprops.

Below: The Antonov An-24V, one of a family of designs that achieved considerable export success in civil and military versions.

vehicles, or swung down and forward beneath the fuselage to permit straight-in loading of freight from ground vehicles at truck-bed height. The An 26 is primarily used in military guise but can be easily adapted for passenger-carrying.

A specialized aerial survey derivative of the An-24RT, the An-30 initiated its test programme during the summer of 1973 and has entered service with Aeroflot for mapping tasks in the remoter areas of the Soviet Union. The An-30 is structurally identical with the An-24RT apart from the forward fuselage which has been entirely redesigned.

For its primary task of aerial photography for map-making, the An-30 is provided with four large survey cameras mounted in the cabin and operated by remote control by the crew photographer. Equipment includes a pre-programmed computer to control aircraft speed, altitude and direction throughout the mission. Five camera hatches are provided as well as hatches permitting the use of laser, thermographic, gravimetric, magnetic and geophysical sensors. A crew of seven is normally carried and sufficient oxygen to permit a high-altitude mission of eight hours endurance.

A further derivative of the basic aircraft appeared in 1977 as the An-32, this being the An-26 powered by two 4,250shp AI-20M engines and having some aerodynamic changes to handle the large increase in power. The An-32 was intended primarily as a military freighter for use at high-altitude and high-ambient-temperature airfields and although the prototype bore Aeroflot markings, this variant is unlikely to be used for any but highly-specialized civil operations.

Beechcraft Commuter C99
USA

The following specification relates to the C99.
Power Plant: Two 715shp Pratt & Whitney PT6A-36 turboprops.
Performance: Max cruising speed, 285mph (459km/h) at 8,000ft (2440m); initial rate of climb, 2,221ft/min (11·3m/sec); service ceiling, 28,080ft (8559m); range with max payload, 665mls (1070km), range with max fuel, 910mls (1466km).
Weights: Empty equipped, 5,872lb (2663kg), max take-off, 10,900lb (4944kg).
Dimensions: Span, 45ft 10½in (14·00m); length, 44ft 6¾in (13·58m); height, 14ft 4¼in (4·38m); wing area, 279·7sq ft (25·98m²).

The Beech 99 Airliner was evolved from the original piston-engined Queen Air during 1965, primarily for commuter airline use. In this rôle, it carried up to 15 passengers in single seats each side of the central aisle, and an air-stair was incorporated in the main cabin door. A wide cargo-loading door in the fuselage adjacent to the main passenger door was offered as an option to facilitate the use of the Beech 99 in mixed passenger-cargo operations.

Beech flew a long-fuselage prototype of the Queen Air in December 1965, and PT6A-20 turboprops were fitted in this aircraft in July 1966, providing a basis for FAA Type Approval to be obtained on 2 May 1968, with production deliveries beginning at the same time. Initial aircraft were powered by 550shp PT6A-20 engines, with 680shp PT6A-27s introduced in the Model 99A. Beech temporarily stopped production in 1975 after 164 had

Below: The prototype of the Beechcraft C99, a modernised version of the original Model 99 which re-entered production in 1980.

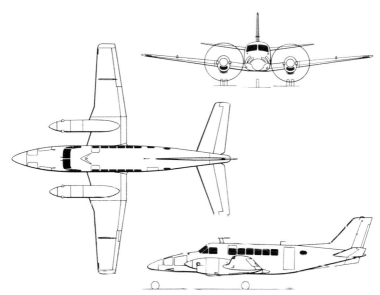

Above: Three-view of the Beech 99, developed as a 15-seat commuter airliner and widely used as such in the USA.

been built, and in 1979 announced its intention to build the improved C99 version, with PT6A-36 engines. Dimensionally the same as the 99A, the Commuter C99 first flew on 20 June 1980, the prototype being a converted Model 99. Certification was obtained in July 1981 and first customer deliveries were made on the 30th of that month to Christman Air System and Sunbird Airlines.

Beechcraft Commuter 1900
USA

Power Plant: Two flat rated, 1,000shp Pratt & Whitney PT6A-65 turbo-props.

Performance: Max cruising speed, 303mph (487km/h) at 10,000ft (3050m); initial rate of climb, 2,280ft/min (11·6m/sec); service ceiling 30,000ft (9150m); range at max cruise power, with full 19-passenger payload, 639mls (1028km) at 10,000ft (3050m) and 977mls (1572km) at 25,000ft (7620m).

Weights: Standard empty weight, 8,500lb (3855kg); payload, 4,000lb (1815kg); take-off and landing weight, 15,245lb (6915kg).

Dimensions: Span 54ft 6in (16·61m); length 57ft 10in (17·63m); height 14ft 10¾in (4·53m).

At the same time that it relaunched production of the Commuter C99, Beech announced plans to develop one or more new types in order to consolidate its position in the market for commuterliners. While studies for a larger, pressurized aircraft in the 30/40-seat category continued, variants of the Super King Air 200 business aircraft were planned to follow more immediately upon the C99.

Scheduled to make its first flight in the spring of 1982, the Commuter 1900 is a stretched-fuselage derivative of the Super King Air, designed — as the designation suggests — for 19 passengers. A 13-passenger 1300 was also studied, using the original fuselage without any stretch, but this no longer figures in Beech plans; the company is, however, interested in the longer term in a Model 1200, which would offer the lengthened fuselage for corporate use. Flight testing of its PT6A-65 engines for the Commuter 1900 began on 30 April 1981, in a Super King Air test-bed.

With a fuselage width adequate for single seats to be track-mounted each side of a central aisle, the Commuter 1900 offers a number of interior arrangements, providing for up to 19 passengers, or two tons of cargo, or

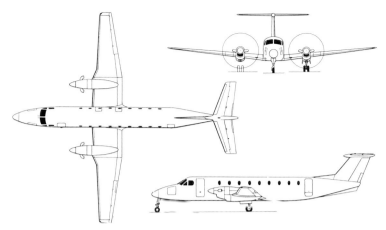

Above: Three-view drawing of the Beechcraft Commuter 1900, an enlarged derivative of the Super King Air 200 business twin.

mixed loads, with the option of an enlarged rear door for cargo loading. Air stairs are incorporated in the standard passenger doors at front and rear, and the cabin is pressurized to a differential of 4·8/lbsq in (0·34kg/cm²); maximum certificated operating altitude will be 25,000ft (7620m).

For its commuter rôle, the 1900 is designed for multi-stop operations without refuelling — typically, a 467st ml (752km) range can be achieved, cruising at 10,000ft (3050m) and with 45-min fuel reserve, making four intermediate stops. Max take off and landing weights are the same, so there is no minimum distance before the first stop can be made.

Below: An impression of the Beechcraft Commuter 1900, a 19-seat commuter-liner which was entering flight testing in 1982.

39

Boeing 707 (and 720)
USA

The following specification refers to the Boeing 707-320C:
Power Plant: Four 18,000lb st (8165kgp) Pratt & Whitney JT3D-3 or 19,000lb st (8618kgp) JT3D-7 turbofans.
Performance: Max cruising speed, 600mph (965km/h); best economy cruise, 550mph (886km/h); initial rate of climb, 4,000ft/min (20·3m/sec); service ceiling, 39,000ft (11,885m); range with max payload, 4,300mls (6920km); range with max fuel, 7,475mls (12,030km).
Weights: Basic operating, 136,610–146,000lb (62,872–66,224kg); max payload (passsenger), 84,000lb (38,100kg), (cargo), 91,390lb (41,453kg); max take-off, 333,600lb (151,315kg).
Dimensions: Span, 145ft $8\frac{1}{2}$in (44·42m); length, 152ft 11in (45·6m); height, 42ft $5\frac{1}{2}$in (12·94m); wing area, 3,050sq ft (283·4m²).

The following specification refers to the Boeing 720B.
Power Plant: Four 17,000lb st (7718kgp) Pratt & Whitney JT3D-1 or 18,000lb st (8165kg) JT3D-3 turbofans.
Performance: Max cruising speed at 25,000ft (7620m), 608mph (978km/h); best economy cruise, 533mph (858km/h); initial rate of climb, 3,700ft/min ·(18·7m/sec); service ceiling, 40,500ft (12,344m); no-reserves range with max payload, 4,110mls (6614km); range with max fuel, 6,450mls (10,380km).
Weights: Basic operating, 115,000lb (52,163kg); max payload, 41,000lb (18,600kg); max take-off, 234,000lb (106,140kg).
Dimensions: Span, 130ft 10in (39·87m); length, 136ft 9in (41·68m); height, 41ft 7in (12·67m); wing area, 2,521sq ft (234·2m²).

Through its production in the late 'forties of the C-97 and KC-97 family of transports and tankers for the USAF, the Boeing company was well placed to assess the future requirement for aircraft of this type; and production of 56 Stratocruisers for the airlines in the same timescale had given the company a feel for the commercial market too. With both these future possibilities

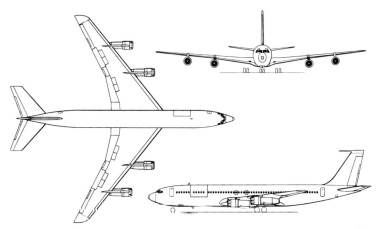

Above: The Boeing 707-320C, with freight door, and the similar 707-320B were the final production versions of Boeing's first jetliner.

in mind, Boeing had project studies under way before 1950 to investigate a turboprop- or turbojet-powered successor to the KC 97/Stratocruiser family. The studies were conducted under the C-97 Model number of 367 and by the beginning of 1952, the 367-80 study had emerged as the most promising, this being for a large transport with a swept-back wing, four turbojet engines in individual underwing pods and a large-diameter fuselage.

On 20 May 1952, the Boeing company decided to proceed to prototype construction of the 367-80, and the first flight was made at Renton, near Seattle, Washington, on 15 July 1954, opening the era of the Boeing jet transports which by 1977 had achieved sales of more than 3,000. Powered by 10,000lb st (4540kgp) Pratt & Whitney JT3C turbojets, this prototype, which became known in later years as the Dash 80, emerged as the proto- ▶

Below: The Boeing 707-320B version, with turbofan engines. The 707 is the most successful four-jet airliner to date.

type Boeing 707. This new model number had been assigned to the projected commercial jet transport based on the prototype, and was allocated in sequence (numbers up to 499 having been assigned to earlier Boeing aircraft, and 500 to 699 being reserved meanwhile for industrial products and gas turbines, with the aircraft types resuming at 700). The number 707 proved to be especially felicitous from a marketing point of view, however, and the Model 727, 737, 747 sequence used for later Boeing jet airliners followed as a direct result of this, and not by chance.

The Boeing 707 prototype, with the appropriate civil registration N70700, was extensively demonstrated to airlines and the USAF, and the latter placed an initial order for production of a tanker/transport version on 5 October 1954, this appearing in due course as the KC-135A (Boeing Model 717). Another year was to elapse before an airline order was to be placed for the Boeing transport, however, this order being from Pan American, which contracted to buy 20 Boeing 707s on 13 October 1955, a similar contract being placed with Douglas for 20 DC-8s at the same time. For the airlines, Boeing had meanwhile redesigned the fuselage of the Dash 80 to be 4in (10cm) wider to permit six-abreast seating, and alternative short-body and long-body versions were offered, this being an early indication of the Boeing philosophy to offer many different variants of the basic design to meet different airline requirements. The engines were to be 13,000lb st (5896kgp) JT3C-6s and with a gross weight of about 240,000lb (108,860kg), the new airliner would carry up to 179 passengers (one class, high density) and have sufficient range for US transcontinental operation.

The Pan American order triggered off a "jet buying spree" by the world's airlines that allowed Boeing (and other manufacturers which had meanwhile proposed their own jet airliners) to launch full-scale production, and the first two 707s off the line flew on 20 December 1957 and 3 February 1958 respectively. Full Type Approval was obtained on 23 September 1958 and the Boeing 707 entered service with Pan American on 26 October – this marking the introduction of the first US commercial jet transport and the world's third (after the Comet and Tu-104). Under the impetus of competition from BOAC with the Comet 4, Pan American used its first Boeing 707s on the New York–London route, although they had insufficient range for consistent non-stop operation over so long a sector. Domestic US operation of the Boeing 707 began on 10 December 1958. National Airlines using aircraft leased from Pan American, and American Airlines began using its own 707s within the USA on 25 January 1959.

All these early Boeing 707s were of the long-body type, only one operator, Qantas, choosing the short-body alternative – respective lengths were 144ft 6in (44·04m) and 134ft 6in (41·00m). Each customer variant was identified by a dash number, commencing at –121 for the JT3C-powered aircraft, which were known generically as 707-120s; several different fuel capacities were available, depending on the number of flexible bag tanks in the centre section, and weights up to 256,000lb (116,120kg) were eventually approved. To provide improved take-off performance, Boeing also produced a version of the basic domestic model as the 707-220 with 15,800lb st (7166kgp) JT4A-3 or -5 turbojets and gross weight of 257,000lb (116,573kg), but this was purchased by only one airline, Braniff. The first example flew on 11 June 1959 and Type Approval was obtained on 5 November, permitting service to begin on 20 December.

Boeing offered a long-range version of the 707, as the Intercontinental, from the outset of the programme, this having increased wing span and area,

Above: The Boeing 720, seen here operating in Air Malta colours, was a short-fuselage, shorter-range version of the original 707.

lengthened fuselage to seat up to 189 passengers, more fuel, higher weights and either JT4A or Rolls-Royce Conway engines. Depending on engine type, these were designated 707-320 or 707-420 respectively. The first 707-320 flew on 11 January 1959 and certification was obtained on 15 July 1959, with 15,800lb st (7167kgp) JT4A engines and a gross weight of 302,000lb (136,985kg); subsequently, the 16,800lb st (7620kgp) JT4A-9 and -10, and the 17,500lb st (7940kgp) JT4A-11 and -12 became available, alternative fuel capacities were introduced and gross weights up to 316,000lb (143,335kg) were certificated. Pan American put the 707-320 into service on 26 August 1959 on routes out of the US West Coast, and across the North Atlantic on 10 October 1959.

With the same overall features as the -320, the 707-420 first flew on 20 May, being one of a fleet ordered by BOAC with 16,500lb st (7480kgp) Conway 505 engines. Considerable flight testing was required to achieve British certification, leading to the introduction of several new features concerned with aircraft handling, including a taller fin and rudder and a ventral fin, which became applicable to all 707 variants in due course. The 707-420 was type approved on 12 February 1960, with British ARB certification on 27 April and BOAC began services in May. The 17,500lb st (7940kgp) Conway 508 was introduced later and weights up to 316,000lb (143,335kg) were approved. ►

Below: The tone drawing depicts a Boeing 707-370C of Iraqi Airways, an airline that uses a mixed fleet of Western and Soviet airliners in Europe, the Middle East and the Far East. The -370C is a customer designator, each airline having its own two-digit suffix.

In addition to BOAC, four airlines specified the Conway-engined 707-420, and 37 were built. Production of the 707-320 totalled 69, and 60 707-120s were built for airlines. These, with the five 707-220s, represented the first phase of Boeing jetliner development and production; aerodynamic refinements, and the introduction of turbofan engines, were to bring major improvements in subsequent models, and consequently many of the earlier aircraft have now been retired as being at the end of their useful life, or have been modified to later standards.

The first aerodynamic refinements introduced by Boeing were applied to a short-to-medium range variant offered in 1957 under the designation 707-020. Also known for a time as the Model 717 (this being the type number already allocated to the military KC-135) it was eventually marketed as the Boeing 720. It shared a common fuselage length with the short-body 707-120 as first offered (but the latter, as built, was shortened by another 1ft 8in (0·51m) and it was designed to operate at lower gross weights, carrying less fuel, having a lightened structure in certain respects and using lighter, lower-powered JT3C engines. To achieve an increase of 0·02 in cruising Mach number, the effective thickness/chord ratio on the inner wing sections was reduced by adding an inner wing "glove" that extended the leading edge forwards between the fuselage and inner pylons, and leading edge flaps were added on the outer wings. The Boeing 720 first flew on 23 November 1959 and was type approved on 30 June 1960; first services were flown by United on 5 July and by American on 31 July 1960. The engines were 12,000lb st (5443kgp) JT3C-7 or -12, and weights up to 229,000lb (103,873kg) were eventually approved; the maximum passenger capacity was 149, although Eastern Air Lines later obtained approval to carry 165 passengers in their aircraft. Production of the Boeing 720 totalled 65, of which many were later converted to have turbofan engines.

Development of a front fan version of the JT3C engine by Pratt & Whitney brought the promise of greater power and reduced specific fuel consumption, and versions of the Boeing 707-120, 707-320 and 720 were all quickly offered with the new power plant, which entered production as the 17,000lb st (7710kgp) JT3D-1. These versions were identified by the addition of a letter "B" as a suffix to the type designation. First to fly was a Boeing 707-120B, on 22 June 1960; in addition to the fan engines, distinguished by new cowlings with an annular exhaust for the front fan, it had the inner wing glove and extra leading edge flaps of the 720, and taller fin and ventral fin as already introduced on 707-320s in production. Type approval was obtained on 1 March 1961 and American Airlines put the type

into service on 12 March 1961. Boeing built 78 Model 707-120Bs, and several airlines had their -120s modified; these included Qantas, with the result that the short-body version of the -120 also appeared with fan engines. Gross weights up to 258,000lb (117,027kg) were approved and the 18,000lb st (8164kgp) JT3D-3 or -3B engines were also used.

The first Boeing 720B flew on 6 October 1960 and certification followed on 3 March 1961, American Airlines starting service with this type alongside its -120Bs on 12 March 1961. Only JT3D-1 engines were used, and the gross weight was 234,000lb (106,141kg). Production totalled 89, plus some 720s converted.

Fitting turbofan engines to the Boeing 707-320 produced what was to become the most universally used version, in all-passenger (-320B) and passenger/cargo convertible (-320C) variants, the latter having a large side-loading freight door in the forward fuselage and associated freight floor and handling equipment. As well as the turbofan engines, these models featured new low-drag wing tips that extended the span by 3ft 3½in (1·0m), slotted leading-edge flaps and improved trailing-edge flaps, but the inner wing "glove" and ventral fin were not used. Boeing flew the first 707-320B on 31 January 1962 and after type approval on 31 May, this version entered service with Pan American in June. It could use JT3D-1, -3 or -7 engines and was initially approved to operate at 327,000lb (148,325kg) but all aircraft built after February 1964 had structural provision for weights up to 335,000lb (151,953kg).

The first 707-320C flew on 10 February 1963 and was type approved on 30 April, entering service with Pan American in June. A few examples, such as those used by American Airlines, operated as pure freighters, with the cabin windows blanked off. The same engine choice was available as for the 707-320B but the maximum flight weight was slightly reduced.

Excluding the 46 examples of the Boeing E-3A Sentry ordered by the end of 1981 (this AWACS aircraft being based on the 707 airframe) Boeing had sold 917 examples of the 707/720 family, including some 35 to military customers and non-airline users. Commercial production has ended, Boeing having studied but dropped a 707-500 project with lengthened fuselage and CFM-56 turbofans. One 707 was fitted with these engines for a flight development programme, making its first flight on 27 November 1979.

Below: A Boeing 707-348C of Australian operator Qantas, which eventually disposed of its 707s to operate an all-Boeing 747 fleet.

Boeing 727
USA

The following specification relates to the Advanced 727-200:

Power Plant: Three 15,000lb st (6804kgp) Pratt & Whitney JT8D-11 or 15,500 lb st (7030kgp) JT8D-15 or 16,000lb st (7257kgp) JT8D-17 turbofans.

Performance: Max cruising speed, 599mph (964km/h) at 24,700ft (7530m); economy cruise, 570mph (917km/h) at 30,000ft (9145m); initial rate of climb, 2,600ft/min (13·2m/sec); service ceiling, 33,500ft (10,210m); range with max payload over 2,800mls (4500km).

Weights: Operating weight empty, 100,000lb (45,360kg); max payload, 42,800lb (19,414kg); max take-off, 209,500lb (95,027kg).

Dimensions: Span, 108ft 0in (32·92m); length, 153ft 2in (46·69m); height, 34ft 0in (10·36m); wing area, 1,700sq ft (157·9m²).

Design studies to evolve a medium-to-short range partner for the Model 707 were begun by Boeing as early as February 1956, two years before the first 707 entered service. Many configurations were studied, with nearly 70 alternatives actually reaching the stage of wind-tunnel testing, but maximum commonality with the 707 was one of the major design objectives, in order to achieve economy in first cost and operating cost. Boeing designers eventually concluded that a three-engined configuration best suited the size and performance requirements, and the new type therefore evolved along lines closely resembling those of the de Havilland 121 Trident which was intended for the same segment of the airline market.

After three years in Preliminary Design, during which time the designation 727 was adopted to continue the family series begun with the 707, the new transport became an active project early in 1959 and all major design decisions had been finalized by 18 September in that year. For another twelve months or so the favoured engine was the Allison-built version of the Rolls-Royce Spey, but the Pratt & Whitney JT8D was eventually chosen, and in this form the Boeing 727 moved from project to production on 5 December 1960 when United Airlines and Eastern Air Lines each ordered 40 examples. Boeing expressed its confidence in the future market for medium-sized aircraft of the 727 type with an estimate of sales totalling at least 300; by late 1981, however, the sales total stood at 1,815, making the 727 the world's best-selling jet airliner by a substantial margin. More than 100 airlines had by then purchased examples of the 727 from Boeing, three of these each having acquired fleets of more than 100, and many other operators had acquired examples on lease or through second-hand purchases.

Commonality with the Boeing 707 included the entire upper lobe of the fuselage, based on a cabin floor of identical width and therefore permitting the use of the same interior arrangements, and similar flight decks. Special attention was paid to the field performance, and the wing design incorporated the most advanced high lift devices ever adopted for a commercial transport at the time the 727 was launched. With a sweepback of 32 deg, the 727's wing had leading-edge slats and flaps, triple-slotted trailing edge flaps, inboard (high-speed) and outboard (low-speed) ailerons and flight and ground spoilers. With accommodation for up to 125 passengers (high-density) the 727 was designed to operate over stage lengths of up to

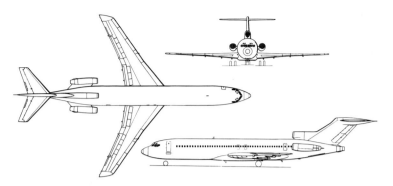

Above: The Boeing 727-200, developed as a stretched-fuselage version of the original design and soon established as the most popular of the two.

1,700mls (2,736km) and to be able to fly from 5,000ft (1524m) runways.

The first Boeing 727, in United colours, flew on 9 February 1963 from Seattle, followed by a company demonstrator in Boeing's canary yellow and brown house colours on 12 March. With two more production aircraft soon joining the flight test programme, FAA Type Approval was obtained on 24 December 1963 and the first commercial service was operated on 1 February 1964 by Eastern between Miami, Washington and Philadelphia, followed by United's first service on 6 February. Later in the same month, the first export delivery was made, to Lufthansa, and the German airline flew its first service with the type on 16 April. Thus, the Boeing 727 completely eroded the lead that the D.H.121 Trident had gained with its go-ahead in 1958, and was quickly to achieve ascendance in the sales battles that were to follow, not least because of the larger capacity and greater range offered by Boeing from the outset.

Following the precedent set with the 707, Boeing offered the 727 in a number of variants. At first, these were concerned primarily with fuel capacity and operating weights, the original certificated gross weight of 152,000lb (68,950kg) soon being increased to 160,000lb (72,575kg) and then, in the 727C version, to 169,000lb (76,655kg). Progressive increases in engine thrust also became available, starting with the 14,000lb st (6350kgp) JT8D-1 or -7, followed by the 14,500lb st (6577kgp) JT8D-9. The 727C was announced in July 1964 as a convertible passenger/cargo version, with the same side-loading freight door and cargo handling systems already developed for the Boeing 707-320C. Northwest Orient was the first to order the 727C; the first example flew on 30 December 1965, Type Approval was obtained on 13 January 1966 and Northwest flew the first service with the type on 23 April. A further refinement of the convertible idea was to mount passenger seats and galleys on pallets to achieve fast conversions, allowing ▶

Below: A Boeing 727-206 of Air Algérie, one of about 100 airlines that have bought this best-selling tri-jet.

the same aircraft to fly passengers by day and freight by night, although there was a weight penalty. This became known as the QC (Quick Change) version and was in service by May 1966, with United.

Meanwhile, in August 1965, Boeing had announced a "stretched' version as the 727-200 (the original production version then becoming the 727-100, or 727-100C or QC in convertible form). The "stretch" comprised exactly 20ft (6·10m) in two equal sections fore and aft of the wing, which remained unchanged, and maximum accommodation increased to 189. The JT8D-7 or -9 engines were specified at first, the gross weight being 169,000lb (76,655kg), but 15,000lb st (6804kgp) JT8D-11s became available in 1972 and the 15,500lb st (7030kgp) JT8D-15 was offered as a further alternative in later models. The first customer for the Boeing 727-200, which was to become the most important variant, was Northeast Airlines, with an order placed on 10 August 1965; the first example flew on 27 July 1967; Type Approval was obtained on 29 November and the first service was flown on 14 December 1967.

During 1970, when sales of the 727 were temporarily at a low ebb, Boeing began to plan a series of additional improvements, which led to introduction of the Advanced 727 with a wide option of gross weights, fuel capacities, engine powers and other features. Basic to the Advanced model were an increase in fuel capacity, new and improved aircraft systems, a "wide-body look" interior modelled on that of the Boeing 747 and additional noise reduction features to comply with new FAA regulations. First orders for the Advanced 727 were placed in December 1970 by TAA and Ansett of Australia, and the first example, destined for All-Nippon Airways, flew on 3 March 1972, with JT8D-15 engines and a gross weight of 191,000lb (86,636kgp). Type Approval was obtained on 14 June and All-Nippon flew the first service in July 1972.

On 26 July 1973, Boeing made the first flight of an Advanced 727 at a

new gross weight of 207,500lb (94,120kg), this being destined for delivery to Sterling Airways before the end of 1973, with sufficient range to fly a full 189-passenger payload on routes from Scandinavia to the Canary Islands. Yet another option became available in 1974 with the introduction of 16,000lb st (7260kgp) JT8D-17 engines, first flown in a 727 in March of that year and first delivered, on 24 June, to Mexicana. Boeing also introduced, in 1976, the JT8D-17R engine with automatic thrust reserve, operating normally at 16,400lb st (7440kgp) with an extra 1,000lb (454kg) available from the remaining engines in the event of one engine failing during a critical stage of the flight. The first 727 with ATR flew on 27 May 1976 and was later delivered to Hughes Airwest. Another variant emerged in 1981 when Federal Express ordered the Boeing 727F, a pure cargo version with cabin windows blanked off, side-loading freight door, cargo restraint and handling systems and a maximum cargo payload of 62,000lb (28,118kg).

Between 1974 and 1978, Boeing studied a number of possible "stretched" versions of the 727, initially as the 727-300A and 727-300B with 18ft 4in (5·59m) more fuselage length and either JT8D-17R or JT8D-217 engines. These projects were eventually superseded by the decision to develop the Boeing 7N7, which was launched as the Boeing 757. During 1981, however, Boeing was actively considering launching a programme to convert 727-200s to the new 727RE configuration, in which two Pratt & Whitney PW2037 or Rolls-Royce RB.211-535 turbofans (the engines selected to power the Boeing 757) would replace the three JT8Ds. Conversion would require structural modification of the rear fuselage and would provide a 150-seat airliner with modern fuel and noise characteristics at relatively low cost.

Below: Icelandair's Boeing 727-108C, a passenger/cargo convertible version of the original short-fuselage model.

Boeing 737
USA

The following specification relates to the Advanced 737-200:

Power plant: Two 14,000lb st (6350kgp) Pratt & Whitney JT8D-7 or 14,500lb st (6577kgp) JT8D-9 or 15,500lb st (7030kgp) JT8D-15 or 16,000lb st (7257kgp) JT8D-17 turbofans.

Performance: Max cruising speed, 576mph (927km/h) at 22,600ft (6890m); best economy cruise, 553mph (890km/h); initial rate of climb, 3,760ft/min (19·1m/sec); range with max payload, 2,370mls (3815km); range with max fuel, 2,530mls (4075km).

Weights: Operating weight empty, 59,300lb (26,898kg); max payload, 35,700lb (16,193kg); max take-off, 119,500lb (54,195kg).

Dimensions: Span, 93ft 0in (28·35m); length, 100ft 0in (30·48m); height, 37ft 0in (11·28m); wing area, 980sq ft (91·05m²).

Boeing's decision to add a short-haul airliner to its family of jet transports including the various models of 707 and 727 was taken in November 1964, by which time the BAC One-Eleven was already in flight test and the DC-9 was nearing first flight. With what became known as the Model 737, Boeing was competing for, broadly, the same portion of the airline market as that covered by the One-Eleven and DC-9, but the design approach was quite different. Whereas both BAC and Douglas had chosen a rear-engined, T-tail layout, Boeing decided to keep an underwing engine location and a conventional tail unit; not only did this keep the 737 clear of the aerodynamic problems associated with T-tails, but it also helped to achieve maximum commonality between the "baby" Boeing and its big brother. Most importantly, Boeing decided to retain the same overall fuselage width as that used in the 707/727; this resulted in a somewhat stubby appearance for the aircraft when the cabin length was sized to carry about 100 passengers, but provided for relatively spacious seating arrangements and permitted airlines already using the 707 or 727 to standardize on seats, galleys, etc.

The "launching order" for the Boeing 737, announced on 19 February

Right: A Boeing 737-2M9 of Zambia Airways. The 737 is the smallest of the extensive family of Boeing jetliners available in 1982, and is the second best-seller, exceeded in sales total only by the 727. The "M9" in the designation indicates Zambia Airways configuration: Boeing originally used two digits for its customer designators but was forced to introduce letter/number combinations as the customer list grew. The "-2" indicates that this is a -200 model of the 737.

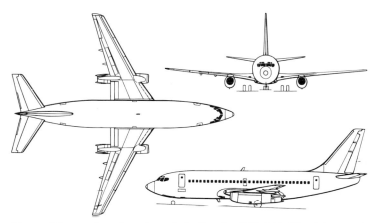

Above: Three-view drawing of the Boeing 737-200. The Advanced 737, incorporating numerous new features, is externally the same as the basic -200; the original -100 has a shorter fuselage.

1965, came from Lufthansa in Germany, marking the first occasion on which an airline outside the USA had ever been the initial customer for a new airliner put into production in the USA. Although passenger capacities of 60–85 had been projected for the 737 during most of the early stages of design, the size was increased to allow for 100 seats in the final stages of negotiation with Lufthansa; powered by Pratt & Whitney JT8D-1s at 14,000lb st (6350 kgp) each, the Model 737 was to have a gross weight of 85,000lb (38,535kg) and a full-payload range of 700mls (1,126km).

This aircraft was to emerge in due course as the Boeing 737 Srs 100, with an initial gross weight of 97,000lb (44,380kg) and up to 111,000lb (50,350kg) eventually in a special model produced for Malaysia-Singapore Airlines. The JT8D-7, with the same power as the 1 but flat rated for higher temperatures, was also introduced instead of the initial engine variant, and the ►

14,500lb st (6577kgp) JT8D-9 was offered for use in later versions of the 737-100. Boeing soon discovered, however, that there was a strong demand for slightly larger passenger capacity, and to meet this need the 737-200 was announced on 5 April 1965 when United Air Lines ordered 40, this also being the first order from a US airline for the type. The fuselage was lengthened by 6ft (1·82m) to provide two more seat rows, which, with some internal redesign, increased accommodation to 119 or eventually, in high-density layouts, 130. With JT8D-7 engines, the 737-200 began its life at a gross weight of 97,000lb (43,998kg) with two centre-section fuel tanks, which were optional. Subsequent developments have taken the gross weight of the standard 737-200 to 117,000lb (53,070kg), with either the JT8D-9, JT8D-15 or JT8D-17 turbofans also being available.

First flight of the Boeing 737 was made at Seattle on 9 April 1967, this aircraft being a company demonstrator, followed about a month later by the first of Lufthansa's 737-100s. The first 737-200 in United configuration was the fifth 737 to fly, on 8 August 1967. Full FAA Type Approval was obtained for the 737-100 on 15 December 1967, and for the 737-200 on 21 December 1967, services being inaugurated with the two models, respectively, by Lufthansa on 10 February and by United on 28 April 1968.

Sales of the Boeing 737 proceeded somewhat more slowly than those of the earlier Boeing jetliners, but the company pursued a concentrated programme of improvement and refinement to keep abreast of the competition. A passenger/cargo convertible version of the 737-200 was soon offered, with side-loading freight door and other features similar to those in the 727C. The first 737-200C was flown in August 1968 and after certification in October entered service with Wien Consolidated before the end of the year.

Because of some deficiencies in the specific range of the 737 as first delivered, plus poor efficiency of the thrust reversers on the JT8D engines, Boeing introduced a series of modifications commencing with aircraft No 135 delivered (to United) in March 1969, and offered conversion kits for earlier customers who wished to update their aircraft. The changes included target-type thrust reversers instead of clamshell design, with redesign of the aft engine nacelle; some drag-reduction modifications to the wing and changes in the flap settings and structure. Another series of changes was offered by Boeing later in 1969, and these were combined in the specification of what became the Advanced 737-200, with deliveries starting in 1971. The new features comprised changes to the leading edge flaps and slats, wider nacelle struts, optional use of JT8D-15 engines and optional nose-wheel brakes.

The first Advanced 737-200 flew on 15 April 1971; certification was obtained on 3 May and All Nippon Airways inaugurated service in June 1971. Later that year, a "wide-body look" interior was also developed for the 737, the first example being delivered to Air Algerie in December 1971, and this eventually became widely adopted by customers for the Advanced 737. A "Quiet Nacelle" modification was added to the Advanced 737 specification in 1973, to allow compliance with latest FAA regulations, the first delivery being made in October to Eastern Provincial Airways. Later options on the Advanced 737 introduced the JT8D-17 engine at 16,000lb st (7264kgp) and a gross weight of 117,000lb (53,070kg) or 119,500lb (54,253kg), the first example at the latter weight going to Braathens SAFE in Norway in latè 1977.

A separate series of modifications was also developed by Boeing to permit the 737 to operate from gravel and dirt runways, so that full advantage could be taken of its short field performance. These modifications comprised gravel deflection shields on the main and nosewheel gears, blow-away jets beneath the engine intakes to prevent debris ingestion, fuselage abrasion protection, flap protection and other features.

By the end of 1981, Boeing had sold over 950 Boeing 737s, including a few for military and non-commercial use; of the total, only 30 were 737-100s, and 64 of the remainder were 737-200Cs. Included in the sales total were 20 Boeing 737-300s, this being the designation of a new variant launched by Boeing on 26 March 1981 when US Air and Southwest Airlines each ordered 10. The 737-300, to fly in April 1984 with first deliveries at the end of that year, features an 8ft 8in (2·64m) fuselage stretch to increase seating capacity by up to 20 seats; a 1ft 10in (56cm) increase in wing span; a revised leading edge and extended dorsal fin and a pair of 20,000lb st (9072kgp) turbofans in revised nacelles. Variants at gross weights of 124,500lb (56,473kg), 130,000lb (58,968kg) and 135,000lb (61,236kg) are on offer, with varying fuel capacities.

Above: A Boeing 737-2H4 in the very striking orange, red and ochre livery of Texas-based Southwest Airlines.

Below: "White Nile" is one of a pair of Boeing 737-2J8C convertible passenger/cargo versions used by Sudan Airways, the other being named "Blue Nile".

Boeing 747
USA

The following specification relates to the 747-200:

Power Plant: Four 43,500lb st (19,730kgp) Pratt & Whitney JT9D-3, 45,000lb st (20,410kgp) JT9D-3W, 45,500lb st (20,635kgp) JT9D-7, 47,000lb st (21,320kgp) JT9D-7W or 47,670lb st (21,620kgp) JT9D-7A turbofans.

Performance: Max speed, 608mph (978km/h) at 30,000ft (9150m); best economy cruise, 580mph (935km/h); cruise ceiling, 45,000ft (13,705m); no-reserves range with max payload, 4,985mls (8023km); range with max fuel, FAR reserves, 7,090mls (11,410km).

Weights: Basic operating, 367,900lb (166,876kg); max payload, 158,600lb (71,940kg); max take-off, 785,000lb (356,070kg).

Dimensions: Span, 195ft 8in (59·64m), length, 231ft 4in (70·51m); height, 63ft 5in (19·33m); wing area, 5,500sq ft (511m²).

The first of the "wide-body" jet transports, and the largest airliner put into service to date, the Boeing 747 was developed as a logical extrapolation of the Boeing 707 concept, the basis of the design being Boeing's project work to meet a USAF requirement for a large logistics transport (eventually satisfied by the Lockheed C-5A). A number of possible configurations were studied, including mid-wing, double-bubble layouts, but the project eventually chosen as the most promising was essentially an enlargement of the 707, with a fuselage providing a long, single passenger deck with sufficient width to permit up to 10 seats across, and two aisles; the flight deck was located on a higher level, with space for a small passenger lounge behind.

By 1965, Boeing had defined the concept for this very large airliner, with accommodation for up to 500 passengers (but about 350 as a more typical load in mixed-class configuration) and a range of about 4,000 miles (6437km) with full payload. Gross weight was expected to be 680,000lb (308,440kg) and the new transport, which was inevitably designated Boeing 747 in continuation of the Boeing family of jet airliners, was to be powered by the completely new Pratt & Whitney JT9D turbofan rated initally at 41,000lb st (18,600kgp) and mounted in underwing pods.

The launching order for the 747, which quickly became known as the "Jumbo Jet", was placed by Pan American on 14 April 1966 and was for 25 aircraft with deliveries to start in 1969. Boeing waited for more orders to be placed before actually committing the type to production, however, this step being taken on 25 July after Lufthansa and JAL had each ordered three. Right from the start, Boeing planned to offer all-cargo and convertible versions, with upward-hinged nose to permit straight-in loading, but the introduction of these versions was, in the event, delayed because of difficulties encountered with the initial passenger versions, particularly related to structure weight growth and JT9D problems. The first flight of the 747 was made at Everett, where a new production facility for the "Jumbo" had been established, on 9 February 1969, by which time 27 airlines had ordered 160 examples of the new transport. FAA Type Approval was obtained on 30 December 1969 and Pan American launched service with the 747 across the North Atlantic on 21 January 1970; JT9D-3 engines rated at 43,500lb st

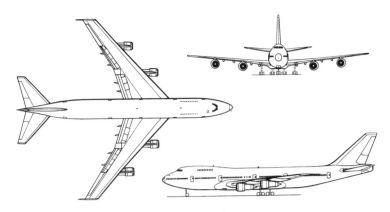

Above: The Boeing 747-200 with JT9D engines. The 747SP has a shorter fuselage but all other variants are dimensionally similar.

(19,730kgp) had replaced the original -1 engines used at the start of flight tests and the certificated gross weight was 710,000lb (322,050kg). Considerable difficulties with the engine prevented the 747 from being fully exploited for some months, until the modified JT9D-3A engine was introduced; eventually the 45,000lb st (20,410kgp) JT9D-3W, the 45,500lb st (20,635kgp) JT9D-7 and 47,000lb st (21,320kgp) JT9D-7W became available for use in the 747 and the permitted gross weight grew to 735,000lb (333,390kg) for some versions of the basic model.

A second variant had been announced, meanwhile, on 25 November 1967, to provide greater range but with no change in overall dimensions or passenger capacity. Extra fuel was carried in the wing centre section and ▶

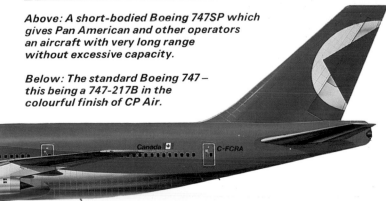

Above: A short-bodied Boeing 747SP which gives Pan American and other operators an aircraft with very long range without excessive capacity.

Below: The standard Boeing 747 – this being a 747-217B in the colourful finish of CP Air.

structural changes were made, together with changes in the undercarriage design, to permit certification at a gross weight of 775,000lb (351,540kg), with JT9D-7 or -7W engines — later increased to 785,000lb (356,070kg) when the 47,670lb st (21,620kgp) JT9D-7A became available in 1973. The uprated 747 was introduced as the 747B but Boeing later adopted its customary designation system, the early models being 747-100 and the high gross weight version the 747-200. First flight of the Boeing 747-200 was made on 11 October 1970 and after certification on 23 December 1970 the type entered service with KLM early in 1971.

The first example of the 747 with hinged nose for freight loading flew on 30 November 1971 and entered service with Lufthansa on 19 April 1972 following certification on 7 March 1972, with the designation 747F as a pure freighter. A year later, on 23 March 1973, the first convertible variant, also with hinged nose, made its first flight and this entered service with World Airways after certification as the 747C on 24 April. Only Series 200 airframes were offered in F or C configurations. Another convertible/freighter option offered by Boeing comprises a side-loading freight door in the fuselage aft of the wing, usually without the nose-loading feature and known as the 747 Combi. The first such aircraft was delivered to Sabena in 1974 and by 1981, more than 60 747-200s, and 16 747-100s, had been delivered with, or modified to have, the side freight door. The 200th 747 was delivered on 23 April 1973, this being a 747-200 for El Al with JT9D-7A engines which was also the first at a new high gross weight of 775,000lb (351,530kg).

Also in 1973, Boeing introduced the 747SR, a variant for high-density short-haul operations — primarily in Japan. Structural changes were made to permit a higher frequency of take-offs and landings, with restricted gross weight, JT9D-7AW engines and 747-100 fuel capacity. There was no dimensional change, and Japan Air Lines, the only airline to order this variant, had its aircraft arranged to accommodate 498 passengers — the largest capacity in use on a regular basis anywhere. Services began on the Tokyo—Okinawa route on 9 October 1973 and these aircraft operate at gross weights of 570,000lb (258,780kg) or (two aircraft only), 610,000lb (276,940kg). The 747SR designation was changed in 1978 to 747-100B, with a wide choice of engine variants and gross weight options of 735,000lb (333,690kg) and 750,000lb (340,500kg). All Nippon Airways received the first 747-100Bs early in 1979, with CF6-45 engines and 500 passenger seats.

To provide an aircraft suitable for use on very long ranges with only modest traffic, Boeing launched the 747SP (Special Performance) in August 1973, the first order being placed a month later by Pan American. The first variant to have different dimensions from the original 747, the SP has a fuselage shortened by 48ft (14·6m) to give a typical mixed-class accommodation of 288 and maximum high-density layouts for 360. Other

Above: The Boeing 747 is shown here in its -270C Combi version, in the distinctive livery of Iraqi Airways.

changes include lighter-weight structure in parts of the wing, fuselage and landing gear, a taller fin and rudder with double hinged rudder and new trailing edge flaps. Gross weight is 663,000lb (301,000kg) and with JT9D-7A turbofans the 747SP offers improved take-off performance, higher cruising speeds and a full-payload range of nearly 6,900mls (11,000km) The first 747SP flew on 4 July 1975 and after certification on 4 February 1976, Pan American put the type into service in May. Eleven airlines had ordered 41 examples of the 747SP by the end of 1981.

To permit further weight growth of the 747, Pratt & Whitney, General Electric and Rolls-Royce offered advanced models of their respective large turbofans for use in variants delivered in 1975 and beyond. Boeing converted its original prototype to fly with 51,000lb st (32,135kgp) General Electric CF6-50D engines, flight testing starting on 26 June 1973, and the first airline order was announced in 1974 when KLM ordered two with 52,500lb st (23,850kgp) CF6-50Es and side-loading freight doors and convertible interiors for up to 428 passengers, or 200 passengers plus 110,000lb (49,895kg) of freight. This variant was certificated at a gross weight of 800,000lb (362,874kg) and a similar weight became available in 1975 for variants powered by the 52,000lb st (23,586kgp) JT9D-70, the first examples of which were ordered by Seaboard World in 747F configuration.

During 1975, British Airways ordered the first examples of the 747 to be powered by 50,000lb st (22,700kgp) Rolls-Royce RB.211-524Bs and this variant made its first flight on 3 September 1976. The RB.211 version entered service with British Airways in 1977 at a gross weight of 800,000lb (363,200kg). The availability of more powerful versions of the three engine types led to still higher weights being certificated subsequently. By the end of 1981, at which time 578 Boeing 747s were on order, the engine options included the 50,000lb st (22,680kgp) JT9D-7J, the 51,600lb st (23,406kgp) RB.211-524C, the 52,500lb st (23,814kgp) CF6-50E2, 53,110lb st (24,090kgp) RB.211-524D4 and 54,750lb st (24,835kgp) and the highest gross weight options were 820,000lb (371,950kg) and 833,000lb (377,850kg). The first aircraft delivered at the latter weight, with 53,000lb st (24,040kgp) JT9D-7Q engines, was delivered to Cargolux on 10 October 1980.

In mid-1980, Boeing obtained the first orders (from Swissair) for a new variant known as the 747SUD (stretched upper deck). The upper front fuselage fairing in this variant is extended aft to provide up to 69 seats on the upper deck; overall dimensions, weight and engine options are unchanged. The first 747SUD was to fly in October 1982, for March 1983 delivery.

Boeing 757
USA

Power Plants: Two Rolls-Royce RB.211-535C turbofans each rated at 37,400lb st (16,980kgp).
Performance: Max cruising speed, 569mph (915km/h) at 29,000ft (8840m); long-range cruise, 528mph (850km/h) at 37,000ft (11,280m); range with max payload, no reserves, 1,380mls (2220km); range with max fuel, no reserves, 5,600mls (8631km).
Weights: Typical operating weight empty, 130,670lb (59,270kg), max take-off weight, 220,000lb (99,880kg); max zero fuel weight, 184,000lb (83,536kg); max landing weight, 148,000lb (67,120kg).
Dimensions: Span, 124ft 6in (37·95m); overall length, 155ft 3in (47·32m); overall height, 44ft 6in (13·56m); wing area, 1,951sq ft (181·25m²).

After several years during which various "stretched" versions of the Boeing 727 were studied and attempts were made to obtain sufficient airline orders to launch production, Boeing finally was able to launch the Boeing 757 in mid-1978. This new airliner retains the fuselage width of the 707/727/737 series and therefore maintains commonality with the 727, but it has a new wing, with two engines in underwing pods, and a low-mounted tailplane. After it had been launched, the Boeing 757 design was further revised to incorporate the same nose and flight deck as the Boeing 767, with the result that it ended up having greater commonality with the latter than with the 727 on which it was originally based.

As finally launched, the Boeing 757 was designed to carry a maximum of 233 passengers six-abreast in a high-density layout at 29-in (73·7-cm) seat pitch, or, more typically, 196 in all-tourist or 178 in two-class layouts, and to have a maximum range of 2,300mls (3700km) with a full passenger load. With some 13,200lb (6000kg) of cargo, the maximum payload was 64,000lb (29,025kg). The 757 was designed primarily as a replacement for the Boeing 727 tri-jet and with the Rolls-Royce RB.211-535C engines initially specified was claimed to offer the best fuel efficiency per passenger carried of any aeroplane in its class.

The two launching airlines, British Airways and Eastern Air Lines, announced their intention of ordering Boeing 757s in August 1978, at which time Boeing confirmed its decision to offer the new aircraft with the Rolls-Royce engines, these being smaller-fan derivatives of the RB.211 already in production for the Lockheed TriStar and the Boeing 747.

British Airways signed a definitive order for 19 Boeing 757s on 2 March, valued at some £300m, later taking an option on 18 more, and the Eastern Air Lines contract was signed on 23 March, covering 21 aircraft with an option on 24. Although Boeing had been proceeding with preliminary activities for production of the 757, the formal decision to initiate full-scale production was not taken until the Eastern contract had been signed. Subsequent to the launch, Boeing offered increased gross weight options of 230,000lb (104,328kg) and 240,000lb (108,863kg), and the 36,330lb st (16,480kgp) CF6-32C was nominated as an alternative engine. However, the third and fourth major customers for the Boeing 757, Delta and American Airlines, both selected the Pratt & Whitney PW2037 and the CF6-32 was subsequently withdrawn from development by General Electric. By the end of the 1981, seven airlines had ordered 136 757s, with 61 more on order. First flight was made on 19 February 1982, with customer deliveries starting on December 1982 at the time of certification.

Right: The Boeing 757 was rolled out at Renton, Washington, on 13 January 1982 to become Boeing's sixth major jet transport. Four aircraft were being used for flight test and development leading to certification and entry into service before the end of 1982.

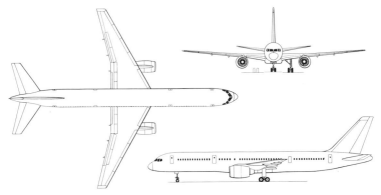

Above: Three-view drawing of the Boeing 757-200, which is the basic version as launched in mid-1978; the projected 757-100 was shorter.

Boeing 767
USA

The following specification refers to the basic Boeing 767-200:

Power Plant: Two Pratt & Whitney JT9D-7R4D turbofans each rated at 47,700lb st (21,637kgp) for take-off.

Performance: Max cruising speed, 582mph (937km/h) at 30,000ft (9150m); long-range cruise, 528mph (850km/h) at 39,000ft (11,887m); range with max payload, no reserves, 2,550mls (4100km); range with max fuel 5,640mls (9075km).

Weights: Operating weight empty, 180,300lb (81,770kg); max payload, 67,700lb (30,708kg); max take-off weight 300,000lb (136,050kg); max zero fuel weight 248,000lb (112,470kg); max landing weight, 270,000lb (122,450kg).

Dimensions: Span, 156ft 4in (47·70m); length 159ft 2in (48·48m); overall height, 52ft 0in (15·88m); wing area, 3,050sq ft (283m²).

The Boeing Company announced on 14 July 1978 that it was launching full-scale production of the Model 767, an all-new wide-body twin-jet that had emerged after several years of intense design and sales activity during which time a variety of alternative projects was studied under the designations 7X7, 7N7 and 757. As finally launched, the 767 was aimed primarily at meeting the requirements of US airlines for domestic operations, with a one-stop transcontinental capability. Maximum one-class capacity in a seven-abreast, two-aisle layout was established at 252, with a typical mixed-class layout for about 200. Using an eight-abreast layout (2+4+2), the maximum capacity was 289 at a seat pitch of 30in (76·2cm).

The Boeing 767 was designed to make extensive use of "state-of-the-art construction materials", including advanced aluminium alloys that offer light weight, improved stress capabilities and better resistance to corrosion. Lightweight components — mostly using graphite particles bonded with epoxy — are specified for the spoilers, landing gear doors and components of the engine pods. Capable of being operated by a three-man flight crew, the Boeing 767 has an advanced flight management computer system

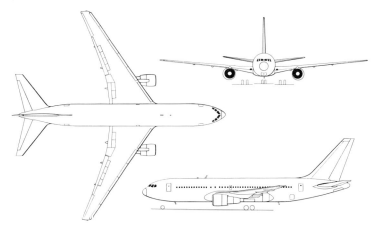

Above: The Boeing 767 is shown by this three-view in its basic form, in which guise it was entering service in 1982.

integrated with the auto-pilot and auto-throttle to achieve maximum fuel economy in all phases of the flight. An automatic landing system is also specified, including roll-out guidance, to permit operations in Cat III conditions.

Boeing initially offered two versions of the 767, the -200 as launched, and a shorter-body 767-100. Also offered was a choice of engines in the 45–50,000-lb (20,430–22,700kgp) class from Pratt & Whitney, General Electric and Rolls-Royce. By choice of the launching airlines, the JT9D-7R became the lead engine for the 767 certification programme with the CF6 adopted subsequently.

To produce the 767, Boeing set up a final assembly line at Everett, the production centre for the Boeing 747. Actual manufacture was widely ▶

Below: The first example of the Boeing 767 to fly, bearing Boeing's "house" colours. Subsequent test aircraft wore United livery.

sub-contracted, with major components produced by other US companies and Canadair Ltd. In addition, Aeritalia concluded an agreement with Boeing providing for production in Italy of the wing moving surfaces (slats, flaps and ailerons) and the fin, rudder, tailplane and elevators; a similar deal between Boeing and a consortium of Japanese companies was made in respect of fuselage and main undercarriage components. Both Aeritalia and the Japanese CTDC group became risk-sharing partners in the Boeing 767, helping to reduce Boeing's initial commitment.

The launch order on which Boeing based its go-ahead for the 767 was placed by United Airlines, and covered 30 aircraft; subsequently, options were secured by this airline on 37 more. Later in the year, American Airlines ordered 30 and Delta Air Lines announced it would buy 20 (confirmed by contract in February 1979); these airlines also securing options on 20 and 22 respectively. Both American and Delta ordered an increased gross weight version of the 767, at 310,000lb (140,740kg) compared with the 282,000lb (127,915kg) of the initial variant for United; this weight increase was accompanied by an increase in fuel capacity to achieve non-stop trans-continental service. Both these customers also selected the 47,900lb st (21,756kgp) CF6-80A engine. Dimensionally the same as the version ordered by United, these aircraft were also basically 767-200s but after they had been ordered Boeing announced that it would not continue to offer the short-body 767-100. The basic 767-200 then became a version with gross weight of 300,000lb (136,050kg), while the United variant at a gross weight of 290,000lb (131,520kg), was described as the medium range option and versions with increased gross weights of 320,000lb (145,125kg) and 330,000lb (149,660kg) were to be available from September 1983 and October 1984 respectively, the latter having optional extra fuel to achieve a range of 4,600mls (7400km) with full passenger payload. The 44,300lb st (20,112kgp) JT9D-7R4A is an alternative to the version quoted above.

First flight of the 767 was made at Everett on 26 September 1981, followed on 4 November by the first of three 767s in United Airlines configuration, with JT9D-7R4 engines; fifth to fly was the first for Delta, with CF6-80A engines. By end-1981, Boeing held orders for 173 767s from 17 airlines, with options on 138 more.

Below: The first Boeing 767 after roll-out at Everett, Washington. This example has Pratt & Whitney JT9D engines, but the first examples with CF6 turbofans were also under test in 1982.

Boeing 7-7
USA

To compete in the market for a new 150-seat short/medium-range transport, Boeing studied a number of options from 1980 onwards. These alternatives included re-engined variants of the 727, such as the 727RE; the 757-100 (with shorter fuselage than the 757-200 as launched) and even the stretched 737-300 which was under full-scale development by the end of 1981; these are all referred to under appropriate entries elsewhere in this volume.

Recognising that derivatives of the 727 and 737 were unlikely to be able to compete in the longer term with such projected new types as the Airbus A320 and McDonnell Douglas-Fokker MDF-100, Boeing also had under study in 1981 a new aircraft, which is tentatively identified as the 7-7 (Seven Dash Seven). This project also became the subject of discussions between Boeing and the group of Japanese manufacturers seeking a project in which to share development (as the Y-XX).

Preliminary details of the 7-7 were revealed by Boeing at the Paris Air Show in June 1981, showing that the company favoured, at that time, a twin-engined type of generally similar configuration to the Boeing 737, but with a larger fuselage cross section — perhaps the same as that of the 757. As much commonality as possible would be sought with Boeing 767 components such as the flight deck, front fuselage, rear fuselage, tail unit and many of the systems. The wing and engine installation would be new, together with the undercarriage.

Because of its preoccupation with the 757, 767, 737-300 and 727RE, Boeing was in no hurry to go ahead with the 7-7 and indicated that the earliest in-service date was likely to be 1988. Development of suitable engines in the 25,000lb st (11,340kgp) class was in any case likely to be a pacing factor, as it was for the other 150-seat programmes. Whatever engines eventually become available, Boeing was planning to optimise the design of the 7-7 to achieve its lowest fuel burn over ranges of 500naut mls (925km), while the design range would be 1,500naut mls (2776km) and the design speed would be Mach 0·75-0·78.

Below: This model represents the Boeing 7-7 project as it was in mid-1981. The 7-7 was one of several options being considered by Boeing to meet the demand for a modern 150-seat jetliner.

British Aerospace 748
United Kingdom

The following specification refers to the HS.748 Srs 2A:

Power Plant: Two 2,280ehp Rolls-Royce Dart 532-2L or -2S turboprops.
Performance: Max cruising speed, 278mph (448km/h) at 10,000ft (3050m); initial rate of climb, 1,320ft/min (6·7m/sec); service ceiling, 25,000ft (7600m); range with max payload, 530mls (852km); range with max fuel, 1,987mls (3150km).
Weights: Basic operating, 26,700lb (12,110kg); max payload, 11,800lb (5350kg); max take-off, 44,495lb (20,182kg).
Dimensions: Span, 98ft 6in (30·02m); length, 67ft 0in (20·42m); height, 24ft 10in (7·57m); wing area, 810·75sq ft (73·35m²).

After concentrating upon military aircraft development for a decade after World War II, A V Roe and Co Ltd (Avro — later absorbed in Hawker Siddeley Aviation and therefore now a part of British Aerospace, making up the Manchester Division) decided to re-enter the commercial aircraft field in 1957, primarily as a result of the Sandys White Paper on Defence in that year, with its prediction that the RAF would have no more new manned aircraft. After a study of the market, the company elected to develop a twin turboprop transport for the short-haul market — in general terms, a replacement for the DC-3 and Viking. Thus, the new aircraft would inevitably be a competitor for the Fokker F-27 which was already in flight test, and one of the design objectives set by Avro was to offer an aircraft that was cheaper and had a better performance.

One early study (mid-1958) under the Avro 748 designation was for a high wing design resembling the F-27 in general configuration but having only 20 seats and a gross weight of 18,000lb (8165kg). Airline reaction, however, led to a general scaling-up of the project to use two Rolls-Royce Darts, and to a decision to adopt a low-wing layout. In this form, with capacity for 36 passengers (four abreast) and a gross weight of 33,000lb (14,968kg), the project went ahead, the Hawker Siddeley board approving, in January 1959; construction of two flying prototypes and two test specimens. Special features of the design were the use of fail-safe principles in structural design, rather than the more usual (at that time) safe-life (this being the first medium-sized aircraft so designed) and the use of an unusual single-slotted flap to help provide a very good field performance.

The two prototypes made their first flights on 24 June 1960 and 10 April 1961 respectively. They had Dart R.Da.10 Mk 514 engines and were generally similar to the production Series 1 standard, the first example of which flew on 30 August 1961. The first customer for the Avro 748 was Skyways Coach-Air, which wanted three to use on its short cross-Channel routes, and following British certification on 7 December 1961, Skyways inaugurated services in 1962. Second operator of the type was Aerolineas Argentinas, the first overseas customer of many that were to sign up to buy the 748 in subsequent years.

After 18 Srs 1s had been built (plus the prototypes), production switched to the Avro 748 Srs 2, which introduced uprated Dart R.Da.7 Mk 531 engines and had a gross weight, eventually, of 44,495lb (20,182kg), compared with the 39,500lb (17,915kg) eventually approved for the Series 1. The prototype Srs 2 (a Srs 1 converted) flew at Woodford on 6 November 1961 and deliveries began after certification in October 1962, the first operator being BKS Air Transport. Improved performance was achieved with the introduction, from mid-1967, of the Dart Mk 532-2L or 532-2S, changing the designation to Srs 2A, and on 31 December 1971, a modified Srs 2A made its first flight, incorporating a large freight door in the fuselage aft of the wing. This door was offered together with a strengthened cabin floor and an optional air-transportable cargo hoist; sometimes

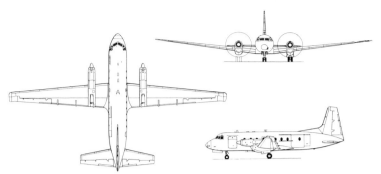

Above: Three-view of the British Aerospace HS.748 Series 2B showing the extended wing-tips and optional freight door.

referred to as the Srs 2C, this variant was of primary interest to military users.

An improved version of the HS.748 entered production in 1979, this being the Srs 2B. Its new features were a 4ft (1·22m) increase in wing span (at the tips), Dart 536-2 engines, an automatic water methanol system for use in case of engine failure and some aerodynamic refinements. The first production Srs 2B flew on 22 June 1977 and this version could carry up to 2,000lb (907kg) more payload from "difficult" airfields. During 1981, British Aerospace was completing plans to launch a stretched derivative of the HS.748, which would have a longer fuselage for up to 60 passengers, a swept-back fin and rudder and new-technology engines — probably Pratt & Whitney Canada PW100s.

In addition to production by the parent company in the UK, the HS.748, as the Avro 748 eventually became, was assembled under licence by Hindustan Aeronautics Ltd at Kanpur, primarily for the Indian Air Force but also for Indian Airlines. The first Srs 1 assembled in India flew on 1 November 1961 and the first Srs 2 on 28 February 1964. By the end of 1981, 357 HS.748s had been sold and the type was in widescale use, having been purchased by some 78 operators in 49 countries, and had proved of special interest to smaller operators using airfields with limited facilities, as well as for feeder-line use by larger airlines on their secondary routes.

Below: Sales of the HS.748 had totalled 360 by early 1982, mostly to smaller airlines around the world.

British Aerospace One-Eleven
United Kingdom

The following specification refers to the One-Eleven 500:

Power Plant: Two 12,550lb st (5692kgp) Rolls-Royce Spey 512-DW turbofans.

Performance: Max cruising speed: 541mph (871km/h) at 21,000ft (6400m); best economy cruise, 461mph (742km/h) at 25,000ft (7620m); initial rate of climb, 2,400ft/min (12·2m/sec); range with typical capacity payload, 1,480mls (2380km); range with max fuel, 2,149mls (3458km).

Weights: Basic operating, 54,582lb (24,758kg); max payload, 26,418lb (11,983kg); max take-off, 104,500lb (47,400kg).

Dimensions: Span, 92ft 6in (28·50m); length, 107ft 0in (32·61m); height, 24ft 6in (7·47m); wing area, 1,031sq ft (95·78m²).

As a jet successor to the turboprop Viscount, the BAC One-Eleven proved somewhat less successful than its illustrious forebear, although by 1970 the sale of some 200 One-Elevens had established the type as largest earner of foreign exchange among the British civil aircraft then being exported. Sales totalled 230 by the end of 1981, not counting the additional aircraft being assembled in Romania, as noted below.

The One-Eleven had its origins in a project study by the Hunting Aircraft Ltd design team at Luton, which was working on a small jet airliner as early as 1956. Identified as the Hunting H-107, the early project was for a 48-seat (four-abreast) aircraft with a range of up to 1,000mls (1610km); the layout, following the style set by the Sud Caravelle, featured a low wing with modest sweepback, a T-tail and engines on the rear fuselage. The choice of suitable engines was severely restricted in 1956 and Hunting designers based their project upon two Bristol Orpheus turbojets. Wind tunnel tests were made and a mock-up was built, and in September 1958 the design was revised around two BS.61 or BS.75 turbofans.

During 1960, the Hunting company was acquired by the British Aircraft Corporation, which was set up at the beginning of that year to merge Vickers, Bristol and English Electric, and work proceeded on the H-107 as a joint effort between the Vickers-Weybridge and Hunting design teams. By early 1961, following an assessment of potential airline interest, the design had been enlarged to provide five-abreast seating for about 65 passengers and an optimum range of about 600mls (272km), using two of the commercial Rolls-Royce Spey turbofans that had been specified for the D.H.121 Trident. In this enlarged form the airliner became known as the BAC-111 (One-Eleven).

An order for 10 One-Elevens was placed with BAC by British United Airways and announced on 9 May 1961, a few weeks after the company had decided to lay down a batch of 20 aircraft in order to achieve the target delivery date of autumn 1964. The order book grew rapidly and by the time the first aircraft (intended for use as a company demonstrator and development machine) flew from Hurn on 20 August 1963, it stood at a total of 60. By that date, the aircraft had grown to have a gross weight of 73,500lb (33,340kg) and its maximum seating capacity was put at 79 in a high-density layout.

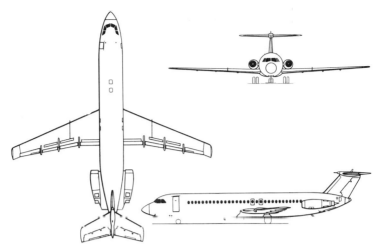

Above: The BAC One-Eleven 500, the largest of the variants put into production, with longer fuselage and increased span.

The North American market, in which the Viscount had always done so well, was regarded as a prime outlet for the One-Eleven, and orders were soon accepted from Braniff (a trunk operator) and Mohawk (a local service airline). The seal was put on the success of the One-Eleven in the US in July 1963, however, when American Airlines, one of the "big five" US operators, ordered 15, with options on 15 more to be taken up later.

The American Airlines order was the first for the One-Eleven Series 400, a specially "Americanized" version with some features required to meet the then applicable FAA certification requirements. In May 1963, BAC had adopted the designation One-Eleven 200 for the initial production standard and had introduced the Series 300 with uprated Spey engines, a centre-section fuel tank and higher gross weights — up to 87,000lb (39,463kg) — to provide a better range with full payload. The Series 400 had the same engines as the Srs 300, and the same structure, but was initially restricted to a gross weight of 79,000lb (35,834kg) to permit two-crew operation in the USA (this limit being lifted subsequently).

Flight development of the BAC One-Eleven was ill-fated, the first aircraft being lost, with a highly experienced crew, on 22 October 1963 when a hitherto unsuspected deep-stall problem was encountered, related to the T-tail, rear-engined layout. The subsequent investigation and corrective action, including installation of a stick-pusher to prevent excessive (nose-high) angles of incidence being achieved inadvertently, was of great value to all manufacturers, including those competing with BAC for the same airline orders. Certification was achieved on 6 April 1965. British United ▶

Below: A British Aerospace One-Eleven in the original livery of British Airways, for which operator this version was developed.

flew the first One-Eleven services on 9 April, and Braniff flew the first in the US on 25 April, following the granting of FAA Type Approval on 15 April.

The next One-Eleven milestone was reached on 13 July 1965, when the first of American Airlines' fleet — distinctive in a natural metal finish without the usual white upper surfaces to the fuselage — made its first flight. FAA Type Approval was obtained on 22 November 1965, and this type was to become one of the numerically most important One-Eleven variants (the other being the Series 500 which emerged in 1966) with 69 examples being built. Only nine Series 300s were built, and 56 Series 200s were delivered.

Whereas the Series 200, 300 and 400 were all dimensionally similar, the Series 500 introduced a lengthened fuselage to increase maximum passenger accommodation to 97 — and eventually, when higher weights were certificated, to 119. Stretched One-Elevens had been studied by BAC since before the first flight, but it was not until BEA decided to order the Series 500 that a go-ahead was given.

The fuselage of the Series 500 was lengthened by 13ft 6in (4·11m), and the wing span was increased by 5ft (1·2m) to cope with the increased weights, which also required a further uprating of the engine thrust, to 12,000lb st (4443kg) in the Spey 512-14 version. A company-owned Series 400 demonstrator was converted to the new configuration and flew as the prototype Series 500 on 30 June 1967 (initially retaining Spey 511 engines). The first production Series 500 flew on 7 February 1968 and was certificated on 18 August for BEA at a max weight of 92,483lb (41,950kg). Subsequently, the Series 500 was recertificated with 12,550lb st (5562kgp) Spey 512-14DW engines (with water injection) and the max weight went up to 99,650lb (45,200kg) or, to permit the use of a supplementary fuel tank in the aft end of the rear freight hold, 104,400lb (47,400kg). Orders for the Series 500 totalled 80 by the end of 1976, major users being British Airways, B. Cal., Philippine Air Lines, Tarom and several IT operators.

BAC developed the Series 475 as a "hot and high" version using the Spey 512-14DW engine and the extended span of the Series 500 with the original fuselage length, plus large-diameter low-pressure tyres which called for some modification of the wheel bays in the fuselage. The original Series 400/500 development aircraft was converted back to have the short fuselage and made its first flight as the Srs 475 prototype on 27 August 1970. The first production 475 flew on 5 April 1971 and certification was completed in July, when the first delivery was also made — to Faucett of Peru. The specialized characteristics of the One-Eleven Srs 475 proved, however, to be of rather limited airline interest and only a few examples were built.

In an effort to extend the useful life of the One-Eleven, BAC developed a "hush kit" for application to its Rolls-Royce Spey 512 engines, comprising an intake duct lining, a by-pass duct lining, an extended acoustically-lined jet pipe and a six-chute jet mixing exhaust silencer. The Srs 475 prototype fitted with these hush-kits made its first flight on 14 June 1974. Also during 1974, a freight door installation was designed for the One-Eleven for retrospective installation. The final One-Eleven variant to reach flight testing was the Series 670, which was similar to the Series 475 but had a refined wing profile and other changes to improve the field performance in line with Japanese requirements. The original Srs 475 prototype flew in late 1977 as the Series 670, but no production ensued.

In 1979, British Aerospace concluded an agreement with the National Centre of the Romanian Aircraft Industry (CNIAR), providing for the latter to establish a One-Eleven production line in Romania. The deal included the purchase of three complete One-Elevens and 22 kits from the British production line, the latter in various stages of completion, for assembly in Romania. The first of the UK-built trio of aircraft, a Srs 525/1, was delivered in January 1981, followed by a Srs 487 freighter in July and a second Srs 525/1 early in 1982. As the ROMBAC One-Eleven Series 550, the first of the 22 aircraft to be assembled in Romania was to fly also early in 1982. After completion of this batch, CNIAR has the right to undertake complete licence-manufacture of the One-Eleven.

Below: A Series 475 BAC One-Eleven, combining the original fuselage with the lengthened wing and uprated engines of the Series 500.

British Aerospace Jetstream
United Kingdom

The following data refer to the Jetstream 31:

Power Plant: Two Garrett TPE 331-10 turboprops flat-rated at 900shp each.

Performance: Max cruising speed, 303mph (488km/h); normal cruise, 291mph (469km/h); initial rate of climb, 2,231ft/min (11·1m/sec); service ceiling, 31,600ft (9480m); range, 483mls (778km) with 18 passengers.

Weights: Empty equipped, 8,840lb (4010kg); max take-off, 14,550lb (6600kg); max landing, 14,550lb (6600kg).

Dimensions: Span, 52ft 0in (15·86m); length, 47ft 1½in (14·35m); height, 17ft 6in (5·30m); wing area, 270sq ft (25·05m²).

The last aeroplane to bear the respected Handley Page name, and the project that was largely responsible for the financial collapse and demise of that illustrious company, the Jetstream was designed in the mid-sixties to provide an 8/18-seat transport suitable for third level airline as well as executive use. Two Turboméca Astazou XIV engines were chosen to power the HP.137 Jetstream, as the new type was named, and by the time the first of four prototypes flew on 18 August 1967, full-scale production had already been launched. A fifth prototype was powered by Garrett AiResearch TPE331 engines and flew on 21 November 1968.

Jetstreams with Astazou engines were in operation, both for business use and as airliners, by mid-1969, with the principal demand coming from the USA, but when Handley Page ceased operating in 1970 only 38 Jetstreams had been delivered; another 10 were completed subsequently from components already manufactured. Many of these Jetstreams remained in service subsequently, although the Astazou engine proved unpopular among American operators and several alternatives have been offered. These include at least one conversion to have Pratt & Whitney PT6A-34 turboprops by Riley Aeronautics Corporation, and the Century Jetstream III featuring 904eshp Garrett AiResearch TPE331-3U-303s offered by Century Aircraft and engineered by Volpar Inc. The first Century Jetstream III flew in August 1976.

Right: Photographed while in flight test, this is the prototype Jetstream 31, representative of the new production variant.

Below: Produced initially as a business transport, the Jetstream has been used as a commuter-liner by several airlines.

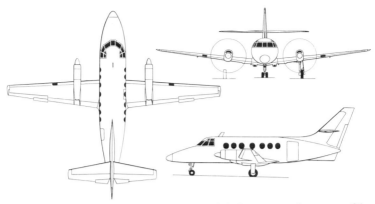

Above: Three-view drawing of the British Aerospace Jetstream 31, an updated version of the original Handley Page design.

In 1978, British Aerospace announced plans to re-launch production of the Jetstream, the manufacturing rights for which had been acquired by Scottish Aviation, now part of BAe. As the Jetstream 31, the new variant is powered by 900shp TPL331-10 turboprops and has higher operating weights, as quoted above. A prototype of the Jetstream 31, converted from an earlier airframe, first flew on 28 March 1980. The first production Jetstream 31 was to fly in 1982, with customer deliveries starting in July of that year. As a commuter airliner, the Jetstream 31 seats 18 passengers and early orders for the aircraft in this rôle were placed by Mall Airways in the USA, Partnair in Norway and Contactair in Stuttgart.

British Aerospace 146
United Kingdom

The specification below refers to the BAe 146-100:

Power Plant: Four Avco Lycoming ALF502 R-3 turbofans rated at 6,700lb st (3049kgp) for take-off. Fuel capacity, 2,540gal (11,540l).

Performance: Typical max cruising speed, 482mph (776km/h); typical long-range cruising speed, 427mph (687km/h); range with max payload, 588mls (946km); range with 82 passengers, 840mls (1352km).

Weights: Typical operating weight empty, 45,570lb (20,670kg), max take-off, 74,600lb (33,840kg); optional max take-off, 80,750lb (36,628kg); max landing weight, 71,850lb (32,590kg); max zero-fuel weight, 63,250lb (28,690kg).

Dimensions: Span, 86ft 6in (26·36m); length, 85ft 10in (26·16m); height 28ft 3in (8·61m); wing area, 832sq ft (77·3m²).

As the HS.146, this feederjet transport was launched on 29 August 1973 when the British government agreed to provide 50 per cent of the estimated launching costs of £92m as a risk-sharing investment. The HS.146 was the outcome of a lengthy period of design development that had embraced a series of twin-engined aircraft starting with the high-wing DH.123 with turboprops and passing through a number of low-wing rear-engined layouts up to the HS.144. Finally, in April 1971, attention switched to a high wing layout and, from a number of possible power plants, the Avco Lycoming ALF 502 high by-pass turbofan emerged as the most promising, although this led to a four-engined layout.

The HS.146, as launched in 1973, was designed to provide a 70—100-seat aircraft for the short-haul feederline market, which appeared to be growing vigorously. Good field performance was required, although not so good as to call for special STOL capability, and ease of maintenance, simplicity of operation and extreme reliability were considered to be prerequisites to make the aircraft attractive to smaller airlines in underdeveloped countries. Unfortunately, however, the launch decision was taken only just before the world-wide recession that occurred in 1974/75 in the wake of the oil crisis, and within a year it had become clear that the market was not going to develop as rapidly as originally forecast, while inflation pushed the cost of development up dramatically. Consequently, Hawker Siddeley terminated the programme in October 1974, although development was allowed to continue at a slow pace under government contract in order to retain the option of relaunching.

After Hawker Siddeley had become part of the nationalized British Aerospace Corporation, the 146 was subjected to a thorough review and the potential market was carefully re-analysed, as a result of which the management decided to recommend a resumption of full-scale development. Government approval for this step was obtained on 10 July 1978, and the British Aerospace 146 thus became the first new aircraft undertaken by the state Corporation. Apart from some changes in design weight, the 146 remained substantially the same as originally launched.

The BAe 146 has a relatively wide fuselage for an aircraft of its size, allowing six-abreast seating, and is available in two versions, the basic -100 and the lengthened -200. Respectively, these seat up to 93 and 109 passengers in one-class high-density layouts, more typical figures being 71—88 for the -100 and 82—96 for the -200. Final assembly of all versions is based at Hatfield; Avco Corporation, which provides the Lycoming engines, is a risk-sharing partner in the programme with responsibility for the main wing box; other sub-contractors are Saab-Scania, making the tailplane, elevators, rudder and some wing moving parts; and Shorts with responsibility for the engine pods. Other major airframe components are produced by factories within the British Aerospace group.

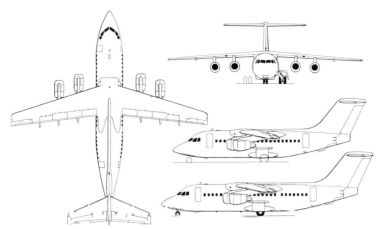

Above: Three-view drawing of the British Aerospace 146 Srs 200 with additional side-view of the shorter fuselage Srs 100.

Below: The first example of the BAe 146 on its maiden flight. The registration G-SSSH was chosen to emphasise the low noise levels.

First flight of the BAe 146 was made at Hatfield on 3 September 1981 and a second aircraft flew on 25 January 1982, both these being Srs 100 aircraft, as was the third, also dedicated to the flight test and certification programme. The first Srs 200, No 4 in the final assembly sequence, flew early-1982, by which time British Aerospace had recorded 11 firm orders and 12 options for the stretched variant and two orders for the Srs 100. Certification was expected before the end of 1982 for the Srs 100 and early in 1983 for the Srs 200.

Britten-Norman Trislander
United Kingdom

Power Plant: Three 260 Lycoming O-540-E4C5 piston engines.
Performance: Max speed, 183mph (294km/h) at sea level; max cruising speed (75 per cent engine power), 176mph (283km/h) at 6,500ft (1988m); typical cruise (67 per cent engine power), 174mph (280km/h) at 9,000ft (2750m); best economy cruise (59 per cent engine power), 168mph (270km/h) at 13,000ft (3960m); initial rate of climb, 980ft/min (4·98m/sec), service ceiling, 13,150ft (4010m); range with max payload (VFR reserves) 210mls (338km); range with max fuel, 860mls (1384km).
Weights: Basic operating, 6,178lb (2800kg); max payload, 3,550lb (1610kg); max take-off, 10,000lb (4536kg).
Dimensions: Span, 53ft 0in (16·15m); length, 43ft 9in (13·34m); length (extended nose), 47ft 6in (14·48m); height, 13ft 5¾in (4·11m); wing area, 337sq ft (31·25m²).

The uniquely configured Trislander was evolved directly from the best-selling Islander, having the same fuselage cross section and same mainplane and power plant. Its new features were increased fuselage length, and a third engine — necessary to cope with the higher operating weights — located in a nacelle carried on the fin. The tailplane — larger than that of the Islander — was located high on the fin instead of being on the fuselage.

Evolution of the Trislander began in 1968, when a long-fuselage Islander was test-flown (starting on 14 July). The prototype Trislander flew on 11 September 1970 and after some changes in tail unit shape and area, it entered small-scale production alongside the Islander; the first production model flew on 6 March 1971, British and US certification being obtained on 14 May and 4 August 1971 respectively. Up to 18 passengers are carried, two-abreast.

Deliveries began on 29 June 1971, and the first Trislanders were known as BN-2A Mk IIIs at the gross weight of 9,350lb (4245kg), but this was soon increased to 10,000lb (4540kg) in the BN-2A Mk III-1. On 18 August 1974, the first Trislander with the lengthened nose of the BN-2S Islander made its first flight and this feature then became standard on the BN-2A Mk III-2. About 50 Trislanders had been sold by 1979, when the Britten-Norman company was acquired by Pilatus; production continued at Bembridge, IoW, but sales remain at a modest level compared with the success of the Islander (nearly 1,000 examples of which had been built by the end of 1981) and were still a little short of 100 in 1981.

Right: A Britten-Norman Trislander (production of which is continued at Bembridge on the Isle-of-Wight under the Pilatus company) operated by Loganair. The longest-established independent airline in Scotland, Loganair had three Trislanders in its fleet in 1982 and flew scheduled services to many small communities.

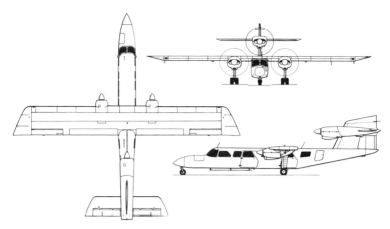

Above: The Trislander, showing its unique configuration, with two engines on the wing and one located high on the fin.

Below: The Britten-Norman Trislander, used by a number of smaller airlines for "third-level" operation.

Casa Aviocar
Spain

The specification below refers to the C-212-200:

Power Plant: Two 900shp Garrett-AiResearch TPE331-10-501C turbo-props.

Performance: Max speed 240mph (386km/h) at 10,000ft (3050m); cruising speed, 219mph (353km/h) at 10,000ft (3050m); initial rate of climb, 1,700ft/min (8.6m/sec); service ceiling, 28,000ft (8540m); range, 470mls (760km) with max payload and no reserves.

Weights: Empty equipped, 8,630lb (3915kg); max cargo payload, 4,960lb (2250kg); max take-off weight, 16,093lb (7300kg).

Dimensions: Span, 62ft 4in (19.0m); length, 44ft 9in (15.16m); height, 21ft 11in (6.68m); wing area, 430.6sq ft (40.9m²).

The Aviocar was developed by the Spanish company Construcciones Aeronauticas SA (CASA) primarily to meet Spanish Air Force requirements for a multi-rôle transport, and its initial construction and production was in this guise, although civil applications were in prospect from the start of design. A high-wing monoplane of simple and rugged construction, the C.212 follows conventional lines for a light transport, with the cabin providing a basically uninterrupted box shape to which straight-in access can be obtained by means of a rear loading ramp.

Powered by 776shp Garrett-AiResearch TPE331 turboprops, two prototypes of the Aviocar were built, making their initial flights on 26 March and 23 October 1971. Production was then launched against Spanish Air Force contracts, the Aviocar being adopted to replace such elderly transports still in service as the Junkers Ju 52/3m, Douglas DC-3 and CASA-207 Azor. As well as serving as a 16-paratroop carrier, the military C.212 could be adapted as an ambulance, photo-survey aircraft, freighter or crew trainer. The first production aircraft flew on 17 November 1972.

As the C.212C, the Aviocar has been marketed as a 19-seat passenger transport for civil operation, initial sales being made to Pertamina in Indonesia for operation by its subsidiary Pelita Air Service. CASA also con-

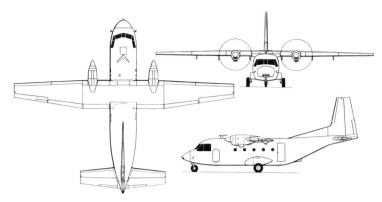

Above: Three-view drawing of the CASA 212 Aviocar. Civil and military variants are externally similar, but a lengthened version is projected for civil use.

cluded an agreement with the PT Nurtania company in Djakarta whereby the latter undertook to assemble Aviocars in Indonesia for supply to customers throughout the Far East. This step led to a substantial expansion of the market for the Aviocar, especially among civil operators in Indonesia and other countries in the Far East. By the end of 1981, CASA had sold 202 Aviocars in 27 countries (for military and civil use) and of these 82 had been sold and assembled by Nurtanio.

Initial civil Aviocars were of the C.212CA standard, having a gross weight of 12,500lb (5675kg) but this was increased later to 14,330lb (6500kg). In 1978, CASA completed aircraft Nos 138 and 139 as prototypes of the C-212 Series 200 (the earlier version then becoming known as the C-212-5); these prototypes first flew on 30 April and 20 June 1978. Principal new features of the Srs 200 are the use of 900shp Garrett TPE331-10-501C engines and a gross weight of 16,093lb (7300kg).

Below: The CASA C-212 Aviocar, seen here in its Series 200 version, has proved successful in both military and civil roles.

Casa-Nurtanio CN-235
International

Power Plant: Two flat-rated 1,700shp General Electric CT7-7 turboprops.
Performance: Max cruise (ISA) 288mph (463km/h) at 20,000ft (6095m);
initial rate of climb, 2,165ft/min (11m/sec); range (with 34 passengers at
200lb/91kg) 920mls (1482km) and (with 38 passengers) 690mls (1112km)
at max cruise power at 20,000ft (6095m).
Weights: Max payload 9,920lb (4500kg); max take-off, 28,658lb
(13,000kg); max landing, 28,218lb (12,800kg).
Dimensions: Span 84ft 7$\frac{1}{2}$in (25·8m); length 69ft 10$\frac{1}{4}$in (21·3m); height,
25ft 11in (7·9m).

Launched on the international market at the Paris Air Show 1981, with
announced orders for 54 aircraft plus 18 options from Indonesian, Spanish
and Argentinian operators, the CN-235 34/38-seat commuterliner and
utility transport is the subject of joint development and production by the
Spanish Construcciones Aeronauticas SA (CASA) and the Indonesian PT
Nurtanio concern on a 50-50 basis. No duplication of component manufacture is planned between the Spanish and Indonesian partners in the
programme, CASA being responsible primarily for the equipped front
fuselage and centre wing, with Nurtanio providing the rear fuselage, outer
wing panels and tail surfaces. Tooling manufacture was to begin in December
1981, followed by the start in May 1982 of detail parts production. Integra-
tion of the first complete fuselages for the initial pre-series aircraft in both
Spain and Indonesia was planned for March—April 1983, with final assembly
in July and simultaneous roll-out of the first aircraft from each of the
Spanish and Indonesian assembly lines foreseen for 1 September 1983.
Initial flight testing was planned to begin one month later, with both certification and first flight of the production CN-235 following in 1984.

The CN-235 differs from its competitors in being aimed equally at civil
and military markets, the requirements of the latter having strongly influenced
several aspects of the design. Owing much to experience gained with the
smaller C-212 Aviocar, the CN-235 places emphasis on simplicity and
sturdiness, and the ability to operate from semi-prepared fields. Unusual
among aircraft in its category in having a large rear ventral ramp and
retractable, tandem-wheel main undercarriage members suitable for rough
field operation — both features selected primarily to endear the aircraft to
potential military operators despite weight and drag penalties — the CN-235
is offered in a variety of configurations, ranging from a straight commuter-
liner for 34-passengers with seats at 32-in (81-cm) pitch seating, through
combi and quick-change versions to a pure freighter carrying cargo on 88-in
(2·23-m) wide pallets or accommodating five standard LD-2 or four
standard LD-3 containers.

The oval-section fuselage of the CN-235 is claimed to provide a high
standard of comfort for commuter-liner operations with four-abreast
seating, a central aisle with a height of 6ft 2$\frac{3}{4}$in (1·9m), 13$\frac{3}{4}$ by 11in (34·8 by
28cm) windows, toilet, galley and 247cu ft (6·99m^3) baggage container,
the last-mentioned being aft of the pressurized cabin. As a freighter, the
CN-235 will carry 9,920lb (4500kg) of cargo.

CASA and Nurtanio market studies indicated a market within the 1984—94
timeframe for some 1,800 aircraft in the CN-235 category, of which the
partner companies hope for 20 per cent, plus a further 600 similar aircraft
for the military market within the same period, and of these 40 per cent are
expected to be supplied by the CASA-Nurtanio transport. Thus, CASA-
Nurtanio was looking for the sale of 600 CN-235s over the decade following
first customer delivery, and has already started to study the potential for a
stretched derivative of the CN-235 accommodating 51—59 passengers for the
late 'eighties.

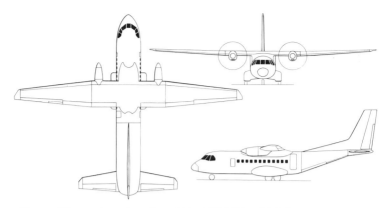

Above: Three-view drawing of the CN-235, which incorporates a rear-loading ramp to cater particularly for cargo carrying.

Below: An impression of the CN-235, which was launched jointly by CASA and Nurtanio after successful collaboration on the C-212 Aviocar.

Convair 240, 340, 440
USA

The following specification relates to the Convair 440:
Power Plant: Two 2,500hp Pratt & Whitney R-2800-CB16 or -CB17 piston radials.
Performance: Max cruising speed, 300mph (483km/h) at 13,000ft (3962m); best economy cruise, 289mph (465km/h) at 20,000ft (6100m); initial rate of climb, 1,260ft/min (6·4m/sec); service ceiling, 24,900ft (7590m); range with max payload, 285mls (459km); range with max fuel, 1,930mls (3106km).
Weights: Basic operating, 33,314lb (15,110kg); max payload, 12,836lb (5820kg); max take-off, 49,700lb (22,544kg).
Dimensions: Span, 105ft 4in (32·12m); length, 81ft 6in (24·84m); height, 28ft 2in (8·59m); wing area, 920sq ft (85·5m²).

In view of the success enjoyed by the Douglas DC-3 in the years immediately preceding World War II, it was natural that airlines and manufacturers alike should be interested in the concept of a "DC-3 replacement" for use immediately after the war. A specification for such an aeroplane was set out by American Airlines early in 1945, for use on routes of up to about 1,000mls (1600km) in length to complement the four-engine types becoming available for the longer hauls.

Negotiations between American and Convair led the latter company to go ahead with construction of its first commercial airliner, the Model 110. Powered by 2,100hp Pratt & Whitney R-2800 radial engines, it provided accommodation for 30 passengers and was first flown on 8 July 1946 at San Diego. Before that event, however, American had decided that a somewhat larger aircraft was required, and placed an order with Convair for 75 of the Model 240 design, based on the prototype Model 110. No prototype of the 240 was built as such, production jigs and tools being used from the outset and the first aircraft being flown on 16 March 1947. The overall dimensions of the 240 – which retained the same power plant – were somewhat larger than those of the 110, and passenger accommodation was increased to a basic 40 in single class, although the fuselage diameter was actually reduced by 4in (10cm) to keep drag down.

American Airlines put the Model 240, often known as the Convairliner, into service on 1 June 1948 and the type quickly settled down as a modern companion to the four-engined generation represented by the DC-4 and early models of the Constellation. Although the availability of large numbers of surplus DC-3s probably restricted the market for Convair 240s to some extent, the type sold well, with sales totalling 176 for airline use and another 39 for other customers – primarily the USAF which acquired it for use both as a transport (C-131) and a trainer (T-29). A few Convair 240s are still used in various parts of the world, together with larger numbers of the improved Model 340 and 440.

Convair set about to improve the basic Model 240 in 1951, and on 5 October in that year flew the first Convair 340 at San Diego. This was a straightforward "stretch" of the original design, with the fuselage lengthened by 4ft 6in (1·38m) and the wing area also increased to cope with the higher operating weights. The passenger accommodation was increased by one seat row, to a basic 44, and the use of uprated engines – 2,500hp R-2800-CB16 or -CB17 – resulted in a slightly improved performance. The first airline service by Convair 340 was flown on 28 March 1952 and production totalled 212 for airline use, plus 99 non-airline.

Further refinement of the Model 340 led to the appearance of the Model 440 Metropolitan in 1955: the prototype flew on 6 October, and the first production model on 15 December in that year. Having the same overall dimensions as the Model 340, the 440 had redesigned engine nacelles and

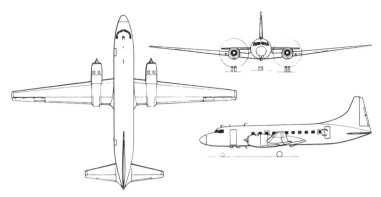

Above: A three-view of the Convair 440 in its standard production version, with weather radar in a lengthened nose

other refinements to improve performance and passenger comfort. Seating capacity was eventually increased to a maximum of 52 as high-density arrangements became more acceptable, and most Convair 440s had nose radar, lengthening the fuselage by another 2ft 4in (0·70m).

The Convair 440 entered airline service, with Continental Airlines, in February 1956 and production totalled 153 for the airlines and 26 for other users. The name Metropolitan was used primarily for Convair 440s supplied to European airlines, several of which used the Convair series in substantial quantities prior to the introduction of turboprop equipment. Substantial numbers of Convairliners were still in service in the early 'eighties primarily in North and South America in the hands of smaller airlines. Many had also been converted to have turboprop engines, as described on the next page.

Below: The Convair 240/340/440 series of piston-engined 44/52-seat transports enjoyed reasonable success in the intended role as a DC-3 replacement, although by 1982 fewer examples of the Convair types remained in service than of the original Douglas twin. The illustration shows a Convair 440 in the colours of Great Lakes, an operator typical of the third-level airlines that proliferated in the USA in the 'seventies.

Convair 580, 600, 640
USA

The following specification relates to the Convair 580:
Power Plant: Two 3,750shp Allison 501-D13H turboprops.
Performance: Cruising speed, 342mph (550km/h); range with max fuel, 2,866mls (4611km).
Weights: Max payload 8,870lb (4023kg); max take-off, 58,140lb (26,371kg).
Dimensions: Span, 105ft 4in (32·12m), length, 81ft 6in (24·84m); height, 29ft 2in (8·89m); wing area, 920sq ft (85·5m²).
The following specification relates to the Convair 640:
Power Plant: Two 3,025eshp Rolls-Royce Dart 542-4 turboprops.
Performance: Cruising speed, 300mph (482km/h); range with max payload, 1,230mls (1975km) at 15,000ft (4575m); range with max fuel, 1,950mls (3138km) at 15,000ft (4575m).
Weights: Basic operating, 30,275lb (13,732kg); max payload, 15,800lb (7167kg); max take-off, 55,000lb (24,950kg) or 57,000lb (25,855kg) if Model 440 with outer wing fuel and fuel dumping.
Dimensions: Span, 105ft 4in (32·12m); length, 81ft 6in (24·84m); height, 28ft 2in (8·59m); wing area, 920sq ft (85·5m²).

Over 230 examples of the Convair 240/340/440 family (see previous page) were later converted to have turboprop engines in one or other of three such programmes undertaken between 1955 and 1967. Although other piston-engined aircraft have also been converted to turboprop power, only the Convair achieved success on this scale — a tribute to the sound structural and engineering design of the basic aircraft that allowed it to be given a new lease of life.

The primary reason for converting Convair airframes in this way was to improve performance and operating economics and thus prolong the useful life of an ageing aircraft type. To investigate the possibilities, Convair flew a Model 240 with Allison T38 (501-A2) turboprops on 29 December 1950, this prototype being known as the Turboliner. The T38 was developed into the T56 for military use, and two Convair 340s were converted to have these engines (similar to the commercial 501-D13) as part of a USAF investigation into the value of turboprops for transport aircraft in general; designated YC-131C, the first of these flew on 29 June 1954.

The first conversion programme aimed specifically at airline applications was launched by the former UK engine company D Napier & Son, Ltd, in 1954. A Convair 340 with two of that company's 3,060ehp Eland NEl.1 turboprops flew on 9 February 1955, and six more conversions were made, entering service with Allegheny Airlines in the USA in July 1959 as Convair 540s. Production and development of the Eland was terminated in 1962, however, and these conversions reverted to their original piston-engined f or m. Canadair also built ten Canadair 540s (using Convair's original jigs) as CL-66B Cosmopolitans for the RCAF, with Eland engines and converted three others, two going into service for a time with Quebecair.

Next to appear was the Allison-Convair, sometimes also referred to as the Super Convair, and eventuall designated the Convair 580. This had two 3,750eshp Allison 501-D13 turboprops and the conversion work was done by Pacific Airmotive, first flight being made on 19 January 1960. FAA certification — started with one of the YC-131Cs — was obtained on 21 April 1960, followed by first delivery (to a corporate owner) on 6 May 1960 and first airline service (by Frontier) in June 1964. Of 130 Allison-Convairs converted, 110 were for airline use in the first instance, with Allegheny and Lake Central (subsequently merged under the former name) having a combined fleet of over 40 at one time. Other major airline users were Frontier, North Central and Avensa, all still using the Convair 580 in 1974, and

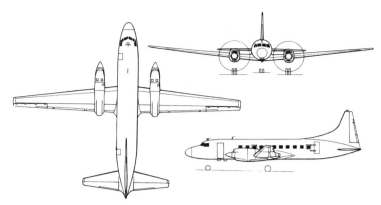

Above: The Convair 580, a conversion of the original piston-engined Convairliner with Allison 501D turboprops.

Below: A Convair 580 in the livery of North Central Airlines, a US local-service airline which merged in 1979 with Southern Airways to form Republic Airlines. Nearly 20 of the Allison turboprop-engined Convair 580s remained in Republic's fleet in 1982.

SAHSA-Honduras, which acquired two second-hand.

Final turboprop programme for the Convair family comprised installation of the Rolls-Royce Dart 542 rated at 3,025eshp, this being the only programme in which Convair Division of General Dynamics was directly involved, offering kits or converted airframes. These conversions were at first referred to as the Convair 240D, 340D and 440D, but the 240D later became the Convair 600, while Dart-engined 340s or 440s became Convair 640s. Central Airlines initiated the programme by ordering 10 Convair 600s, first flight being made at San Diego on 20 May 1965; FAA certification was obtained on 18 November 1965 and the type entered service on 30 November. The Convair 640 was launched by orders placed by Caribair and Hawaiian Airlines; the type entered service with the former airline on 22 December 1965. In all, 39 Convair 600s and 28 Convair 640s were converted and most were still in service in 1981, although in the hands of operators other than those for which they had first been converted.

Convair (General Dynamics) 880 and 990
USA

The following specification relates to the Convair 990A:
Power Plant: Four 16,050lb st (7280kgp) General Electric CJ805-23B turbofans.
Performance: Max level speed (M = 0·871), 615mph (990km/h) at 20,000ft (6100m) at a weight of 200,000lb (90,720kg); long-range cruising speed (Mach = 0·84), 556mph (895km/h) at 35,000ft (10,670m); service ceiling, 41,000ft (12,500m); range with max payload, 3,800mls (6115km); range with max fuel, 5,446mls (8770km).
Weights: Basic operating, 120,900lb (54,840kg); max payload, 26,440lb (11,992kg); max take-off, 253,000lb (114,760kg); max landing, 202,000lb (91,625kg).
Dimensions: Span, 120ft 0in (36·58m); length, 139ft 2½in (42·43m); height, 39ft 6in (12·04m); wing area, 2,250sq ft (209m²).

The Convair Division of General Dynamics became the third US manufacturer to enter the jet transport market when it launched the construction of a medium-range, high performance airliner in September 1956. By that date, Boeing and Douglas were already committed to the 707 and DC-8 respectively and Convair was seeking to retain a foothold in the commercial market, following its success with the Convair 240/340/440 family. The attempt proved an extremely expensive one for the company and after only limited development of the basic design, all civil aircraft production by Convair came to an end.

Market surveys during 1955 led Convair to choose an aircraft of smaller capacity (90 in mixed class, up to 124 high density), but higher performance than the Boeing and Douglas types, although of the same overall configuration. Powered by four General Electric CJ805 engines (versions of the military J79) it was intended to operate primarily on US domestic trunk routes, and the fuselage diameter was sufficient only for five-abreast seating, compared with the six-abreast arrangements in the 707 and DC-8.

Designed as the Model 22, the new transport was at first called the Convair Skylark, and then the Golden Arrow; when this name was in turn dropped, the appellation Convair 600 was chosen, derived from the cruising speed of 600mph plus: this speed expressed as feet per second led to the definitive name of Convair 880. The first flight was made on 27 January 1959 at San Diego, certification being obtained on 1 May 1960 and Delta inaugurating Convair 880 service later that month.

The Convair 880 achieved little sales success compared with the larger Boeing and Douglas jets and only 65 were built, including 17 Convair Model 31 or 880-M with extra fuel in the centre section and higher weights. The last major airline to use the 880-M regularly was Cathay Pacific in Hong Kong which had seven in service in 1974, but these are now out of use. In 1979, Gulfstream American converted two 880s to Airlifter configuration for all-cargo or cargo/passenger convertible use, and this company in 1981 had more than 20 more CV-880s available for conversion.

A growth version of the Convair 880 was first projected in 1958 as the Model 30, with a longer fuselage (of the same cross section), to seat up to 106 passengers, a longer wing, more fuel capacity and turbofan engines. An unusual feature was the use of four anti-shock fairings on the wing trailing edge to achieve higher cruising speeds for the same engine power. American Airlines placed a launching order for this new model on 30 July 1958, the name Convair 600 being used again for a time before it was changed to Convair 990.

First flight was made on 24 January 1961, but flight development proved

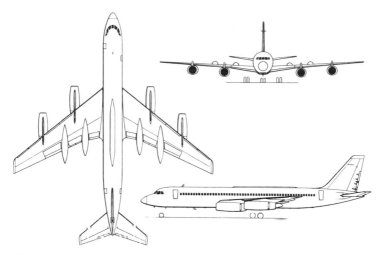

Above: The Convair 990, showing the four fairings on the wing that were designed to improve efficiency in cruising flight.

to be protracted and expensive and a series of modifications had to be engineered and test flown to allow the Convair 990A — as it became when fully modified — to meet its guaranteed speed and range performance.

American Airlines accepted its first (unmodified) aircraft on 8 January 1963 and modified 990As entered service later in the same year. Production ended after only 37 had been built, the original operators, other than American, being Swissair, SAS, Garuda Indonesian and Varig. Spantax, a Spanish charter company, and Modern Air Transport, a US supplemental airline, acquired fleets of Convair 990As from American, from 1967 onwards. In 1981 Spantax was the last major operator of the Convair transport, with 12 in service.

Below: The Convair 990, least successful of the first-generation jet transports. This is one of four used by the Ports of Call travel club.

Dassault-Breguet Mercure
France

Power Plant: Two 15,500lb st (7030kgp) Pratt & Whitney JT8D-15 turbofans.

Performance: Max cruising speed, 579mph (932km/h) at 20,000ft (6100m); best economy cruise, 533mph (858km/h) at 30,000ft (9145m); initial rate of climb, 3,300ft/min (16·76m/sec) at 100,000lb (45,359kg) weight; range with max payload, 466mls (750km); range with max fuel, 1,025mls (1650km).

Weights: Basic operating, 70,107lb (31,800kg); max payload, 35,715lb (16,200kg); max take-off, 124,560lb (56,500kg).

Dimensions: Span, 100ft 3in (30·55m); length, 114ft 3½in (34·84m); height, 37ft 3¼in (11·36m); wing area, 1,249sq ft (116·0m²).

In a bold gamble to enter the airline market at a level considerably above the biz-jet field represented by its highly successful Mystère Falcon 20, the Dassault company launched the construction of a twin-jet transport in the Boeing 737 class in early 1969. This step followed a lengthy study of the potential market and the preparation of several smaller transport projects with the name Mystère 30 or Mercure, leading to the conclusion that there was a market for a large capacity transport (up to 150 seats) optimized for ranges of up to 930mls (1500km). The market between 1973 and 1981 was estimated to be for as many as 1,500 aircraft.

The French government agreed to provide a loan – to be repaid by a levy on sales – of 56 per cent of the launching costs and Dassault contributed 14 per cent; the balance of 30 per cent was obtained from risk-sharing partners in Italy (Aeritalia); Spain (CASA), Belgium (SABCA), Switzerland (F+W) and Canada (Canadair). While two prototypes were put in hand, Dassault set about building up major new production facilities for the Mercure, which took shape as a conventional low-wing aeroplane with 25 deg sweepback and two podded Pratt & Whitney JT8D turbofan engines.

The first of two prototypes flew on 28 May 1971 from Bordeaux, powered by 15,000lb st (6800kgp) JT8D-11 engines. After 20 flights, the definitive JT8D-15 engines were fitted, flying in the prototype for the first time on 7 September 1971, and on 18 November the first flight was made with di-hedral on the tailplane. The second prototype flew on 7 September 1972 from the new factory at Istres, with new leading-edge slats fitted.

Below: In the colours of Air Inter – the only airline to operate the type – is the second prototype Dassault-Breguet Mercure.

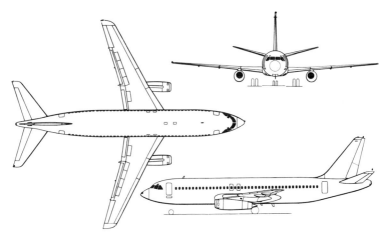

Above: Three-view drawing of the Dassault-Breguet Mercure 100, the initial production version and, in the event, only variant built.

Although Dassault had originally indicated that it would put the Mercure into production only if reasonably firm orders for at least 60 were in prospect, the programme was in fact launched on the strength of a single order for 10 examples placed by the French domestic airline Air Inter on 29 January 1972. Operated by a flight crew of two, the Mercure was to be able to seat 155 passengers in a typical mixed class layout and would carry this maximum payload a distance of about 450mls (750km). Air Inter remained the only Mercure customer despite Dassault attempts to launch an enlarged version as the Mercure 200, this project also being the basis for a joint Dassault McDonnell Douglas design study and market survey in 1976/77.

The first production Mercure flew at Istres on 17 July 1973 and the French C of A was awarded on 12 February 1974, permitting operation in Cat II weather conditions. Delivery of the first two aircraft was made to Air Inter on 16 May and 11 June 1974 respectively, and the first commercial service was flown on 4 June.

Certification for Cat III operation was granted on 30 September 1974, by which time Air Inter had received four aircraft. The equipment for Cat III comprised a Bendix auto-pilot and a Thomson-CSF Head-up Display, permitting operations with a runway visual range of 500ft (150m) and a decision height of 50ft (15m). Two aircraft equipped to this standard (Nos 5 and 6) were delivered to Air Inter in 1974 and the remainder of the fleet entered service in 1975.

De Havilland Canada DHC-6 Twin Otter
Canada

The following specification refers to the Twin Otter Series 300:

Power Plant: Two 652eshp Pratt & Whitney PT6A-27 turboprops.
Performance: Max cruising speed, 210mph (338km/h); initial rate of climb, 1,600ft/min (8·1m/sec); service ceiling, 26,700ft (8140m); range with max payload, 115mls (160km); range with max fuel, 1,103mls (1775km).
Weights: Basic operating, 7,320lb (3320kg); max payload, 4,430lb (2010kg); max take-off, 12,500lb (5670kg).
Dimensions: Span, 65ft 0in (19·81m); length, 51ft 9in (15·77m); height, 18ft 7in (5·66m); wing area, 420sq ft (39·02m²).

The de Havilland Aircraft of Canada Ltd (originally a subsidiary of the British de Havilland company and until 1974 a member company of Hawker Siddeley Group) has specialized in the production of STOL utility aircraft and light transports since 1947, when the single-engined Beaver made its first flight. Continuing the Beaver theme, the company went on to produce the larger Otter (also single-engined, and known originally as the King Beaver) and then evolved the Twin Otter to use many of the wing and fuselage components of the Otter, but with two engines.

Whereas the company's earlier twin-engined types, the Caribou and the Buffalo, had been aimed primarily at the military user, the Twin Otter was intended specifically for commercial use, especially in the rôle of third-level airliner or commuter, operating from restricted areas. The Twin Otter used the same basic fuselage cross section as the Otter, with new nose and tail assemblies, and the cabin section extended in length to seat up to 20 passengers in individual seats with a central aisle. The basic wing section was also similar to that of the Otter, with the span increased from 58ft (17·68m) to 65ft (19·81m). STOL performance was achieved, as in the earlier DHC types, by aerodynamic lift only, using double-slotted full-span trailing edge flaps, the outer sections of which also operated differentially as ailerons. A fixed tricycle undercarriage was adopted, the small performance penalty that this involved being offset by the reduced first cost and simpler maintenance.

Turboprop power was chosen for the Twin Otter in the form of the then-new Pratt & Whitney PT6As developed in Canada by United Aircraft of Canada Ltd. The decision to proceed with development of the Twin Otter was taken early in 1964, and construction of an initial batch of five aircraft

Right: De Havilland Canada Twin Otter 300 LN-BEC was the first of 13 of these light transports that made up the principal component of the Widerøe's Flyveselskap fleet in Norway by 1982. The Twin Otter has proved to be the most successful, to date, of de Havilland's range of STOL aircraft.

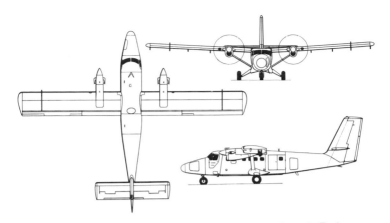

Above: Three-view drawing of the de Havilland Canada Twin Otter Series 300; the Srs 200 is externally similar but the original Srs 100 had a shorter nose fairing.

began in November of that year. Assembly proceeded rapidly, thanks to the commonality of many components with the Otter, and the first Twin Otter, appropriately registered CF-DHC, made its first flight at Downsview, near Ontario, on 20 May 1965. The first three examples had 579shp PT6A-6 turboprops, but the production standard incorporated the improved PT6A-20s of similar power. Type approval was obtained in May 1966 and deliveries began in July. When the Series 200 version of the Twin Otter was introduced in due course, the first production standard became known as the Series 100, production of this version totalling 115.

Delivery of the Twin Otter Series 200 began in April 1968, this version differing from the first in having a lengthened nose fairing with larger baggage capacity. Production of this variant also totalled 115.

About a year after the Twin Otter 200 appeared, de Havilland introduced the Series 300, which differed in having 652ehp PT6A-27 engines and an increase of nearly 1,000lb (454kg) in max take-off weight. By the end of 1981, sales of the Twin Otter were approaching 800, of which more than 700 had been delivered. The type was in use with many scheduled airlines throughout the world for commuter-style operations and for services on routes with low traffic densities. Floatplane and wheel/skiplane versions had also been delivered, all floatplanes having the original Series 100 short nose, irrespective of particular model concerned. Also available and used by a few operators was a ventral pod carrying up to 600lb (272kg) of baggage or freight.

De Havilland Canada DHC-7 Dash 7
Canada

Power Plant: Four 1,120shp Pratt & Whitney (UACL) PT6A-50 turbo-props.

Performance: Max cruising speed, 261mph (420km/h) at 15,000ft (4570m); initial rate of climb, 1,220ft/min (6.2m/sec); service ceiling, 21,000ft (6400m); range with 50 passenger payload, 840mls (1352km); range with max fuel, 1,335mls (2148km).

Weights: Operating empty, 27,650lb (12,542kg); max payload, 11,350lb (5148kg); max take-off, 44,000lb (19,958kg).

Dimensions: Span, 93ft 0in (28.35m); length, 80ft 8in (24.58m); height, 26ft 3in (8.00m); wing area, 860sq ft (79.9m²).

The Dash 7 is the largest in a series of specialized STOL aircraft originated by the de Havilland Canada company, being intended to make airline-standard flying possible from airfields with runways little more than 2,000ft (610m) in length. Its STOL performance is derived from an aero-dynamic lift system using double slotted flaps operating in the slipstream from four large-diameter, slow-running, five-bladed propellers. These propellers, and the PT6A-50 turboprops, are also designed to minimize noise levels both externally and within the cabin, which provides accommodation for 48–54 passengers in four-abreast layouts.

Construction of two prototypes was launched in 1972 with backing of the Canadian Government, and this was followed by a full production decision announced on 26 November 1974. The prototypes made their first flights on 27 March and 26 June 1975 respectively and the flight test programme was continued with these aircraft throughout 1976. The first production aircraft of an initial batch of 50 approved by the Canadian govern-

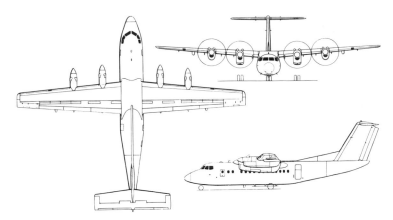

Above: Three view drawing of the de Havilland Canada DHC-7 Dash 7 STOL (short take-off and landing) airliner in its basic Series 100 form as initially produced.

ment (which had acquired DHC from Hawker Siddeley in June 1974) flew on 30 May 1977 and was one of a pair ordered by Rocky Mountain Airways. The Dash 7 entered service with the latter company on 3 February 1978 and by the end of 1981, sales had reached a total of nearly 130. The basic passenger version is the Series 100, with a few aircraft used in the all-cargo rôle designated Series 101. Projected future developments include the Series 200 with 1,230shp PT6A-55 engines and 46,000lb (20,866kg) gross weight and the Series 300 with a stretched fuselage.

Below: An eye-catching colour scheme is sported by this early production model of the de Havilland Canada Dash 7, used as a demonstrator. The name Dash 7 is taken from the DHC-7 designation.

De Havilland Canada DHC-8 Dash 8
Canada

Power Plant: Two Pratt & Whitney Canada PW120 turboprops each flat-rated at 1,788shp to 82 deg F (27·7 deg C) for take-off and continuous power.

Performance: Max cruise speed at 15,000ft (4572m), 311mph (500km/h) at 29,000lb (13,154kg). Range with 36 passengers, IFR fuel reserves, at 5,000ft (1524m), four stage lengths each of 115mls (185km) without refuelling.

Weights: Operating weight empty, 20,176lb (9152kg); max payload, 7,824lb (3549kg); max take-off weight (standard), 30,500lb (13,835kg); max landing weight, 30,000lb (13,605kg); max zero-fuel weight, 28,000lb (12,700kg).

Dimensions: Span, 84ft 0in (25·60m); length, 73ft 0in (22·25m); height, 25ft 0in (7·62m); wing area, 585sq ft (54·3m²).

Marketed as the Dash 8, the de Havilland Aircraft of Canada DHC-8 is a logical derivation and extension of successful experience in world markets with turboprop-powered short-haul STOL transports. The Dash 8 is an evolutionary design embodying service-proven features of the Dash 7, Buffalo/Transporter and Twin Otter while taking full advantage of new technology and the latest manufacturing methods. More than 100 had been committed to production by the end of 1981, at the rate of six a month to be reached within 18 months of first delivery. In October 1981, the company announced it had 110 aircraft on option for more than 30 companies. Duplicate tooling and fixtures were being provided from the outset to ensure that the rate would be attained and that eight aircraft a month could be built without having to wait for increased productivity as shopworkers gained experience.

Building on the success of the 50-passenger four-turboprop Dash 7, the 36-passenger Dash 8 makes use of two new-design turboprops but otherwise is basically similar to its forerunner. Like all the de Havilland STOL designs, the Dash 8 is a high-wing aeroplane that provides steep-gradient performance without dependence upon vulnerable wing leading-edge devices for high lift. Following the design of the Buffalo/Transporter and Dash 7, the new aircraft has a "T"-tail with two-element rudder, and has wing spoilers to augment ailerons for lateral control.

The wing has a flat, rectangular centre-section with taper and dihedral on the panels outboard of the engine nacelles like the twin-engined Buffalo/

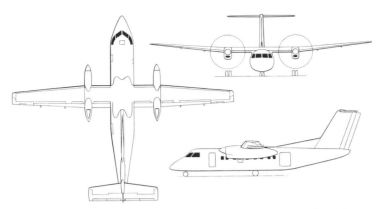

Above: Three-view drawing of the de Havilland Canada Dash 8, latest in the company's series of STOL transport designs.

Transporter, whereas the four-engined Dash 7 has both taper and dihedral from the wing roots. The Dash 8 wing has an aspect ratio of 12.1 compared with 10:1 for the Dash 7. In addition to manually-operated ailerons there are four hydraulically-powered wing spoilers for maximum roll control at low speeds. At high speeds the inboard spoilers are not used. On the ground all four spoilers may be raised together (instead of differentially for rolling) to dump wing lift and four independent ground spoilers dump lift over the inner wing, when the weight is on the main wheels.

First flight of the Dash 8 was set for mid-1983, with first delivery scheduled for mid-1984 to norOntair, the air service of the Ontario Northland Transport Commission which was the first to take options on the new type. Of the first 100 or so aircraft on option, 60 per cent were for customers in the USA, 22 per cent for Canada and 18 per cent for international customers. The Dash 8 was to be certificated by the Canadian Department of Transport to meet the requirements of the US Federal Aviation Regulations Parts 25 and 36, and SFAR 27. A corporate version was also to be made available through Innotech Aviation, which has been made responsible for the interior design. Estimated market for this class of aircraft is 1,200 and de Havilland Canada has indicated it is confident of building at least half of these, despite the vigour of the competition.

Below: An impression of the Dash 8 in the colours of Norwegian operator Widerøe, one of more than 30 customers for the new type.

Dornier Do 228
West Germany

The following specification refers to the Dornier 228-200:
Power Plant: Two 715shp Garrett TPE 331-5 turboprops.
Performance: Max cruising speed, 230mph (370km/h) at sea level and 268mph (432km/h) at 10,000ft (3050m); long-range cruise, 206mph (332km/h) at 10,000ft (3050m); initial rate of climb, 2,050ft/min (10·4 m/sec); service ceiling, 29,600ft (9020m); range with full passenger payload, 715mls (1150km).
Weights: Operating weight empty, 7,370lb (3343kg); max payload, 4,540lb (2057kg); max take-off and landing weight, 12,570lb (5700kg); max zero fuel weight, 11,900lb (5400kg).
Dimensions: Span, 55ft 7in (16·97m); length, 54ft 3in (16·55m); height, 15ft 9in (4·80m); wing area, 344sq ft (32·0m²).

Making its public debut at the Paris Air Show in 1981, the Dornier 228 is an extrapolation from the original Do 28 Skyservant, development having been undertaken under the designation Do 28E until revised nomenclature was adopted during 1980. The current versions of the 10-seat Skyservant then became the Dornier 128-2 with piston engines and Dornier 128-6 with turboprops.

The Dornier 228 represents a considerable stretch of the original Do 28D-2 on which it is based, retaining little but the basic fuselage cross section and the general structural philosophy. Its most important new feature is the wing, which is Dornier's TNT (*Tragflugels Neuer Technologie* or new technology wing), a prototype of which was first flown on a converted Skyservant on 14 June 1979. Associated with this wing is the introduction of turboprop engines, mounted in wing nacelles in place of the piston engines previously carried on sponsons. The undercarriage is also new, now being retractable into fuselage-side fairings.

Two versions of the Dornier 228 were launched in parallel; the 228–100 has an overall length of 49ft 3in (15·03m), almost 12ft (3·5m) more than that of the 128-2, and seats 15 passengers in the longer cabin (part of the increase also being attributable to the lengthened and reprofiled nose). The Dornier 228-200, for which a specification is given above, has another 5ft (1·52m) of length and seats 19 passengers, but in all other respects is identical with the -100, including maximum operating weights. The extra capacity is therefore traded against range with max payload, which in the

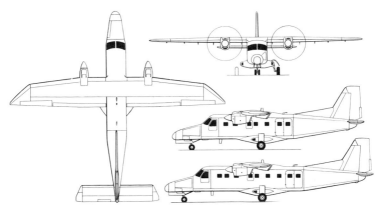

Above: Three-view drawing of the Dornier Do 228-100 with additional side view (bottom right) of the longer-fuselage Do 228-200.

228–100 is 1 224mls (1970km).

The Dornier A-5 aerofoil section as used in the TNT wing is similar to the NASA-developed Whitcomb GA(W)-1 supercritical section, although not quite so thick or so "droopy" over the front 40 per cent of chord. The company claims that this section gives better lift/drag characteristics, especially in the take-off and initial climb, than the GA(W)-1 section and that as applied to a twin-engined aircraft such as the Dornier 228, offers performance improvements of up to 25 per cent compared with older, conventional aerofoils. The Dornier 228 is designed to provide the basis for a family of related aircraft covering a wide variety of civil and military rôles. All cargo and mixed passenger/cargo versions will be available, and executive interiors have been designed. Military and quasi-military rôles include maritime surveillance, observation/calibration, training, air ambulance, search-and-rescue and troop and supply dropping. The uprated Garrett TPE 331-10, and the Pratt & Whitney PT6A-41 and PT6A-135 have been quoted by Dornier as possible future options to power 228 variants.

The prototype Dornier 228-100 made its first flight on 28 March 1981 and this was quickly followed by the first 228-200 flown on 9 May. The company announced during 1981 that it had initial orders for 20 Dornier 228s; delivery of the first example to Norving Flyservice was made early in 1982.

Left: The prototype of the Dornier Do 228-200 on an early test flight. The -200 was first flown in May 1981, some six weeks after the maiden flight of the Do 228-100, and deliveries of both variants were starting in 1982. The Do 228 is based on the original Do 28 Skyservant, but is almost totally new in overall configuration and in detail design.

95

Douglas DC-3
USA

Power Plant: Two 1,200hp Pratt & Whitney R-1830-92 Twin Wasp piston engines.
Performance (typical post-war conversion of C-47): Max speed 215mph (346km/h); high speed cruise 194mph (312km/h); economical cruise, 165mph (266km/h) at 6,000ft (1829m); initial climb, 1,070ft/min (5·4m/sec); service ceiling, 21,900ft (6675m); range with max payload, 350mls (563km); range with max fuel, 1,510mls (2430km).
Weights: Operating weight empty, 17,720lb (8030kg); max payload, 6,600lb (3000kg); max take-off (US passenger), 25,200lb (11,430kg); max take-off (British C of A, freight), 28,000lb (12,700kg).
Dimensions: Span, 95ft 0in (28·96m); length, 64ft 6in (19·66m); height, 16ft 11½in (5·16m); wing area, 987sq ft (91·7m²).

Probably the most famous of all airliners, and certainly the most widely used, the DC-3 (Douglas Commercial 3) brought together in a brilliantly successful manner all the technical innovations in aeronautical engineering of the early 'thirties. Its configuration was similar to that of the DC-1 prototype and the production batch of DC-2s that entered service on 18 May 1934 — starting with TWA on the New York–Los Angeles route. Evolution of the Douglas twin-engined transport design had begun in 1932, primarily to meet a TWA requirement for an aircraft to compete with United Air Lines' Boeing 247s, and the DC-1 flew on 1 July 1933.

The DC-2 flew on 11 May 1934, and useful operational experience had been gained within a year when American Airlines asked Douglas to produce an improved and enlarged version of the transport, initially for use on a sleeper service across the US. The aircraft that emerged, to make its first flight at Santa Monica on 17 December 1935, was somewhat larger overall than the DC-2, with a wider fuselage, larger wing and tail areas and increased power and weights. It was intended to seat 24 passengers, or carry 16 sleeping berths, and was known initially as the DST (Douglas Sleeper Transport) as well as the DC-3.

American Airlines put the DST into service on 25 June 1936 between New York and Chicago, certification having been granted on 21 May. The initial versions had 920hp Wright GR-1820-G5 Cyclone engines but 1,000hp Pratt & Whitney R-1380 Twin-Wasps were soon offered as alternatives in the DST-A and DC-3A, and 1,100hp Cyclone G-102s distinguished the DC-3B. Up to the time that all transport aircraft production in the US was taken over by the US military services, 430 examples of the DC-3 had been delivered for civil use, of which nearly 100 were for export. Even before the USA became engaged in World War II, however, the potential of the Douglas transport had been realized by the USAAC, and after evaluation of prototypes, a production order for 545 military DC-3s was placed in September 1940. These were the first of the C-47 Skytrains; the name Dakota was applied later, by the RAF.

By the time the war ended and further production of the DC-3 was terminated, 10,655 examples had been built at three Douglas-operated factories; the original Santa Monica works and new facilities at Long Beach and Oklahoma. The total includes the pre-war civil production, and 28 aircraft delivered post-war by Douglas as DC-3Ds and assembled from parts of military airframes then in production. The C-47 (and other variants of the design designated C-53, C-117, R4D etc) and the Dakota had been deployed to every Allied war zone, and thousands became available for civil use overnight, in many different parts of the world. The Douglas transport became the universal workhorse of the world's airline industry and few companies that have operated in the 1945–1965 period have not had at least one in their fleet at some time. In the early post-war years, DC-3s were used

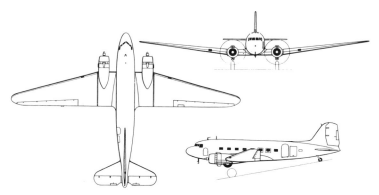

Above: The Douglas DC-3, all-time best-seller to the world's airlines, thanks to large-scale wartime production.

on many primary routes, and various efforts were made to improve the performance and the standard of passenger comfort, leading to some aircraft being known as Super DC-3s and by other names.

Lacking a pressurized cabin, the DC-3 was soon outmoded as a first-line transport, but the sheer numbers available combined with the very low first cost, the sound engineering design, and ability to fly into and out of small, unimproved airfields, ensured that the type would not quickly disappear from the airline scene. In 1975, over 400 were reported to be still actively engaged in air transport operations – for the most part with smaller operators in North and South America, and in many cases for freighting rather than passenger carrying. Up to 28 passengers could be carried by the DC-3 in its post-war variants.

A licence for production of the DC-3 was obtained pre-war by the Soviet government, and these licence-built aircraft were designated Li 2, production being the responsibility of a team led by B Lisunov. They were powered by Shvetsov M-621R or M-63R engines and had numerous differences in detail from the US version. Some DC-3s purchased from Douglas by Aeroflot in 1937 were designated PS-84, and 707 US-built C-47s were supplied to the Soviet Union through lend-lease. The latter and the Li-2s have the NATO reporting name *Cab*, and some examples were reported to be still in use in the late-seventies in the Northern, Polar and Far East Directorates of Aeroflot.

Below: Douglas DC-3 VP-LVJ, one of five of the Douglas transports serving with Air BVI, is seen here landing at Beef Island.

Douglas DC-4 (and Carvair)
USA

The following specification refers to the DC-4:
Power Plant: Four 1,450hp Pratt & Whitney R-2000-2SD-13G Twin Wasp piston radial engines.
Performance: Max speed, 265mph (426km/h); cruising speed, 207mph (333km/h) at 10,000ft (3050m) at 65,000lb (29,484kg) mean weight; service ceiling, 19,000ft (5791m); range with max payload, 1,150mls (1850km); range with max fuel, 2,180mls (3510km).
Weights: Empty equipped, 46,000lb (20,865kg); max payload, 14,200lb (6440kg); max take-off weight, 73,000lb (33,112kg); max landing and max zero fuel weight, 63,500lb (28,800kg).
Dimensions: Span, 117ft 6in (35·82m); length, 93ft 5in (28·47m); height, 27ft 7in (8·41m); wing area, 1,462sq ft (135·8m²).

The twin-engined, all-metal airliner of the mid-'thirties, of which the DĆ-3 was a prime example, brought about a revolution in air transportation, and the major US trunk airlines were the first to appreciate the full implications of that revolution. As early as mid-1935, with the DC-3 only just on the point of entering service, a consortium of five of these airlines — American, Eastern, Pan American, TWA and United — drew up specifications for a larger, long-range transport having the same advanced engineering features as the new twins. Out of this requirement grew the DC-4, which was to have as profound an impact upon air transport in the few years after the war as did the DC-3 in the years just preceding it.

Before the DC-4 emerged, however, Douglas made a false start with the DC-4E, a pressurized 52-seat airliner that was developed on a cost-sharing basis between Douglas and the airline consortium. It flew on 21 June 1938 and had a range of 2,000mls (3220km) cruising at 190mph (306km/h). Airline testing of the DC-4E led to demands for many modifications before production could begin, and with the worsening international situation casting a cloud over future planning, Douglas decided in 1939 to make a second, less ambitious, attempt to produce a four-engined airliner, this time with an unpressurized fuselage and only 42 seats, but still with enough range for transcontinental performance. Powered by four 1,450hp Pratt & Whitney R-2000 engines, this new model was known as the DC-4A and American Airlines and United Airlines both placed orders without waiting for a new prototype to be built.

Douglas laid down a batch of 24 DC-4As, but the entire production line was commandeered by the USAAF shortly after Pearl Harbor and the first of the new transports to fly — on 14 February 1942 — emerged in warpaint

Right: Seen here landing at Miami, this DC-4 is an original USAAF C-54B, operated in 1982 by Turks Air Ltd in an all-cargo configuration. It had previously operated on the Brazilian civil register — aircraft as elderly as the DC-4 still in service almost all have had a succession of owners.

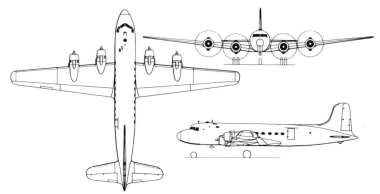

Above: The Douglas DC-4, built primarily for military use in World War II but much used commercially post-war

as a C-54 Skymaster. Over 1,000 military examples were built by Douglas by 1945, and the company then built 79 specifically for airline use; American Overseas Airlines became the first commercial operator of the type, in October 1945.

Many of the military C-54s were civilianized in 1946 and went into service as the initial long-haul equipment of airlines building up their operations in the austerity of the late 'forties. The excellent economy of the DC-4 was of particular significance at that time, helping airlines to make a profit out of which to finance the production of the new post-war generation of transports. The size of the DC-4 also made it suitable for high density layouts, eventually increased to a maximum of 86 seats, and for freighting, for which large side-loading doors could be fitted. Several dozen DC-4s were still in airline service at the end of the 'seventies, mostly for low-cost charter, freighting and other miscellaneous transport duties, and as recently as 1974 ex-USAF examples were still being offered for sale by the US government.

Another DC-4 derivation was the Carvair, developed by Aviation Traders in the UK to meet the needs of its associated company Channel Air Bridge for a vehicle ferry. First flown on 21 June 1961, the Carvair had an entirely new forward fuselage incorporating an hydraulically-operated sideways-opening nose door to permit up to five cars to be driven into the hold, and a new raised flight deck over the forward part of the cargo hold. The remainder of the DC-4 airframe was unchanged apart from increases in height and area of the vertical tail surfaces. A total of 21 DC-4s was converted and the Carvair entered airline service in March 1962. Examples were used in Luxembourg, Eire, Canada, France, Spain, Dominica and Australia but only a handful of these were still in service in 1981.

Douglas DC-6
USA

The following specification relates to the DC-6B; the DC-6A is similar:
Power Plant: Four 2,500hp Pratt & Whitney R-2800-CB17 piston radial engines.
Performance: Typical cruising speed, 316mph (509km/h); initial rate of climb, 1,120ft/min (6·2m/sec); no reserves range with max payload, 3,000mls (4828km); no reserves range with max fuel, 4,720mls (7596km).
Weights: Basic operating, 58,635lb (26,595kg); max payload, 24,565lb (11,143kg); max take-off, 107,000lb (48,534kg).
Dimensions: Span, 117ft 6in (35·81m); length, 105ft 7in (32·2m); height, 29ft 3in (8·92m); wing area, 1,463sq ft (135·9m²).

Like its arch-rival Lockheed, with the Constellation, the Douglas Aircraft Company acquired its preliminary experience of four-engined transport design and operation through the USAAF in World War II, which intervened to prevent the introduction of the commercial DC-4 (see previous page) as planned. Out of this experience, and with possible future military requirements as much in mind as the expected demand for such an aircraft by the airlines as soon as the war ended, Douglas set about developing an enlarged successor to the DC-4 during the war years. As the DC-6, it was destined to play a significant rôle in the post-war evolution of air transport.

Using the same wing as the DC-4, the DC-6 had a fuselage lengthened by 81 inches (2·06m) to increase the passenger capacity to a basic 52 — at the rather exaggerated seat pitches commonly used in the 'forties. The other major improvement was the introduction of pressurization, which the Constellation already offered; more powerful engines and system improvements were also featured. Construction of a prototype was ordered by the USAAF, which gave the new transport the designation XC-112; however, first flight was not made until 15 February 1946, by which time military requirements had evaporated, and only one other military example was purchased, as the C-118 *Independence* Presidential transport.

The first commercial order for the DC-6 was placed late in 1944 by American Airlines (for a fleet of 50) and United followed soon after, both airlines being faced by competition from TWA with the Constellation. The first production DC-6 flew in June 1946, deliveries to American and United began in November 1946 and the first commercial service was flown on 27 April 1947. Operating on the primary US transcontinental routes, the DC-6 offered coast-to-coast times of 10 hours eastbound and 11 hours

Below: Douglas DC-6Bs in their heyday, when these classic aircraft formed the main-line fleet of United Air Lines.

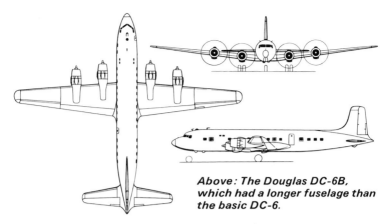

Above: The Douglas DC-6B, which had a longer fuselage than the basic DC-6.

westbound and deliveries to other US and foreign operators quickly followed. Commercial sales of the DC-6 eventually totalled 174, ending in 1951. A number of DC-6s remained in use into the early 'eighties mostly for low-cost charters and freighting, some having side-loading freight doors.

During 1948, Douglas began work on a further "stretch" of the DC-6 fuselage, made possible primarily by the availability of uprated R-2800 engines with water/methanol injection and by structural analysis that allowed the gross weight to be increased. The fuselage was lengthened by 5ft (1·5m), various improvements were made in systems engineering and all-freight and passenger versions were planned in parallel as the DC-6A and DC-6B. The prototype long-fuselage DC-6 flew in DC-6A configuration on 29 September 1949 and the first operator was Slick, starting on 16 April 1951. The DC-6B made its first flight on 2 February 1951, and American was the first to operate the new type, starting on 29 April 1951 on the transcontinental US route. Combining low operating costs with a high standard of comfort and outstanding mechanical reliability, the DC-6B was among the best of the generation of piston-engined airliners, and it saw service with many of the world's foremost airlines.

Production of the DC-6B totalled 288, ending in 1958; commercial deliveries of the DC-6A, ending about the same time, totalled 74 and included a few aircraft with convertible passenger/freight interiors and designated DC-6C. In addition, 166 DC-6As went to the USAF and USN as C-118As and R6D-1s respectively. As the DC-6Bs began to phase-out of front-line service, many were acquired by charter and freight operators, some being converted to DC-6A or similar standard with side-loading doors, 6Bs were converted (by Sabena) to swing-tail freighters. The DC-6A and DC-6B remained in service in considerable numbers in 1981, although no longer used on primary routes.

Douglas DC-7
USA

The following specification refers to the DC-7C:
Power Plant: Four 3,400hp Wright R-3350-EA1 or EA4 piston radial engines.
Performance: Typical cruising speed, 345mph (555km/h); service ceiling, 21,700ft (6615m); range with max payload, 3610mls (5810km); no-reserves range with max fuel, 5,642mls (9077km).
Weights: Basic operating, 80,000lb (36,287kg); max payload, 21,500lb (9752kg); max take-off, 143,000lb (64,865kg).
Dimensions: Span, 127ft 6in (38·8m); length, 112ft 3in (34·23m); height, 31ft 8in (9·65m); wing area, 1,637sq ft (152·0m²).

The success of the DC-6, and the continuing competitive pressure exerted by Lockheed with the Constellation, led Douglas to plan a further "stretch" of the DC-6 airframe in 1951, coupled with the introduction of the new Wright R-3350 turbo-compound piston engine with a big step-up in take-off and cruise powers. Retaining the same basic wing that had started on the DC-4 and had already been associated with three different fuselage lengths, Douglas designed a new fuselage that was 40in (1·02m) longer than that of the DC-6B, with passenger capacity increased to up to 95 in high density layouts. Apart from the new engines, the new aircraft had increased fuel capacity — sufficient to guarantee non-stop transcontinental operations in each direction. The designation DC-7 was logical — although it had been previously used when Pan American ordered a projected commercial version of the C-74 Globemaster I, which was not in the end built.

First flight of the DC-7 was made on 18 May 1953 and certification was completed by November, transcontinental service being started by American on 29 November 1953. Three other airlines, all US domestic operators, bought the DC-7, production of which totalled 105. Some of these passed eventually to other operators, together with the dimensionally similar DC-7B. The latter was a long-range version of the DC-7, with extra fuel carried in saddle tanks in the rear of the engine nacelles and within the wing. Structural modifications were made to permit operation at higher gross weights. The first DC-7B was flown on 25 April 1955 and Pan American was among the operators, using a fleet of seven to inaugurate, on 13 June 1955, the first non-stop New York—London service. Douglas delivered 110 aircraft as DC-7Bs (two others were built but not delivered), but not all had the full range of B features and are sometimes included in DC-7 production totals.

Although Pan American operated DC-7Bs between London and New

Below: Douglas DC-7s were once mainline equipment with many major operators, such as Sabena, but that day is now long gone.

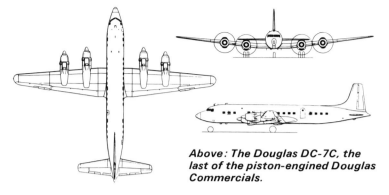

Above: The Douglas DC-7C, the last of the piston-engined Douglas Commercials.

York non-stop, this aircraft's ability to make the crossing under all conditions with a full payload was limited, and strong headwinds often led to intermediate landings or diversions to Gander. Douglas saw a clear demand for a DC-7 variant with greater range, but this could only be achieved by enlarging the airframe to provide additional fuel capacity. This led to development of the DC-7C Seven Seas, the last of the piston-engined Douglas Commercials and perhaps the peak of pre-jet airliner design.

The DC-7C had a 10ft (3·05m) increase in wing span, achieved by adding sections between the fuselage and the inner engine nacelles. Curtiss-Wright had offered a further increase in engine power, to 3,400hp in the Turbo Compound EA1, and Douglas designers were therefore able to increase the operating weights again, and the fuselage was lengthened by another 42in (1·1m) to give a maximum passenger capacity of 105. The first DC-7C flew on 20 December 1955 and production totalled 121. Pan American was the first of 13 airlines to buy the DC-7C from Douglas, starting service with it on 1 June 1956. Another "first" for the DC-7C was its use for "over-the-pole" service between Europe and the Far East, inaugurated by SAS on 24 February 1957.

During 1959, Douglas offered a conversion scheme for DC-7 variants, to be fitted with double freight-loading doors, strengthened floor and other cargo features. These conversions were officially designated DC-7F regardless of basic model converted, but DC-7BF and DC-7CF designations were also used by some airlines. Other companies later made similar conversions as the original DC-7Cs came onto the second-hand market. They have remained in demand in many parts of the world for charter passenger flying and cargo operations, and were still being used in the early 'eighties for scheduled passenger services on a few of the less competitive routes.

Below: A Douglas DC-7, retired from regular airline service, flying in the markings of Ports of Call, a Denver charter company.

EMBRAER EMB-110 Bandeirante
Brazil

The following data apply to the standard EMB-110P2
Power Plant: Two 750shp Pratt & Whitney (Canada) PT6A-34 turboprops.
Performance: Max cruising speed, 259mph (417km/h) at 10,000ft (3050m); initial rate of climb, 1,970ft/min (10m/sec); single-engined rate of climb, 1,788ft/min (9.1m/sec); service ceiling, 24,100ft (7350m); max range, 1,180mls (1900km) at 10,000ft (3050m); range with standard payload, 309mls (497km).
Weights: Empty equipped, 7,751lb (3516kg); max take-off weight, 12,500lb (5670kg); max landing and zero fuel weight, 12,015kg (5450kg).
Dimensions: Span, 50ft 3in (15.32m); length, 49ft 6$\frac{1}{2}$in (15.10m); height, 16ft 1$\frac{3}{4}$in (4.92m); wing area, 313sq ft (29.10m²).

The Bandeirante (named after pioneering Brazilian explorers) emerged in 1968 as the first modern light transport of Brazilian origin, its design having been directed by the French engineer Max Holste (see also Aérospatiale/Nord 262) at the Institute for Research and Development. First flown on 26 October 1968, the Bandeirante met local needs for a third level airliner as well as a Brazilian Air Force requirement, and the EMBRAER organization (Emprêsa Brasileira de Aeronáutica) was set up at São Paulo during 1969 to handle production. Second and third prototypes flew on 19 October 1969 and 26 June 1970 respectively, all three having Pratt & Whitney PT6A-20 turbo-props, circular windows and mainwheels partially exposed when retracted.

The production standard Bandeirante, first flown on 9 August 1972, featured PT6A-27 engines, a slightly lengthened fuselage with square cabin windows and redesigned nacelles that completely enclosed the main wheels when retracted. Early production deliveries were assigned to the Air Force, but the pressing needs of Brazilian airlines for a feeder-liner to replace DC-3s and similar elderly types led to deliveries being made to Transbrasil and VASP during 1973 before Air Force needs had been fully met. Typical airline layout provided accommodation for 15 passengers in single seats with a central aisle, this being the EMB-110C version that entered service (with Transbrasil) on 16 April 1973. Subsequently, a number of specialized

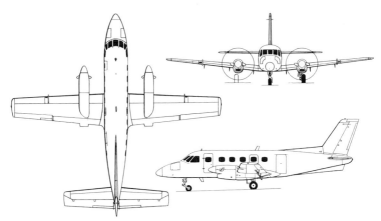

Above: Three-view drawing of the Bandeirante in its EMB-110P2 version, with a longer fuselage than originally offered. Over 300 Bandeirantes had been sold (including military) by 1982.

variants has been developed to meet the needs of airline operators. Most important of these was the EMB-110P, designed primarily to meet the requirements of third level airlines in Brazil; with 18 passenger seats this version entered service with TABA early in 1976. The EMB-110E and EMB-110F are, respectively, executive and all cargo versions and the EMB-110S is a geophysical survey version.

The principal commercial versions since 1980 have been the EMB-110P1 and the EMB-110P2, which have a longer fuselage than the original EMB-110C and -110P; the P2 seats up to 21 passengers as a third-level transport and was first flown on 3 May 1977, while the P1 is a quick-change passenger/cargo version with enlarged cargo door. The Bandeirante sales total was close to 300 by the end of 1981, more than half being for export.

Below: An EMB-110P Bandeirante. Originally developed for a Brazilian Air Force requirement, the EMB-110 has proved successful in several civil rôles, including business transport.

EMBRAER EMB-120 Brasilia
Brazil

Power Plant: Two Pratt & Whitney Canada PW115 turboprops each flat rated at 1,500shp up to 37deg C at sea level.
Performance: Max cruising speed, 340mph (546km/h) at max cruise power at 20,000ft (6100m); long-range cruise, 282mph (454km/h) at 20,000ft (6100m); initial rate of climb, 2,750ft/min (13·97m/sec); range, 575mls (925km) or four 115-mile (185-km) stages with 30 passengers and no intermediate refuelling.
Weights: Operating weight empty, 11,585lb (5255kg); max payload 6,666lb (3024kg); max take-off and landing weight, 21,164lb (9600kg); max zero fuel weight, 18,960lb (8600kg).
Dimensions: Span, 64ft 10¾in (19·78m); length 64ft 8½in (19·73m); height, 20ft 8in (6·3m); wing area, 409·39sq ft (38·025m²).

After successfully establishing the Bandeirante in the export market for commuter aircraft (see previous page), the Brazilian EMBRAER company projected in the mid-seventies several derivations that used, to a varying degree, components of the original design. Largest of these was a project identified as the EMB-120 Araguaia, which was intended to be a 20-seat airliner combining a new wing with the circular fuselage cross-section meanwhile evolved for the EMB-121, a business twin using the Bandeirante wing.

By the middle of 1978, the EMB-120 had evolved, in response to the developing market for slightly larger commuter-liners, into a 30-seat project with two 1,500shp engines and a wider fuselage than at first proposed, to permit three-abreast seating. In this form, the project proceeded into full scale development, the name Brasilia being adopted towards the end of 1979 and a first flight target date of 29 July 1983 being established.

To power the new project, EMBRAER selected the new turboprop engine that was being developed by Pratt & Whitney Aircraft of Canada to complement its highly successful PT6A family. Launched as the PT7A, this

Below: A manufacturer's model of the EMBRAER EMB-120 Brasilia, under development in 1982 as a "big brother" for the Bandeirante. The Brasilia was designed as a pressurized 30-seat commuter liner.

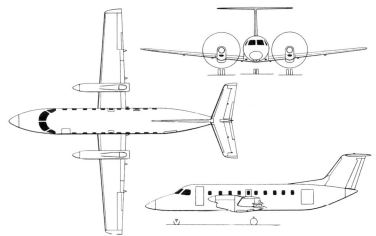

Above: Three-view drawing of the EMB-120 Brasilia, clearly show-ing the family resemblance to the very successful EMB-110.

engine is now known as the PW100 in its basic form, with different variants identified by the final two digits to indicate the take-off rating, eg PW115 for the 1,500shp of the version used in the Brasilia. Flight testing of the PW115, in a Brasilia nacelle mounted on the nose of a Viscount test bed, began at the end of 1981.

With a circular-section fuselage pressurized to a differential of 7psi (0·49kg/cm²), the Brasilia is of conventional low-wing layout, with a T-tail. The wing has double slotted flaps in six sections and all flying controls are manually operated through duplicated control circuits. The standard layout provides 30 seats in a "two-plus-one" arrangement at a pitch of 31in (79cm). Cargo and mixed traffic versions will be offered with an upward-opening cargo loading door aft of the wing, retaining the main passenger door forward.

By the end of 1981, EMBRAER had recorded 110 orders and options for the Brasilia, from 19 operators. Certification was scheduled for completion in the second quarter of 1984, with deliveries commencing immediately thereafter.

Fairchild-Swearingen Metro
USA

The following specification refers to the Metro III.

Power Plant: Two Garrett AiResearch TPE 331-11U-601G turboprops each rated at 1,100shp for take-off, using alcohol/water injection.

Performance: Design operating speed, 285mph (459km/h) CAS/Mach = 0·52; max speed, 345mph (555km/h); max cruising speed, 319mph (513km/h) at 10,000ft (3050m); initial rate of climb, 2,440ft/min (12·4 m/sec); range, 19 passengers, baggage and 45-min reserve, 714mls (1149km).

Weights: Typical operating weight empty (with two crew, avionics and unusable fuel), 8,737lb (3963kg); max useful load, 5,463lb (2478kg); max take-off and landing weight, 14,000lb (6350kg); max zero fuel weight, 12,500lb (5670kg).

Dimensions: Span, 57ft 0in (17·37m); length 59ft $4\frac{1}{4}$in (18·09m); height 16ft 8in (5·08m); wing area, 309sq ft (28.71m²).

The Metro was designed by Ed Swearingen to meet the needs of the third level airlines, and was the first product of wholly original concept produced by the Swearingen company, which had taken the Beechcraft Queen Air to provide the basis for a series of business aircraft named the Merlin I, IIA and IIB. When the Metro was developed, as a 19-passenger transport, a version was also offered for business use, with up to 12 seats in an executive interior. Swearingen was acquired by Fairchild Industries as a subsidiary in November 1971 and the company name has subsequently changed to Fairchild Swearingen.

The Metro first flew on 26 August 1969 and entered service early in 1971, the first major operator being Air Wisconsin, which had a fleet of 10 by 1977. Progressive improvements have kept the Metro in the forefront of the US commuter market and more than 200 had been sold by 1981.

During 1974, the Metro 2 was introduced, with square windows and some internal refinements, plus optional installation of a small rocket unit in the tail to improve take-off performance in hot and high conditions. Like the original model, however, this was confined by the provisions of FAA regulations (SFAR 23) that restricted to 12,500lb (5670kg) the gross weight of aircraft to be operated by US commuter airlines.

This weight restriction was relaxed by Special Federal Aviation Regulation (SFAR) 41, and, on 23 June 1980, the Metro became the first aircraft to be approved by the FAA under the provision of SFAR 41. As the Metro IIA, with a number of additional safety features as prescribed by the FAA, a maximum weight of 13,100lb (5941kg) was approved, but to obtain full benefit from the new regulations for commuter operations, a more extensive

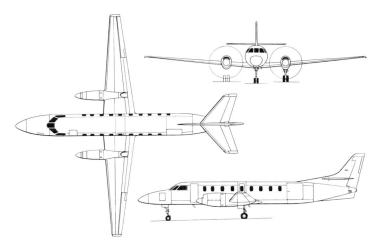

Above: Three-view drawing of the Metro III, which introduces a wing of greater span than that of the Metro II previously built.

modification of the aircraft was required. This led to introduction of the Metro III, the major new features of which were uprated engines and a longer, stronger wing, associated with a gross weight of 14,000lb (6350kg). There was no change in fuselage size or passenger accommodation; as before, the aircraft was approved for up to 20 passengers, but in US operations the effective limit is 19, since a cabin attendant has to be carried if 20 or more passengers are enplaned.

The new wing of the Metro III was 10ft (3·05m) longer than that of the original Merlin, with conical-cambered wing tips to reduce drag and structural strengthening matched to the new weights and flight loads. The engines were Garrett AiResearch TPE 331-11U-601G turboprops, with an optional continuous alcohol/water injection (CAWI) system for those operators requiring the best field performance in hot and high conditions; respective dry and wet ratings of 1,000 and 1,100shp were each 160shp higher than those of the TPE 331-3UW-304G engines in the Metro II.

New Dowty-Rotol supercritical four-bladed propellers were adopted and the nacelle lines were refined to reduce drag and to improve accessibility for rapid engine changes. Another drag-reducing modification concerned the main landing gear doors, which now close after gear extension, as well as retraction. As a further development of the basic Metro III, the company announced during 1981, for 1983 delivery, the Metro IIIA with Pratt & Whitney PT6A-45R engines and gross weight increased to 14,500lb (6576kg).

Left: A Metro II in the markings of Tejas Airlines, a Texas-based local airline that was among the first to use this commuter airliner. Progressive development led to the Metro III in 1981, with extended wing span, and to the Metro IIIA (first flown on 31 December 1981).

Fokker F.27 Friendship and Fairchild FH-227
Netherlands

The following specification refers to the F.27 Mk 200:

Power Plant: Two 2,105eshp Rolls-Royce Dart 528 or 528-7E or 2,230eshp Dart 532-7 turboprops.

Performance: Cruising speed, 302mph (486km/h); initial rate of climb, 1,475ft/min (7·5m/sec); service ceiling, 29,500ft (9000m); range with max payload, 1,285mls (2070km); range with max fuel, 1,374mls (2211km).

Weights: Empty, 22,696lb (10,295kg), operating empty, 24,600lb (11,159 kg); max payload, 10,340lb (4690kg); max take-off, 45,000lb (20,410kg).

Dimensions: Span, 95ft 2in (29·00m); length, 77ft 3½in (23·56m); height, 27ft 11in (8·51m); wing area, 753·5sq ft (70·0m²).

The following specification refers to the FH-227E:

Power Plant: Two 2,300shp Rolls-Royce Dart 532-7L turboprops.

Performance: Max cruising speed, 294mph (473km/h) at 15,000ft (4570m); best economy cruise, 270mph (435km/h) at 25,000ft (7620m); initial rate of climb, 1,560ft/min (7·9m/sec); service ceiling, 28,000ft (8535m); range with max payload, 656mls (1055km); range with max fuel, 1,655mls (2660km).

Weights: Empty, 22,923lb (10,398kg); max payload, 11,200lb (5080kg); max take-off, 43,500lb (19,730kg).

Dimensions: Span, 95ft 2in (29·0m); length, 83ft 8in (25·50m); height, 27ft 7in (8·41m); wing area, 754sq ft (70·0m²).

When the famous Fokker company resumed active work on aircraft design in the years following World War II, high priority was given to the development of a commercial transport, this having been one of the areas in which the company had excelled before the war. Since one of the activities at the Schiphol, Amsterdam, works from 1945 onwards was the overhaul and conversion of ex-military Douglas DC-3s, the company was already in close contact with many European and other airlines, and they were asked, during 1950, to outline their likely requirements for a "DC-3 replacement" aircraft. Out of this survey emerged a series of project studies, one of which, dated August 1950, was for a shoulder-wing, twin-Dart powered 32-seater known as the P.275.

Evolution of the P.275 led to the F.27 of 1952, with a circular-section pressurized fuselage seating up to 40 passengers and a range of 300mls (483km) with full payload. Double slotted flaps were to be used to obtain the required short-field performance. In 1953, Netherlands government backing was obtained for the construction of two flying prototypes and two structural test specimens and a marketing campaign began. First flights of the two prototypes were made on 24 November 1955 and 29 January 1957, respectively, the second of these introducing a fuselage extension of 3ft (0·91m) and having Dart 511s in place of the Dart 507s used temporarily in the first prototype. With the lengthened fuselage, adopted as the production

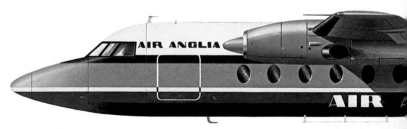

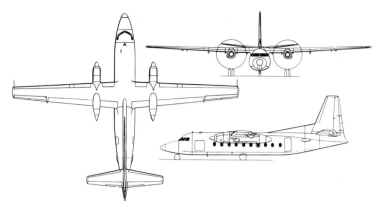

Above. Three-view drawing of the Fokker F.27 Mk 200, a basic version of Europe's best-selling turboprop transport.

standard, the basic seating capacity went up from 32 to 36, the initial gross weight being 35,700lb (16,193kg). Flight testing showed that the double slotted flaps were not needed and single-slotted flaps were adopted instead.

Fokker flew the first production F.27, which meanwhile had been named the Friendship, on 23 March 1958. Meanwhile, a licence agreement had been concluded with Fairchild in the USA and a production line had been laid down to meet a healthy demand from the local service operators, for whom the type offered an economic opportunity to introduce turbine engined equipment. Fairchild introduced a lengthened nose for weather radar (later adopted also by Fokker), increased the basic seating to 40, upped the ▶

Above: An example of the FH-227B, the lengthened-fuselage version of the Friendship developed by Fairchild in the USA.

Below: A Friendship 200 in the markings of Air Anglia.

G-BAUR

fuel capacity and made various other changes. The first two F-27s off the Fairchild line at Hagerstown flew on 12 April and 23 May 1958, and after FAA Type Approval on 16 July 1958, the type entered service with West Coast Airlines on 27 September 1958. Initial services by Fokker-built F.27s followed in December, the operator being Aer Lingus.

Fokker has steadily improved the F.27, which is the Western world's best-selling turboprop transport with 736 sold by the end of 1981 (including Fairchild production), and identifies the variants by mark numbers (100, 200, etc) whereas Fairchild, which undertook its own evolution of the type in collaboration with Fokker, used letter suffixes (F-27A, F-27B etc). The first production batch by Fokker were F.27 Mk 100s, and the basic Fairchild aircraft were plain F-27s. In the F.27 Series 200 and the F-27A, more powerful Dart R.Da.7 Mk 528 engines provided improved cruising speeds and better airfield "hot and high" performance; both Fokker and Fairchild fitted the new engines in development airframes for certification during 1958, and subsequently the permitted maximum take-off weight went up to 45,000lb (20,410kg).

Sometimes referred to as the Combiplane, the F.27 Mk 300 and F-27B introduced a large freight loading door in the forward fuselage, plus a strengthened cabin floor, to permit mixed passenger/freight operations, being otherwise similar to the Mk 100. The first examples came from Fairchild, US certification being completed on 25 October 1958 and initial deliveries being made to Northern Consolidated. The F.27 Mk 400 (no Fairchild equivalent) was a Mk 300 with the Mk 528 engines, sold by Fokker primarily for military use. Some specifically military Friendships were known as F.27M Troopships, being based on the Mk 400. Fokker also found a requirement to produce a version of the F.27 with the large freight door but without the all-metal, watertight, freight floor of the Mk 300 and Mk 400. This emerged as the Mk 600 (with R.Da.7 engines) and provision was made for a quick-change interior to be installed. The designation Mk 700 was reserved for a similar version using the lower rated R.Da.6 engines of the original production standard.

Fairchild closed its Friendship line down in 1960 after meeting initial

Above: An F.27 in the colours of Air Congo, a one-time operator of the twin turboprop transport that has become Europe's best-selling airliner, with sales approaching 750 in 1982.

airline demand, but re-opened it in 1961, initially to produce the F-27F version for business users. This differed primarily in having Dart 529-7E engines rated at 2,190ehp, and was type approved on 24 February 1961. There were no airline buyers, and an F-27G variant, with cargo door, was not built. On 3 August 1965, Fairchild obtained type approval for the F.27J with Dart 532-7 engines and on 12 June 1969, for the F-27M with Dart 532-7N and larger diameter propeller; some examples of both these types went to airlines — 10 F-27Js to Allegheny and two F-27Ms to Lloyd Aero Boliviano. The last-mentioned brought Fairchild production of the F-27 to an end, with 128 built

All versions of the Friendship from Mk 100 to Mk 400, plus the 600 and 700, had the same overall dimensions and maximum seating for 48 passengers. A long-fuselage variant was proposed in 1961 as the Mk 500, with a 4ft 11in (1·5m) stretch and forward freight door, but no orders were forthcoming until 1966, when the French government ordered 15 as DC-3 replacements, for use in the highly-developed Postale de Nuit mail delivery operation in France. The first Fokker F.27 Mk 500 flew on 15 November 1967 and deliveries began in June 1968. Meanwhile, however, Fairchild had taken up Fokker's idea and had introduced its own version of a stretched F.27 in the form of the FH-227. In this case, the fuselage stretch was 6ft (1 83m), and other special features were introduced to make the aircraft more specifically suited to the US market.

Fairchild flew the first of two prototypes on 27 January 1966 and then built 10 FH-227s for Mohawk, but later exchanged these on a one-for-one basis for FH-227Bs, which introduced higher weights and revised structure. Some FH-227s were later converted to FH-227C with some features of the B model but the original weights, or to FH-227E with uprated Dart 532-7L turboprops. The FH-227Bs became FH-227Ds when fitted with these same engines and other improvements. Production totalled 79.

Fokker F28 Fellowship
Netherlands

The following specification refers to the F.28 Mk 4000:

Power Plant: Two 9,850lb st (4468kgp) Rolls-Royce Spey 555-15H-turbofans.

Performance: Max cruising speed 502mph (808km/h) at 33,000ft (10,060m); best economy cruise, 489mph (787km/h) at 32,000ft (9755m); long-range cruise, 407mph (656km/h) at 30,000ft (9150m); max operating ceiling, 35,000ft (10,675m); range with max payload, 956mls (1538km); range with max fuel, 2,100mls (3380km).

Weights: Operating empty, 38,825lb (17,611kg); max payload, 23,317lb (10,556kg); max take-off, 69,500lb (31,523kg).

Dimensions: Span, 82ft 3½in (25·07m); length, 97ft 2in (29·6m); height, 27ft 9½in (8·47m); wing area, 850sq ft (76·3m²).

The Fokker company announced plans in April 1962 for a new short-haul jet airliner that would complement its F.27 Friendship, which was destined to become, a few years later, the world's best-selling turboprop airliner when sales passed the Viscount's previous record-holding figure total of 444. As originally conceived, the F.28 was to carry about 50 passengers over ranges of up to 1,000mls (1600km) and was to have a good short-field performance. The use of Bristol Siddeley BS.75 engines was studied but an early decision was made in favour of the Rolls-Royce RB.183 Spey Junior, a lighter and simpler version of the commercial Spey already committed to production for the Trident and BAC One-Eleven. Fokker had gained extensive experience of the potential airline market for an F.28-type aircraft through sales of the F.27, and planned development and production of the new aircraft on the assumption that sales would be made in small batches over a relatively long period, rather than in large fleets to airlines all wanting delivery at the same time, as tended to apply to the larger transport aircraft. In configuration, the F.28 followed the popular trend of the early 'sixties, with a low, slightly swept-back wing, T-tail and rear-fuselage mounted engines. The passenger capacity was set at 60 for the basic model.

Production was launched in July 1964 following completion of financing arrangements that included a loan from the Netherlands government, repayable from a levy on sales, and risk-sharing participation by Short Bros in the UK, the then-HFB (now MBB) and VFW companies in Germany and several equipment manufacturers in the UK and USA. Construction of three test and development airframes was put in hand at Schiphol, quickly backed up by the ordering of long lead-time items for production aircraft, the first of which was earmarked for the German IT operator LTU when it placed an order in November 1965.

First flights of the three prototypes were made on 9 May, 3 August and 20 October 1967, respectively, and the No 4 aircraft (first production and first for LTU) flew on 21 May 1968. Dutch certification was obtained on 24 February 1969, on which day the first delivery to LTU formally took place. The original production aircraft are known as Mk 1000, and are to the original specification for a 65-passenger (one-class, five-abreast) aircraft, the certificated gross weight having increased since 1969 from 62,000lb ▶

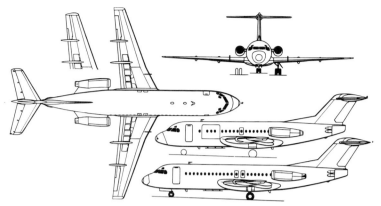

Above: The basic three-view drawing above depicts the F.28 Mk 4000, one of the three production versions in 1982. The upper side view and scrap wing view relate to the original Mk 1000; the Mk 3000 has the latter's fuselage with the long span wing.

Above: A pair of F.28 Mk 4000s in the blue livery of Swedish domestic operator Linjeflyg, first airline to use this high-density version.

Above: A Fokker F.28 Mk 2000 of Nigeria Airways.

(28,123kg) to 64,000lb (29,510kg). A version of the F.28 Mk 1000 with a forward side freight loading door is available for mixed passenger/freight operations as the Mk 1000-C.

To provide an alternative for operators requiring more capacity over shorter ranges. Fokker developed the Mk 2000, with the fuselage stretched by 7ft 3in (2·21m). Started in 1970, this variant carries up to 79 passengers and the first prototype F.28 converted to the new standard first flew on 28 April 1971, being certificated in August 1972. The first production example was delivered to Nigeria Airways in October 1972.

Also in 1972, Fokker announced the first details of the Mk 5000 and Mk 6000, with improvements aimed at permitting the F.28 to operate from shorter runways. Respectively equivalent to the Mk 1000 and Mk 2000 in passenger accommodation, the Mk 5000 and the Mk 6000 have an increase of 6ft 11½in (1·51m) in wing span, leading-edge slats, and improved versions of the Spey, designated Mk 555-15H, with additional noise reduction features. The original Mk 2000 prototype of the F.28 was fitted with the new wings and first flew in the guise of a Mk 6000 on 27 September 1973.

After obtaining certification of the Mk 6000 on 30 October 1975, Fokker went on to develop the Mk 3000 (short fuselage) and Mk 4000 (long fuselage) with the same increased wing span and the engine improvements, but without the leading-edge slats. A redesigned interior increases the seating capacity of the Mk 4000 to 85 and at a max gross weight of 71,000lb (32,200kg) it can carry this load a distance of 1,125mls (1814km). The Mk 3000 can carry 65 passengers for 1,725mls (2777km). Deliveries of the Mk 4000 (to Linjeflyg in Sweden) began at the end of 1976, and Garuda placed the first contract for the Mk 3000 in mid-1977, these subsequently becoming the principal production versions. The F-28 sales total by the end of 1981 was 189 to 46 operators.

Above: Martinair Holland, which specializes in charter and IT flights from its Amsterdam base, operates this F28 Mk 1000.

Below: A successful short-haul jet airliner, the Fokker F28 is also used as a transport by some air forces.

GAF Nomad
Australia

The following specification refers to the N22B:

Power Plant: Two Allison 250-B17B turboprops, each rated at 400shp for take-off.

Performance: Normal cruising speed, 193mph (311km/h); initial rate of climb, 1,460ft/min (7·4m/sec); service ceiling, 21,000ft (6400m); max range, 840mls (1352km).

Weights: Operating weight empty, 4,741lb (2150kg); standard fuel load, 1,770lb (803kg); max fuel, 2,350lb (1066kg); max take-off weight, 8,500lb (3855kg).

Dimensions: Span, 54ft 2¼in (16·52m); length, 41ft 2½in (12·56m); height, 18ft 1½in (5·52m); wing area, 324·0sq ft (30·10m²).

With headquarters at Fishermen's Bend, near Melbourne, the Government Aircraft Factories make up the principal aircraft production unit in Australia, being operated by the Department of Industry and Commerce primarily as a source of defence supplies. During the mid 'sixties, the GAF began design of a small utility transport intended to provide a continuing production activity as well as meeting local military and civil needs. This type emerged in prototype form as the N2, the first two examples of which made their first flights on 23 July and 5 December 1971.

The N2 was of conventional high wing layout with an almost-square fuselage cross section, large side-loading doors, a retractable under-carriage and Allison 250 turboprop engines. After gaining Australian certi-

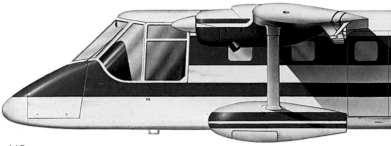

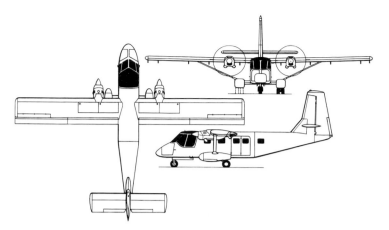

Above: Three-view drawing of the GAF Nomad N22, Australia's first recent attempt to design and produce a transport aircraft.

fication on 11 August 1972, the type entered production as the N22 for both military and civil use and, named Nomad, went into commercial service on 18 December 1975 with Aero Pelican. Although the majority of more than 100 N22s and N22Bs (the latter with increased gross weight) so far produced have been for military use, others are used by civil operators for air taxi and third level services and for special duties such as aerial survey and mapping.

The Nomad N24, first flown in 1976, has the fuselage lengthened by 3ft 9in (1.14m), increasing the seating capacity from 12 to a maximum 17. Power plant remain unchanged but the gross weight, in the N24A variant, increases to 9,400lb (4263kg). The N24 was intended primarily for commercial use and one of the first customers was the Northern Territory Aeromedical Service, which has a fleet of six N24s equipped as air ambulances. About 40 N24As had been sold by the end of 1981.

Left: A GAF Nomad 22 on a European tour displays its clean and functional lines. The N22 and N24 have been selling steadily since production began in Australia in 1972.

Below: A GAF Nomad in service with IAT in Papua New Guinea, where the ability of the Nomad to operate from small, unprepared strips has proved to be of considerable advantage.

Grumman Mallard
(Goose and Widgeon)
USA

Power Plant: Two 600hp Pratt & Whitney R-1340-S3H1 radial engines.
Performance: Max speed, 215mph (346km/h) at 6,000ft (1830m); cruising speed, 180mph (290km/h) at 8,000ft (2438m); service ceiling, 23,000ft (7010m); range with max fuel, 1,380mls (2220km).
Weights: Empty, 9,350lb (4241kg); max take-off, 12,750lb (5783kg).
Dimensions: Span, 66ft 8in (20·32m); length, 48ft 4in (14·73m); height (on landing gear), 18ft 9in (5·72m); wing area, 444sq ft (41·25m).

Having achieved reasonable success pre-war with its small amphibians, the Widgeon and the Goose — both of which also served in military rôles during the war — the Grumman company embarked soon after the war ended upon the design of a modernised civil amphibian, the G-73 Mallard. Of the same overall configuration as the Goose, the Mallard first flew in 1946, but production ended after only 61 had been built, primarily for business or private users.

In 1981 about a dozen Mallards were in airline service. The principal user was Chalks International Airline, based in Miami and flying scheduled and charter services in the Bahamas. This company had six Mallards, including a single example converted to have two Pratt & Whitney PT6A-34 turboprops replacing the piston engines. This conversion originated with Frakes Aviation of Dallas, Texas, and Chalks planned to acquire up to nine more of this version.

The Grumman G-21 Goose, which was first flown in June 1937 also remained in airline service in small numbers in 1981. The G-21 received US Type Approval on 29 September 1937 and was followed by the G-21A production model on 5 February 1938. These were commercial amphibians with up to eight seats (including the pilot) built primarily for private and business use. Post-war, the amphibious capability of the Goose was found to be particularly useful in certain airline applications, especially in Alaska, parts of Canada, New Zealand, Scandinavia and other areas with lengthy coastlines.

Because of the lack of new amphibians to replace the Goose in this rôle, a market developed for reconditioned and improved versions of the original Grumman design, as modified and marketed by McKinnon Enterprises since 1958. The G-21C and G-21D had four 340hp Lycoming engines, replacing the original two 450hp R-985 Wasp Juniors, the G-21D also featuring a lengthened bow. The G-21E introduced 579eshp PT6A-20 turboprops and the G-21G had 715eshp PT6A-27s, with optional wing-tip floats and accommodating up to 11 passengers. After moving its facilities from the

Above right: A Grumman Mallard landing at St Thomas in the Virgin Islands during the time that services were being operated there by Antilles Air Boats. This company, specialising in the use of flying-boats and amphibians, ceased flying during 1981.

Right: A Grumman G-21A Goose in the markings of Catalina Airlines (now Air Catalina), a small airline that flies regularly between the Californian coast and the island of Catalina.

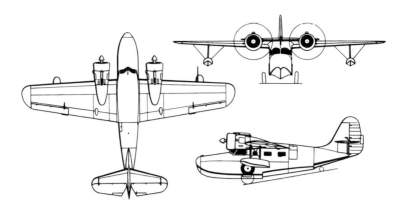

Above: The Crumman G-21 Goose in its original piston-engined form, as still used by several airlines.

USA to Canada, McKinnon-Viking Enterprises was continuing to offer the G-21G conversion in 1981, as well as the Super Widgeon conversion of the smaller Grumman amphibian, more than 70 of which McKinnon had already delivered.

Grumman G-111 Albatross
USA

Power Plant: Two 1,475hp Wright 982CH9HE3 radial engines.
Performance: Normal operating speed, (VNO) 237mph (382km/h); initial rate of climb, 1,250ft/min (6·3m/sec); max operating altitude, 8,000ft (2438m); range with 28 passengers and reserves, at 5,000ft (1525m), 575mls (926km) as a seaplane, 345mls (555km) as a landplane.
Weights: Empty equipped, 23,500lb (10,660kg); useful load (seaplane), 7,965lb ·(3613kg), (landplane), 7,205lb (3268kg); max take-off (seaplane), 31,365lb (14,227kg), (landplane), 30,605lb (13,882kg); max landing weight (seaplane), 31,365lb (14,227kg), (landplane), 29,160lb (13,227kg).
Dimensions: Span, 96ft 8in (29·46m); length, 61ft 3in (18·67m); height, 25ft 10in (7·87m); wing area, 1,035sq ft (96·15m²).

In conjunction with Resorts International, Grumman Aerospace has developed a conversion of the military HU-16 Albatross amphibian for use as a commuter, with 28 passenger seats. A prototype of the civil variant, which is identified by the original Grumman design number for the HU-16B of the Albatross, G-111, was first flown on 13 February 1979 and Resorts International obtained an FAA Type Certificate on 29 April 1980. Commercial service with the G-111 began in July 1981 when Chalks International Airlines, a subsidiary of Resorts, put the type into operation on its routes between Fort Lauderdale, Florida, and Paradise Island, Nassau.

The modification includes a complete overhaul of the airframe, replacement of some parts of the wing structure subject to corrosion, new systems and avionics, the passenger interior and improved entry doors. An initial batch of five G-111s was converted by Grumman for Chalks and for other

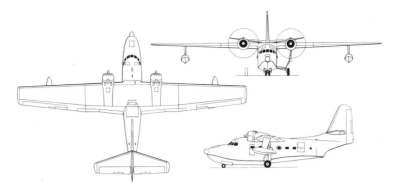

Above: Three-view drawing of the Grumman G-111, a "civilianised" conversion of the GU-16 Albatross military amphibian.

customers in 1981/82; the company also had acquired about 50 surplus HU-16s to meet possible future demand for the only amphibian of its size available for commercial operation. To extend the utility of the basic type, Grumman also had completed preliminary design of a turboprop conversion; this would be powered by a pair of Garrett TPE331-15UAR engines driving Dowty-Rotol four-bladed propellers. It was anticipated that such a turboprop variant would be certificated at a gross weight of 37,500lb (17,010kg), making it possible to double the cabin load, or to double the range with the same payload.

Below: This prototype of the HU-16 Albatross to G-111 standard was used for certification trials and then entered service during 1981 with Chalks International Airlines between Florida and Nassau.

Gulfstream American G-1C Commuter
USA

Power Plant: Two Rolls-Royce Dart 529 turboprops, each rated at 2,210eshp for takeoff.

Performance: Max cruising speed, 356mph (573km/h); initial rate of climb, 2,150ft/min (10·9m/sec); service ceiling, 30,400ft (9265m); range (max passenger load), 600mls (965km); range (max cargo load) 440mls (708km); ferry range, 2,015mls (3242km).

Weights: Basic operating weight (passenger version), 23,550lb (10,692kg); basic operating weight (cargo version), 23,750lb (10,783kg); max payload (passenger), 7,600lb (3450kg); max payload (cargo), 8,500lb (3859kg); max take-off, 36,000lb (16,344kg); max landing weight, 34,285lb (15,565 kg); max zero fuel weight, 32,250lb (14,642kg).

Dimensions: Span, 78ft 4in (23·87m); length, 74ft 3in (22·63m); height, 22ft 11in (6·98m); wing area, 610sq ft (56·67m²).

Following completion of a survey among commuter airlines, Gulfstream American decided to launch a stretched version of the Gulfstream I business twin as a 32/38-seat commuterliner. Production of the Gulfstream I had ended in 1958 after production of 200 for use as business aircraft; they were certificated to carry a maximum of 19 passengers and a few examples were used for scheduled services, by Air South in particular; in 1981. Orion Air was also using ten of the original Gulfstreams for an all-cargo service based on Atlanta, Ga.

Gulfstream American (which acquired the former Grumman American operation at Savannah, including design rights in the Gulfstream I) studied the possibility of putting the type back into production for third-level

Right: Flying on certification trials during 1980, this is the prototype conversion of a Gulfstream I business transport to G-1C Commuter configuration, with the fuselage lengthened to permit up to 32 passengers to be carried. Further conversions were made during the period 1980/81 and the G-1C is now in small-scale service with several US commuter airlines. The original Gulfstream I could accommodate only 19 passengers, limiting its utility as an airliner, but in 1982 Orion Air was operating 10 Gulfstreams to fly cargo.

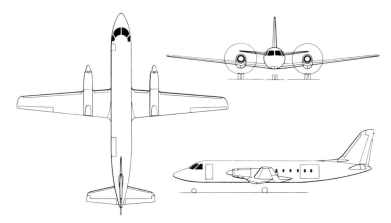

Above: Three-view drawing of the Gulfstream American G-1C, showing the lengthened fuselage and cargo door.

airline use, but up to the end of 1981 had opted only to convert existing airframes to the new GAC 159-C or Gulfstream G-1C configuration. Apart from a redesigned interior, the GAC 159-C features a fuselage stretch of 9ft 0in (2 00m) and an optional freight door in the rear fuselage side. Three-abreast seating at a pitch of 29in (74cm) provides accommodation for 38, at 34in (86cm) pitch, the aircraft seats 32, and in both cases there is a baggage compartment of 144cu ft (4·078m³) at the rear of the cabin and a toilet and carry-on baggage compartment at the front.

The first G-1C conversion flew on 25 October 1979, and this aircraft was subsequently delivered to Air North, which put the type into service at the end of 1980. By end-1981, five G-1Cs had been ordered, by Air North, Air US and Chaparral Airlines.

Handley Page Herald
United Kingdom

The following specification relates to the Herald 200:

Power Plant: Two 2,105ehp Rolls-Royce Dart 527 turboprops.

Performance: Max cruising speed, 274mph (441km/h) at 15,000ft (4572m); best economy cruise, 265mph (426km/h) at 23,000ft (7010m); initial rate of climb, 1,805ft/min (9·1m/sec); service ceiling, 27,900ft (8504m); no-reserves range with max payload, 1,110mls (1786km); no-reserves range with max fuel, 1,620mls (2607km).

Weights: Operating empty, 25,800lb (11,700kg); max payload, 11,242lb (5100kg); max take-off, 43,000lb (19,505kg).

Dimensions: Span, 94ft 9in (28·88m); length, 75ft 6in (23·01m); height, 24ft 1in (7·34m); wing area, 886sq ft (82·3m²).

Like the Aérospatiale (Nord) 262 and the Short Skyvan, the Herald was designed around piston engines but went into production with turboprops. The design was started as the company's first post-war essay into the civil market since the Hermes, and after market study the decision was taken to build a feeder-line aircraft with about 44 seats in a pressurized fuselage, with a range of about 400 miles (644km) — or up to 1,400mls (2253km) with reduced payload. Design was made the responsibility of the Reading branch of the company, previously the Miles Aircraft organization. Details of the HPR 3 Herald were first published in 1954, at which time the aircraft was based upon the use of four Alvis Leonides Major piston radial engines.

By the time the first of two prototypes flew at Woodley on 25 August 1955, orders had been placed for a total of 29 Heralds by Queensland Airlines, Australian National Airways and Lloyd Aereo Colombiano. A second prototype flew in August 1956 and a production batch of 25 was put in hand, but by 1957 the success of the turboprop engine, particularly in the Viscount, made it apparent that future prospects for the Herald were bleak and even the initial customers were reluctant to proceed with their commitments. In May 1957, consequently, Handley Page announced plans to offer an alternative version of the Herald with two Dart turboprops in place of the four radials, and subsequently the original version was dropped altogether.

Both the Herald prototypes were converted to take the Dart engines, flying in their revised form on 11 March and 17 December 1958 respectively. Initially, the name Dart Herald was used, but the prefix was soon dropped. The first production aircraft flew on 30 October 1959 and was identified as a Srs 100, being used as a company demonstrator. Earlier in 1959, the UK government had ordered three Heralds for use by BEA on its Scottish Highlands and Islands routes, and the next three aircraft to appear were also of the Srs 100 type (specifically, Srs 101, individual numbers being adopted for each customer) for BEA. No more Srs 100s were built.

In September 1960, Jersey Airlines (now British Island Airways) placed an order for six of a lengthened and improved version of the Herald known as the Srs 200. The overall length increased by 3ft 7in (1·09m) and gross weight by 2,000lb (907kg); maximum passenger capacity increased from 47 in the Srs 100 to 56 in the Srs 200, although more usual arrangements were 40 and 44 respectively. The second prototype Herald/Dart Herald was converted to the new standard and flew as a Srs 200 on 8 April 1961. British certification was obtained on 1 June 1961.

Handley Page flew the first production Herald Srs 200 on 13 December 1961 and deliveries to Jersey Airlines began in January 1962, this airline eventually increasing its fleet to 12 after becoming part of the BUA group. Production of the Herald 200 continued at a very low rate until mid-1968, by which time the company had delivered 36 Srs 200s and eight Srs 400s, the latter being a military variant sold to the Royal Malaysian Air Force. At the time the Handley Page company collapsed, six more Heralds were in hand

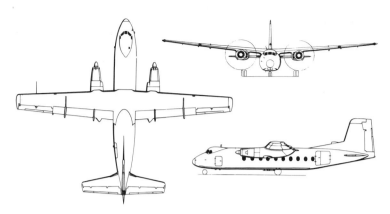

Above: Three-view drawing of the Handley Page Herald 200, the longer-fuselage variant that became definitive for production.

as speculative production but were not completed.

The Heralds were acquired by a variety of operators in small batches, and became the subject of much second-hand trading from an early stage. By 1982, the commercial utility of the Herald appeared to be waning, although a number were still being used on regional ferries by UK operators and a few others in Europe.

Below: The Herald 200 G-APWE was one of 15 retained in the fleet of Air UK in 1982; a similar quantity was operated by British Air Ferries.

Hawker Siddeley HS. 121 Trident
United Kingdom

The following specification refers to the Trident 2E:

Power Plant: Three 11,960ib st (5425kgp) Rolls-Royce Spey 512-5W turbofans.

Performance: Max cruising speed, 596mph (960km/h); long-range cruise, 505mph (812km/h); no-reserves range with max payload, 3,155mls (5078km); no-reserves range with max fuel, 3,558mls (5726km).

Weights: Basic operating, 73,250lb (33,250kg); max payload, 29,600lb (13,426kg); max take-off, 143,500lb (65,090kg).

Dimensions: Span, 98ft 0in (29·9m); length, 114ft 9in (34·98m); height, 27ft 0in (8·23m); wing area, 1,461sq ft (135·7m²).

Although the Trident short-medium haul transport achieved only modest success compared with that enjoyed by the Boeing 727 of similar concept and characteristics, it provided a steady line of businees for the Hawker Siddeley division at Hatfield for some 20 years. Like most commercial transports of the post-war period, the Trident suffered a somewhat involved period of conception and gestation before emerging in 1958 as BEA's first pure-jet transport.

The requirement for such an aeroplane to operate over BEA's routes, few of which were of more than 1,000mls (1610km) in length, was first drawn up in July 1956, and an initial de Havilland proposal was made as the D.H.119, using four Rolls-Royce Avon RA.29 engines. This was followed by the D.H.120, an attempt to meet with one aeroplane both the BEA requirement and BOAC's need for a long-haul jet (eventually met by the VC10). Concentrating again on the BEA requirement, de Havilland then evolved the D.H.121, which the airline chose on technical merit over the competing Avro 540 and Bristol 200. To meet political requirements at that time, de Havilland then set up the Airco consortium, with Fairey and Hunting, to produce the D.H.121, for which BEA placed a preliminary order for 24 in February 1958.

At that stage, the aircraft was to have been powered by three 13,790lb st (6255kgp) RB.141/3 Medway engines grouped in the rear fuselage, have 111 seats and a range of 2,070mls (3330km). In 1959, however, BEA scaled down its requirement and a smaller version of the design emerged, with three 9,850lb st (4470kgp) RB.163 Spey 505 engines, 97–103 seats and range of 930mls (1500km), and in this form production went ahead. The Airco consortium was dissolved later in 1959 when de Havilland joined the Hawker Siddeley Group, and the aircraft was named Trident 1.

No prototypes were built, and the first Trident 1 flew on 9 January 1962; the first revenue flight was made on 11 March 1964 in BEA service, with full scheduled operations starting on 1 April. From the start, the Trident was designed to have suitable equipment to permit its operation in very low weather minima, this equipment comprising the Smiths Autoland system. BEA Trident 1s were certificated in September 1968 to make automatic landings in Cat II weather conditions.

In addition to the 24 Trident 1s, Hawker Siddeley built 15 Trident 1Es for other operators (Kuwait, Iraqi, Pakistan, Air Ceylon, Channel and Northeast). This version had 11,400lb st (5170kgp) Spey 511s, gross weight increased from 115,000lb (52,165kg) to 128,000lb (58,060kg), span increased from ▶

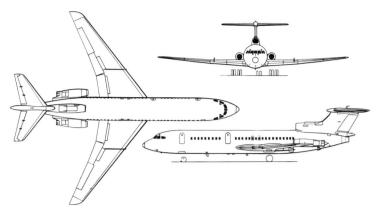

Above: The HS 121 Trident 2E, the principal production version of the tri-jet for British Airways and China's CAAC.

Below: A Trident 2E on a pre-delivery flight in the UK, in the markings of the Civil Aviation Administration of China.

Below: One of the 33 Hawker Siddeley Trident 2Es purchased by CAAC. Some have been transferred to the air force.

89ft 10in (27·41m) to 95ft (28·95m) and accommodation increased to 140 (six abreast).

In 1965, BEA ordered 15 Trident 2s (maker's designation, 2E), which had the same fuselage as the Srs 1s but a further small increase in span to 98ft (29·9m) and more fuel; weights went up and 11,960lb st (5425kgp) Spey 512-5Ws were used. With internal re-arrangements, the Trident 2E could carry up to 149 passengers (six-abreast). First flight was made on 27 July 1967 and BEA operated the first scheduled service on 18 April 1968. Two Trident 2Es were sold to Cyprus Airways and in 1971 the Chinese Peoples' Republic selected this variant in a major re-equipment drive for CAAC, following initial experience with four Trident 1Es acquired from Pakistan International. Successive orders brought the total ordered by China to 33 by the end of 1974; the first was flown on 20 October 1972 and handed over on 13 November; the last was delivered in June 1978, bringing Trident production to an end at an overall total of 117.

Third of the Trident variants for BEA was the Trident Three (maker's designation, 3B), which had the fuselage lengthened by 16ft 5in (5·00m) in order to accommodate up to 180 passengers (six-abreast) and operate on BEA's high-density short-haul routes. The wing span remained as on the

Above: A Trident Three in the 1982 livery of British Airways, showing omission of the word "Airways" from the fuselage marking.

2E but changes were made in the control surfaces, and to improve the take-off performance at the higher operating weights, a fourth, "booster", engine was added, this being a 5,250lb st (2381 kgp) Rolls-Royce RB.162-86 in the tail above the fuselage. The Trident Three first flew on 11 December 1969 and the first flight with boost engine operating was made on 22 March 1970. The first of 26 ordered by BEA entered service on 1 April 1971, and in December of that year, approval was given for autoland operations by the Trident Three down to 12ft (3·66m) decision height and 885ft (270m) runway visual range, plus take-offs in full Cat IIIA conditions, with an RVR of 295ft (90m). Operations to these standards were begun by BEA (now British Airways) in May 1973. After fatigue cracks had been found in several of British Airways' Tridents, the Srs Twos and Threes were modified to have a 3ft (91cm) reduction in span, lessening the bending moments; the Trident Ones are now out of service. Two other Trident Threes were ordered by CAAC in 1972, as Super Trident 3Bs, these differing from the BEA model in having higher fuel capacity and operating weights.

Ilyushin Il-14
Soviet Union

The following specification relates to the Il-14M:
Power Plant: Two 1,900shp Shvetsov ASh-82T 14-cylinder radial air-cooled engines.
Performance: Max speed, 259mph (417km/h); high-speed cruise, 239mph (385km/h); long-range cruise, 193mph (311km/h); initial climb, 1,220ft/min (6·2m/sec); service ceiling, 22,000ft (6705m); range with max payload, 810mls (1034km), with max fuel, 1,988mls (3202km).
Weights: Operational equipped, 27,776lb (12,600kg); max take-off, 39,683lb (18,000kg).
Dimensions: Span, 104ft 0in (31·69m); length, 73ft 2in (22·30m); height, 25ft 11in (7·90m); wing area 1,075sq ft (99·70m²).

The Il-14 was the first post-WWII design from the bureau led by Sergei V Ilyushin to achieve production status and, by comparison with its predecessor the Il-12, embodied a refined structure, improved aerodynamics and up-rated engines. Flown in prototype form in 1952, the Il-14 entered production for both military use and Aeroflot, the commercial version for the latter being designated Il-14P (*Passazhirskii*) and providing accommodation for 18–26 passengers.

A "stretched" variant, the Il-14M (*Modifikatsirovanny*), appeared in 1956, this having a 3ft 4in (1·0m) additional section inserted in the forward fuselage and accommodation being increased to 24–28 passengers. A substantial number of Il-14P and Il-14M airliners were later adapted as

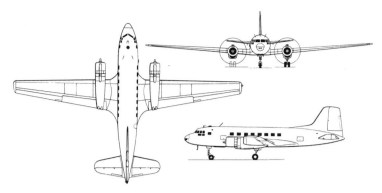

Above: Three-view drawing of the Ilyushin Il-14, the transport developed in the Soviet Union to succeed the Douglas DC-3.

freighters under the designation of Il-14T (*Transportny*)

Production of the Il-14 in the Soviet Union reportedly exceeded 3,500 aircraft, 80 were built by the VEB Flugzeugwerke in East Germany and approximately 80 Il-14Ps were manufactured in Czechoslovakia where production continued with several different versions of the Avia 14.

By the end of the 'seventies, the Ilyushin Il-14 was no longer in service with the airlines of the East European countries that had originally used the type in some numbers. However, as many as 100 or so were believed to be still in service with Aeroflot, especially in its Polar division, and CAAC, the airline of the People's Republic of China, had about 30 in its fleet.

Left: An Ilyushin Il-14 in the markings of the Czechoslo-vakian air line CSA which, in common with the air lines of the other Soviet-bloc nations in Eastern Europe, relied heavily upon the type in the early post-war years for the re-establishment of air services. By the end of the 'seventies the Il-14 was no longer in airline use outside of the Soviet Union, although a few military examples were still to be seen here and there. With Aeroflot, about 100 Il-14s were reported to be still serving in 1982, mostly in remote areas well away from the trunk routes, and includ-ing some in the Polar regions.

Ilyushin Il-18
Soviet Union

The following specification relates to the Il-18D:

Power Plant: Four Ivchenko AI-20M turboprops each rated at 4,250ehp.
Performance: Max cruise (at max take-off weight), 419mph (675km/h); economy cruise, 388mph (625km/h); operating altitude, 26,250–32,800ft (8000–10,000m); range (max payload and one hour's reserves), 2,300mls (3700km), (max fuel and one hour's reserves), 4,040mls (6500km).
Weights: Empty equipped (90-seater), 77,160lb (35,000kg); max take-off, 141,000lb (64,000kg).
Dimensions: Span, 122ft 8½in (37·40m); length, 117ft 9in (35·90m); height, 33ft 4in (10·17m); wing area, 1,507sq ft (140m²).

Numerically the second most important airliner in the Aeroflot inventory in the mid-seventies, the Il-18 entered service with the Soviet carrier on 20 April 1959, and was reported to have carried 60 million passengers by the spring of 1969, when it was being utilized on 800 international and domestic services. The prototype Il-18, which was known as the *Moskva*, was flown for the first time in July 1957, being followed by two pre-production examples. Series production aircraft, with accommodation for 75 passengers, were initially delivered with the Kuznetsov NK-4 or Ivchenko AI-20 turboprop providing optional power plants. The 21st and subsequent aircraft standardized on the latter engine and the initial version was quickly supplanted by the Il-18B which had an increase in max take-off weight of 4,409lb (2000kg) from 130,514lb (59,200kg) and accommodated 84 passengers.

Further development resulted in the Il-18V in 1961, with accommodation for 89–100 passengers, this being followed three years later, in 1964, by the Il-18I with 4,250eshp AI-20M turboprops in place of the 4,000 eshp AI-20Ks of previous versions, accommodation for 110–122 passengers made possible by the lengthening of the pressurized section of the fuselage through deletion of the unpressurized tail cargo hold, and a 32 per cent increase in total fuel capacity as a result of the introduction of additional centre-section fuel tankage. Redesignated Il-18D, this model entered Aero-

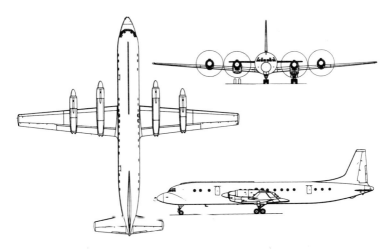

Above: Three-view drawing of the Ilyushin Il-18, one of the key types in the modernization of Aeroflot.

flot service in 1965, together with the Il-18Ye (usually referred to in Western circles as the Il-18E) which was similar apart from having the same fuel capacity as the Il-18V. Both the Il-18D and Il-18V were operated by a flight crew of five, and in their standard 110-seat high-density arrangement had 24 and 71 seats in six-abreast rows in the forward and main cabins respectively, and 15 seats five-abreast in the rear cabin.

Production of the Il-18 reportedly exceeded 800 aircraft of which more than 100 were exported for commercial and military use. Foreign commercial operators included Air Guinee, Air Mali, Air Mauritanie, Balkan, CAAC, CSA, Cubana, Egyptair, Interflug, LOT, Malev, Tarom and Yemen Airways. Many of these remained in use in 1981 although most of these operators have acquired Soviet jet equipment for their primary routes.

Below: The Il-18 was produced in substantial numbers in the Soviet Union and was put into service by all the East European airlines

Ilyushin Il-62
Soviet Union

The following specification relates to the Il-62M:

Power Plant: Four 24,250lb st (11,000kgp) Soloviev D-30KU turbofans.
Performance: Typical cruising speed, 508—560mph (820—900km/h) at 33,000—39,400ft (10,000—12,000m); range with max payload, and 1-hr fuel reserve, 4,847mls (7800km); range with max fuel 6,215mls (10,000km).
Weights: Operating weight empty, 153,000lb (69,400kg); max payload, 50,700lb (23,000kg); max fuel load, 183,700lb (83,325kg); max take-off, 363,760lb (165,000kg); max landing, 232,000lb (105,000kg).
Dimensions: Span, 141ft 9in (43·20m); length, 174ft 3½in (53·12m); height 40ft 6¼in (12·35m); wing area, 3,010sq ft (279·6m²).

Entering service with Aeroflot on 15 September 1967, the Ilyushin Il-62 was the first long-range four-engined jet transport developed in the Soviet Union for commercial use to achieve production status, and had become an essential component in the Aeroflot fleet by the end of the 'seventies. The introduction into service — initially as a replacement for the Tupolev Tu-114 on the Moscow—Montreal transatlantic service — came almost exactly five years after the Il-62 had been publicly unveiled in Moscow.

The Il-62 design featured an all-manual flying control system, with a yaw damper in the rudder circuit, and an automatic flight control system that allowed it to operate in weather minima similar to those defined as Cat II by ICAO standards. Like many other aircraft with a rear-engined, high tail layout, the Il-62 was found to have slender control margins at low speed, and an extensive flight test programme was undertaken to refine the wing design, resulting in the adoption of a fixed, drooped extension of the leading edge over approximately the outer half of each wing. The first flight was made in January 1963, and this prototype was fitted with 16,535lb st (7500kgp) Lyulka AL-7 turbojets pending the development of a new turbofan unit by the Kuznetsov engine design bureau. This new engine, the 23,150lb st (10,500kgp) NK-8-4, became available in time to power some of the later trials aircraft, comprising a second prototype and three pre-production examples. Cascade-type thrust reversers were fitted on the outer engines only.

With six-abreast seating and a central aisle, the Il-62 accommodated 186 passengers in a high-density layout or 168 in a one-class tourist layout. A typical mixed-class layout had 20 seats four-abreast in the forward cabin and 102 six-abreast in the rear cabin, separated by a large galley amidships. Two passenger doors, one immediately aft of the flight deck and the other just ahead of the wing leading edge, gave access to the cabin.

Aeroflot was believed to have over 100 Il-62s in service by early 1974. Following its introduction on the Moscow—Montreal service, the Il-62 went into service on the Moscow—New York prestige route in July 1968, and subsequently replaced Tu-114s and Tu-104s on many of the longer international routes as well as the trunk routes within the Soviet Union. The first user of the Il-62 outside the USSR was Czechoslovakian Airlines CSA, which leased a single example from Aeroflot for its Prague—London service in May 1968. Subsequently CSA procured its own fleet of Il-62s, and most of the East European bloc airlines followed suit, including Interflug (East Germany), Balkan Bulgarian, LOT (Poland) and Tarom of Rumania. Under a 1970 trade agreement, China procured five examples for use by CAAC, and United Arab Airlines (later Egyptair) acquired seven, although these

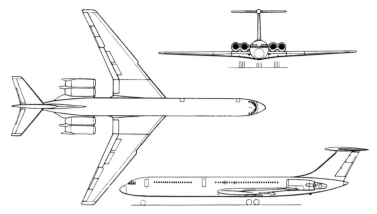

Above: Three-view drawing of the Ilyushin Il-62M, which shared its four engined rear-mounted configuration with the BAC VC10.

were later returned to Russia.

During 1970, the Ilyushin design bureau evolved an improved version of the basic design with increased seating and more range. Known as the Il-62M (and sometimes referred to as the Il-62M-200), this newer version is powered by four Soloviev D-30KU turbofans rated at 24,250lb st (11,000kgp) each and with clamshell-type instead of cascade-type reversers on the outer engines. The extra power permits operation at a higher gross weight and additional fuel capacity is provided by a tank in the fin. These improvements give Il-62M a better payload-range performance, the max range increasing to 6,400mls (10,300km); internal redesign makes it possible to accommodate up to 198 passengers. The flight control system permits operation in Cat II weather minima and is capable of development for Cat III operation. Aeroflot introduced the Il-62M in 1974 and this model has subsequently been adopted by other operators also for long range subsonic operations. A further variant appeared in 1978 as the Il-62MK, with a strengthened wing to increase the fatigue life, higher operating weights including a max take-off weight of 308,170lb (167,000kg) and a redesigned interior for up to 195 passengers.

Above: An Ilyushin Il-62 in service with Interflug makes its final approach.

Below: An Ilyushin Il-62 of LOT Polish Airlines.

Ilyushin Il-86
Soviet Union

Power Plant: Four Kuznetsov NK-86 turbofans each rated at 28,635lb st (13,000kgp) for take-off.
Performance: Cruising speed, 560—590mph (900—950km/h) at 30,000ft (9000m); range 2,235 miles (3600km) with full passenger payload and 2,858mls (4600km) with max fuel.
Weights: Max payload, 92,500lb (42,000kg); max take-off weight, 454,150lb (206,000kg); max landing weight, 385,800lb (175,000kg).
Dimensions: Span, 157ft 8¼in (48·06m); length, 197ft 6½in (60·21m); height, 5qft 5½in (15·68m); wing area, 3,444sq ft (320m²).

The rapid growth of air transport within the Soviet Union led Aeroflot to initiate the development of a whole range of new aircraft types for service during the 'seventies. Among this new generation of transports was the first wide-body "airbus" type designed in the Soviet Union. When the requirement for this type was formulated in the late 'sixties, design proposals were made by the Antonov, Tupolev and Ilyushin bureaux, the last-mentioned winning official backing for construction of what became known as the Il-86. As first projected, it had four rear-mounted engines, in an arrangement similar to that of the Il-62, but as design proceeded it became clear to the Soviet engineers that this layout incurred structure weight penalties that were unacceptable in so large an aircraft. Consequently, before construction began, the design was changed to have four engines in individual underwing pods, making the Il-86 the first Soviet airliner to use this "classic" layout.

A unique feature of the Il-86 is the provision of entrance vestibules on a lower level beneath the main cabin floor, allowing passengers to embark and disembark by way of airstairs incorporated in the doors and making it

Below: Established in the cruise at altitude, one of the prototypes of the Il-86 is seen during development flying. This large capacity airliner entered service with Aeroflot late in 1980.

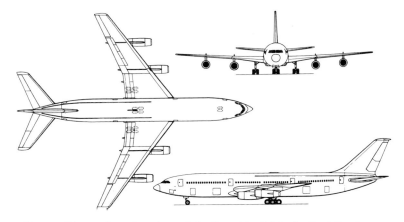

Above: Three-view drawing of the Ilyushin Il-86, the first Soviet wide-body airliner, with accommodation for 350 passengers.

unnecessary to provide complex ground handling equipment at every airport. Stowage space is provided in the vestibules for outer coats and carry-on luggage and passengers then proceed by internal stairways to the main deck.

Originally designed to be powered by Soloviev D-30KP turbofans, the Il-86 in fact makes use of Kuznetsov NK-86 engines of new design, flight testing of which began in 1975 beneath the wing of an Il-86. First flight of the prototype Il-86 was made on 22 December 1976 and a second prototype was followed by the first production Il-86 on 24 October 1977, this aircraft being the first to be completed at the production facility at Voronezh. Proving flights over Aeroflot routes began in September 1978 but the target of getting the Il-86 into service in time for the 1980 Olympic Games in Moscow was not achieved. It was late 1980 before the new aircraft was carrying passengers on a regular basis on long trunk routes within the Soviet Union. Furnished to carry 350 passengers, the Il-86 went into international service on 3 July 1981 on the Moscow–East Berlin route.

Let L-410 Turbolet
Czechoslovakia

The following specification refers to the L-410 UVP:

Power Plant: Two 730eshp Walter M-601 B turboprops.

Performance: Cruising speed, 224mph (360km/h) at 9,850ft (3000m); initial rate of climb, 1,535ft/min (7·8m/sec); service ceiling, 29,360ft (8950m); range with max payload, 285mls (460km); range with max fuel, 646mls (1040km).

Weights: Basic empty, 8,212lb (3725kg); max fuel, 2,127lb (965kg); max payload 2,888lb (1310kg); max take-off, 12,566lb (5700kg); max landing, 12,125lb (5500kg).

Dimensions: Span, 63ft 10¾in (19·48m); length, 47ft 5½in (14·47m); height, 19ft 1½in (5·83m); wing area, 378·7sq ft (35·18m²).

The L-410 was developed by the Czech National Aircraft Industry at its Kunovice works, being the first indigenous design to emerge from that factory. It was intended to be used as a commuter or third-level airliner, seating 15 to 19 passengers in a 2+1 arrangement, and development of a suitable turboprop engine, the M-601, was put in hand in Czechoslovakia at the same time.

As the M-601 was not cleared for flight in time for installation in the prototype L-410, Pratt & Whitney PT6A-27s were fitted and with these the first flight was made on 16 April 1969. Production aircraft, similarly powered and designated L-410A, began to appear in 1971 and had small increases in wing span and overall length. Initial deliveries were made to Slov-Air, which took over responsibility from CSA for some domestic air routes in Czechoslovakia, and four were in service by the end of 1972. The L-410 was also selected by Aeroflot after competitive evaluation with the Beriev Be-30, but deliveries to the Soviet Union were delayed until the L-410M version with M-601 engines became available in 1976. Production of the L-410A totalled 31, and of the L-410M, 110 (including a prototype flown in 1973).

From 1979, the standard production version has been the L-410 UVP, the prototype of which first flew on 1 November 1977. This incorporates a number of changes and refinements made primarily to meet Aeroflot's criticism of the tail unit with dihedral on the tailplane and many systems improvements. Production of up to 100 a year was planned at the LET works at Kunovice, principally for export to Aeroflot.

Below: The colour profile depicts an early production example of the L-410 in the markings of Slov-Air, which operates domestic flights within Czechoslovakia. These operations were taken over from CSA, which now has 11 Turbolets in its fleet including OK-CDS shown here, and were added to Slov-Air's primary activities in agricultural, air taxi and cargo flying.

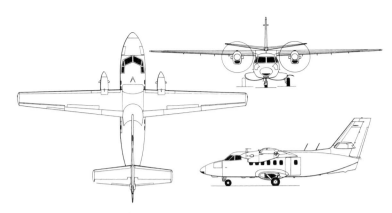

Above: Three-view drawing of the L-410 UVP, the definitive production version of the Turbolet featuring a revised rear fuselage and tail unit.

Above: One of the early production model L-410As as operated by CSA on domestic routes in Czechoslovakia in the early 'seventies.

Lockheed Electra
USA

The following specification relates to the L-188A:
Power Plant: Four 3,750ehp Allison 501-D13A turboprops.
Performance: Max cruising speed, 405mph (652km/h) at 22,000ft (6700m); best economy cruise, 374mph (602km/h); initial rate of climb, 1,670ft/min (8·5m/sec); service ceiling, 27,000ft (8230m); range with max payload, 2,200mls (3540km); range with max fuel, 2,500mls (4023km).
Weights: Basic operating, 61,500lb (27,895kg); max payload, 22,825lb (10,350kg); max take-off, 116,000lb (52,664kg).
Dimensions: Span, 99ft 0in (30·18m); length, 104ft 6in (31·81m); height, 32ft 10in (10·0m); wing area, 1,300sq ft (120·8m²).

The only major US airliner to make use of turboprop engines, the Lockheed Electra proved — like the Vickers Vanguard which was closely comparable in size, performance and timescale — to be an expensive venture for its manufacturer, being overtaken by the development of pure-jet transports before its expected sales potential could be realised. By the time the first Electra flew, orders had been placed for 144, promising a bright future for the type, but only 26 more were sold subsequently, leaving the production total far short of the break-even figure. The design did, however, provide the basis for the P-3 Orion maritime reconnaissance aircraft, which was still in production in 1982.

Design of the Electra began in 1954 primarily to meet requirements set out by American Airlines for a short-medium range transport for US domestic operation, with a larger capacity than was available in the Vickers Viscount or similar types. Both Vickers and Lockheed were among the companies that attempted — at first unsuccessfully — to meet the requirement, but in 1955 American Airlines re-issued the specification in modified form and Lockheed then succeeded in selling its revised L-188 design to American Airlines and, simultaneously, to Eastern Airlines.

The combined "launching" orders from these two companies, placed in June 1955, were for 75 aircraft and the design was for a 100 seat transport with a non-stop range of about 2,300mls (3700km). By the time the first Electra flew, on 6 December 1957, the gross weight had been established at 113,000lb (57,260kg); three further aircraft were flown in quick succession in 1958 and the fifth, to be the first for airline delivery, flew on 19 May 1958. FAA Type Approval for the Electra was obtained on 22 August 1958 and the type entered service with Eastern Airlines on 12 January 1959 and with American Airlines on 23 January 1959. The Electra thus became the first turbine-engined airliner of US design and production to operate regular services, and was to be the only US turboprop to achieve this status. The engines were Allison 501-D13s, commercial versions of the T56.

Once the Electra had been launched into production, orders accumulated rapidly — primarily from other US domestic airlines, but including several from Australasian airlines and one European order, from KLM. In this period, 1955–56, the Vickers Vanguard was competing for the same market, but with markedly less success. It was also the period of the so-called "jet buying spree" when major airlines all over the world were placing their first orders for pure-jet equipment, with the Electra being chosen in several cases as the complementary short-haul type. Ansett-ANA in Australia became the first non-US operator to introduce the Electra, in March 1959.

Within 15 months of the Electra's first service, two fatal accidents had occurred in similar circumstances and on 25 March 1960 the FAA introduced a speed limitation of 275 knots (510km/h) IAS, reduced further to 225 knots (417km/h) a few days later. Painstaking investigations revealed that the problem lay in the structural strength of the power plant mounting which could suffer damage in, for example, a heavy landing and this could then

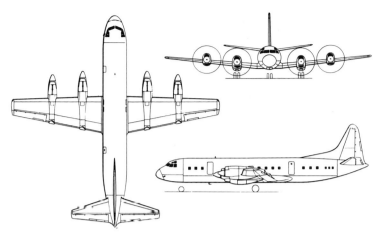

Above: Three-view of the Lockheed Electra, which was the only major airliner of American origin to use turboprop engines.

Below: The Lockheed Electra entered service in 1959 with Eastern Airlines, but it achieved only limited commercial success.

result in an oscillation of the engine and propeller being allowed to develop, with catastrophic structural failure following. Lockheed undertook a structural modification programme, flying a modified aircraft in October 1960, obtaining FAA certification on 5 January 1961 and then putting in hand a programme to modify all Electras delivered or in production.

For some customers — initially Northwest and Western — Lockheed developed the L-188C version of the Electra with additional fuel and higher gross weight. This was primarily an overwater variant, with a max fuel range increased to 3,020mls (4860km). Fifty-five of the 170 Electras built were of this model. By the end of the 'seventies, most Electras had been retired from front-line service but the type was still being used for secondary service, almost wholly in North and South America, a substantial number having been modified for use as pure freighters with large side-loading doors.

Lockheed Hercules
USA

The following specification relates to the L-100-30:
Power Plant: Four 4,508eshp Allison 501-D22A turboprops.
Performance: Max cruising speed, 377mph (607km/h); initial rate of climb, 1,900ft/min (9·65m/sec); range with max payload, 2,130mls (3425km); range with max fuel, 4,740mls (7630km).
Weights: Operating empty, 71,400lb (32,386kg); max payload, 51,400lb (23,315kg), max take-off, 155,000lb (70,308kg).
Dimensions: Span, 132ft 7in (40·41m); length, 112ft 8½in (34·35m); height, 38ft 3in (11·66m); wing area, 1,745sq ft (162·12m²).

The Hercules freighter was designed in 1951 to meet USAF requirements for a tactical airlift transport powered by turboprop engines, and development under USAF contract proceedings from July 1951 onwards at the company's California headquarters. Two prototype YC-130s flew at Burbank, the first on 23 August 1954, and the entire programme was then transferred to the Lockheed-Georgia Company at Marietta, near Atlanta, where the first production C-130 flew on 7 April 1955. The C-130 featured straight-in loading through doors and ramps in the rear fuselage, and could carry large freight loads.

The commercial potential of the Hercules was realized at an early stage in its development, but early efforts to market the type as the L-100 met with relatively little success. On 21 April 1964, however, Lockheed flew a civil demonstrator, based on the military C-130E and known as the Model 382-44K-20, the second and third cyphers in the designation indicating its specific configuration. FAA certification was obtained on 16 February 1965, and deliveries of commercial Hercules variants began later in 1965.

The Hercules delivered for commercial use in 1965–1967 were basically Model 382B. The designation L-100 was also used, specifically for Hercules delivered to Delta Air Lines which had a special cargo loading system, and the designation L-100-10 was applied to a proposed version with 4,500shp Allison 501-D22A turboprops in place of the usual 4,050shp 501-D22s.

During 1967, Lockheed embarked on development of a stretched version

*Right: A Lockheed
L-100-20 Hercules in
service with Philippine
Aerotransport for
scheduled cargo
services within the
Philippines and
charter flights world-
wide. The L-100-20
was the first
"stretched" version
of the Hercules; a
longer fuselage is
featured by the
L-100-30, which had
become the principal
commercial version
by the early 'eighties.
Primarily a cargo
aircraft, the Hercules
is also used for
passenger services.*

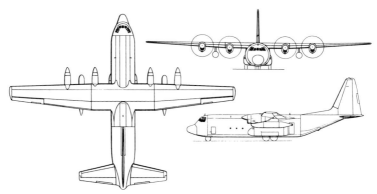

Above: Three-view drawing of the Hercules in its L-100-20 version, with a longer fuselage than the basic Hercules.

of the Hercules offering better operating economics by increasing the fuselage length by 8ft 4in (2·54m). The D22A power plant was adopted, although the maximum take-off weight remained unchanged at 155,000lb (70,307kg). The original commercial Hercules demonstrator was converted to the new standard as Model 382E or L-100-20 and flew in this guise on 19 April 1968, obtaining FAA Type Approval on 4 October that year.

Another stretch of the Hercules was undertaken in 1969, producing the Model 382G or L-100-30. The L-100-30 had various of the original military features deleted, including the rear cargo windows, paratroop doors and rocket ATO provision, and the first example flew on 14 August 1970. Type Approval was obtained on 7 October 1970. Further developments of the basic Hercules had been proposed for the civil market by 1977, including the L-100-50 with the fuselage lengthened by another 20ft (6·1m) from the L-100-30, and the L-400, a twin-engined derivative. None of these had materialized up to the end of 1981, and the great majority of some 70 Hercules delivered for civil use were for pure freighters. Six L-100-30s purchased by the Government of Indonesia were for passenger-carrying in that country's transmigration scheme, and both Air Algérie and the government of Gabon had purchased kits allowing 91 seats, plus galley and toilet units, to be quickly installed on pallets in their L-100-30s.

Lockheed L-1011 TriStar
USA

The following specification refers to the L-1011-1:

Power Plant: Three 42,000lb st (19,050kgp) Rolls-Royce RB.211-22B or 43,500lb st (19,730kgp) RB.211-22F turbofans.

Performance: Max cruising speed, 575mph (925km/h) = Mach 0·85 at 35,000ft (10,670m); best range cruise, 544mph (875km/h) = Mach 0·82 at 35,000ft (10,670m); initial rate of climb, 2,800ft/min (14·3m/sec); service ceiling, 42,000ft (12,800m); range with max payload, 2,878mls (4629km); range with max fuel, 4,467mls (7189km) with payload of 40,000lb (18,145 kg).

Weights: Operating empty, 234,275lb (106,265kg); max payload, 90,725lb (41,150kg); max take-off, 430,000lb (195,045kg).

Dimensions: Span, 155ft 4in (47·34m); length, 178ft 8in (54·35m); height, 55ft 4in (16·87m); wing area, 3,456sq ft (320·0m²).

For the Lockheed company, the ending of production of the turboprop Electra in 1962 meant that for the first time since World War II it had no airliner in production at its Burbank, California, headquarters, and that its hard-earned expertise in the commercial field (gained particularly with the Constellation) was in danger of being lost. To fill the vacuum at Burbank, Lockheed mounted a major effort to re-enter the commercial market, setting in train a sequence of events that was to bring the company to the brink of bankruptcy as well as presenting the airlines with a family of advanced high capacity wide-bodied transport aircraft.

The trigger for Lockheed's design activities leading to production of the L-1011 TriStar came in 1966 when American Airlines (which had previously sponsored the Electra) drew up a specification for a large capacity, short-to-medium haul transport of the "airbus" type, using the new-technology turbofan engines then becoming available. Although American eventually decided, after months of intensive and competitive design effort by Lockheed and McDonnell Douglas, to order the DC-10, Lockheed was in a position to offer its L-1011 to other US domestic operators that were in the market for a similar aircraft, and on 29 March 1968, TWA and Eastern Airlines announced that they were placing contracts which, combined with a deal between Lockheed and the British Air Holdings company, promised the eventual production of 144 aircraft.

The name TriStar was adopted to continue Lockheed's stellar theme and to emphasize the three-engined layout. As launched, the TriStar was an aeroplane of 409,000lb (185,520kg) gross weight, with a Mach = 0·85 cruising speed, able to carry a 345-passenger payload and to be powered by three Rolls-Royce RB.211 engines. The choice of British engines was made easier by the arrangement for Air Holdings (parent company of BUA) to buy 50 TriStars for resale outside of the UK, and the decision was responsible for launching development of the RB.211, at a projected initial thrust rating of 42,000lb st (19,050kgp). The cost of this programme was to lead Rolls-Royce into bankruptcy on 4 February 1971, placing the whole TriStar future in jeopardy and having repercussions from which Lockheed did not fully recover until the end of the decade. ▶

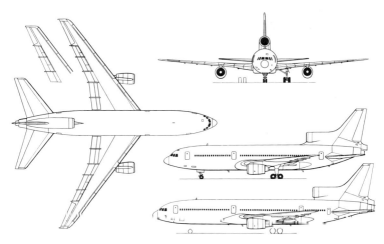

Above: A three-view drawing of the L-1011-500 version of the Tri-Star with an extra side view (bottom right) of the basic L-1011-1 version and a scrap view of the latter's wing, with a slightly shorter span.

Above: A TriStar L-1011-1 in Lockheed company livery. Production of the TriStar is to end in 1984.

Below: One of Gulf Air's fleet of "Golden Falcons" – L-1011-100 TriStars.

The first L-1011 had flown on 17 November 1970, with the second flying a month later, the third on 17 May 1971, the fourth in September and the fifth on 2 December 1971 — with varying standards of RB.211. After intensive financial and political negotiations, a firm basis for continuing with the RB.211 and the TriStar was established in September 1971, and on 8 September engines of 42,000lb st (19,050kgp) were flown in the L-1011 for the first time.

Lockheed delivered the first TriStar (No 7 aircraft) to Eastern on 5 April 1972; FAA Type Approval was obtained on 14 April and the first revenue service was flown on 26 April; TWA flew its first TriStar service on 25 June. Thereafter, production and deliveries continued steadily, with initial service standard RB.211Cs being followed in due course by RB.211Bs, with the same rating but a wider range of ambient temperatures at which full power could be delivered. Following Lockheed custom, aircraft were identified by a "dash number" based on configuration: the full designation of the original version was L-1011-385-1, customer suffixes including 193A, Eastern; 193B, TWA; 193M, Haas Turner; 193E, Air Canada; 193K, Court Line; 193R, LTU; 193C, British Airways and 193P, All Nippon. Other customers for the type included Delta, Saudia and Cathay Pacific.

Several developed versions of the TriStar were proposed by Lockheed from 1971 onwards, with fuselage "stretch", more fuel, and more powerful engines. None of these became firm, however, until 1974, when a go-ahead was confirmed for the RB.211-524 engine with an initial service thrust of 48,000lb st (21,772kgp), increasing to 50,000lb (22,680kg) after one year. The TriStar with these engines is known as the L-1011-200, and is available with three alternative fuel capacities and gross weights of 450,000lb (204,120kg), 466,000lb (211,374kg) or 477,000lb (216,363kg). With the same weights and fuel capacities, but RB.211-22 engines, the TriStar is designated L-1011-100, the basic L-1011-1 having a gross weight of 430,000lb (195,045kg). First customer for the L-1011-200 was Saudia,

Above: Air Canada was among the first non-US customers for the TriStar, and by 1982 had a fleet comprising eight L-1011-1s, four -100s and six short-fuselage -500s. An L-1011-1 is illustrated.

and for the L-1011-100, Cathay Pacific. A TriStar prototype with RB.211-524s first flew on 12 August 1976 and the first -200 for Saudia followed before the end of the year, entering service in mid-1977. Other airlines acquiring -200s included British Airways, Delta, Gulf Air and Trans Carib Air.

Also in August 1976, Lockheed launched the L-1011-500 when British Airways ordered six of this extended range version with 50,000lb st (22,700kgp) RB.211-524Bs, fuselage shortened by 13ft 6in (4 11m), extra fuel and still higher gross weight of 496,000lb (224,982kg) Delta Airlines became the second customer for the TriStar 500 in 1978 and this variant was also subsequently ordered by Pan American, BWIA, Air Canada, Aero Peru, Air Lanka, Alia, LTU and Air Portugal. These airlines also specified the use of active controls, a feature designed to improve the efficiency in cruising flight and reduce fuel consumption; aircraft with this new feature had an increase of 9ft (2·74m) in overall span, a modification first flown on the TriStar demonstrator in 1978. The first L-1011-500 flew on 16 October 1978 and the new version entered service with British Airways in May 1979. The first production -500 with extended wing tips and active controls flew in November 1979 and the few aircraft delivered without this feature were subsequently updated. By the end of 1981, firm sales of the TriStar totalled 247 with 45 more on option. Several derivative versions of the TriStar were at that time in the project stage, including a -500LR (long range), a -500F (freighter), and a -300 with lengthened fuselage, but the slow-down in the rate of new airline orders in 1980/81 led Lockheed to announce at the end of 1981 that production of the TriStar would end in 1984, when outstanding orders had been fulfilled.

McDonnell Douglas DC-8
USA

The following specification refers to the DC-8 Srs 50:
Power Plant: Four 17,000lb st (7945kgp) Pratt & Whitney JT3D-1 or 18,000lb st (8172kgp) JT3D-3 or -3B turbofans.
Performance: Max cruising speed, 580mph (933km/h); no-reserves range with max payload, 6,185mls (9950km).
Weights: Basic operating, 132,325lb (60,020kg); max weight limited payload, 46,500lb (21,092kg); max take-off, 325,000lb (147,415kg).
Dimensions: Span, 142ft 5in (43·41m); length, 150ft 6in (45·87m); height 42ft 4in (12·91m); wing area, 2,868sq ft (266·5m²).

The following specification refers to the DC-8 Srs 63:
Power Plant: Four 17,000lb st (7945kgp) Pratt & Whitney JT3D-1 or 18,000lb st (8172kgp) JT3D-3 or -3B or 19,000lb (8618kgp) JT3D-7 turbofans.
Performance: Max cruising speed, 583mph (938km/h); best economy cruise, 523mph (842km/h); initial rate of climb, 2,165ft/min (11·0m/sec); range with max payload, 4,500mls (7240km).
Weights: Basic operating, 153,749lb (69,739kg); max payload, 67,735lb (30,719kg); max take-off, 350,000lb (158,760kg).
Dimensions: Span, 148ft 5in (45·23m); length, 187ft 4in (57·12m); height, 42ft 5in (12·92m); wing area, 2,927sq ft (271,9m²).

In the continuing effort to maintain its competitive position as a supplier of transport aircraft to the world airline industry (versus Lockheed and Boeing in particular), Douglas Aircraft Company began the search for a successor to the DC-7 in the early 'fifties. Like Boeing, Douglas concluded that the future lay with a turbojet-powered long-range airliner and projected designs along lines very similar to those chosen by Boeing for its military tanker/transport prototype, the Model 367-80. The first flight of the latter in July 1954 heightened Douglas' awareness that the large-scale adoption of jet transports was imminent and on 7 June 1955 the company took the decision to proceed immediately with construction and certification of the DC-8. Details were first published in August 1955, revealing a sleek, low-wing monoplane with 30deg of wing sweepback (less than the Boeing 707), four Pratt & Whitney J57 (JT3C) turbojets in underwing pods and a gross weight of 211,000lb (95,710kg) for domestic US operation (with trans-continental non-stop range) or up to 257,000lb (116,570kg) for projected overwater variants with greater range.

Pan American was the first airline to order the DC-8, placing orders with both Douglas and Boeing for 20 each of their new jet transports on 13 October 1955. United followed with a contract less than two weeks later, and before the end of the year National Airlines, KLM, Eastern, SAS and JAL had joined the queue. Douglas announced that the intercontinental version would have J75 (JT4A) engines, with Rolls-Royce Conways as an alterna-tive, and the gross weights began to rise, to 265,000lb (120,200kg) for the domestic model and 287,500lb (130,410kg) in the intercontinental version — both these figures being increased still further after the aircraft entered service.

Series numbers were adopted for the DC-8 variants at the end of 1959,

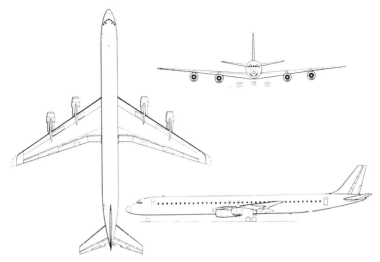

Above: The DC-8 Srs 61, with the longest of the three fuselage lengths applied to the different DC-8 variants.

when the initial domestic model became the Srs 10, and a similar version with JT4A engines for improved take-off performance became the Srs 20. The intercontinental model with JT4As was Srs 30 and with Conway engines, Srs 40. A further variant was also in the planning stage by the time these designations were introduced, being the Srs 50 with JT3D turbofans. All these variants had substantially the same overall dimensions (although some changes in wing span and chord were introduced in the course of production) and provided accommodation for 117 passengers in a typical mixed-class layout or up to 189 in one-class high-density layouts, subject to suitable emergency exit provisions being made.

Flight testing of the DC-8 began on 30 May 1958, with a Srs 10, and the second aircraft to fly was a Srs 20, on 29 November 1958, two more Srs 10s flying in December — by which time the order book stood at 142. Certification of the Srs 10 was obtained on 31 August 1959 and initial services were flown by both United and Delta on 18 September, almost a year later than the commercial introduction of the Boeing 707.

The first DC-8 Srs 30 had flown meanwhile, on 21 February 1959, and Douglas introduced increased fuel capacity in this version, with the weight going up to 310,000lb (140,615kg) initially and 315,000lb (142,880kg) after entry into service. Extended wing tips and a new leading edge that added 4 per cent to the wing chord were also evolved during flight testing, and ▶

Below: The DC-8 Srs 62 was the very long range version of the McDonnell Douglas DC-8, shown here in the sun-bright colours of Air Jamaica, which at one time had four DC-8s in service. Some Srs 62s are becoming Srs 72s with CFM-56s.

6Y-JII

17,500lb st (7945kgp) JT4A-11 or -12 engines became available in place of the 15,500lb st (7167kgp) -3 or -5 and 16,500lb st (7620kgp) -9 or -10 units used originally. The Srs 30 was certificated on 1 February 1960 and entered service with Pan American and KLM in April across the North Atlantic, although the first international services by DC-8 had been flown on 14 March 1960 with a United Air Lines Srs 20.

Douglas flew the first Conway-powered DC-8 on 23 July 1959 and obtained Type Approval for this version on 24 March 1960, TCA (now Air Canada) being the first operator, starting in April. Only two other airlines, Alitalia and Canadian Pacific, specified this variant.

The DC-8 Series 50 was essentially a fully-developed Srs 30 airframe with JT3D turbofan engines, these being derivatives of the JT3C with a front fan offering a considerable improvement in thrust and specific fuel consumption. The original DC-8 was re-engined and flew as the Srs 50 prototype on 20 December 1960 and initial certification was obtained on 10 October 1961 at a gross weight of 276,000lb (125,190kg), with 17,000lb st (7945kgp) engines; subsequently, weights up to 325,000lb (147,415kg) were approved, with 18,000lb st (8172kgp) JT3D-3 or JT3D-3B engines. Some earlier DC-8s were converted to Srs 50s, in addition to new-built aircraft.

In April 1961, Douglas announced the development of a passenger/cargo variant of the DC-8 Srs 50 called the Jet Trader. This had a side-loading freight door in the forward fuselage and a reinforced floor with built-in cargo handling provision, and used the same power plant and gross weights as the Srs 50 described above. The first production Jet Trader flew on 29 October 1962, being one of four ordered by TCA (Air Canada), and certification was obtained on 29 January 1963.

Sales of the DC-8 consistently lagged behind those of the Boeing 707, partly because of its later entry in the market but also because the family of DC-8s, all of the same capacity, was less flexible in meeting varying airline requirements than the variety of Boeing 707 models on offer. Production of the DC-8 Srs 10 to Srs 50 inclusive in fact totalled 293, comprising, in addition to one company prototype/demonstrator, 28 Srs 10 (of which 21 were first converted to Srs 20 and 11 later converted to Srs 50); 34 Srs 20; 57 Srs 30 (of which three later converted to Srs 50); 32 Srs 40; 87 Srs 50 and 54 Srs 50 Jet Traders.

To overcome the sales disadvantage resulting from the standardization on one size of fuselage, the Douglas company finally decided in April 1965 to offer three new models of the DC-8, to be known as the Sixty Series and

providing different combinations of fuselage stretch and payload/range performance. Based initially on the JT3D-1 or JT3D-3 turbofans as used in the Series 50, the Sixty Series comprised the Srs 61 with the fuselage lengthened by 36ft 8in (11·18m) to provide accommodation for up to 259 passengers; the Srs 62 with a fuselage stretch of only 6ft 8in (2·03m) for up to 189 passengers combined with extra fuel and aerodynamic refinements to achieve a very long range; and the Srs 63 combining the long fuselage of the Srs 61 with various of the improvements developed for the Srs 62, including a 6ft (1·82m) increase in span, to give maximum flexibility of operation over medium-to-long ranges.

The first DC-8 Srs 61 flew from Long Beach on 14 March 1966 and was Type Approved by the FAA on 2 September 1966; the Srs 62 flew on 29 August 1966 and was certificated on 27 April 1967; and the Srs 63 flew on 10 April 1967, being approved on 30 June 1967. All three versions entered airline service in 1967 – respectively on 25 February, 22 May and 27 July. In addition to the full passenger variants, Douglas offered convertible and all-freight versions with a forward cargo door as used in the Jet Trader; these were identified by a CF suffix for the convertible (all three series) and AF for all-freight Srs 62s and Srs 63s. Some of the latter were built with the structural provision of the Srs 63CF, to permit subsequent modification and enhance the resale value, but did not have the freight door or floor fitted, and these were designated Srs 63PF.

The addition of the Sixty Series to the DC-8 range brought a spurt of new orders in the mid-sixties, and resulted in the sale of an additional 263 examples by the time production ended in May 1972. This total was made up of 78 Srs 61; 10 Srs 61CF; 52 Srs 62; 16 Srs 62CF and AF; 41 Srs 63 and 66 Srs 63CF, AF and PF, and brought the grand total of DC-8s produced to 556. By the end of the 'seventies, some of the early turbojet-powered versions had been retired but over 400 DC-8s were still in airline service and in 1979 Cammacorp in association with McDonnell Douglas launched a programme to retrofit the 22,000lb st (10,000kgp) CFM-56 in Sixty Series aircraft, which are then redesignated Series 71, 72 or 73 according to the model converted. The first DC-8 Srs 71, converted from a Srs 61 for United Airlines, flew on 15 August 1981, by which time about 10 airlines had contracted for the conversion of 135 DC-8s to have the new engines. The second conversion, a Srs 72, first flew late in 1981.

Below: A DC-8 Series 63CF, one of the second "family" of DC-8s with greatly lengthened fuselages and other improvements.

McDonnell Douglas DC-9
USA

The following specification refers to the DC-9 Srs 30:
Power Plant: Two 14,500lb st (6580kgp) Pratt & Whitney JT8D-9 or 15,000lb st (6800kgp) JT8D-11 or 15,500lb st (7030kgp) JT8D-15 turbofans.
Performance: Max cruising speed, 572mph (918km/h); long-range cruise, 496mph (796km/h); range with max payload, 1,100mls (1770km).
Weights: Operating empty, 58,500lb (26,535kg); max weight-limited payload, 29,860lb (13,550kg); max take-off, 108,000lb (49,000kg).
Dimensions: Span, 93ft 5in (28·5m); length, 119ft 4in (36·37m); height, 27ft 6in (8·38m); wing area, 1,001sq ft (92·97m²).

The following specification refers to the DC-9 Srs 50:
Power Plant: Two 15,500lb st (7030kgp) Pratt & Whitney JT8D-15 or 16,000lb st (7257kgp) JT8D-17 turbofans.
Performance: Max cruising speed, 564mph (908km/h) at 27,000ft (82000m); economical cruising speed, 535mph (861km/h) at 33,000ft (10,000m); long range cruise, 509mph (819km/h) at 35,000ft (10,700m); no-reserves range with max payload, 1,470mls (2360km) at Mach = 0·80 cruise; no-reserves range with max fuel, 2,787mls (4480km) with payload of 21,400lb (9700kg).
Weights: Operating weight empty, 65,000lb (29,500kg); max take-off, 120,000lb (54,400kg); max landing, 110,000lb (49,900kg); max zero fuel, 98,000lb (44,400kg).
Dimensions: Span, 93ft 4in (28·40m); length, 132ft 0in (40·30m); height 28ft 0in (8·50m); wing area, 1,001sq ft (92·97m²).

The following specification refers to the basic DC-9 Super 80:
Power Plant: Two 18,500lb st (8400kgp) Pratt & Whitney JT8D-209 turbofans.
Performance: Max speed, 576mph (927km/h) at 31,000ft (9450m); max cruising speed, 554mph (892km/h) at 25,000ft (7620m); normal cruise, 515mph (829km/h) at 30,000ft (9145m); range with 137 passenger load, 2,055mls (3306km) at 35,000ft (10,668m); range with max fuel, 3,060mls (4925km).
Weights: Operating weight empty, 79,757lb (36,177kg) max take-off weight 140,000lb (63,503kg), max landing weight 128,000lb (58,060kg), max zero fuel weight, 118,000lb (53,524kg).
Dimensions: Span, 107ft 10in (32·85m); length, 147ft 10in (45·08m), height, 29ft 8in (9·04m); wing area, 1,279sq ft (118·8m²).

The designation DC-9 was in use from the early 'fifties onwards to indicate the Douglas company's plans to develop a medium-range jet transport partner for the DC-8. At first, the idea was to produce what would essentially have been a scaled-down DC-8, of similar configuration and about two-thirds the capacity, but continuing contacts with airlines throughout the world in the late 'fifties and early 'sixties served to extend the timescale for launching the DC-9, and led eventually to a complete re-appraisal of the project and its development as a new design unrelated to the DC-8.

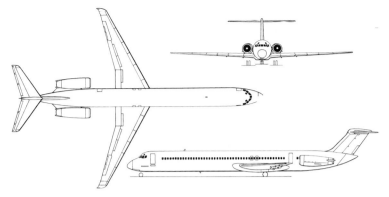

Above: The McDonnell Douglas DC-9 Super 80, the longest of the five different versions produced to date

By 1962, Douglas had defined the potential market more clearly and was emphasizing the short rather than medium-range aspect, aiming, like BAC with the One-Eleven, to produce an aeroplane to replace the smaller, piston-engined and turboprop transports; and the project took shape along similar lines to the One-Eleven, with a T-tail and rear-mounted engines. The decision to proceed with development and production was announced by Douglas on 8 April 1963 without the backing of a firm airline order, but this followed less than three weeks later when Delta signed a contract for 15 with 15 more on option. The initial DC-9 variant was therefore aimed at the requirements of the US airlines, but the company planned from the start to offer a range of variants with differing passenger capacities and ranges, this being in contrast to the policy followed in respect of the DC-8 and giving Douglas a significant edge over BAC in the sales battles that were to follow in the mid-'sixties.

The first DC-9 flew at Long Beach on 25 February 1965, two more following in May, one in June and one in July to complete the test fleet. As for the DC-8, the DC-9 variants were distinguished by Srs numbers, all these early examples being Series 10 with Pratt & Whitney JT8D-5 engines rated at 12,000lb st (5443kgp), and having a gross weight of 77,000lb (34,930kg), or 83,000lb (37,650kg) when extra centre section fuel was carried. In typical mixed-class arrangements, the DC-9 Srs 10 carried 72 passengers, the maximum high-density accommodation being for 90 (five-abreast). FAA Type Approval was obtained on 23 November 1965 and Delta put the DC-9 into service on 8 December. Subsequently, some Series 10s were delivered with 14,000lb st (6350kgp) JT8D-1 or -7 engines and a gross weight of 90,700lb (41,140kg) was approved.

The first order for a "stretched" DC-9 was placed by Eastern Air Lines, on 25 February 1965, at which time it was referred to as the DC-9B or ▶

Below: A DC-9 Srs 32CF convertible freighter in the imaginative livery of Hawaiian Air, an airline with more than half a century of service in the Hawaiian islands.

DC-9 Srs 20, the fuselage being lengthened by 9ft 6in (2·9m). However, the stretch was later increased to 14ft 11in (4·6m) and the designation changed to Srs 30; the Srs 20 designation was re-used subsequently for another version. To preserve performance at higher weights, the DC-9 Srs 30 was given extended wing tips — adding 4ft (1·21m) to the span — full-span leading edge slats and uprated engines. The first flight was made on 1 August 1966, and after certification on 19 December, this variant entered service with Eastern early in 1967. Initially, with 14,500lb st (6580kgp) JT8D-9 engines, the gross weight was 98,000lb (44,444kg), but uprated JT8D-11 or -15 engines could also be used and the max permitted weight increased to 108,000lb (49,000kg) and, eventually, to 121,000lb (54,885kg). Accommodation varied from a typical mixed class layout for 97 up to a maximum of 119.

Sales of the DC-9 proceeded vigorously during the 'sixties, helped by the company's willingness to respond to specific airline needs by developing special versions. For SAS, the Srs 40 was developed as a further stretch of the Srs 30, having 6ft 4in (1·87m) more fuselage length to seat 107–125 passengers with improved payload/range performance. Using 15,500lb st (7030kgp) JT8D-15 engines, the Srs 40 had a gross weight of 114,000lb (51,800kg) and was flown on 28 November 1967; it entered service with SAS in 1968 and has also been used by Swissair (leased from SAS) and purchased by TDA of Japan.

Another SAS requirement resulted in the re-introduction of the Srs 20 designation at the end of 1966 for a "hot and high" version of the Srs 10. This had the Srs 30 wings and JT8D-9 or -11 engines, but the original fuselage length and capacity and a max weight of 100,000lb (45,360kg). The first Srs 20 flew on 18 September 1968 and was ordered only by SAS, which bought 10.

The fifth major variant of the DC-9 was announced in July 1973, when Swissair placed an order for 10 Srs 50s, several other airlines ordering this type subsequently. The major difference, once again, was in fuselage length, which grew by another 6ft 4in (1·87m) over the Srs 40, representing a total increase of 27ft 7in (8·41m) on the original length of the Srs 10. Offering a passenger capacity of 122–139, the Srs 50 was made possible by the availability of additional thrust from the JT8D engine, being based on the use of either the 15,500lb st (7030kgp) -15 or the 16,000lb (7257kgp) -17. Other changes included the introduction of Hytrol Mk IIIA skid control and canting the engine thrust reversers 17 deg from the vertical to avoid the risk of exhaust gas ingestion. With an initial gross weight of 120,000lb (54,400kg), the Srs 50 made its first flight on 17 December 1974 at Long Beach and entered service with Swissair on 24 August 1975.

Versions of the DC-9 were offered with a forward, side-loading freight door, for use in convertible or all-freight configuration. For certification purposes, these were identified by an F suffix to the series number, but the manufacturer used a C or RC (for rapid change) suffix in reference to these versions also. The first order for a convertible DC-9C, with freight door, was placed by Continental Airlines, in March 1965, and the first delivery was made on 7 March 1966, this being a Srs 10 aircraft; the first Srs 30 convertible was delivered in October 1967, to Overseas National. A few all-freight DC-9Fs have also been delivered, the first, a Srs 30F, going to Alitalia.

On 9 January 1975, McDonnell Douglas flew a DC-9 fitted with JT8D-109 (refanned) engines in a programme to develop a quieter engine installation for retrofit to existing DC-9 models. As an outcome of this programme, a number of new DC-9 variants were studied between 1975 and 1977, including the DC-9 Srs 50 RS with the refanned JT8D-209 engines and an increase of 7ft 11in (2·41m) in fuselage length; the DC-9 Srs 60 with more powerful CFM-56 or JT10D turbofans and fuselage stretch of 17ft 4in (5·30m), the DC-9 Srs 50-17R, with JT8D-17Rs and 7ft 11in (2·41m) fuselage stretch and the DC-9SC, similar to the Srs 50RS but with an improved wing of supercritical design.

From these considerations, the DC-9 Srs 55 took shape in 1977 with JT8D-207s and a fuselage stretch of 12ft 8in (3·86m), but final negotiations with the prospective customers led to the stretch being increased to 14ft 3in (4·34m) and the thrust of the -207 engine being further increased to 18,500lb (8400kgp). In this guise, the new variant was renamed the DC-9 Super 80 and was given a go-ahead by the company in October 1977, at which time initial orders were announced by Swissair (for 15), Austrian Airlines (8) and Southern Airways (4), with others on option. First flight of a Super 80 was made on 18 October 1979, followed by the second and third aircraft on 6 December 1979 and 29 February 1980. FAA certification was obtained on 26 August 1980 and the initial variant of the Super 80 (the Srs 81) entered airline service with Swissair on 5 October 1980. McDonnell Douglas also offered a Srs 82 variant with 20,850lb st (9457kgp) JT8D-217 engines (including emergency thrust reserve) and a max take off weight of 147,000lb (66,680kg). First flight of a Srs 82 was made on 8 January 1981 and this variant entered service with Republic Airlines.

By the end of 1981, McDonnell Douglas had sold 1,108 DC-9s, including 23 on option or conditional sale (this total including 32 for the USAF and USN). The type was being operated by well over 50 world airlines.

Below: One of two DC-9 Srs 50s put into service by BWIA in 1978, showing the longer fuselage of this version.

McDonnell Douglas DC-10
USA

The following specification refers to the DC-10 Srs 30:

Power Plant: Three 51,000lb st (23,134kgp) General Electric CF6-50C turbofans.

Performance: Max cruising speed at 31,000ft (9450m), 570mph (917km/h); initial rate of climb, 2,320ft/min (11·8m/sec); service ceiling, 32,700ft (9965m); range with max payload, 4,272mls (6875km); range with max fuel, 6,910mls (11,118km).

Weights: Basic operating, 263,087lb (119,334kg); max payload, 104,913lb (47,587kg); max take-off, 555,000lb (251,744kg).

Dimensions: Span, 165ft 4in (40·42m); length, 181ft 7in (55·35m); height, 58ft 1in (17·7m); wing area, 3,921sq ft (364·3m²). ▶

Below: Laker Airways "Eastern Belle", one of the four DC-10 Srs 10s with which the company launched its Skytrain service in 1977. They were up for sale after Laker collapsed in January 1982.

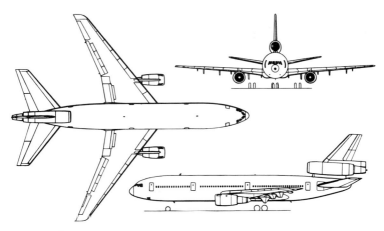

Above: The McDonnell Douglas DC-10 Srs 30, principal production version of the trijet, total sales of which neared 400 in 1982.

Spurred by an outline specification for a "Jumbo Twin" issued by American Airlines in March 1966, the Douglas Aircraft Company embarked upon a series of design studies for a possible addition to the Douglas Commercial series of airliners. By the middle of 1967, the company (which meanwhile had become a division of McDonnell Douglas Corporation) had concluded that the requirement, and the potential future market, for such a type required the use of three engines and a larger capacity than American had originally indicated. American Airlines concurred, issuing an amended "Jumbo Trijet" specification in July 1967 and after further refinement of the Douglas proposal. American placed an order on 19 February 1968 for 25 DC-10s with options on 25 more and a forecast need for 100 by 1975.

This order gave the DC-10 first honours in the intensive sales battle versus the Lockheed TriStar, but was not sufficient evidence of an adequate market to allow the company to launch full production, that stage being reached only at the end of April 1968 when United Air Lines ordered 30 DC-10s and took an option on 30 more. The DC-10, as then defined, was a wide-body transport seating about 270 passengers in typical mixed-class layouts or up to 380 in one-class high density arrangements. Powered by four 40,000lb st (18,144kgp) General Electric CF6 turbofans, it shared with the TriStar the previously untried configuration of two underwing engine pods and a third engine in the rear — in the case of the DC-10, carried above the fuselage in an independent nacelle integrated with the fin. Aimed specifically at meeting the requirements of the US trunk airlines, the initial DC-10 had enough range for transcontinental non-stop operation with full payload. Longer-range versions were planned to be made available in due course however.

The first order for such a range-extended variant came from Northwest Orient Airlines at the end of 1968. Extra fuel was carried in the wing centre section and fuselage tanks, and the gross weight increased from 386,500lb (175,000kg) at which the original version had been launched, to 530,000lb (240,000kg) — further increases in both these weights having been made subsequently. The higher weights required the use of a third main under-carriage unit to spread the load more evenly on the runway, this unit being added on the fuselage centreline; more engine power was also needed, and Northwest opted to use the Pratt & Whitney JT9D-15 to obtain standardization with its Boeing 747s. Designations were introduced by Douglas at this stage to differentiate between the variants, the initial version being the Srs 10, the Northwest variant being Srs 20 and a similar long-range version with CF6-50 engines being Srs 30. Both the Srs 20 and Srs 30 had a small increase in wing span and area, and the overall length varied slightly.

The DC-10 Srs 30 gained its go-ahead in June 1969 when it was selected by the KSSU consortium of European airlines; subsequently, three of the four ATLAS group airlines also chose the Srs 30, confirming its lead over the TriStar at least so far as Europe was concerned. For marketing reasons, the Srs 20 was later redesignated Srs 40, and its engines were redesignated JT9D-20. Later variants of both the CF6-50 and the JT9D have been evolved for introduction in the DC-10 in due course.

First flight of the DC-10 was made on 29 August 1970, with a second aircraft (in American Airlines finish) joining the test programme on 24 October and the third (in United colours) on 23 December. Full FAA Type Approval was obtained on 29 July 1971, and the DC-10 entered service with American Airlines on 5 August, operating a daily non-stop flight be-

Above: This DC-10 Srs 30, is operated by SAS, a consortium of airlines in Sweden, Denmark and Norway.

Below: A colourfully finished DC-10 Srs 30 used by Thai International.

HS-TGA

161

tween Los Angeles and Chicago. The work of certificating the Series 40 began with the first flight of this version on 28 February 1972 and was completed on 27 October, with first delivery to Northwest on 10 November. The first Series 30 flew on 21 June 1972 and was certificated on 21 November.

Maximum weights approved for DC-10 operation have progressively increased and by the end of 1981, the Srs 10 was certificated at 440,000lb (199,580kg), and the Srs 30 and 40 at 572,000lb (259,457kg), these increases being made possible in part by the progressive growth in available engine thrust. Some of the higher weight options were also associated with extra centre-section fuel capacity.

Extending the utility of the DC-10, Douglas offered a convertible freighter as the DC-10CF, featuring a side-loading cargo door ahead of the wing and provision for freight carrying in the forward part of the fuselage. The first convertible model, a DC-10 Srs 30CF, flew on 28 February 1973 and deliveries began on 17 April 1973, when both Overseas National and Trans International accepted their first examples. Pure freight versions were also on offer to airlines but none had been ordered up to the end of 1981. In 1979, McDonnell Douglas introduced the DC-10 Srs 15, with a Srs 10 airframe and 52,500lb st (23,814kgp) CF6-50C2F engines, for "hot and high" operations by Aeromexico and Mexicana. A further stage in DC-10 growth was reached in July 1980 when Swissair ordered the Srs 30ER, with 54,000lb st (24,500kgp) CF6-50C2B engines and increased fuel capacity.

By late 1981, McDonnell Douglas had sold 383 DC-10s (including 12 KC-10A tanker/transports for the USAF). Following an accident to a DC-10 at Chicago on 25 May 1979, the FAA suspended, for a period of 38 days, the Type Certificate that licensed the DC-10 to fly in the USA — an action without precedent in the history of civil air transportation. The Certificate was restored after extensive tests and examinations had failed to reveal any fundamental design faults. Falling orders during 1980/81 had reduced the backlog of orders to about 20, all to be delivered in 1982, and the possibility of a temporary halt in production was being faced by the company. At the same time, a number of new DC-10 variants were under study for possible future production, perhaps using Pratt & Whitney PW2037 or Rolls-Royce RB.211-535F4 engines as an alternative to CF6-80As, and probably incorporating winglets, as first flown for test purposes on a DC-10 Srs 10 on 31 August 1981

Below: A DC-10 Srs 30 of the West German national airline, Lufthansa, photographed at Frankfurt Main.

McDonnell Douglas-Fokker MDF-100
International

The MDF-100 was launched as a new 150-seat short/medium haul transport in May 1981, when McDonnell Douglas and Fokker signed an agreement to cover collaboration on a final definition phase. The target then established was to achieve a first flight in 1985 with entry-into-service a year later, although a full-scale launch depended on final definition and adequate customer backing.

At the time they signed the agreement, both McDonnell Douglas and Fokker had independent projects for aircraft in the 150-seat category. Fokker had been studying such an aircraft for many years, in the guise of F.28 Fellowship derivatives, including the F.28-2, the Super F.28 and finally the F.29. McDonnell Douglas (through the Douglas Aircraft Company at Long Beach) similarly had studied a series of possible new designs, any one of which was likely to have become the DC-11 if launched but which carried such designations as the ATMR (advanced-technology medium range transport), ATMR-II, DC-XX and NCA (new commercial airplane) prior to the launch of the MDF-100.

Between June and December 1981, a joint team from the two companies worked to combine features of the F.29 and the DC-XX, leading to an aeroplane which by the end of the year was projected as a 153-seater in standard mixed-class configuration (or up to 174 one-class), with a twin-aisle arrangement and six-abreast seating. This had long been favoured by McDonnell Douglas as a means of offering "wide-body" comfort in a relatively small aeroplane, but airline acceptance for such a layout had yet to be proven.

The overall configuration of the MDF-100 was conventional, with a modestly swept-back wing, podded engines and a T-tail. Much use was expected to be made of composite materials for such components as the rudder, elevators, wing moving surfaces, engine nacelles and fuselage skins.

On 5 February 1982, the two companies announced that market conditions were such that it would be imprudent to proceed further with the MDF-100, and the partnership was dissolved. McDonnell Douglas intimated, however, that it remained interested in the 150-seat class of aircraft and would continue independent design work at a low key.

Below: An impression of the McDonnell Douglas-Fokker MDF-100 project for a 150-seat short/medium range jetliner.

Martin 404
USA

The following sqecification refers to the Martin 404.

Power Plant: Two 2,400hp Pratt & Whitney R-2800-CB-16 Double Wasp piston engines.

Performance: Max speed 312mph (500km/h) at 14,500ft (4420m); typical cruise, 276mph (442km/h) at 18,000ft (5486m); initial rate of climb, 1,905ft/min (9·6m/sec); service ceiling, 29,000ft (8845m); range with payload of 10,205lb (4633kg), 310mls (500km); range with max fuel, 1,070mls (1715km).

Weights: Empty equipped, 29,126lb (13,223kg); max payload, 11,692lb (5263kg); max take-off, 44,900lb (20,385kg); max landing, 43,000lb (19,522kg).

Dimensions: Span, 93ft 3½in (28·44m); length, 74ft 7in (22·75m); height, 28ft 2in (8·61m); wing area, 864sq ft (79·89m²).

The Martin 404 was the final model in a series of twin-engined transport aeroplanes developed by the Martin company in an early post-war bid to provide a replacement for the DC-3. The first of the series was the Martin 202, which flew as a prototype on 22 November 1946 and was an unpressurized short-range transport with seats for 48–52 passengers. Forty-three examples were built for airline use, and a pressurized prototype, the Martin 303, flew on 20 June 1947. Further improvements were made in the Martin 404, first flown on 21 October 1950, and 103 examples of the latter were produced, starting in July 1951.

All but two of the Martin 404s entered airline service, initially with TWA on 5 October 1951, but the majority had been phased out by the mid-sixties, some then passing to executive use and others to smaller airlines. By the

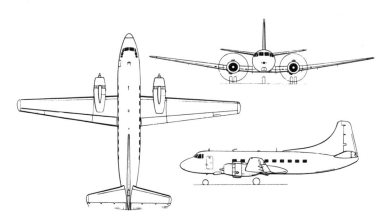

*Above: Three-view drawing of the Martin 404, the only civil
aircraft produced post-war by this famous US manufacturer.*

mid seventies, fewer than 20 remained in airline service, the last major
user being Southern Airways of Atlanta, Georgia. When this airline began to
replace its Martin 404s at the end of 1977, the type was relegated to
operating a handful of routes in the hands of small operators, and was still so
used in 1981.

*Below: Marco Island Airways operates scheduled services between
Miami and Marco Island off the west Florida coast, using six
Martin 404s of the type shown here.*

NAMC YS-11
Japan

The following specification refers to the YS-11A-200:

Power Plant: Two 3,060hp Rolls-Royce Dart 542-10K turboprops.

Performance: Max cruising speed at 15,000ft (4575m), 291mph (469km/h); best economy cruise at 20,000ft (6100m), 281mph (452km/h); initial rate of climb, 1,220ft/min (6·2m/sec); service ceiling, 22,900ft (6980m); no-reserves range with max payload, 680mls (1090km); no-reserves range with max fuel, 2,000mls (3215km).

Weights: Operating empty, 33,993lb (15,419kg); max payload, 14,508lb (6581kg); max take-off, 54,010lb (24,500kg).

Dimensions: Span, 104ft 11¾in (32·00m); length, 86ft 3½in (26·30m); height, 29ft 5½in (8·98m); wing area, 1,020·4sq ft (94·8m²).

Although production of the YS-11 ended when only 182 examples had been built — substantially fewer than the manufacturers had hoped when the programme was launched — the type earned its place in aviation history as the first commercial transport of Japanese design and manufacture to achieve production status at all. The programme to develop a short-to-medium range civil airliner was launched in Japan in 1956 by the Ministry of International Trade and Industry, which encouraged the local aerospace companies to combine their resources to tackle what would be their most challenging project since World War II.

Initial project design activity was shared by six companies, comprising Mitsubishi, Kawasaki, Fuji, Shin Meiwa, Japan Aircraft Manufacturing and Showa, and these six later became participants in the Nihon Aircraft Manufacturing Co Ltd (NAMC). in which the Japanese government held the majority shareholding. Manufacturing activities related to the new transport were in due course shared by the six companies in proportion to their shareholding in NAMC.

The requirements of the Japanese domestic airline industry played a large part in defining the specification to which the new transport was to be built, and this led NAMC to make the aircraft somewhat larger than the turboprop twins already on the market, such as the Fokker F.27 and HS.748. Basic passenger accommodation was set at 60. Some early studies considered a high-wing layout similar to that of the F-27, but the more popular low-wing arrangement was eventually chosen, and an evaluation of the Allison 501, Napier Eland and Rolls-Royce Dart left the last-mentioned as the favoured power plant, in a version developed specially for the Japanese aircraft as the RDa.10/1.

The transport was designated YS-11 and work on four prototypes (two flying and two structural test) began following the creation of NAMC in May 1957. The two prototypes flew on 30 August and 28 December 1962 respectively and after more than 1,000hr of flight testing the YS-11 received Japanese certification on 25 August 1964 followed by FAA Type Approval on 7 September 1965. The first production YS-11 had flown, meanwhile, on 23 October 1964 and this was delivered to the Japan Civil Aviation Bureau in March 1965. Airline use of the YS-11 began a month later, the first user being Toa Airways of Hiroshima (now TDA), followed by Japan Domestic in May and All Nippon in July.

Export sales of the YS-11 began only slowly, starting with the purchase of two by Filipinas Orient in September 1965, three by Hawaiian Airlines in 1966 and three by LANSA of Peru in 1967. A major effort to sell the YS-11 in the USA was then mounted, resulting in the appearance of the YS-11A which, with the same overall dimensions, had higher operating weights and an increase of 2,800lb (1270kg) in the payload. The YS-11A was offered in three sub-variants identified as the Srs 200, 300 and 400, of which the Srs 200 was the basic passenger variant with the same 60-passenger

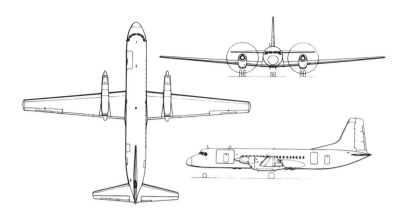

Above: NAMC YS-11 Srs 300/600, with the forward freight door that distinguished those versions of the Japanese transport.

Below: An NAMC YS-11A-200, in service with Toa Domestic Airlines (TDA) on domestic routes in Japan.

capacity (five abreast) as the original production variant, construction of which ended in October 1967 when 48 (plus the two prototypes) had been built.

A significant order was obtained from the US local service airline Piedmont for the YS-11A-200, the first example of which flew on 27 November 1967 and was FAA-approved on 3 April 1968. Deliveries to Piedmont began in 1968 and over 90 Series 200s were built in all, for some nine different airlines and for Japanese armed services and government agencies.

The Srs 300, flown in 1968, was a mixed-traffic version of the 200, with a forward cargo door and provision for 46 passengers plus 540cu ft (15·3m/) of cargo space. Some 16 were delivered, to several different airlines. The Srs 400, used only by military forces, was an all-cargo version, first flown on 17 September 1969. Three further variants, the Srs 500, 600 and 700, were designated, being respectively similar to the 200, 300 and 400 but having a 1,105-lb (500-kg) increase in max take-off weight. In 1981, the YS-11 remained an important type in service on domestic routes in Japan and was still being flown by several other operators in the Far East, Australasia and North America.

Saab-Fairchild SF-340
International

Power Plant: Two 1,675shp General Electric CT7-5A turboprops (with max continuous rating of 1,234eshp at 150kts (279km/h) at 15,000ft (4572m)).

Performance: Max cruising speed, 311mph (500km/h) at 15,000ft (4572m) and 276mph (444km/h) at 25,000ft (7620m); range with 34 passengers, 1,150mls (1850km).

Weights: Operating weight empty, 14,700lb (6668kg); weight limited payload, 8,300lb (3765kg); max take-off and landing weight, 26,000lb (11,794kg); max zero fuel weight, 23,000lb (10,433kg).

Dimensions: Span, 70ft 4in (21·44m); length 64ft 6in (19·67m); height, 22ft 6in (6·87m).

An agreement signed on 25 January 1980 between Saab-Scania of Sweden and Fairchild Industries of the USA served to launch the SF-340 commuter airliner as the first fully collaborative venture between an American and a European company. The SF-340, flight testing of which was scheduled to begin at the start of 1983, is also the first commercial aircraft with which Saab has been associated for many years.

To handle this project, the two companies set up a jointly-owned Swedish company (Saab-Fairchild HB) with a sales office in Paris to co-ordinate marketing outside North America. Within the North American area, Fairchild-Swearingen is responsible for marketing and this company will also furnish and finish, at its San Antonio, Texas, works, the SF-340s destined for customers in the USA, Canada and Mexico. Saab-Scania is handling all final assembly in a new facility built for the purpose at Linköping. The fuselage is also built in Sweden, with design and construction of the wing, engine nacelles and tail unit handled by the Republic Division of Fairchild Industries at Farmingdale, New York.

The SF-340 has a circular cross-section fuselage and a cabin pressurized to a differential of 7·0psi (0·49kg/cm²), providing for a standard all-

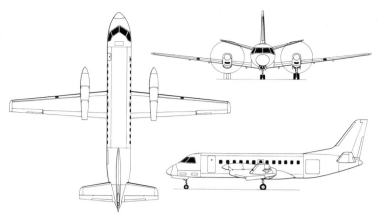

Above: Three-view drawing of the Saab-Fairchild SF-340, the first collaborative commercial project between Europe and the USA.

passenger layout with 34 seats three-abreast. A cargo version is planned, with a cargo door aft of the wing and passenger door forward, permitting mixed-traffic operations. The SF-340 is designed to a combination of fail-safe and safe life criteria, with extensive use of adhesive metal bonding, based on the USAF-developed Primary Adhesive Structural Bonding System (PASBS). A 45,000-hr fatigue life is planned, including 90,000 flight cycles. The high aspect ratio wing features large span single-slotted flaps

By mid-1981, Saab-Fairchild was able to announce an initial order book totalling 101 SF-340s, of which 25 were for US corporate owners. In the executive rôle, the aircraft typically seats 12 passengers and this version has 1,645shp CT7 7E engines, offering more power in the cruise at higher altitudes. Two SF-340s were to be used during 1983 for the bulk of certification testing, with the second aircraft based in the USA. Deliveries were scheduled to begin in the first quarter of 1984, building to a rate of six a month by 1985.

Left. An impression of the Saab-Fairchild SF-340 in the colours of Crossair, a Swiss commuter airline that was among the first to order the Swedish/American aircraft. Development of the SF-340 was launched in 1980, on the basis of project designs prepared by Saab coupled with the engineering and marketing expertise of the Fairchild Corporation which, through its Swearingen subsidiary, was already closely involved with the commuter airline market.

Shorts Skyvan and Skyliner
United Kingdom

The following data refer to the Skyvan Srs 3:

Power Plant: Two Garrett-AiResearch TPE331-201 turboprops each rated at 715shp for take-off.

Performance: Max crusing speed, 203mph (327km/h); initial rate of climb 1,640ft/min (8·3m/sec); service ceiling, 22,500ft (6858m); range, up to 694mls (1115km); range with 4,000lb (1814kg) of freight, 187mls (300km).

Weights: Basic operating, 7,344lb (3331kg); max payload, 4,600lb (2086kg); max take-off weight, 12,500lb (5670kg).

Dimensions: Span, 64ft 11in (19·79m); length, 40ft 1in (12·21m); height, 15ft 1in (4·60m); wing area, 373sq ft (34·65m²).

First flown in 1963, the Shorts Skyvan set a fashion for small utility transports, featuring a high wing, fixed tricycle undercarriage and uncluttered box-section fuselage with provision for straight-in loading from the rear. The prototype was powered by two 300hp Continental piston engines but after an initial phase of flight testing which began on 17 January 1963, it was re-engined with 730shp Turboméca Astazou XII turboprops, flying in this guise as the Skyvan Srs 1A on 2 October 1963. Nineteen Skyvan IIs followed, with the same engines, the first of these flying on 29 October 1965, and these saw limited service in the hands of civil operators, carrying up to 19 passengers or about 4,000lb (1814kg) of freight.

The definitive production version of the Skyvan is the Srs 3 with 715shp Garrett AiResearch TPE331-201 turboprops. The first TPE331 installation flew on 15 December 1967 and deliveries began in mid-1968, some Srs 2s also being converted to this standard. The Skyvan Srs 3 has a gross weight of 12,500lb (5670kg) and is the basic version for use in various civil rôles including passenger transport, ambulance, aerial survey, freighting and police duties; the Srs 3A operates at an increased gross weight of 13,700lb (6215kg) and complies with British airworthiness requirements in the Passenger Transport Category. The Skyliner is similar but is equipped to a higher standard exclusively as a passenger carrier for 19–22 passengers. By the end of 1981, Shorts had delivered more than 130 Skyvans of all models including some 70 Srs 3s, nine Skyliners and about 50 Skyvan 3M military models.

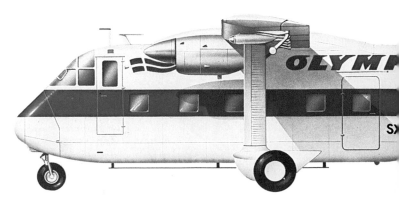

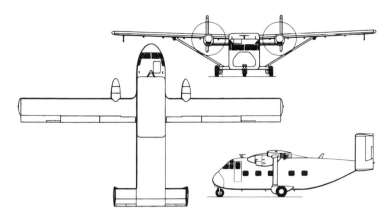

Above: The Shorts Skyvan, which like the Handley Page Herald began life with piston engines before acquiring turboprop power.

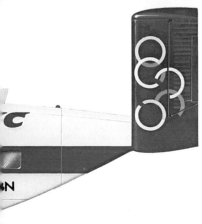

Above: A Shorts Skyvan on test prior to delivery to Venezuela, bearing both British and Venezuelan registrations. More than 130 of these utilitarian transports had been sold by the beginning of 1982.

Left: One of a pair of Shorts Skyvan 3s used by Olympic Airways and its light aircraft division, Olympic Aviation. Together with an assortment of smaller aircraft and helicopters, the Skyvans are used principally for charter flights.

Shorts 330
United Kingdom

The following specification refers to the Shorts 330-200:

Power Plant: Two Pratt & Whitney PT6A-45R turboprops each flat-rated at 1,198shp (with reserve power) and at 1,020shp for max continuous use.

Performance: High speed cruise at 21,000lb (9525kg) weight, 219mph (352km/h) at 10,000ft (3050m); long-range cruise at 21,000lb (9525kg) weight, 181mph (291km/h) at 6,000ft (1830m); initial rate of climb, 1,180ft/min (5·99m/sec); range with 30 passengers, 320mls (515km); range with max fuel, 775mls (1247km).

Weights: Operating weight empty, 15,000lb (6805kg); design payload (cargo), 7,500lb (3400kg); standard fuel, 3,840lb (1740kg); max take-off, 22,900lb (10,385kg); max landing, 22,600lb (10,250kg).

Dimensions: Span, 74ft 8in (22·76m); length, 58ft 0in (17·68m); height, 16ft 3in (4·95m); wing area, 453sq ft (42·08m²).

This third-level/commuter airliner is an outgrowth of the Skyvan. It features similar outer wing panels, with a new centre section, and a lengthened fuselage of the same cross section as the Skyvan. A switch was made from Garrett-AiResearch engines to Pratt & Whitney PT6A-45s driving five-blade propellers, these being similar to the engines developed for the de Havilland Canada Dash 7.

The SD3-30, as the type was at first known, was given official approval for go-ahead on 23 May 1973 with a UK government grant towards the launching costs. A primary objective of the design team was to achieve a

Below: A Shorts 330 carrying the markings of New York-based Command Airways, one of the first airlines to use the type, with a fleet of six by 1982.

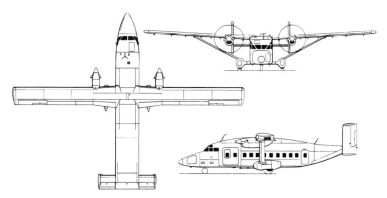

Above: Three-view of the Shorts 330 (originally known as the SD3-30), a commuter liner derived from the smaller Skyvan.

selling price of not more than $1m (£400,000) in 1973 values, and a rapid prototype programme was established, with first flight achieved on 22 August 1974. A second prototype, first flown on 8 July 1975, was also used for certification flying, which was completed soon after the first flight of the production SD3-30 on 15 December 1975. Initial contracts for the SD3-30 were placed by Command Airways and Time Air, respectively US and Canadian operators of third-level airlines, and the latter was the first to put the type into service, on 24 August 1976. Sales were made at a steady rate subsequently, and had reached a total of 105 by the end of 1981 During 1981, Shorts also announced the introduction of the Series 200 version, differing primarily from the original model in having the PT6A-45R engines that had been selected for use on the Shorts 360 (see next page). With a reserve power system and an increase in the flat-rated power, the PT6A-45R allowed the max take-off weight to be increased from 22,690lb (10,250kg) to the values given above.

Shorts 360
United Kingdom

Power Plant: Two Pratt & Whitney (Canada) PT6A-65R turboprops, each having a maximum rating of 1,294shp.
Performance: High speed cruise, 243mph (391km/h) at 10,000ft (3050m); range (max passenger payload), 265mls (426km) at high speed cruise at 10,000ft (3050m) with allowances for 100-mile (160-km) diversion and 45 min hold; range (max fuel), 655mls (1054km) same conditions.
Weights: Operational empty, 16,490lb (7480kg); max useful load, 9,210lb (4178kg); passenger payload, 7,020lb (3184kg); max take-off, 25,700lb (11,657kg); max landing, 25,400lb (11,521kg).
Dimensions: Span, 74ft 8in (22·76m); length, 70ft 6in (21·49m); height, 22ft 7in (6·88m); wing area, 453sq ft (42·08m²).

A growth version of the Shorts 330 commuterliner offering a 20 per cent increase in passenger capacity and enhanced cruise performance, the Shorts 360 was announced in mid-1980 and made its first flight on 1 June 1981. It differs from its progenitor primarily in having some 10 per cent more power, a 3ft (91cm) plug in the fuselage ahead of the wing, and an entirely redesigned and aesthetically more attractive rear fuselage and tail surfaces. Considered by the manufacturers to be complementary to the 330, rather than a successor, the 360 is the end product of a programme estimated to involve a total of £15m in non-recurring costs. The manufacturers were confident that, at a unit price of $3m—$3·25m (as compared with about $2·7m for the smaller-capacity 330) in 1980 terms, the 360 would have a significant first-cost advantage over the potential competition and would also benefit from at least a year's lead in the market. Sales of 275—350 aircraft up to the end of the 'eighties were projected by Shorts; the first order

Right: The prototype Shorts 360, a close relative of the previously-illustrated Shorts 330. The revised contours and lengthening of the fuselage made possible two additional seat rows in the cabin, the roominess of which was emphasised by the registration letters G-ROOM adopted on this prototype. The fuselage cross-section remains the same as that of the original Skyvan, from which the Shorts 330 was in turn developed. Deliveries of the Shorts 360 from the company's Northern Ireland works were starting in 1982.

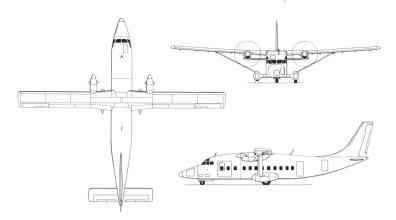

Above: Three-view drawing of the Shorts 360, showing the longer rear fuselage and single fin-and-rudder of this model.

came from Suburban Airlines, a member of the Allegheny Commuter Group in the USA, and several other customers brought the total to 21 by the end of 1981.

The most noteworthy design change featured by the Shorts 360 is the new rear end which is now gracefully tapered with a swept single tail, in marked contrast to the characteristic "sawn-off" appearance of the 330's rear fuselage with its angular twin fins and rudders. Two additional seat rows raise capacity to 36 passengers and considerable importance has been attached to the provision of adequate baggage space, 6cu ft (0·17m³) being available per passenger, or 7·2cu ft (0·204m³) if the overhead lockers are included.

Transall C-160P
International

Power Plant: Two Rolls-Royce Tyne RTy 20 Mk 22 turboprops each rated at 6,200ehp for take-off.
Performance: Max speed, 367mph (592km/h) at 16,000ft (4875m); economical cruising speed, 282mph (454km/h) at 20,000ft (6100m); rate of climb, 1,300ft/min (6·6m/sec); service ceiling, 25,500ft (7770m); range, 2,982mls (4800km) with 17,637lb (8000kg) payload and 1,056mls (1700km) with 35,274lb (16,000kg).
Weights: Operating weight empty, 63,815lb (28,946kg).
Dimensions: Span, 131ft 3in (40·00m); length, 106ft 3½in (32·40m); height, 40ft 6¾in (12·36m); wing area, 1,723sq ft (160·10m²).

Four examples of the Transall C-160 — which is primarily a military tactical transport — have been in operation with Air France since 1973 on night mail services within France. The operation of these services, under contract to the Centre d'Exploitation Postal Metropolitan (CEPM), has long been an Air France speciality, and a formidable record of regularity and punctuality has been achieved despite the difficulties, in the early days, inherent in night flying in all types of weather. The DC-3s used at first gave way, eventually, to DC-4s and then Fokker F27 Mk 500s and the four Transall supplement the fleet of the last-mentioned type. For mail carrying, the C-160s were modified to allow 13·5tons of mail to be loaded or off-loaded in about 12 minutes. Operating between Paris and Bastia, Corsica (with two aircraft permanently stationed at each end of the route), the Transalls have been carrying an average of 1·8 million letters each night and in the first three years of service achieved a regularity of 98 per cent while flying a total of 10,000hrs.

The C-160 Transall was developed originally to meet the joint requirements of the *Luftwaffe* and the *Armée de l'Air*, with the AG Transall concern being set up to handle its production. Assembly lines were established in both France and Germany and these turned out three prototypes — the first of which flew on 25 February 1963 — six pre-production C-160s, 110 C-160Ds for the *Luftwaffe*, 50 C-160Fs for the *Armée de l'Air* and nine C-160Zs for the South African Air Force. Delivery of the military Transalls was completed by 1970 and the four C-160Ps for Air France were converted by SOGERMA from *Armée de l'Air* C-160Fs.

Primarily to meet the requirements of the *Armée de l'Air* for an additional 25 Transalls, production was relaunched in 1977 and the first of these new-batch aircraft made its initial flight in 1981. The Indonesian government has ordered three Transalls to be used in that country's transmigration programme, for delivery in 1982. Up to 90 passengers can be carried.

Right: One of the four Transall C-160Ps operated by Air France on the Aéropostale services between Paris and Corsica, with one flight in each direction every night with outstanding regularity.

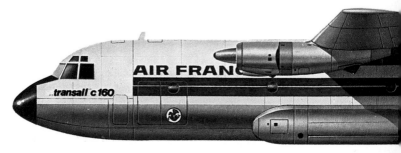

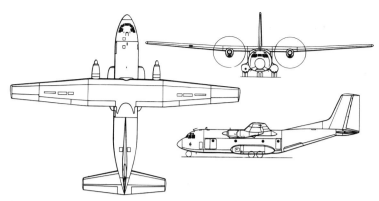

Above: Three-view drawing of the Transall C-160, developed as a military transport and with some specialized civil applications.

Above: For operations as mail-planes by Air France, four C-160Ps were converted in 1970 from military transport versions.

Tupolev Tu-104 and Tu-124
Soviet Union

The following specification relates to the Tu-104A:
Power Plant: Two 21,385lb st (9700kgp) Mikulin AM-3M 500 turbojets.
Performance: Max cruising speed, 560mph (900km/h); best economy cruise, 497mph (800km/h); service ceiling, 37,750ft (11,500m); range with max payload at 33,000ft (10,000m), 1,645mls (2650km); range with max fuel, 1,925mls (3100km).
Weights: Empty, 91,710lb (41,600kg); max payload, 19,840lb (900kg); max take-off, 167,550lb (76,000kg).
Dimensions: Span, 113ft 4in (34·54m); length, 127ft 5½in (25·85m); height, 39ft 0in (11·90m); wing area, 1,877sq ft (174·4m²).

Of the various Soviet aircraft design bureaux, that originally headed by the late Andrei Tupolev, and still bearing his name, has played the most significant rôle in the modernization of Aeroflot. This process began in 1956 when the Tu-104 entered service, becoming only the second jet airliner in the world to achieve this status (after the Comet). As the Soviet Union's first jet transport, the Tu-104 was of historic importance; five other commercial Tupolev designs have followed with "1×4" designations, making this bureau the nearest thing in the USSR to the Boeing Company with its "7×7" The following specification refers to the Tu-134:

The Tu-104 was, in fact, a simple adaptation of the Tu-16 bomber, using the same wings and a new fuselage. The first batch were 50-seaters, followed in 1958 by the Tu-104A, with improved engines and a 70-passenger interior. The final production version had a small fuselage "stretch", higher weights and up to 100 seats, and some earlier aircraft were later fitted with a similar interior and operated at the higher weights, in which guise they were designated Tu-104V.

At least 200 Tu-104s were reported to have been built, all but six being for Aeroflot; the only other user was CSA in Czechoslovakia. By the mid 'seventies, those Tu-104s still operating in the Soviet Union had been relegated to secondary routes in which rôle they continued to serve, in dwindling numbers, in 1981.

The second Tupolev jet transport was the Tu-124 (the Tu-114, no longer in service, being turboprop-powered). Although the Tu-124 was very similar in overall appearance to the Tu-104, it was some 25 per cent smaller and consequently was a completely new design insofar as structural detail was concerned.

The first Tu-124 was flown in June 1960, and following flight trials with a small number of prototypes, production was initiated in time for deliveries to be made to Aeroflot in mid-1962. The first commercial service was flown on the Moscow-Tallinn route on 2 October 1962, this being the first use anywhere in the world of an airliner with turbofan engines — the 11,905lb st (5400kgp) D-20Ps specially developed by the Soloviev engine bureau. Originally, the Tu-124 was designed to carry 44 passengers in three separate cabins; seating was increased to 56, however, in the standard Aeroflot version, designated the Tu-124V.

Apart from Aeroflot, only two airlines operated the Tu-124, CSA Czechoslovakian Airlines having acquired three and East Germany's Interflug, two. Fewer than 200 were built and few, if any, remained in service in the Soviet Union by 1981.

Above right: A Tupolev Tu-104 in its original Aeroflot markings, as used to fly the Soviet Union's first jet services in 1956.

Right: Produced only in relatively small numbers, the Tu-124 was operated for a time by East Germany's Interflug, as illustrated.

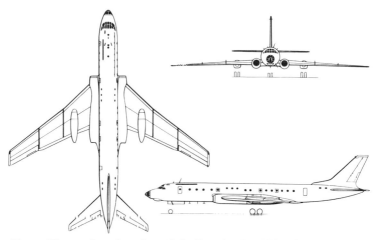

Above: Three-view drawing of the Tupolev Tu-104, which used the same wings and tail unit as the Tu-16 bomber, with a new fuselage.

Tupolev Tu-134
Soviet Union

The following specification refers to the Tu-134A:

Power Plant: Two 14,490lb st (6800kgp) Soloviev D-30 or D-30-II turbofans.

Performance: Max cruising speed, 550mph (885km/h) at 32,800ft (10,000m); economical cruise, 466mph (750km/h) at 36,000ft (11,000m); initial climb rate, 2,913ft/min (14·8m/sec); normal operating ceiling, 39,000ft (11,900m); range 1,174mls (1890km) with max payload and 1,876mls (3020km) with 11,025lb (5000kg) payload.

Weights: Operating weight empty, 64,045lb (29,050kg); max payload, 18,075lb (8200kg); max take-off, 103,600lb (47,000kg); max landing, 94,800lb (43,000kg).

Dimensions: Span, 95ft 1¾ (29·00m); length, 121ft 6½in (37·05m); height, 30ft 0in (9·14m); wing area, 1,370·3sq ft (127·3m²).

With the Tu-104 and the Tu-124, the Tupolev design bureau allowed Aeroflot to take a major step forward and to enter the jet age, but in a number of respects both these types lagged behind the standards being established by contemporary products of western companies. Recognizing the need to overcome these discrepancies and to match the standards of the equipment of other airlines in all respects, Aeroflot established a new requirement for a short-haul medium capacity airliner almost as soon as the Tu-124 had entered service, and to meet this requirement the Tupolev bureau evolved the Tu-134. The design was undertaken at the time that "compact jets" such as the Caravelle, One-Eleven and DC-9 were receiving much publicity, and Tupolev adopted a similar rear-engined, T-tail layout.

Initially, an attempt was made to use the Tu-124 fuselage with minimum change, and the designation Tu-124A was applied, but a complete redesign was eventually found to be required, and the designation was then changed. The Tu-134 did retain, however, the short-field and rough-field capabilities of the Tu-124, with a similar undercarriage and high-lift features. Avionics and flight control system were suitable for operation in conditions approximately equivalent to those of ICAO Cat II, and an airbrake was fitted beneath the fuselage to permit steeper approaches to be flown.

Prototype testing began in late 1962, and the test programme used a total of six aircraft. Production was launched in 1964 at the Kharkhov factory where the Tu-104 had also been built, and early production aircraft underwent a series of proving flights over Aeroflot routes before full commercial services were launched in September 1967, on the Moscow—Stockholm route. In its standard version, the Tu-134 seats 72, four-abreast in a single class layout, alternative arrangements seating 68 one-class or 64 (eight first-class and 56 tourist).

In the second half of 1970, Aeroflot introduced the Tu-134A into service, this version differing from the Tu-134 in having the fuselage "stretched" by 6ft 10½in (2·10m) and being fitted with Soloviev D-30 Series II engines and an APU. The standard layout in this version seats 76, with up to 80 seats at reduced pitch or 68 in a mixed-class layout (12 first class and 56 tourist). Although all early Tu-134s and some Tu-134As had the distinctive glazed nose of earlier Tupolev designs, containing a navigator's station, some later examples dispensed with this crew position and had a "solid"

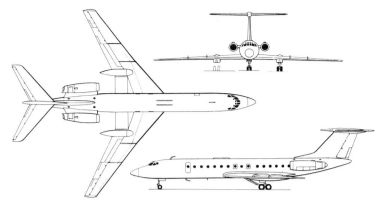

Above: The Tupoley Tu-134A, which has a slightly longer fuselage and nose radar to distinguish it from the Tu-134.

nose fairing containing radar. A version known as the Tu-134B-1 was reported under development in 1981, with improved D-30 engines, updated systems and avionics and a revised interior for up to 100 passengers.

The Tu-134 and Tu-134A have proved to be among the most popular of Soviet airliners for export, matching the earlier success of the Il-18, which in many instances the Tu-134 has been purchased to replace. By the end of 1981, several hundred Tu-134s and Tu-134As had been delivered for service with Aeroflot. In addition, substantial fleets of this twin-jet had been acquired by CSA, Interflug, Balkan Bulgarian, LOT, Malev and Aviogenex in Yugoslavia.

Above: A Tu-134A twin-jet operated by the Czech national airline CSA.

Below: A Tu-134A in the markings of Malev — Hungarian Airlines; 10 were serving by 1982.

Tupolev Tu-144
Soviet Union

Power Plant: Four 44,000lb st (20,000kgp) with reheat Kuznetsov NK-144 turbofans.

Performance: Max cruising speed, up to M = 2·35 (1,550mph/2500km/h) at altitudes up to 59,000ft (18,000m); normal cruise, M = 2·2 (1,430mph/2300km/h); typical take-off speed, 216mph (348km/h); typical landing speed, 150mph (241km/h); balanced field length (ISA, sl, max take-off weight), 9,845ft (3000m); landing run, 8,530ft (2600m); max range with full 140-passenger payload, 4,030mls (6500km) at an average speed of M = 1·9 (1,243mph/2000km/h).

Weights: Operating weight empty, 187,400lb (85,000kg); max payload, 30,865lb (14,000kg); max fuel load, 209,440lb (95,000kg); max take-off weight, 396,830lb (180,000kg); max landing weight, 264,550lb (120,000 kg); max zero-fuel weight, 220,460lb (100,000kg).

Dimensions: Span, 94ft 6in (28·80m); length overall, 215ft 6½in (65·70m); height (wheels up), 42ft 2in (12·85m); wing area, 4,714·5sq ft (438m²).

Holding a secure place in history as the world's first supersonic airliner to fly, the Tupolev Tu-144 has often been described in the popular press as the "Soviet Concorde" or the "Concordskii" — an appellation that underlines the similarity of the two types. There is little doubt that Aeroflot was led to initiate design of an SST by the launching of the Concorde by Britain and France in 1963, and the Tupolev design bureau, having been selected to undertake this important programme, reached design conclusions similar to those of the Concorde's designers. The first public indication of the Tu-144's appearance came in May 1965, when a model was exhibited in Paris, revealing that it was a large ogival-wing transport with provision, like the Concorde, for the nose and visor to be hinged down ahead of the cockpit to improve the forward view in the nose-high approach angle. Unlike Concorde, the chosen engines were turbofans rather than turbojets, and were arranged side by side across the underside of the fuselage in a single large nacelle; the overall dimensions were also somewhat greater than those of its western counterpart and the design cruising speed a little higher, at M = 2·2 to 2·3.

The first of three prototypes of the Tu-144 to be assembled at the Zhukovsky works, near Moscow, made its first flight on 31 December 1968,

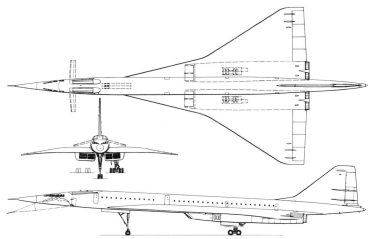

Above: Three-view drawing of the production form of the Tupolev Tu-144, differing in many details from the prototype.

Left: The registration CCCP-77109 identifies this as the ninth of a total of 11 production examples of the Tu-144 believed to have been built for Aeroflot and used for much development flying before regular service began on routes within the Soviet Union at the end of 1975. Persistent technical difficulties have prevented the Tu-144 from being fully utilized.

and supersonic speed was achieved for the first time on 5 June 1969, followed by the first excursion beyond M = 2·0 on 26 May 1970. All these three events were world "firsts", but the rate of flight testing with the prototypes was relatively slow with only about 200hrs achieved in the first $3\frac{1}{2}$ years after initial flight. During this period, and based on early flight test results, a major redesign of the Tu-144 was put in hand, the production configuration appearing early in 1973 in the Soviet Union and in May 1973 at the Paris Air Show. Compared with the prototypes, this production model had larger overall dimensions; a new wing; relocated engine nacelles; uprated engines; a new undercarriage and retractable noseplanes for improved slow-speed handling.

The wing of the Tu-144 was changed from the original ogival form (with curved leading edges) to a compound delta, with straight leading edges and sweepback angles of about 76 deg on the inboard portions and 57 deg on the outer panels. The whole wing incorporates complex camber from leading to trailing edge, with anhedral towards the tips.

Addition of noseplanes to the production Tu-144 was an indication of the difficulties of achieving acceptable low-speed control, since they provide unwanted drag and weight penalties in cruising flight. The noseplanes ▶

are stowed in the upper fuselage just behind the flight deck, pivoting to open to an overall span of about 20ft (6·1km); they have anhedral when open, and incorporate fixed double leading edge slots plus double slotted trailing edge flaps.

Each pair of engines is housed in an individual nacelle (unlike the prototype arrangement) The engines have been improved since first being flown in the prototype to have a dry thrust rating of 33,000lb st (15,000kgp) and an afterburner thrust of 44,000lb st (20,000kg). The cruising technique called for about 35 per cent of maximum reheat boost to be maintained throughout the supersonic cruise, and the intakes incorporate fully-automatic movable ramps.

The Tu-144 was designed to be operated by a crew of three (two pilots and an engineer) and can carry up to 140 passengers. Typically, the forward cabin seats 11 at first-class standards and the centre and rear compartments, separated by galleys, toilets and cloakrooms, accommodate 30 and 99

Below: An early production version of the Tu-144, as exhibited at the Paris Air Show in 1976. In this view, the nose planes are retracted and the nose is drooped for improved forward view.

passengers at tourist class standards, basically five abreast. There are no under-floor freight or baggage holds, but provision is made for containerized baggage in a compartment behind the cabin.

On 26 December 1975, Aeroflot began a regular service with Tu-144s between Moscow and Alma Ata (a distance of about 2,200mls/3500km), but only freight was carried, in accordance with normal Aeroflot procedure for the in-service testing of a new type. On 22 February 1977, testing began on the Moscow—Khabarovsk route, a total of 50 flights being made on the two routes up to 1 November 1977, when the Tu-144 inaugurated a twice-weekly passenger service on the Moscow—Alma Ata route. From then until 1 June 1978, 51 round-trip flights were completed; the service was then suspended, however, immediately following an accident to one of the 13 Tu-144s built.

Further development of the Tu-144 was then undertaken, and on 23 June 1979 a proving flight was made between Moscow and Khabarovsk by a variant described as the Tu-144D, with new engines — perhaps of variable by-pass type developed by Koliesov. The Tu-144D was reported to be able to fly a stage length of 4,350mls (7000km), but up to the end of 1981, it had not entered regular passenger-carrying service with Aeroflot.

Tupolev Tu-154
Soviet Union

Power Plant: Three 20,950lb st (9500kgp) Kuznetsov NK-8-2 turbofans.
Performance: Max cruising speed, 605mph (975km/h) at 31,150ft (9500m); best-cost cruise, 560mph (900km/h); long-range cruise 528mph (850km/h); range with max payload and 1-hr reserve, 2,150mls (3460km); range with max fuel and 30,100-lb (13,650-kg) payload, 3,280mls (5280km).
Weights: Operating weight empty, 95,900lb (43,500kg); max payload, 44,090lb (20,000kg); max fuel load, 73,085lb (33,150kg); max take-off weight, 198,416lb (90,000kg); max landing weight, 176,370lb (80,000kg); max zero fuel weight, 139,994lb (63,500kg).
Dimensions: Span, 123ft 2½in (37·55m); length, 157ft 1¾in (47·90m); height, 37ft 4¾in (11·40m); wing area, 2,169sq ft (201·45m²).

The sixth and latest of the Tupolev bureau's commercial airliners, the Tu-154, can be considered as a direct counterpart of the Boeing 727-200/HS Trident Three transports, having a similar three-engined T-tail layout. Compared with its western contemporaries, however, the Tu-154 was designed to have a higher power-to-weight ratio, giving it a better take-off performance, and a heavy duty undercarriage suitable for use from Class 2 airfields with surfaces of gravel or packed earth. These features are common to most Soviet transports and indicate the importance of air transport in the Union's remoter areas, where airfield facilities are minimal. Lacking the characteristic glazed nose of the earlier Tupolev transports, the Tu-154 nevertheless retained the wing pods for main undercarriage stowage that are a feature of all the Tupolev series except the Tu-144.

First flight of the Tu-154 was made on 4 October 1968, and six prototype/ pre-production models were used for flight development. Production was launched soon after first flight, the Tu-154 having been selected by Aeroflot as a replacement for the Tu-104, Il-18 and An-10 on domestic and international routes of medium length, in partnership with the Il-62 and Il-62M on longer stages. The first delivery was made to Aeroflot early in 1971 and there followed the customary period of route proving with freight and mail, plus a few passenger services on an *ad hoc* basis, from May 1971 onwards, but full commercial exploitation began only on 9 February 1972, initially on the route from Moscow to Mineralnye Vady. First international services were flown on 1 August 1972, between Moscow and Prague.

The Tu-154 was normally laid out to accommodate 158 or 164 passengers in a single-class layout, six abreast in two cabins separated by the galley. If a mixed-class layout was required, 24 seats could be provided four abreast in the forward cabin, with 104 tourist class seats in the rear cabin. Maximum high density seating was for 167. Standard avionics and flight control system permit operation to Cat II levels, with projected future development for fully automatic landings. During 1973, flight testing of a new version, the Tu-154A, began, and this entered service in 1975 after proving flights with the prototype over Aeroflot routes in 1974. The Tu-154A was dimensionally unchanged from the Tu-154 but had uprated NK-8-2U engines giving 23,150lb st (10,500kgp), increased internal fuel capacity and higher take-off and landing weights of 207,235lb (94,000kg) and 171,960lb (78,000kg) respectively. Many systems and equipment changes were

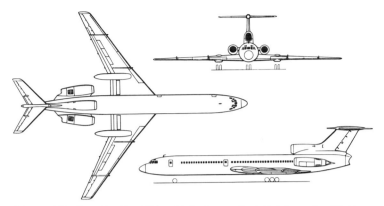

Above: The Tupolev Tu-154, which shares its trijet layout with the Boeing 727 and HS Trident and is of comparable size.

made, and the standard Aeroflot layout provided 144–152 seats. Further improvements were introduced with the Tu-154B in 1977, this having the same engines and dimensions, but another increase in maximum weight to 211,650lb (96,000kg) and internal changes to allow up to 169 passengers to be carried. The flight control and navigation systems were also improved and further refinements of this model led to the designation Tu-154B-2 being adopted. A version known as the Tu-154M was reported in 1981, with a side-loading freight door.

After the initial requirements of Aeroflot had been met, deliveries of Tu-154s for export began in 1973. By the end of 1981, more than 400 Tu-154s of all versions had been built and the type was in service with Balkan Bulgarian Airlines, Malev and Tarom in addition to Aeroflot.

Above: A Tupolev Tu-154B in service with Balkan Bulgarian Airlines.

Below: An early Tu-154 of Balkan Bulgarian.

LZ-BTC

Vickers Viscount
United Kingdom

The following specification refers to the Viscount 810:

Power Plant: Four 2,100ehp Rolls-Royce Dart 525 turboprops.

Performance: Cruising speed, 350mph (563km/h) at 20,000ft (6100m); service ceiling, 25,000ft (7620m); no-reserves range with max payload, 1,725mls (2775km); no-reserves range with max fuel, 1,760mls (2830km).

Weights: Basic operating 41,565lb (18,753kg); max payload, 14,500lb (6577kg); max take-off, 72,500lb (32,886kg).

Dimensions: Span, 93ft 8½in (28·50m); length, 85ft 8in (26·11m); 26ft 9in (8·16m); wing area, 963sq ft (89·46m²).

An order confirmed by BEA on 3 August 1950 for 20 Vickers Viscounts ensured that production of this four-turboprop short-to-medium haul transport would go ahead, and thus put in train a sequence of events that would establish the Viscount as Britain's most-produced commercial transport to date and one that was to be the means of introducing gas turbine operations to a large proportion of the world's airlines. The event came more than six years after the first steps had been taken that were to lead to the design and production of the Viscount, during which time the future of the aircraft was at times in jeopardy.

The idea of developing a turboprop transport emerged late in 1944 in discussions between the Brabazon Committee and Vickers designers, who were already working on a transport derivative of the Wellington bomber as the VC1 Viking. By March 1945, Vickers had projected possible pressurised transports to seat 24–27 passengers, with a gross weight of 35,000lb (15,875kg) under the designation VC2 and in May the Brabazon Committee set out the requirements in greater detail as the Type IIB, specifying 24 seats, a 1,000 mile (1610km) range and a 7,500lb (3400kg) payload. By the end of the year, Vickers had chosen the Rolls-Royce Dart as the potential power-plant and on 9 March 1946 the company received a government contract to build two prototypes, one with Armstrong Siddeley Mamba engines and one with Rolls-Royce Darts. The name Viceroy was adopted, but was dropped after the partition of India and Viscount was chosen instead.

Right: A Viscount 800 series in the markings of Arkia Israel Inland Airlines Ltd which was using five such Viscounts and four Metro IIs in 1982 on its domestic routes. Once the main-stay of regional airlines throughout the world, the Viscount had been largely relegated to minor routes and less developed areas by the early 'eighties, but was still giving excellent service in the latter role, as well as in the corporate and business transport category.

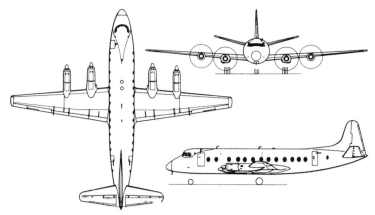

*Above: **The Vickers Viscount 800, with longer fuselage and more power than the original 700 series.***

By the time the first Viscount prototype (with Dart R.Da.1 engines) was ready to fly, it had grown in size to seat 32 passengers. First flight was made at Wisley on 16 July 1948, but airline interest remained lukewarm and progress on the other prototype was slowed down. When Rolls-Royce offered a new Dart variant, the R.Da.3, with 40 per cent more power, however, Vickers was able to redesign the Viscount with a 6ft 8in (2·03-m) fuselage stretch and 5-ft (1·52-m) increase of span, and seats for 40 passengers (four-abreast). The economics of this new variant, the Vickers Type 700 or Viscount 700, looked much more attractive to the airlines and once the BEA order had set the ball rolling, the order book for this version of the Viscount grew rapidly, helped by demonstration flights by the new prototype, which had made its first flight on 19 April 1950.

The first production Viscount flew on 20 August 1952, to BEA standard, having a gross weight of 53,000lb (14,040kg), 47 seats (five-abreast) and Dart 505s in place of the 504s in the prototype. A full certificate of airworthiness was granted on 17 April 1953 and BEA inaugurated Viscount services the next day, between London and Cyprus. This marked the in ►

auguration of regular passenger services by a turboprop aircraft, although the original Viscount 630 prototype had been used in 1950 for a month-long trial on the London—Edinburgh route.

As the world's first, and for some time only, turboprop transport, the Viscount quickly gained a favourable passenger reaction and important airline orders were achieved, notably from TCA (now Air Canada) in November 1952 and from Capital Airlines of the USA in June 1954. The latter company eventually bought 60 Viscounts and TCA bought 51; other early sales were made to operators throughout the world. Each customer variant was distinguished, in accordance with Vickers practice, by an individual type number, ranging from 701 (BEA's first variant) to 798. Significant changes were introduced in the Type 724 for TCA, including a new fuel system, a two-pilot cockpit, US styling and a 60,000lb (27,215kg) gross weight. The Type 745 for Capital marked another stage in Viscount development, introducing uprated Dart R.Da.6 Mk 510 engines, full compliance with US regulations and a gross weight (eventually) of 64,500lb (29,256kg); FAA approval was obtained on 7 November 1955. Subsequent Viscounts fitted with the R.Da.6 engines were known generically as Type 700Ds.

To improve the payload/range performance of the Viscount and to take advantage of possible increases in engine power, Vickers developed a stretched-fuselage variant as the Type 800, the fuselage being 3ft 10in (1·17m) longer but the effective cabin length being 9ft 3in (2·82m) greater through relocation of the rear bulkhead. Passenger capacity therefore increased to 65 (or 71 high-density) and with Dart R.Da.6 engines the gross weight was 64,500lb (29,256kg). A prototype flew on 27 July 1956 and first delivery was made, to BEA, on 11 January 1957. In addition to 22 Viscount 802s, BEA bought 19 similar 806s, with Dart R.Da.7 Mk 520 engines.

A further stage in Viscount evolution came in 1957 with the Type 810, which was dimensionally the same as the 800 but with R.Da.7/1 engines and structural strengthening to allow the gross weight to increase to 72,500lb (32,885kg). A prototype flew on 23 December 1957 and most of the final production batch of Viscounts were of this type. The last order of all came

Above: A Viscount 813 of British Midland Airways, which had 10 of these transports in its fleet in 1982 for domestic and charter flights.

from China, buying six as the first Western equipment ever acquired by CAAC. Deliveries of these aircraft were completed in 1964, bringing the total of Viscounts built to 444 (of which 438 were sold to customers, the others being prototypes or rebuilds). The only turboprop transports to have exceeded this sales record to date are the Fokker F.27 and, within the Soviet Union, the Antonov An-24, the Ilyushin Il-18 and the Antonov An-10/12 family, many of which were built for military use.

Since the beginning of the 'seventies, growing numbers of Viscounts of the earlier series have been withdrawn from service and scrapped, and few of any variant remain in use on primary routes. On secondary routes and in less developed areas of the world, however, about a hundred were still in airline service in 1981, and others were used for corporate transportation.

Below: Two classic transport aircraft—a Viscount (the world's very first turboprop airliner) and a DC-3 (the most widely used airliner ever produced).

Vickers Vanguard
United Kingdom

The following specification refers to the Vanguard Type 952:

Power Plant: Four 5,545ehp Rolls-Royce Tyne 512 turboprops.

Performance: High speed cruise, 425mph (684km/h) at 20,000ft (6100m); long-range cruise, 420mph (676km/h) st 25,000ft (7620m); initial rate of climb, 2,700ft/min (13·7m/sec); service ceiling, 30,000ft (9145m); range with max payload (no reserves), 1,830mls (2945km) at 25,000ft (7620m); range with max fuel, 3,100mls (4990km) at 25,000ft (7620m).

Weights: Empty equipped 82,500lb (37,422kg); max payload, 37,000lb (16,785kg); max take-off, 146,500lb (66,448kg); max landing, 130,500lb (61,238kg).

Dimensions: Span, 118ft 7in (36·15m); length, 122ft 10½in (37·45m); height, 34ft 11in (10·64m); wing area, 1,529sq ft (142·0m²).

The Vanguard, first flown on 20 January 1959, was designed primarily to meet BEA requirements for a "big Viscount", of similar overall configuration and using turboprop engines. It was, however, overtaken by the advent of pure-jet airliners able to operate economically on medium stage lengths and initial sales were made only to BEA (now British Airways European Division) and to TCA (now Air Canada). The latter bought the Type 952 with Tyne 513 engines while BEA had a mixture of 951s and 953s with Tyne 506s, the 953 having increased weights. Up to 139 passengers could be carried in one-class layouts.

Above: A Vanguard in the final livery of British European Airways before that airline was absorbed into British Airways.

Below: One of Air Canada's original Vanguard 952s, after it had been acquired by Europe Aero Service in France.

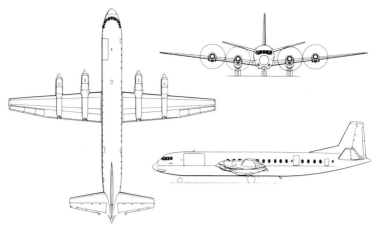

Above: Three-view drawing of the Vickers Vanguard, showing its family likeness to the Viscount, depicted on page 189.

By 1974, Air Canada had retired all its Vanguards and two years later British Airways had in service only five, all converted to Merchantman freighting standard, with a large side-loading door. These were finally retired in 1980. Several other operators had acquired Vanguards second-hand, however, including Air Bridge Carriers in the UK, Merpati Nusantara in Indonesia and Europe Aero Services in France, the last named being the principal remaining user of the type in 1981, with a fleet of 10.

Above: The Vanguards were finally withdrawn from British Airways' fleet in 1980, the last five serving as Merchantmen freighters.

193

Yakovlev Yak-40
Soviet Union

The following specification refers to the standard 27-seat Yak-40 with AI-25 engines.

Power Plant: Three 3,300lb st (1500kgp) Ivchenko AI-25 turbofans.

Performance: Max speed, 373mph (600km/h) at sea level; max cruising speed, 342mph (550km/h) at 19,685ft (6000m); initial climb rate, 1,575ft/min (8·0m/sec); range with max fuel, 45-min reserve, 590mls (950km) at max cruise speed; max range, no reserves, 900mls (1450km) at 261mph (420km/h) at 26,247ft (8000m).

Weights: Empty, 20,140lb (9135kg); max payload, 5,070lb (2300kg); max fuel load, 8,820lb (4000kg); max take-off weight, 35,280lb (16,000kg).

Dimensions: Span, 82ft 0¼in (25·0m); length, 66ft 9½in (20·36m); height, 21ft 4in (6·50m); wing area, 753·5sq ft (70·0m²).

First flown on 21 October 1966, the Yak-40 marked the first venture of the Yakovlev design bureau into the civil transport field, although several light transport designs had previously been produced under the Yakovlev banner in addition to its better-known fighters and trainers. The task confronting the bureau was to evolve a small, economic short-haul transport that could replace many of the Lisunov Li-2 (DC-3) transports still being used in the Soviet Union, and this requirement meant that the new aircraft had to be able to operate at Class 5 airfields, with grass runways.

The emphasis on good field performance led the design team to adopt a three-engined layout rather than the usual twin-engined configuration for aircraft of this size; this meant that take-off weights and runway lengths could be calculated on the basis of losing only one-third, and not one-half, of total power in the case of an engine failure. The 3,300lb (1500kg) turbofan engines were specially developed for the Yak-40 at the Ivchenko engine bureau, and the high thrust-to-weight ratio that they bestow on the aircraft is especially beneficial for operations at high-altitude airfields, of which there are many in the remoter regions of the USSR. The standard range of avionics and flight control system provided for operation down to Cat II standards, and future development for Cat III was projected.

The basic Yak-40 was designed as a 27-passenger short-haul feeder-liner, seating being three abreast (2+1) with an off-set aisle. A variety of alternative layouts has been evolved by the design bureau, including one with 32 seats at reduced pitch, mixed-class arrangements with 16 or 20 seats, and an executive model with 11 seats in two separate cabins. An all-cargo version was also developed, with a loading door in the port side of the cabin. All versions have a ventral airstair as the main access to the cabin, and an APU is mounted above the rear fuselage, primarily for engine starting.

Following construction of a batch of five prototypes, production of the Yak-40 was launched at a factory at Saratov, some 300 miles (500km) SE of Moscow, in 1967 and deliveries to Aeroflot began during the following year. Regular operations on scheduled services began on 30 September 1968, and production increased to eight a month by 1973 to meet the very large domestic demand. Approximately 1,000 Yak-40s have been built, primarily for service with Aeroflot, and the type has been the subject of a major export campaign by Aviaexport, the Soviet state aircraft marketing organization; production ended in 1978. Among the users of the Yak-40 are or have been Avioligure in Italy; General Air of Hamburg; Bakhtar Afghan; CSA in Czechoslovakia and its internal subsidiary Slovair; Balkan Bulgarian Airlines and Hang Khong in Vietnam. Other examples have been delivered for use by government agencies and air forces within the Soviet Bloc, and the Yugoslav Air Force has two.

Since the Yak-40 entered service, it has undergone some modifications, the most noticeable of which are the addition of a clam-shell thrust reverser

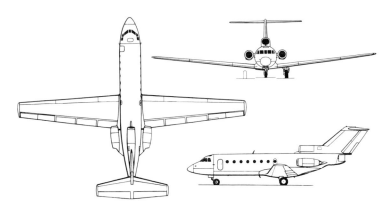

Above: The Yak-40, which applies the three-engined layout to a smaller airframe than in any contemporary airliner.

on the centre engine, and deletion of the acorn fairing at the fin/tailplane leading-edge junction. During 1970, a version with a lengthened fuselage was projected as the Yak-40M, to carry 40 passengers, but this apparently did not proceed. During 1974, the Yak-40V became available for export, this having 3,858lb st (1750kgn) Al-25T engines and fuel capacity increased from 6,614lb (3000kg) to 8,820lb (4000kg). This increased power permitted the gross weight to be raised from 34,410lb (14,700kg) for the original 27-seater to 35,274lb (16,000kg) with a similar layout or 36,376lb (16,500kg) with a 32-seat high-density layout, when the payload was 6,000lb (2720kg). To make the Yak-40 more acceptable in the North American market, a version with Garrett-AiResearch TFE731-2 turbofans has also been projected as the X-Avia, to be marketed by ICX Aviation in Washington In 1980, three versions of the X-Avia were being studied: the LC-3A with a 30-passenger layout, the LC-3B seating 40 in a high-density layout and the all-cargo LC-3C.

Below: The Czech airline CSA had nine Yak-40s in service in 1982, as well as eight of the improved Yak-40CFs.

Yakovlev Yak-42
Soviet Union

Power Plant: Three Lotarev D-36 high by-pass turbofans each rated at 14,330lb st (6500kgp).
Performance: Normal cruising speed, 510mph (820km/h) at 25,000ft (7620m); high speed cruise, 540mph (870km/h); range, 1,150mls (1850km) with 23,150lb (10,500kg) payload; range with max fuel, 1,860mls (3000km).
Weights: Empty, 63,845lb (28,960kg); max payload, 31,940lb (14,500kg); max take-off, 114,535lb (52,000kg).
Dimensions: Span, 112ft 2½in (34·20m); length, 119ft 4in (36·38m); height, 32ft 3in (9·83m); wing area, 1,614·6sq ft (150m²).

The Yak-42 was the second jet transport to emerge from a design bureau that has been famous for many years for its fighters serving with the Soviet Air Force. Resembling, in overall configuration, the Yak-40 with its three engines grouped in the rear, the Yak-42 was designed to replace the Tu-134 and Il-18 on the shorter-range trunk routes and An-24s on local routes operated by Aeroflot within the USSR. Its development began in the early 'seventies, a mock-up being displayed to Western correspondents visiting Yakovlev's works near Moscow in mid-1973, and the prototype made its first flight on 7 March 1975.

Two versions of the Yak-42 have been designed — a 100-seater for the local routes, with provision for passengers to stow carry-on baggage and outer garments as they board the aircraft (using the same concept adopted in the Il-86) and a 120-seater for the trunk routes with baggage preloaded into containers for stowage under the cabin floor. Like the Yak-40, the Yak-42 has a rear-loading integral stairway, but there is also a forward fuselage door. According to Soviet reports, the first and second prototypes of the Yak-42 have different degrees of sweepback — 11 and 25 respectively — for comparative flight testing, the latter having been adopted for the production aircraft featuring also on the third prototype.

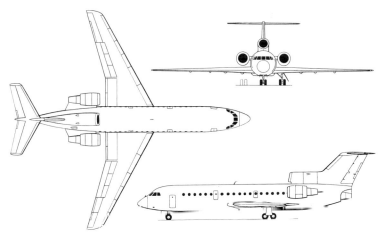

Above: Three-view drawing of the Yak-42, the largest commercial aircraft to date from the Yakovlev design bureau.

The D-36 engines for the Yak-42 were developed at the former Ivchenko design bureau under the direction of V. A. Lotarev and are claimed to have a very low specific fuel consumption. Although the passenger capacity of the Yak-42 is about the same as that of the Douglas DC-9 Srs 40 or 50, it has almost 50 per cent more power, indicating the emphasis placed upon field performance to allow the aircraft to operate from relatively short achieving long fatigue life and low maintenance man hours. Aeroflot is reported to have an initial requirement for 200 Yak-42s and the first of these appeared during 1980, differing from the prototypes in having bogey main undercarriages and in a number of other small details. First passenger proving flights were flown by the Yak-42 towards the end of 1980 on the Moscow–Krasnodar route.

Left: An early production example of the Yakovlev Yak-42, which entered preliminary service with Aeroflot on routes within the Soviet Union during 1980. Prototypes were tested with two different angles of wing sweepback in order to establish the optimum, and production aircraft introduced twin bogey mainwheels, whereas the prototypes had only single pairs. Large scale production of the Yak-42 is planned, to allow this type to replace the Tu-134 and older types still in Aeroflot service.

Airlines Section

Contents

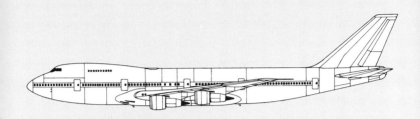

Introduction

The airlines featured in this section represent the world's major passenger carriers which operate predominantly international services. It also includes the larger carriers which specialise in domestic operations. The USA is naturally well represented, all the US "majors" and one leading "national", Frontier Airlines, being included. (Under the new CAB designations "majors" are defined as airlines with annual revenues of more than $ US 1000 million and "nationals" are airlines with annual revenues of $ US 75-1000 million). The major Communist airlines with long haul equipment are also covered, including the world's largest operator, Aeroflot-Soviet Airlines, for whom only approximate statistics are available.

The airline fleet information is correct to the end of 1981, and wherever possible account has been taken of confirmed aircraft transactions announced during the early part of 1982. Each fleet data list includes all the airline's major passenger-carrying aircraft, ie: the aircraft featured in the first section of this book. Light trainers and helicopters, however, have been excluded. The eighty airlines selected represent a fair cross section of worldwide air transportation and I have attempted to include comparable passenger, route distance and employee statistics in as many of the entries as possible. Of note are the substantial new order commitments undertaken by a number of airlines despite the lengthy market recession and harsh economic conditions prevailing in the early 1980s, and also the growing influence of Airbus Industrie in supplying commercial aircraft throughout the world.

John Mowinski

Aer Lingus

Aer Lingus is the trade name under which the combined operations of Aer Lingus Teoranta and Aerlinte Eireann are known. Aer Lingus Teoranta was formed on 22 May 1936 as the national airline of the Irish Republic to operate scheduled services between Ireland and Great Britain. BEA and BOAC both acquired holdings in the carrier in April 1946, and during the same year the Anglo-Irish air agreement gave Aer Lingus sole responsibility for developing a number of air services from Dublin to London, Liverpool and other UK points. Revision of the agreement ten years later resulted in BEA obtaining traffic rights to Dublin in return for which Aer Lingus gained fifth freedom rights to operate from Dublin through Manchester to several European destinations. Aer Lingus was the first carrier outside of Great Britain to order the Viscount and was the first European operator of the Fokker F.27 Friendship. The carrier initiated short haul jet services in May 1965 with BAC One-Elevens.

Aerlinte Eireann was formed on 26 February 1947 to operate transatlantic services but due to a change in Government policy the proposed services (initially to Boston and New York) were shelved and the 5 Constellations acquired were later sold to BOAC. The carrier finally began operations with the inauguration of a Dublin—Shannon—New York service on 28 April 1958 using Super Constellations leased from Seaboard. Jet operations on the route began in December 1960 with the delivery of 3 Boeing 720-048 aircraft. The carrier upgraded to the Boeing 707-348C from June 1964, and introduced wide-bodied service in March 1971 with the delivery of 2 Boeing 747-148 aircraft.

The operations of the two carriers are now fully integrated into an international and regional 29-point network of passenger and cargo services from Dublin, Shannon

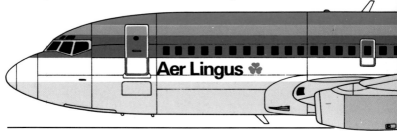

Aeroflot

The Soviet state airline is the world's largest carrier. In addition to operating scheduled passenger and freight services and international charter flights, over one hundred additional activities are undertaken. These include agricultural work, survey operations, fishery and ice reconnaissance, forest fire patrol and aeromedical services. Between 400,000 and 500,000 personnel are employed.

The carrier was formed in March 1923 under the name of Dobrolet, and services were operated from Moscow to Odessa, Georgia and into Central Asiatic Russia. Dobrolet merged with the Ukraine airline, Ukvozduchput, in 1929 to form Dobroflot, which was subsequently reorganised as Aeroflot in 1932. However it was not until 1960 that the last remaining separate entity, the Polar Aviation division operating services in the Arctic regions, became part of Aeroflot. During the 1930s emphasis was placed on developing the domestic route network; very few international services were operated at this time. On 15

September 1956 Aeroflot initiated jet services, on the Moscow-Irkutsk route, with the Tupolev Tu-104. From 1958 onwards substantial development of international routes was undertaken, initially to West European cities and subsequently to the underdeveloped Third World countries in Asia and Africa under the organisation of the Directorate of International Air Routes. The carrier operated its first transatlantic service on 7 January 1963.

Aeroflot currently operates to some 3,600 points within its domestic network and 106 points in 86 countries within Europe, Africa, Asia, North and South America, and Canada. International services are operated from Moscow (Sheremetiyevo) and nine other international airports including Leningrad (Pulkovo), Kiev, Tashkent and Khabarovsk. Unduplicated route length now exceeds 621,400 miles (1,000,000km) of which 136,700 miles (220,000km) are international. Approximately 103 million passengers were carried in 1980 of which 2·7 million were on

and Cork to London and several provincial centres throughout the UK, 14 European cities, and New York and Boston in North America, representing a total route distance of 33,570 miles (54,022km). The carrier's major shareholder is the Ministry of Finance for the Irish Government with management holding a small number of qualifying shares. Aer Lingus currently employs 6,830 personnel, and carried a total of 2,136,007 passengers in the fiscal year ending in April 1981.

Fleet Data
4 BAe (BAC) One-Eleven 208AL
1 Boeing 707-349C
5 Boeing 737-248
3 Boeing 737-248C
2 Boeing 737-248 Advanced
1 Boeing 737-248C Advanced
1 Boeing 737-281
2 Boeing 747-148
1 Boeing 747-130

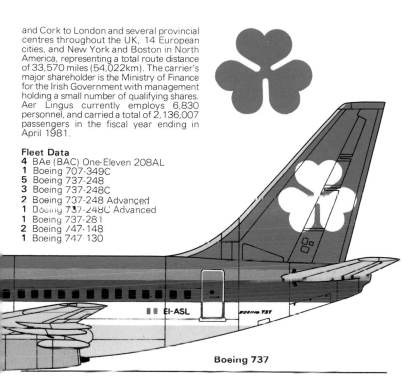

Boeing 737

international services. Aeroflot is aiming to carry approximately 106 million passengers and 3·25 million tonnes of freight and mail during 1981.

The Tupolev Tu-154B, Tu-134A and Ilyushin Il-62M aircraft are the present mainstay of Aeroflot's international operations with the Antonov An-12 and more recently the Ilyushin Il-76 appearing more frequently on international cargo services. The newly developed Yakovlev Yak-42 and Ilyushin Il-86 are gradually being phased into service with the Yak-42 having begun international service on the Leningrad-Helsinki route in July 1981.

Fleet Data (In the absence of official data the figures are provided as a guide only)
4,000 Antonov An-2
150 Antonov An-12
700 Antonov An-24, 26, 30
200 Ilyushin Il-14
100 Ilyushin Il-18
160 Ilyushin Il-62
50 Ilyushin Il-76
6 Ilyushin Il-86
400 Tupolev Tu-134
400 Tupolev Tu-154
550 Yakovlev Yak-40
8 Yakovlev Yak-42
Over 2,000 helicopters including Mil Mi-6, Mi-8, and Mi-10k, and Kamov Ka-26.

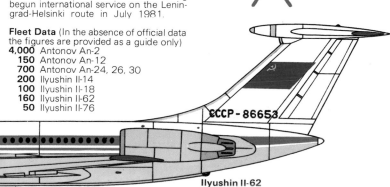

Ilyushin Il-62

Aerolineas Argentinas

Aerolineas Argentinas was founded on 14 May 1949 as a state corporation by the Argentine Ministry of Transport. It superseded four separate operators: Flota Aerea Mercante Argentina (FAMA), Aviacion del Litoral Fluvial Argentino (ALFA), Zonas Oeste y Norte de Aerolineas Argentinas (ZONDA) and Aeroposta Argentina. Of these, Aeroposta Argentina was the oldest having begun operations in late 1928. ALFA had inaugurated flying boat services in 1938 as Corporacion Sudamericana de Servicios Aereos while ZONDA was established in February 1946 operating domestic and regional routes with DC-3 aircraft. FAMA, the largest of the four operators, was founded on 8 February 1946 and had been established as the Argentine flag carrier. FAMA initiated services to London in September 1946 with DC-4 aircraft. The four companies ceased operations on 31 December 1949 and were merged to form the new carrier. Services from Buenos Aires to New York were initiated in March 1950 and domestic services were significantly expanded. Jet operations to Europe began in May 1959 following the acquisition of Comet 4 aircraft and in 1962 Caravelle VI-R aircraft provided domestic and regional jet services. Aerolineas Argentinas, employing some 9,300 personnel, now operates an extensive network of scheduled passenger and cargo services to points in North, Central and South America, Europe, South Africa and New Zealand with the long haul routes being served primarily by Boeing 747 aircraft, seven of which are currently operated.

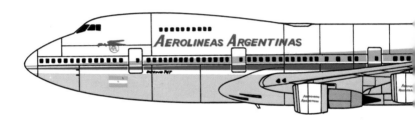

Aeromexico

The carrier was formed on 1 September 1934 as Aeronaves de Mexico. Domestic operations were initiated with the opening of services between Mexico City and Acapulco. Between 1952 and 1962 Aeronaves took over Lineas Aereas Mexicanas SA (LAMSA), Aerovias Reforma SA, Aerolineas Mexicanas SA, and Guest Aerovias Mexico (which had been operating transatlantic services). Aeronaves was nationalised in July 1959 and the Pan American holding was acquired by the Mexican Government. The first major international route, from Mexico City to New York, was opened up in December 1957 by Britannia 302 aircraft—later DC-8 aircraft were used. In 1970, as part of a Government plan, domestic operators in Mexico were rationalised into an integrated system consisting of eight smaller operators under the control of Aeronaves de Mexico. Aeronaves changed its name to Aeromexico in February 1972. Aeromexico, employing some 6,770 personnel, operates a 55 point domestic network and international services from Mexico City to Panama City, Caracas, Lima, Bogota, Buenos Aires, Los Angeles, Tucson, Houston, Miami, New York, Toronto, Montreal, Madrid and Paris.

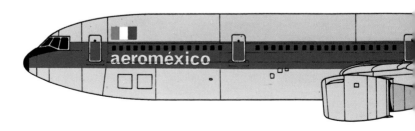

Fleet Data
4 Boeing 707-387B
1 Boeing 707-387C
1 Boeing 707-372C
4 Boeing 727-287 Advanced
4 Boeing 737-287
2 Boeing 737-287C
6 Boeing 737-287 Advanced
1 Boeing 747SP-27
6 Boeing 747-287B
3 Fokker F.28-1000
2 Fokker F.28-4000 (1 leased)

On Order
3 Boeing 727-287 Advanced

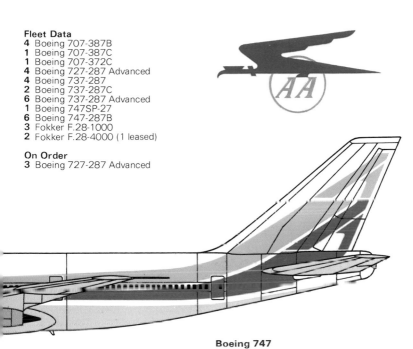

Boeing 747

Fleet Data
5 McDonnell Douglas DC-8-51
8 McDonnell Douglas DC-9-15
17 McDonnell Douglas DC-9-32
3 McDonnell Douglas DC-9-82
2 McDonnell Douglas DC-10-15
2 McDonnell Douglas DC-10-30

On Order
1 McDonnell Douglas DC-9-82

McDonnell Douglas DC-10

Aerovias Nacionales de Colombia

Avianca is the oldest airline in the Americas with the longest unbroken record of scheduled operation in the world. The carrier was founded on 5 December 1919 under the name of Sociedad Colombo-Alemana de Transportes Aereos (SCADTA) by a group of German and Colombian businessmen. Scheduled operations commenced with the opening in September 1921 of services between the capital, Bogota, and the northerly port Barranquilla using Junkers F13 seaplanes. Pan American acquired an 80% shareholding in the carrier in 1931 and in June 1940 SCADTA merged with Servicio Aereo Colombiano, a small domestic airline established in 1933, adopting the current name, Avianca. Aerovias Ramales Colombianos (ARCO), was taken over by the carrier in April 1941, and in August 1946 Avianca began to operate a domestic route network on behalf of Ecuador with connections to Bogota, which continued until 1951.

Transatlantic services to Madrid and Hamburg were started in March 1950 using DC-4 aircraft. Further expansion took place when in September 1951 the carrier purchased Lineas Aereas Nacionales (LANSA), an operator servicing a domestic network covering all major points in Colombia and also Caracas, Venezuela. An additional five domestic operators were taken over by Avianca between 1947 and 1952. Boeing 707-121 aircraft leased from Pan American enabled Avianca to initiate jet services to Miami and New York in October 1960 prior to the carrier taking delivery of Boeing 720B aircraft. Pan American's remaining shareholding was purchased by Avianca in 1978.

Employing some 7,300 personnel, Avianca currently operates a large domestic network from Bogota, and international services to Madrid, Paris and Frankfurt in Europe; to Miami, New York and Los Angeles in North America; and to major

Air Afrique

Air Afrique (Société Aérienne Africaine Multinationale) was formally constituted on 28 March 1961 with the signing of the Treaty of Yaoundé in Cameroon. The carrier was formed by Air France, the French independent airline UAT (now UTA) and eleven African states (Benin [then Dahomey], Cameroon, Central African Republic, Chad, Gabon, Ivory Coast, Mauritania, Niger, Republic of the Congo, Senegal and Upper Volta) which were formerly French colonies. The state of Togo joined the Air Afrique consortium in 1965, but Cameroon withdrew in September 1971 and Gabon in 1977, each to develop its own international carrier. Sierra Leone joined in 1978. Each of the member states contributes 6.54% of Air Afrique's capital with the balance held by Société

pour le Développement du Transport Aérien en Afrique (Sodetraf). The carrier began services on 1 August 1961, taking over the route structure operated by Air France and UAT in French Africa and using 707 and DC-8 aircraft leased from the two carriers. Air Afrique subsequently acquired its own DC-8 aircraft, and introduced DC-10-30 aircraft into service in 1972.

As black Africa's largest carrier, Air Afrique currently operates a route network encompassing twenty-two African states and linking these with Paris, Bordeaux, Lyons, Marseilles, Nice, Geneva, Zurich, Rome, Las Palmas and New York. In all, some 140 points in the system are served. Some 5,100 personnel are employed by Air Afrique and nearly 631,000 passengers were carried in 1980.

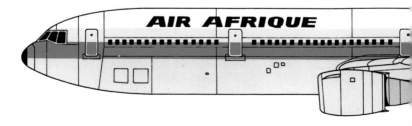

points in Central and South America. Sociedad Aeronautica de Medellin Consolidad SA (SAM), a scheduled operator, and Helicopteros Nacionales de Colombia SA (Helicol) are wholly-owned subsidiaries.

Fleet Data
2 Boeing 707-359B
3 Boeing 707-321B
(1 leased from Atasco)
3 Boeing 707-321C
(2 leased from Atasco)
1 Boeing 720-030B
2 Boeing 720-059B
4 Boeing 727-59
4 Boeing 727-21
2 Boeing 727-2A1 Advanced
(leased from Boeing)
2 Boeing 727-209 Advanced
(leased from Itel Air)
3 Boeing 727-259 Advanced
1 Boeing 747-259B (SCD)

1 Boeing 747-124
(leased from Boeing)

On Order
3 Boeing 767-259

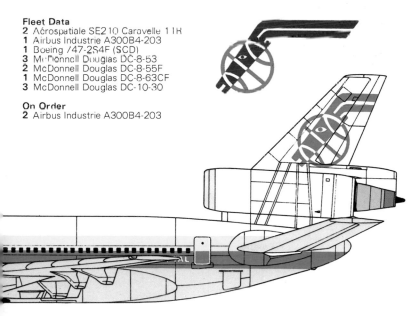

Boeing 747

Fleet Data
2 Aérospatiale SE210 Caravelle 11R
1 Airbus Industrie A300B4-203
1 Boeing 747-2S4F (SCD)
3 McDonnell Douglas DC-8-53
2 McDonnell Douglas DC-8-55F
1 McDonnell Douglas DC-8-63CF
3 McDonnell Douglas DC-10-30

On Order
2 Airbus Industrie A300B4-203

McDonnell Douglas DC-10

Air Algérie

The carrier was formed as a result of the merger of the original independent Air Algérie (established in 1947) and the French operator Compagnie Air Transport in June 1953. Air Algérie officially became the country's national carrier in 1963, and was wholly government-owned by 1972.

Air Algérie (Société Nationale de Transport et de Travail Aérien), employing some 6,000 personnel, currently operates scheduled passenger and cargo services to Paris and other destinations in France, Brussels, Madrid, Barcelona, Palma, Alicante, Rome, London, Frankfurt, Geneva, Cairo, Belgrade, Sofia, Moscow, Tripoli, Bucharest, Prague, Jeddah, Damascus and points in West Africa as well as an

extensive domestic network. Société de Travail Aérien, which was founded in March 1968 and provided agricultural, air taxi and third-level services, became a subsidiary of Air Algérie in May 1972 and is now an integral part of the carrier. Boeing 727 and 737 aircraft provide the backbone of Air Algérie's operations, having replaced the carrier's Caravelle aircraft which initiated jet operations for Air Algérie in January 1960. The carrier has also leased Airbus capacity for the denser international services such as the Algiers-Paris route, and has also acquired Lockheed L-100-30 Hercules aircraft equipped for both passenger operation and cargo duties.

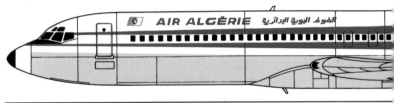

Air Canada

Air Canada was formed as Trans-Canada Air Lines (TCA) by the Canadian government on 10 April 1937 to function as a wholly-owned affiliate of Canadian National Railways. The carrier began scheduled operations on 1 September of that year with a passenger and air mail service between Vancouver and Seattle with Lockheed 10A Electra aircraft. Transcontinental passenger services on the Vancouver-Montreal route were inaugurated on 1 April 1939 using Lockheed 14H2s, and expansion of the network included the opening of a Toronto-New York route in May 1941. Transatlantic services in support of the Canadian Armed Forces overseas began on 22 July 1943 between Montreal and Prestwick with Avro Lancastrian aircraft. DC-3s entered service on domestic routes in 1945, and on 7 May 1947 TCA began operating its North Atlantic services on a commercial basis, with Canadair DC-4M North Stars subsequently replacing the Lancastrians. TCA was firmly established as the national flag carrier during that year. 1954 saw the introduction of Lockheed Super Constellation aircraft on TCA's long haul routes, and TCA became the first operator of turboprop aircraft in the Americas

with the inauguration of Viscount 724 services on 1 April 1955 between Montreal and Winnipeg. A total of 51 Viscounts eventually entered service with the carrier, the last being finally retired in 1974. By the end of 1957 TCA was serving 56 communities in Canada and had initiated non-stop transatlantic service from Toronto.

DC-8-41 aircraft inaugurated jet operations for TCA on 1 April 1960 on the Montreal-Toronto-Vancouver route, and similar services to London were introduced on 1 June of that year. The first of 23 Vanguard 952s entered TCA service on 1 February 1961, and DC-9-14 aircraft commenced operations in April 1966. In the meantime the carrier had adopted its present title on 1 January 1965. On 1 November 1966 Air Canada became the first North American airline to operate to the Soviet Union. Wide-bodied services were started on 25 April 1971 following delivery of Boeing 747-133 aircraft, and Lockheed TriStar 1s entered service on 15 March 1973 between Toronto and Vancouver. Airtransit Canada Limited, a subsidiary of Air Canada, introduced STOL services with DHC-6 Twin Otters between

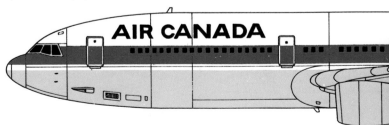

Fleet Data
- **2** Airbus Industrie A300B4-2C (leased from Lufthansa)
- **2** Boeing 727-2D6
- **8** Boeing 727-2D6 Advanced
- **10** Boeing 737-2D6 Advanced
- **3** Boeing 737-2D6C Advanced
- **3** Lockheed L-100-30

On Order
- **1** Boeing 727-2D6 Advanced
- **1** Boeing 737-2D6 Advanced

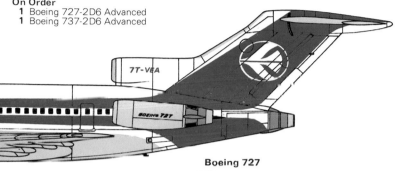

Boeing 727

Montreal and Ottawa in July 1974, but the operation was discontinued in April 1976.

Air Canada currently operates an extensive domestic network and international services to the USA, the Caribbean, Europe and Bermuda. Approximately 13,000,000 passengers were carried in 1980 and a total of 23,418 personnel employed by the carrier. Air Canada has acquired a 29% holding in Guinness Peat Aviation Limited and presently maintains an 86.46% interest in Nordair, a Quebec-based regional airline. The Canadian government, however, has requested Air Canada to dispose of its holding in Nordair.

Fleet Data
- **36** Boeing 727-233 Advanced
- **5** Boeing 747-133
- **2** Boeing 747-233B (SCD)
- **8** Lockheed L-1011-385 TriStar 1 (two leased from Haas-Turner)
- **4** Lockheed L-1011-385 TriStar 100 (converted series 1)

- **6** Lockheed L-1011-385 TriStar 500
- **6** McDonnell Douglas DC-8F-54
- **7** McDonnell Douglas DC-8-61
- **10** McDonnell Douglas DC-8-63
- **?** McDonnell Douglas DC-8-63AF (converted DC-8-63)
- **41** McDonnell Douglas DC-9-32

On Order
- **6** Boeing 727-233 Advanced
- **12** Boeing 767-233

Lockheed L-1011 TriStar

Air France

The carrier was founded on 30 August 1933 when Société Centrale pour l'Exploitation de Lignes Aériennes (formed on 17 May 1933 by the merger of four French operators) purchased the bankrupt Compagnie Générale Aérospatiale. The combination resulted in a fleet of 259 aircraft comprising 35 different types. Following nationalisation after the Second World War, Société Nationale Air France was established on 1 January 1946, succeeded by Compagnie Nationale Air France on 16 June 1948 when the carrier was incorporated by Act of Parliament. Languedoc, DC-4 and Constellation aircraft entered service during the post war period, the Constellation initiating New York and South American services on 24 June 1946. Air France introduced Comet 1A services on 26 August 1953 over their Paris-Rome-Beirut route and Viscount 708 services initially between Paris and London on 15 September 1953. Caravelle services were introduced on the Paris-Istanbul route in May 1959 and the build-up of extensive 707 operations was initiated

with its introduction into service on the Paris-New York route on 2 February 1960. During the fifties the carrier claimed to operate the largest route network in the world, but since that time the granting of independence to many former colonies has led to the establishment of national carriers within these territories and a consequent shrinkage in the network operated by Air France. The French Government currently holds 98.93% of the carrier's shares, with the balance in the hands of public and private interests.

Air France's current route network includes a complex structure of medium haul routes throughout Europe and to North Africa and the Middle East, and a long haul network which extends to North and South America, the Caribbean Islands, Africa, Madagascar and the Indian Ocean, China, Japan and other Far East destinations. Air France also operates the highly efficient Postale de Nuit internal night mail services using Fokker F.27 Friendships and Transall C-160 aircraft. In all, Air France presently serves 145 points in 73 countries, covering an undupli-

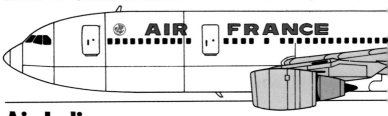

Air-India

Air-India was formed as Air-India International on 8 March 1948 by Air-India Limited (51% holding) and the Indian government (49% holding) to operate international services. Air-India Limited had commenced operations as Tata Sons Limited on 15 October 1932 providing scheduled air mail services on the Karachi-Ahmedabad-Bombay-Bellary-Madras route with De Havilland Puss Moths, the carrier changing its title to Tata Airlines in January 1938. On 29 July 1946 Tata became a public company and was re-named Air-India Limited. Viking aircraft were acquired in 1947 and during that year plans were drawn up with the Indian government for the creation of Air-India International which inaugurated service on 8 June 1948 between Bombay and London, via Cairo and Geneva, with Lockheed Constellation aircraft. A Bombay-Aden-Nairobi route was opened on 21 January 1950, and

following the passage of the Air Corporations Act in March 1953, Air-India International was nationalised on 1 August of that year (Air-India Limited being absorbed into the Indian Airlines Corporation). The Super Constellation was introduced into service on the London route on 19 June 1954. Services to Singapore via Madras commenced on 16 July, and to Hong Kong via Calcutta and Bangkok on 14 August. The Singapore route was extended on 5 October 1956 to Darwin and Sydney, and the carrier inaugurated a Delhi-Moscow service via Tashkent on 15 August 1958.

Jet operations were inaugurated on the Bombay-London route with Boeing 707-437 aircraft on 19 April 1960. A New York service with the type commenced a month later. The carrier's title was abbreviated to Air-India on 8 June 1962 by an amendment to the Air Corporations Act. Wide-bodied services were initiated to

cated route network of 381,590 miles (614,082 km), and employs 33,450 personnel.

The French carrier was the first airline to introduce the A300 Airbus into service (initially on the Paris-London route from 23 May 1974) and also inaugurated commercial supersonic services on 21 January 1976 (simultaneously with British Airways), using Concorde to link Paris with New York, Washington, Caracas, Mexico City and Rio de Janeiro.

Fleet Data
- **7** Aérospatiale/BAC Concorde 101
- **9** Airbus Industrie A300B2-1C
- **4** Airbus Industrie A300B4-2C
- **7** Airbus Industrie A300B4-203
- **5** Boeing 707-328B
- **4** Boeing 707-328C
- **2** Boeing 707-321C
- **20** Boeing 727-228
- **9** Boeing 727-228 Advanced
- **15** Boeing 747-128
- **2** Boeing 747-228B
- **7** Boeing 747-228B (SCD)
- **5** Boeing 747-228F (SCD)

- **15** Fokker F.27 Friendship 500
- **4** Transall C-160P

On Order
- **3** Airbus Industrie A300B4-203
- **5** Airbus Industrie A310-201
- **25** Airbus Industrie A320
- **1** Boeing 727-228 Advanced
- **12** Boeing 737-228 Advanced

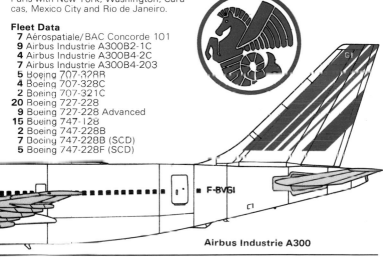

F-BVGI

Airbus Industrie A300

London on 21 May 1971 with Boeing 747-237B aircraft.

Air-India currently operates a network of scheduled passenger and cargo services from Bombay, Delhi, Madras and Trivandrum to 40 destinations in the Middle and Far East, Europe, Africa, Australia and the USA. 1,407,910 passengers were carried in the 1980-81 fiscal year and the airline employs 15,350 personnel. Air-India Charters is a wholly-owned subsidiary formed in September 1971 to undertake charters for the parent company.

Fleet Data
- **2** Boeing 707-437
- **3** Boeing 707-337B
- **2** Boeing 707-337C
- **10** Boeing 747-237B
- **2** McDonnell Douglas DC-8-63CF (leased from Flying Tigers and Icelandair)

On Order
- **3** Airbus Industrie A300B4-200

VT-EBO

Boeing 747

Air Inter

Air Inter (Lignes Aériennes Intérieures) was established on 12 November 1954 to operate domestic services within France. Initial operations began with leased aircraft in 1958 (the first service being Paris-Strasbourg on 17 March) but these proved unsuccessful and were terminated a few months later. Full operations were resumed in June 1960 on a regular basis with aircraft leased from Air France, TAI (now UTA) and Air Nautic (Caravelle, Constellation, Super Constellation, DC-3, DC-6B and Viscount 708 aircraft); and in 1962 Air Inter purchased its first aircraft, five Viscount 708s from Air France. The carrier subsequently acquired more Viscounts, and on 24 July 1964 Air Inter introduced the first of four Nord 262Bs into service between Paris and Quimper. The first of the carrier's own Caravelle III aircraft entered service in March 1967, and the F.27 Friendship began serving with Air

Inter on 11 June of that year. Also in 1967, protocol documents were signed with the State to authorise Air Inter's operations in the French metropolitan region, and with Air France and UTA to define the parameters of the carrier's activities in relation to the operations of the two French airlines. Air Inter attained financial autonomy during 1972 with the termination of subsidies, and the first two Caravelle 12 entered service. Air Inter became the first and only operator of the Dassault-Breguet Mercure 100 when the type entered service between Paris and Lyon on 4 June 1974. The Viscount was retired from Air Inter service on 12 April 1975, and the carrier signed an agreement with Airbus Industrie on 24 December of that year for the purchase of its three Airbus A300B2-1C aircraft, the type entering service on the Paris-Marseille and Paris-Lyon routes on 29 November 1976.

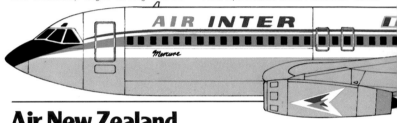

Air New Zealand

Air New Zealand was formed in 1939 as Tasman Empire Airways Ltd (TEAL) by the Governments of New Zealand (50%), Australia (30%) and the United Kingdom (20%). Following delivery of two S30 Empire-class flying boats, operations commenced on 30 April 1940 between Auckland and Sydney. In 1946 the carrier took delivery of four S25 Sandringham flying boats and in 1949 five Mk IV Solents were acquired. The carrier took over the Auckland-Suva, Fiji, route from New Zealand National Airways Corporation on 6 June 1950, and began services to Tahiti the following year. The decision of the British government to withdraw from participation in the carrier in October 1953 left the New Zealand and Australian governments as sole shareholders, each with a 50% holding. DC-6s were acquired in 1954 and introduced on the Auckland-Nandi route. Three Lockheed Electra aircraft were delivered to TEAL in late 1959 with service inauguration of the type on 1 December of that year between Auckland and Sydney followed by Auckland-Melbourne six days later. In July 1961 the

New Zealand government took over sole ownership of TEAL in return for which Qantas was permitted to commence trans-Tasman services in competition with TEAL.

A contract for the carrier's first three DC-8-52 jets was signed on 23 September 1963 and following their delivery in 1965, services with the type began between Christchurch and Sydney on 3 October. TEAL adopted its current title Air New Zealand on 1 April 1965 and introduced DC-8 service to Los Angeles via Nandi and Honolulu on 14 December 1965, with routes to Hong Kong and Singapore being opened the following year. Wide bodied operations commenced in February 1973 following delivery of the carrier's first DC-10-30. Services with the type began to London in 1975 as an extension of the Auckland-Los Angeles service.

In 1977 the New Zealand Government decided to merge Air New Zealand with the other state owned airline New Zealand National Airways Corporation (NZNAC) and the two were amalgamated on 1 April 1978 as Air New Zealand. NZNAC had

Air Inter ceased charter operations in 1977 following an agreement reached with Air France, in return for which the carrier received a 20% holding in Air Charter International, a formerly wholly-owned charter subsidiary of Air France established in 1966.

Air Inter currently operates a 17,245 mile (27,755km) route network within France (including Corsica) covering 30 destinations. The carrier's main base is located at Paris-Orly Airport. Air Inter employs 5,436 personnel and carried 8,238,369 passengers in 1980 of whom 1,103,007 were carried on the Paris-Marseille route alone.

Fleet Data
10 Aérospatiale SE210 Caravelle III
 9 Aérospatiale SE210 Caravelle 12
 6 Airbus Industrie A300B2 1C
 1 Airbus Industrie A300B2K-3C

 1 Airbus Industrie A300B4-102
10 Dassault-Breguet Mercure 100
 9 Fokker F.27 Friendship 500

On Order
 3 Aérospatiale SE210 Caravelle 12
   (from Sterling Airways)
 2 Airbus Industrie A300B4-102

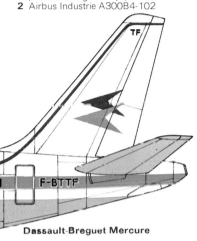

Dassault-Breguet Mercure

been formed as a result of an Act of Parliament in November 1945 to merge three private operators (Union Airways of New Zealand, Cook Strait Airways and Air Travel (NZ) Limited) into one national domestic airline. In the first year of operation NZNAC operated to 18 points and began serving Norfolk Island, Fiji, Tonga, Western Samoa and the Cook Islands a year later. Overseas services were subsequently transferred to TEAL with the exception of Norfolk Island. From 1956 all domestic services were operated by DC-3 aircraft until the acquisition of Viscount 807 aircraft in 1958. The carrier's first F.27 Friendship was delivered in December 1960 and jet operations began with the introduction of 737-219s in September 1968.

Air New Zealand presently operates a route network encompassing 24 domestic points and 15 international destinations. The airline carried 3,288,767 passengers in 1980 and currently employs 8,798 personnel.

Fleet Data
4 Boeing 737-219

2 Boeing 737-214
1 Boeing 737-222
3 Boeing 737-219 Advanced
3 Boeing 747-219B
7 Fokker F.27 Friendship 100
2 Fokker F.27 Friendship 500
8 Fokker F.27 Friendship 500F
2 McDonnell Douglas DC-8-52
1 McDonnell Douglas DC-8-52F
6 McDonnell Douglas DC-10-30

On Order
1 Boeing 737-219QC Advanced
2 Boeing 747-219B

Boeing 747

Air Portugal-TAP

Air Portugal was established by the Portuguese Government as a division of the Civil Aeronautics Secretariat in 1944 under the name of Transportes Aereos Portugueses SARL. Regular commercial services were inaugurated between Lisbon and Madrid on 19 September 1946, and later to Luanda (Angola), Lourenco Marques (Mozambique) and Paris, using DC-3s and subsequently DC-4 aircraft. TAP's first domestic route (Lisbon-Oporto) was opened in 1947. In 1953 the Government sold its interest in the carrier, principally to a private business consortium, and TAP became a limited liability company. Super Constellations were introduced into service from July 1955 and in 1959 TAP embarked on a policy of route expansion to the African continent. Services to Rio de Janeiro via Ilha do Sal and Recife in association with Panair do Brasil (now Varig) began in 1960 using Panair DC-7C aircraft. Caravelle VI-Rs were delivered from July 1962 although jet operations

had started earlier through the operation of Comet 4Bs in association with BEA. A Sabena Boeing 707-329 was also used to inaugurate jet services to Africa prior to delivery of TAP's own 707-382B aircraft in 1965. The carrier's first Boeing 727-82 commenced operations on European routes in the spring of 1967. North Atlantic services were inaugurated on the Lisbon-New York route in 1969 and to Montreal in 1971. Wide-bodied services were initiated in April 1972 on the routes to Luanda and New York following delivery of TAP's first Boeing 747-282B. Following initial Boeing 727-282 (Advanced) deliveries in 1975, the Caravelle fleet was retired from service and disposed of. TAP once again came under state ownership when the carrier was nationalised on 15 April 1975. The carrier adopted its present name in 1979.

Air Portugal currently operates a 86,665 mile (139,468km) route network covering 38 main destinations in Europe, Africa, North and South America, Madeira, the

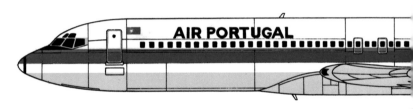

Alia-The Royal Jordanian Airline

Alia was founded in December 1963 as the wholly Government-owned national carrier of Jordan to supersede the previous national airline, Jordanian Airways. Operations commenced in December 1963 with services to neighbouring Middle East countries using a leased DC-7 aircraft and subsequently two Handley Page Heralds. Jet operations began following delivery of Alia's first Caravelle 10R in July 1965 and services were inaugurated to Paris and Rome. Boeing 707 and 720B aircraft were acquired from January 1971 and a fleet of 727-2D3 aircraft was gradually established to meet the needs of Alia's rapidly developing route network. Alia was the first Arab carrier to link the Middle East with North America inaugurating North Atlantic service in July 1977 using

747-2D3B equipment. The carrier's first TriStar 500 began service to London in October 1981.

Alia presently operates services to 33 destinations in Europe, the Middle and Far East, North America and North Africa, representing a total of 43,062 miles (69,299km) in unduplicated route distance. Alia employs nearly 4,000 personnel and carried 1,112,556 passengers in 1980 thereby passing the million figure for the first time. Subsidiary interests of Alia include an 88% shareholding in Arab Wings Company Limited (established in 1975 and operating air taxi, medical and executive jet charter services with a fleet of Gates Learjets), a 20% holding in Arab Air Services, and a number of hotel and travel interests.

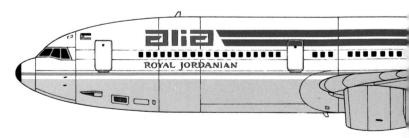

Canary Islands and the Azores. Additional feeder services are provided to several points within Portugal and charter operations are also undertaken. Air Portugal carried 1,718,897 passengers in 1980 and currently employs 10,003 personnel. The Lockheed TriStar 500 has been ordered to replace Boeing 707 aircraft.

Fleet Data
- 7 Boeing 707-382B
- 1 Boeing 707-373C
- 2 Boeing 707-399C
- 2 Boeing 707-3F5C
- 4 Boeing 727-82
- 2 Boeing 727-82C
- 1 Boeing 727-155C (leased from Omni)
- 1 Boeing 727-172C
- 4 Boeing 727-282 Advanced
- 2 Boeing 747-282B
- 2 De Havilland DHC-6 Twin Otter 300

On Order
5 Lockheed L-1011-385 TriStar 500

Boeing 727

Fleet Data
- 2 Boeing 707-321C
- 2 Boeing 707-344C
- 2 Boeing 707-384C
- 1 Boeing 707-3D3C
- 1 Boeing 720-030B
- 6 Boeing 727-2D3 Advanced
- 2 Boeing 747-2D3B (SCD)
- 1 Boeing 747-2D3B
- 2 Lockheed L-1011 TriStar 500

On Order
3 Lockheed L-1011 TriStar 500

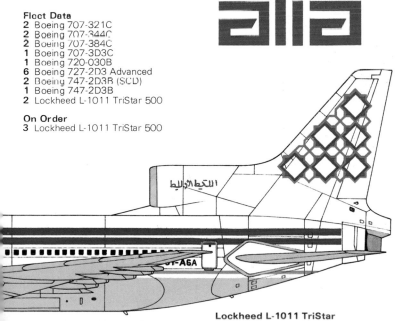

Lockheed L-1011 TriStar

Alitalia

Alitalia (Linee Aeree Italiane) was established in its original form as Alitalia-Aviolinee Italiane Internazionali on 16 September 1946, a joint-capital company in which the Italian government subscribed 47.5% of the capital, BEA subscribed 40% and the remainder came from private interests. The carrier commenced operations between Turin, Rome and Catania on 5 May 1947 using Fiat G.12 aircraft leased from the Air Force. Later that year services were initiated to Cairo, Tripoli and Lisbon, and in 1948 the European route network was developed with the opening of routes to Geneva, London, Nice and Paris. In addition to G.12s, Avro 691 Lancastrian and Savoia Marchetti SM95 aircraft were operating for the carrier until the turn of the decade. These were replaced by DC-4s from 1950. A South America route was inaugurated in 1948 to Rio de Janeiro, Sao Paulo, Montevideo and Buenos Aires, and on 3 July 1950 services commenced between Rome and Caracas via Milan, Lisbon and Ilha do Sal (Cape Verde Islands). The introduction of Convair 340s in 1953 greatly strengthened the carrier's services

in Europe, while the commencement of DC-6B operations in the same year enhanced the longer haul services. By 1955 Alitalia was one of only two carriers in Italy operating scheduled services, the other operator being LAI (Linee Aeree Italiane) which was formed by the Italian Government and TWA in the same year as Alitalia. With the exception of the Rome-Turin route, operated by Alitalia, all domestic services were undertaken by LAI. Both carriers operated European, Mediterranean and transcontinental services. Alitalia changed its corporate designation to Alitalia-Linee Aeree Italiane and absorbed LAI in 1957. By 1 November of that year, the newly created Italian national carrier operated a fleet of 38 aircraft comprising DC-3, DC-6/6B, DC-7C, Convair 340/440 and Viscount 785 aircraft. Alitalia inaugurated jet services in 1960 with the Caravelle VI-N starting on the Rome-London route on 23 May, and the DC-8-43 commencing operations on the Rome-New York route on 1 June. Services to Australia and West Africa were initiated in 1961, and to Chicago, Singapore, Kinshasa, Hong Kong

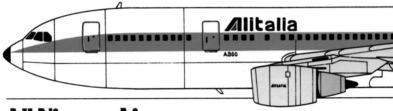

All Nippon Airways

In less than three decades ANA has grown to become Japan's largest airline in terms of fleet size and passengers carried. ANA was founded in 1952 as the Japan Helicopter and Aeroplane Transport Company and began service between Tokyo and Osaka with De Havilland Dove aircraft. The carrier changed its name to All Nippon Airways in December 1957. The carrier merged in March 1958 with Kyokuto Airlines, a domestic airline that had started operations in March 1953 flying from Osaka to points in Southern Japan. Four Convair 340 and 440 aircraft were acquired in late 1960 and Viscount 828 aircraft entered service with the carrier in July 1961. The F.27 Friendship was also introduced into service during the same month between Tokyo and Osaka. In spite of strong competition from Japan Air Lines and railway transportation, ANA experienced vigorous growth with rapid

expansion in domestic travel, and in November 1963 the carrier absorbed Fujita Airlines, followed by Central Japan Airlines in 1965 and Nagasaki Airways in 1967. Jet services with a 727 aircraft leased from Boeing were introduced between Tokyo and Sapporo in May 1964 and the NAMC YS-11 entered service on routes from Osaka in July 1965. 737 aircraft joined ANA's fleet in early 1970, and wide-bodied operations with Lockheed TriStar aircraft commenced in 1974. In recent years a number of YS-11 routes have been transferred to Nihon Kinkyori Airways, a third level operator formed in March 1974 by Japan Air Lines, ANA, Toa Domestic and other Japanese airlines to operate government-subsidised feeder services to isolated island communities and remote mainland destinations.

ANA currently employs 10,382 employees and operates a scheduled passenger

and Tokyo in 1962. DC-9-32 aircraft entered service with Alitalia in 1967 and progressively replaced the Caravelle fleet. The carrier's first Boeing 747-143 inaugurated wide-bodied operations on North America routes from June 1970 and the first DC-10-30 for Alitalia was delivered in February 1973. The Boeing 727-243 (Advanced) entered European service to supplement the carrier's DC-9s from late 1976, and the Airbus A300B4-203 commenced operations on Middle East and European routes in June 1980.

Alitalia currently serves more than 85 destinations in a worldwide network covering Europe, Africa, the Near, Middle and Far East, Australia, North and South America. 7,316,927 passengers were carried in 1980 and the airline employs 18,243 personnel. Subsidiary interests of Alitalia include Aero Trasporti Italiani (100% owned, scheduled domestic and international charter subsidiary formed in 1963), and various hotel, insurance and real estate companies. Alitalia has also an 80% holding in Aermediterranea, an operator formed to replace Aerolinee Itavia.

Fleet Data
- **8** Airbus Industrie A300B4-203
- **17** Boeing 727-243 Advanced
- **4** Boeing 747-243B
- **3** Boeing 747-243B (SCD)
- **1** Boeing 747-243 (SCD)
- **21** McDonnell Douglas DC-9-32
- **8** McDonnell Douglas DC-10-30

On Order
- **1** Boeing 727-243 Advanced
- **1** Boeing 747-243B

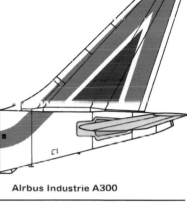

Airbus Industrie A300

---

and cargo network of 72 routes covering 33 points. Although present government policy prohibits ANA from operating scheduled international services, the carrier operates charter flights to Hong Kong, Manila, Bangkok, Singapore, Beijing, Shanghai and other Asian points. ANA carried 22,421,000 passengers in the fiscal year ending March 1981 and has been increasingly employing the 500-seat 747SR aircraft on the densest trunk routes since 1979.

On Order
- **4** Boeing 747SR-81
- **25** Boeing 767-281

Fleet Data
- **9** Boeing 727-281
- **13** Boeing 727-281 Advanced
- **9** Boeing 737-281
- **6** Boeing 737-281 Advanced
- **13** Boeing 747SR-81
- **20** Lockheed L-1011-385 TriStar
- **3** NAMC YS-11
- **25** NAMC YS-11A

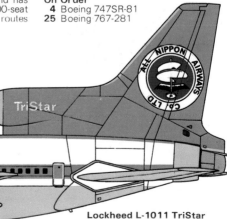

Lockheed L-1011 TriStar

American Airlines

American Airlines was formed in May 1934 as a successor to American Airways which had been established in 1930 by the Aviation Corporation (AVCO) to unify the operations of five operators under AVCO's control. These operators in turn had succeeded many pioneer air operators with roots stretching back to 1926. American represented the conglomeration of 85 original companies. The carrier was heavily dependent upon air mail business in the early thirties, and sponsored development of the DC-3 aircraft in order to develop passenger operations.

Since World War II, American has been responsible for sponsoring the design of a number of significant commercial aircraft, including the Convair 240 and 990, Douglas DC-7 and DC-10 and Lockheed Electra. International services were initiated by the hitherto domestic carrier to Toronto in 1941 and Mexico in 1942. From 1945 American operated a transatlantic division, American Overseas Airlines, serving a number of European countries, but this division was sold to Pan American in September 1950. American began non-stop transcontinental service with DC-7 aircraft between New York and Los Angeles on 29 November 1953. Jet operations with the first of many 707 aircraft began on the same route on 25 January 1959.

The carrier became the largest customer for the BAC One-Eleven aircraft which entered service on American's short haul routes in March 1966, supplementing the 727 aircraft introduced in early 1964. Deliveries of 747 aircraft began in June 1970, and the world's first DC-10 service was operated by American, between Los Angeles and Chicago, on 5 August 1971.

American, one of the world's largest carriers, currently operates a network of scheduled passenger and cargo services encompassing most of the North American continent. In 1971 American absorbed Trans Caribbean Airways and began flying to Caribbean destinations. The greatest single route expansion undertaken by the carrier occurred in January 1979 when

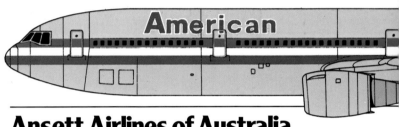

Ansett Airlines of Australia

The carrier was originally formed in February 1936 as Ansett Airways Limited by R.M. Ansett. Operations commenced between Melbourne and Hamilton using a Fokker Universal. By 1939 Ansett was operating additional routes from Melbourne to Adelaide, Broken Hill and Sydney. In late 1945 Ansett acquired three C-47s and extended its network to Hobart and Brisbane. Barrier Reef Airways, which operated seaplane routes radiating from Brisbane to Sydney, Hayman Island and Townsville, was taken over in 1952, and additional routes from Sydney were acquired from the bankrupt Trans Oceanic Airways during the following year. Convair 340 and 440 aircraft were subsequently introduced to provide low-fare services between state capitals in competition with Trans-Australia Airlines (TAA) and Australian National Airways, (ANA). Ansett is a subsidiary of Ansett

Transport Industries Limited (ATI), and in 1957 ATI succeeded in purchasing the financially-ailing ANA to form Ansett-ANA on 4 October of that year. ANA had been founded in May 1936 through the merger of Holyman's Airways and Adelaide Airways. ANA's network finally stretched through Sydney and Melbourne to Tasmania and across Western Australia to Perth.

ATI subsequently took over Butler Air Transport, an intra-state operator in New South Wales which later became Airlines of New South Wales, and its subsidiary, Queensland Airlines, on 5 February 1958. During the same year Ansett acquired Guinea Airways which became Airlines of South Australia. ATI later purchased Mandated Airlines, and its subsidiary, Gibbes Sepik Airways, and Papuan Air Transport in Papua/New Guinea (which became Ansett Airlines of Papua/New Guinea until

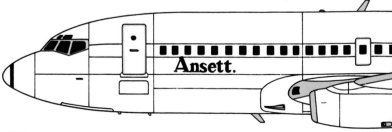

American inaugurated service on 19 new
routes and at 8 new points in the US
mainland, including cities in the southeast,
mid-west and southwest. Further
expansion to strengthen American's hub
and spoke operations from Chicago and
Dallas/Fort Worth during 1981 give the
carrier an 86 point network. The airline
currently employs approximately 37,500
personnel.

On Order
30 Boeing 767-223

Fleet Data
48 Boeing 727-23
 2 Boeing 727-35
 1 Boeing 727-95
 2 Boeing 727-123
 1 Boeing 727-1A7C
41 Boeing 727-223
 1 Boeing 727-2A7
68 Boeing 727-223 Advanced
15 Boeing 727-227 Advanced
 8 Boeing 747-123
 6 Boeing 747-123F (SCD)
34 McDonnell Douglas DC-10-10

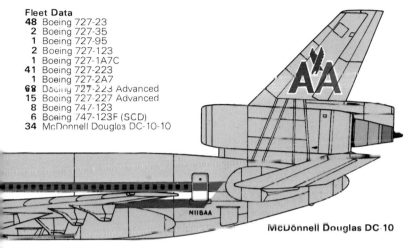

McDonnell Douglas DC-10

---

the formation of Air Niugini in 1973.
 Ansett inaugurated Lockheed Electra
turboprop services between Sydney and
Melbourne on 10 March 1959, and Boeing
727-77 aircraft initiated jet services on 2
November 1964. The carrier's first DC-9-
31 was delivered in April 1967, and the
type is now being replaced by Boeing 737-
277 (Advanced) aircraft. The carrier adopted
its present title in late 1968. Ansett currently
serves an extensive route network throughout all states of Australia, and total personnel
employed is approximately 8,600.

Ansett.

On Order
 5 Boeing 737-277 Advanced
 5 Boeing 767-277

Fleet Data
16 Boeing 727-277 Advanced
 7 Boeing 737-277 Advanced
 5 Fokker F.27 Friendship 200
 4 Fokker F.27 Friendship 600
 3 Lockheed L-188AF Electra
 8 McDonnell Douglas DC-9-31

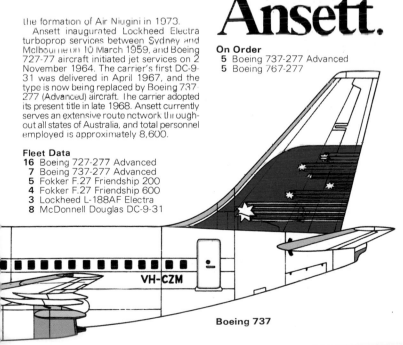

Boeing 737

Austrian Airlines

Austrian Airlines (Österreichische Luftverkehrs AG) was founded on 30 September 1957 by a merger of Air Austria and Austrian Airways, which had been formed but had not started operations. The nation's previous operator, OLAG, had been incorporated into Deutsche Luft Hansa in 1938, and after cessation of hostilities in 1945 the Allies did not permit civil aviation activities until the State Treaty was signed in 1945. Austrian inaugurated services on 31 March 1958 between Vienna and London using chartered Viscount 779 aircraft. The carrier's own Viscount 837 aircraft were acquired in 1960 and commenced operations in March of that year. Jet services were introduced with Caravelle VI-Rs on 20 February 1963 to cope with the carrier's fast-growing European route system. Austrian operated its first domestic service with a DC-3 on 1 May of that year. By early 1965 Austrian had carried its first million passengers, and in June of the following year two Hawker Siddeley 748s entered service to replace the DC-3. Transatlantic service began on 1 April 1969 on the Vienna-Brussels-New York route in co-operation with Sabena and using a Boeing 707-329 chartered from the Belgian airline. This was terminated in March 1971. From 19 June of that year Austrian began to take delivery of DC-9-32 aircraft, and by January 1973 had phased out all other aircraft types previously operated.

Following introduction of the DC-9, Austrian signed an agreement on technical co-operation with Swissair on 29 March 1972. The first DC-9-51 for Austrian, and the second worldwide to be used in regular services, was delivered on 14 September 1975 and in April of the following year new services were initiated from Vienna to Cairo, Düsseldorf, Stockholm and Helsinki as well as on the Vienna-Salzburg-London route. Austrian became

Braniff International

Braniff Airways, which operates under the name of Braniff International, was originally formed in 1928 by Tom and Paul Braniff, and in 1929 the company became part of the Aviation Corporation which subsequently established American Airlines. The present Braniff Airways was re-organised as an independent company on 3 November 1930, and the original Tulsa-Oklahoma City route operated in 1928 was extended to Wichita. DC-2 aircraft entered service in 1937, followed by DC-3s in 1939. Operations from Houston to Lima via Havana commenced on 4 June 1948 with subsequent extensions to Rio de Janeiro, Asuncion and Buenos Aires. By this time both DC-4 and DC-6 aircraft had joined the carrier's fleet. Braniff developed domestic services throughout the mid-western states as far west as Denver, and acquired Mid-Continent Airlines on 15 August 1952. A Dallas/Fort Worth-New York route was inaugurated in February 1956, and DC-7C aircraft entered service later that year.

Lockheed L-188A Electras commenced operations with Braniff on 15 June 1959 between San Antonio, Dallas and New York, and jet services were inaugurated with Boeing 707-227 aircraft on 20 December.

Braniff became the first US operator of the BAC One-Eleven (Series 203) with service inauguration of the type on 25 April 1965. The carrier received its first Boeing 727-27C on 27 May 1966, and absorbed Pan American-Grace Airways (Panagra) on 1 February 1967. As a result of the merger, Braniff acquired a number of additional South American destinations, as well as Panagra's DC-8-62 order. Wide-bodied operations began with the delivery of Braniff's first Boeing 747-127 aircraft on 5 January 1971, the type entering service on the carrier's Honolulu route. A Dallas/Fort Worth-London route was opened in March 1978, and Concorde services between Washington D.C. and Dallas/Fort Worth were initiated on 12 January 1979

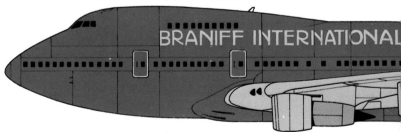

one of the launch customers for the DC-9-81 when the carrier placed an order for its first eight of the type on 30 October 1977. Austrian placed an order for two Airbus A310-220 aircraft on 19 May 1980, having earlier signed a "Memorandum of Understanding" with Airbus Industrie. On 26 October the carrier operated its first DC-9-81 service between Vienna and Zurich.

Austrian currently operates a route network of 28,907 miles (46,519km) covering over 42 cities in 30 countries in Europe, North Africa and the Middle East. The carrier employs 2,670 personnel and carried 1,645,315 passengers in 1980 (including 360,830 on charter operations).

Fleet Data
4 McDonnell Douglas DC-9-32
5 McDonnell Douglas DC-9-51
7 McDonnell Douglas DC-9-81

On Order
2 Airbus Industrie A310-220
3 McDonnell Douglas DC-9-81

McDonnell Douglas DC-9

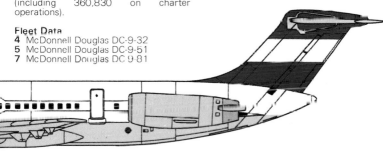

in association with British Airways and Air France, though this was terminated in 1980.

Braniff currently operates a nationwide domestic trunk network including services to Honolulu. Scheduled international passenger and cargo services are operated to Europe and to Central and South America. Approximately 10,500 personnel are employed by Braniff.

Fleet Data
1 Boeing 727-27
2 Boeing 727-27C
2 Boeing 727-30C
(leased from Evergreen International)
1 Boeing 727-172C
3 Boeing 727-191
1 Boeing 727-214
2 Boeing 727-227
54 Boeing 727-227 Advanced
3 Boeing 727-291
2 Boeing 727-2B7
1 Boeing 747-127
1 Boeing 747-227B

1 Boeing 747-230B (leased from ITEL)
1 Boeing 747SP-27
7 McDonnell Douglas DC-8-62
1 McDonnell Douglas DC-8-62CF

Boeing 747SP

British Airways

British Airways was formed on 1 September 1972 through the amalgamation of British Overseas Airways Corporation (BOAC), BOAC Associated Companies, BOAC Engine Overhauls, British European Airways Corporation (BEA), BEA Airtours, BEA Helicopters, Northeast Airlines, Cambrian Airways and International Aeradio which were brought together under the British Airways Group established by the 1971 Civil Aviation Act. The airline subsequently operated in a divisional form and underwent further rationalisation into a single unified structure in 1977.

BEA was formed on 1 August 1946 as a nationalised concern to take over the European routes operated by BOAC's British European Airways division and to absorb a number of British domestic airlines. BEA introduced the world's first turboprop service on 18 April 1953 with Viscount 701 aircraft between London and Nicosia, and began jet operations with Comet 4Bs in April 1960.

BOAC was formed as a result of an Act of Parliament which provided for the acquisition and amalgamation of Imperial Airways (formed on 31 March 1924) and the pre-war British Airways (established in 1935) on 1 April 1940. BOAC took over British South American Airways on 30 July 1949 and became the world's first commercial jet operator when services with the ill-fated Comet 1 were inaugurated between London and Johannesburg on 2 May 1952. Jet operations were restarted with the Comet 4 in 1958. The Boeing 707-436 entered service on 2 July 1960 and wide-bodied services on the North Atlantic route were started in April 1971 with Boeing 747-136 aircraft. Supersonic operations with Concorde were inaugurated in parallel with Air France on 21 January 1976.

British Airways operates the largest route network in the world: in the 1980-1981 fiscal year it covered some 172 cities in 80 countries within Europe, the

British Caledonian Airways

BCAL came into being as Caledonian/BUA in November 1970 through the acquisition of British United Airways (BUA) by Caledonian Airways. The new carrier represented the second force airline which government policy favoured at that time with a view to stimulating stronger competition. BUA had been established more than a decade earlier through the merger of the Airwork Group and Hunting-Clan Air Transport in July 1960. Associates of BUA included British United Air Ferries, which later became British Air Ferries in 1967, and British United Island Airways which became British Island Airways (now part of Air UK). Airwork and Hunting pioneered services to Africa in the 1950s which were to form the basis of BCAL's present route links with that continent. BUA developed routes to Europe and became the launch customer for the BAC One-Eleven, inaugurating service with the type in April 1965. BUA also took over BOAC's former South America route and

in November 1964 commenced VC-10 services to that continent. Caledonian Airways was formed in April 1961 as an international charter airline and operations commenced with leased DC-7C aircraft. Britannias entered service in April 1965 and Caledonian's first Boeing 707 was delivered in July 1967. One-Eleven 500s were delivered in 1969 for European charter work.

A number of routes were assigned from BEA and BOAC to BCAL after the merger, and following the 1976 Government civil aviation review, BCAL took over British Airways' routes to Caracas, Bogota, Lima and Lusaka while giving up to British Airways the routes to East Africa and the Seychelles, and relinquishing traffic rights to New York, Los Angeles, Boston, Toronto and Singapore. BCAL gained from the subsequent increase in the number of US gateway cities and experienced a substantial expansion of its long haul network to North America and also to the Far East,

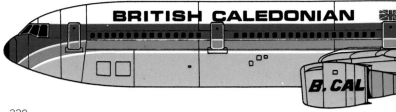

Middle and Far East, Australasia, East and South Africa, North America and Guyana in South America, representing a total route distance of 353,295 miles (568,546km) and over which 15,918,240 passengers were carried. The carrier employs approximately 43,000 personnel.

Fleet Data
- **7** BAe/Aérospatiale Concorde 102
- **2** BAe (HS) 748-287 Series 2A
- **2** BAe (BAC) One-Eleven 401AK
- **2** BAe (BAC) One-Eleven 408EF
- **1** BAe (BAC) One-Eleven 416EK
- **18** BAe (BAC) One-Eleven 510ED
- **3** BAe (BAC) One-Eleven 539GL
- **2** Boeing 707-336B
- **3** Boeing 707-336C
- **1** Boeing 707 365C
- **1** Boeing 707-379C
- **28** Boeing 737-236 Advanced
- **16** Boeing 747-136
- **10** Boeing 747-236B
- **8** HS 121 Trident 2E
- **25** HS 121 Trident 3B
- **9** Lockheed L-1011-385 TriStar 1
- **8** Lockheed L-1011-385 TriStar 200
- **6** Lockheed L-1011-385 TriStar 500

On Order
- **19** Boeing 757-236
- BAe (HS) 748 (Type/number unspecified)

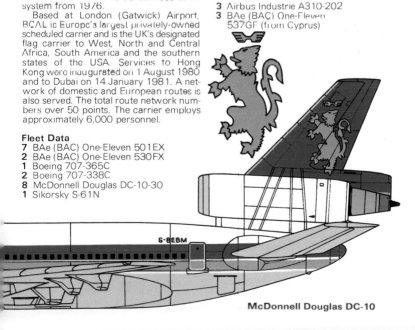

TriStar 500

G-BFCB

Lockheed L-1011 TriStar

and introduced DC-10-30 services to its system from 1976.

Based at London (Gatwick) Airport, BCAL is Europe's largest privately-owned scheduled carrier and is the UK's designated flag carrier to West, North and Central Africa, South America and the southern states of the USA. Services to Hong Kong were inaugurated on 1 August 1980 and to Dubai on 14 January 1981. A network of domestic and European routes is also served. The total route network numbers over 50 points. The carrier employs approximately 6,000 personnel.

Fleet Data
- **7** BAe (BAC) One-Eleven 501EX
- **2** BAe (BAC) One-Eleven 530FX
- **1** Boeing 707-365C
- **2** Boeing 707-338C
- **8** McDonnell Douglas DC-10-30
- **1** Sikorsky S-61N

On Order
- **3** Airbus Industrie A310-202
- **3** BAe (BAC) One-Eleven 537GF (from Cyprus)

G-BEBM

McDonnell Douglas DC-10

CAAC

CAAC (The General Administration of Civil Aviation of China) was established in 1962 and superseded the Civil Aviation Administration of China (also known as CAAC) which had been formed in 1949 after the founding of the People's Republic. The operations of Skoga (People's Aviation Corporation of China), an airline formed as a joint Sino-Soviet undertaking, were taken over by CAAC following the withdrawal of Soviet participation in Skoga during 1954, leading to its dissolution in 1955. CAAC operated primarily domestic routes in the initial stages with the exception of services to the Soviet Union. DC-3, Lisunov Li-2 (Soviet-built DC-3s), Ilyushin Il-12 and Il-14 aircraft were the main types operated, with Ilyushin Il-18 turboprops introduced in 1960, and the first of six Viscount 843 aircraft entering service on 25 March 1964.

Acquisition of four Trident 1E aircraft from Pakistan International Airlines in 1970 allowed jet services to be inaugurated, and the first of a large fleet of new Tridents, a Trident 2E, was delivered to CAAC in November 1972. The first Boeing 707-3J6B was acquired in August 1973, and, with the Il-62, enabled CAAC to develop long haul international routes. Services to Tokyo were started in September 1974 and to Paris in October of the same year. Routes to Teheran and Bucharest were also opened in 1974, followed by services to Zurich, Belgrade, Addis Ababa (via Karachi), and more recently London and New York. Wide-bodied services commenced in 1980 following delivery of Boeing 747 SP-J6 aircraft.

CAAC currently operates an extensive domestic network of more than 160 routes covering a total distance of approximately 118,000 miles (190,000km). CAAC's

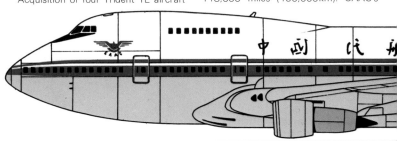

Cathay Pacific Airways

Cathay Pacific was founded on 24 September 1946 and initial operations consisted of freight and passenger services between Asia and Australia and charter flights to the United Kingdom using DC-3 aircraft. In 1948 the Swire Group became the major shareholder and manager of the carrier with Australian National Airways (later absorbed by Ansett Airlines of Australia) as a minority shareholder. By the end of that year Cathay Pacific operated seven DC-3 aircraft and two Catalina flying boats on scheduled services from Hongkong to Manila, Bangkok, Singapore and Rangoon. A DC-4 aircraft was introduced in 1949 to operate the Singapore route and open new services to Saigon, Haiphong and North Borneo. The carrier subsequently introduced DC-6/6B and, later, Lockheed Electra aircraft into service during a period of rapid expansion. In 1959 it acquired Hong Kong Airways

giving Cathay access to northern routes including Japan. Jet service was introduced in 1962 when the first of nine Convair 880-22M aircraft was delivered. These were gradually replaced from 1971 with Boeing 707 aircraft. New services were initiated to the east coast of Australia in 1974 and wide-bodied jet service was introduced from August 1975 with the acquisition of Lockheed TriStar aircraft deployed primarily on the Asian routes. The carrier finally succeeded in obtaining traffic rights to London in 1980, a route now operated daily with Boeing 747 s.

Cathay Pacific currently employs some 5,700 personnel and remains a private company with 70% of its shares owned by the Swire Group and the remainder by the Hong Kong and Shanghai Bank. An extensive route network covering 19 countries is operated from Cathay's Hong Kong base to Osaka, Tokyo, Seoul, Taipei,

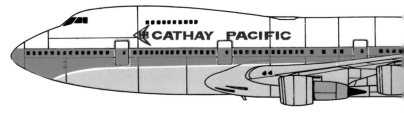

international network covers 17 countries in Asia, Africa, Europe and North America. CAAC controls all civil aviation activities in China and operates a variety of non-airline activities in connection with the national development of industry and agriculture. Such activities include aerial survey, crop-spraying and aero-medical work.

Note: CAAC also operates a number of Il-14, Li-2, An-26 and An-30 aircraft as well as a variety of helicopters and small aircraft including DHC-6 Twin Otters.

Fleet Data
- **1** Antonov An-12
- **30** Antonov An-24 (approx)
- **4** Boeing 707-3J6B
- **6** Boeing 707-3J6C
- **3** Boeing 747SP-J6
- **3** Hawker Siddeley 121 Trident 1E
- **33** Hawker Siddeley 121 Trident 2E
- **2** Hawker Siddeley 121 Trident 3B
- **13** Ilyushin Il 10
- **1** Ilyushin Il 18D
- **5** Ilyushin Il-62
- **6** Vickers Viscount 843

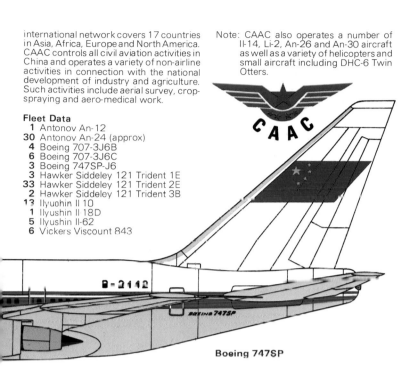

B-2112
BOEING 747SP

Boeing 747SP

Manila, Bangkok, Kuala Lumpur, Singapore, Kota Kinabalu, Brunei, Jakarta, Fukuoka, Perth, Sydney, Bahrain, Melbourne, Penang, Dubai, Kaohsiung, Port Moresby, Shanghai, London, Abu Dhabi, Bombay and Frankfurt. Cathay's network represents 54,794 miles (88,178km) in route distance. The carrier currently operates an average of 400 flights per week and expects to carry in excess of 3,200,000 passengers in 1981.

Fleet Data
- **4** Boeing 707-351C
- **5** Boeing 747-267B
- **1** Boeing 747-236F (SCD)
- **2** Lockheed L-1011-385 TriStar 100
- **7** Lockheed L-1011-385 TriStar 1
  (3 leased from Eastern)

On Order
- **1** Boeing 747-267B

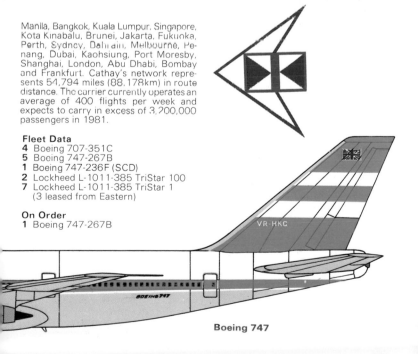

VR-HKC
BOEING 747

Boeing 747

Ceskoslovenske Aerolinie

Ceskoslovenske Aerolinie (CSA), the national airline of Czechoslovakia, was originally formed on 28 July 1923 as Ceskoslovenske Statni Aerolinie. The carrier operated in competition with the privately-owned Cesko-slovenske Letecka Spolecnost (CLS) formed in 1927. The two carriers were absorbed into Deutsche Luft Hansa during World War II. The present carrier came into being on 1 March 1946 and commenced domestic and international operations with DC-3 aircraft. CSA was nationalised by the Communist government in 1949 and subsequently introduced Ilyushin Il-12 aircraft to supplement the DC-3s, followed by Avia 14s in 1955.

Jet operations began in 1957 with the delivery of Tupolev Tu-104A aircraft which inaugurated the first jet link between Prague and Moscow on 9 December. In 1959 CSA became the first Communist carrier to operate international services outside Europe with the opening of a route to Bombay via Cairo and Bahrain. Ilyushin Il-18s were acquired in 1960 to operate the shorter-haul international services, and new routes to Dakar and Guinea were initiated. Services to Jakarta were subsequently introduced, and on 3 February 1962 CSA inaugurated services to Havana in co-operation with Cubana, using a Britannia 318 chartered from the Cuban airline. Ilyushin Il-62 operations were started with the lease of one aircraft from Aeroflot in May 1968, prior to the delivery of CSA's own Il-62s, and a service to New York via Amsterdam and Montreal with the type was inaugurated on 4 May 1970. The Tupolev Tu-134A entered service on European routes in 1972 and in January 1976

China Airlines

China Airlines Ltd (CAL) was founded by a group of retired Air Force officers on 10 December 1959 and commenced charter operations with two PBY Catalina amphibious aircraft. Cargo operations were subsequently initiated and various additional activities undertaken, including fishery patrol, insecticide spraying and aerial photography. Scheduled domestic services were inaugurated in October 1962 between Taipei and Taichung, and subsequently to Hualien, Tainan, Makung and Kaohsiung, for which DC-3, DC-4 and C-46 aircraft were acquired. CAL became the national carrier of Taiwan in 1965, and a year later initiated its first international service between Taipei and Saigon (now Ho Chi Minh City) in December with Super Constellation aircraft. The first Boeing 727-109 for CAL was delivered on 3 March 1967, and new international routes to Fukuoka, Osaka, Tokyo and Hong Kong were opened in April of that year, with extensions to Seoul, Manila, Bangkok, Singapore and Kuala Lumpur commencing in October. Following suspension of all domestic operations in 1968 by Civil Air Transport, CAL took over CAT's traffic rights to enhance its domestic system. Two NAMC YS-11A turboprop aircraft entered service with the carrier in 1970 on short haul routes and in February of that year CAL inaugurated service to San Francisco via Tokyo with a Boeing 707-309C. Operations commenced to Los Angeles through Tokyo and Honolulu in April 1971, and services to Jakarta were started in August. Former Swissair Caravelle IIIs were placed into service in 1971 to provide additional jet services to the rapidly expanding network. Government action resulted in a cessation of services to Japan and Korea on 20 April 1974, and the carrier re-routed its trans-Pacific flights through Guam. Links with Japan were normalised on 9 July 1975; in the previous month CAL had introduced Boeing 747 services on trans-Pacific routes. In 1976 Boeing 737-281 aircraft were purchased from All Nippon Airways. Direct flights to the USA were initiated in April 1977 using Boeing 747SP-09s.

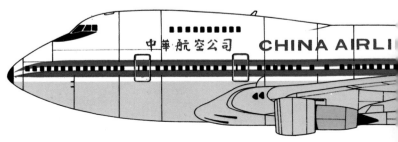

CSA took over the third-level domestic operations of Slov-Air, which was originally formed in 1969.

In addition to its domestic system, CSA operates an extensive network of services to most European capitals and to destinations in the Near, Middle and Far East, North and West Africa, and North and Central America. Approximately 6,000 personnel are employed by CSA.

Fleet Data
- **1** Ilyushin Il-18V
- **1** Ilyushin Il-18E
- **1** Ilyushin Il-18D
- **7** Ilyushin Il-62
- **4** Ilyushin Il-62M
- **10** Let L-410A Turbolet
- **13** Tupolev Tu-134A
- **9** Yakovlev Yak-40
- **8** Yakovlev Yak-40CF

Ilyushin Il-62

CAL operates a domestic route network covering all major cities in Taiwan and to destinations in South East Asia, the Pacific, North America and the Middle East. The 22 point network covers 66,616 miles (107,204km) in total unduplicated route distance. CAL carried 2,163,100 passengers in 1980 and currently has 4,956 employees. The carrier is the first, and so far only, airline to order both the Airbus and Boeing 767 aircraft.

On Order
- **4** Airbus Industrie A300B4-200
- **1** Boeing 747-209B
- **2** Boeing 767-209

Fleet Data
- **1** Boeing 707-309C
- **1** Boeing 707-321C
- **1** Boeing 707-324C
- **1** Boeing 707-351B (F)
- **2** Boeing 727-109
- **1** Boeing 727-109C
- **1** Boeing 727-121C (leased)
- **3** Boeing 737-281
- **1** Boeing 747-132
- **3** Boeing 747-209B
- **1** Boeing 747-209B (SCD)
- **1** Boeing 747-209F (SCD)
- **3** Boeing 747SP-09

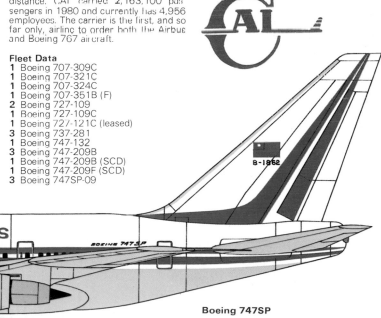

Boeing 747SP

Continental Airlines

Continental's history can be traced to Varney Speed Lines (South West Division) which inaugurated passenger and air mail service on 15 July 1934 from El Paso to Pueblo with Lockheed Vegas. An onward passenger service was operated to Denver but this proved to be uneconomic and was suspended. The former Varney Speed Lines had started air mail services in 1926, but was taken over by the forerunner of the present United Airlines in 1930. In December 1934 the carrier was reorganised as Varney Air Transport. The carrier adopted its present title on 1 July 1937. By 1943 Continental's route system had expanded into Kansas, New Mexico, Oklahoma and Texas. The carrier was granted the Tulsa-Kansas City route in December 1952, and acquired Pioneer Airlines at the end of 1954, thus giving Continental access to Pioneer's extensive network covering 21 cities in Texas and New Mexico. Operations on these routes began in April 1955, and

on 1 May 1957 service was inaugurated between Chicago and Los Angeles via Kansas City and Denver using DC-7B aircraft. This last development marked Continental's full transition to a mainline trunk carrier.

Viscount 812 aircraft entered service between Chicago and Los Angeles on 26 May 1958, and Boeing 707-124s began jet operations for Continental on 8 June 1959. The carrier received its first DC-9-14 aircraft (on lease from McDonnell Douglas) on 4 March 1966, and the first Boeing 727-24C (also leased from the manufacturer) was delivered in June 1967. During the 1960s and early 1970s, Continental undertook a considerable amount of charter business for Military Airlift Command, and formed Continental Air Services, a wholly-owned subsidiary, on 1 September 1965 to operate specialist charter services from Vientiane in Laos. Boeing 747-124s were acquired during

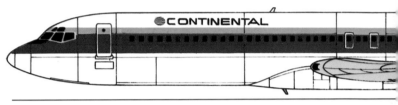

CP Air

CP Air was formed on 16 May 1942 through the purchase and amalgamation of ten small independent operators by Canadian Pacific Railways. These had been primarily operating a network of northern air routes linking isolated communities and potentially rich mining areas with rail terminals. At the time of its formation Canadian Pacific Air Lines Limited (CPAL), as the carrier was then known, had inherited 77 aircraft comprising 14 different types ranging from Rapides to Beech 18s. By 1949 the air fleet was standardised to 47 aircraft comprising 5 types, including 17 DC-3s, which flew a 9,743 mile (15,680km) network of mainland north-south routes in both eastern and western Canada.

In late 1948 CPAL was awarded its first international route, Vancouver to Sydney via Honolulu, Fiji and Auckland, and service commenced on 13 July 1949 with DC-4M North Stars. DC-6Bs were introduced on Pacific routes on 16 October 1953, primarily as a result of problems with the De Havilland Comet for which CPAL had placed an order but subsequently never

operated. Later expansion from Vancouver brought services to Mexico City, Lima, Santiago and Buenos Aires. On 19 September 1949 the Orient service to Tokyo and Hong Kong via the Great Circle route over the North Pacific was inaugurated, and in June 1955 CPAL pioneered a polar route between Vancouver and Amsterdam via Edmonton and Greenland. In return for TCA (now Air Canada) ceasing services to Mexico City, CPAL traded its domestic routes in Ontario and Quebec. Britannia 314 aircraft entered service with the carrier on 1 June 1958 providing non-stop service between Vancouver and Amsterdam.

From 1955 to 1969 CPAL shed many short haul routes inherited from its predecessors and concentrated on the development of longer haul services. In 1959 it was finally successful in securing its first trans-continental route, from Vancouver to Montreal via Winnipeg and Toronto in competition with TCA, and services commenced with Britannias on 4 May. DC-8-43 aircraft replaced the Britannias and

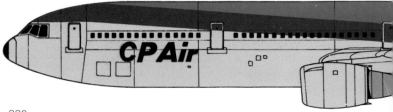

1970 but were subsequently sold. Wide-bodied services are currently provided by a fleet of DC-10-10 aircraft, the first of which was delivered on 14 April 1972.

Continental's current route network stretches from coast to coast and includes services to Hawaii. International services are operated to destinations in Mexico, Australia and New Zealand. Approximately 10,000 personnel are employed by Continental. The carrier has a 30% shareholding in Air Micronesia which was formed in 1966 to operate scheduled inter-island services within the US Trust Territory of the Pacific.

2 Boeing 727-30
1 Boeing 727-76
1 Boeing 727-92C
(operated for Air Micronesia)
21 Boeing 727-224
24 Boeing 727-224 Advanced
7 McDonnell Douglas DC-10-10
4 McDonnell Douglas DC-10-10CF
2 McDonnell Douglas DC-10-30

Fleet Data
10 Boeing 727-22
1 Boeing 727-24C
(operated for Air Micronesia)

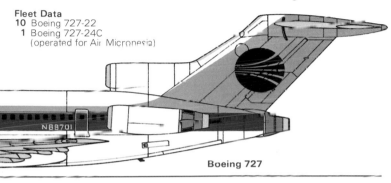

Boeing 727

DC-6Bs on long haul routes from 1961, and 737-217s entered service on the shorter domestic routes in 1968. CP Air's first Boeing 727-17 was delivered in March 1970 and wide-bodied services with 747-217Bs commenced at the end of 1973, to be supplemented by DC-10-30 aircraft from November 1979. The carrier adopted its current title of CP Air in 1968.

CP Air's current route network radiates from Vancouver linking five continents and all major cities in Canada. In addition to a 17 point domestic system, international services are operated to 14 destinations. CP Air carried 3,628,323 passengers in 1980. Over 8,500 people work for CP Air.

Fleet Data
2 Boeing 727-217 Advanced
7 Boeing 737-217
11 Boeing 737-217 Advanced
4 Boeing 747-217B
2 McDonnell Douglas DC-8-43
1 McDonnell Douglas DC-8-53
4 McDonnell Douglas DC-8-63
6 McDonnell Douglas DC-10-30

On Order
2 Boeing 737-217 Advanced
4 Boeing 767-217

McDonnell Douglas DC-10

Delta Air Lines

Delta was formed in 1925 as Huff Daland Dusters: the world's first crop dusting company. In 1928 the company broke from its parent organisation and was renamed Delta Air Service. The carrier commenced passenger operations in 1929 between Birmingham (Alabama) and Dallas with a subsequent extension to Atlanta. The carrier discontinued passenger services in 1930 following the award of the Dallas-Atlanta air mail contract to American Airlines. Crop dusting operations continued and in 1934, when the Post Office department cancelled all airmail contracts and submitted all routes for reallocation, Delta succeeded in regaining its former route from Dallas/Fort Worth to Birmingham and beyond to Atlanta and Charleston. The award of new routes from Atlanta to Savannah, Knoxville and Cincinnati in 1941 led Delta to move its administration offices and maintenance base from Monroe, Louisiana, to Atlanta where they are situated today. At this time operations had been undertaken by five DC-3s and four L-10A

Electras. DC-4 non-stop services began between Chicago and Miami in November 1946 followed by DC-6s in December 1948 and DC-7 aircraft in April 1954. Delta merged with Chicago and Southern Air Lines on 1 May 1953. Jet services were inaugurated with DC-8 aircraft on 18 September 1959, and Delta was the first airline to begin services with the Convair 880, in May 1960.

Delta moved into the ranks of the transcontinental airlines in 1961 with the award of the route from Dallas/Fort Worth to five points in California and Las Vegas. Delta premiered DC-9 service in December 1965, the type superseding the Convair 440. 747 aircraft were delivered to the carrier from September 1970 and DC-10-10 aircraft leased from United joined the fleet in 1972 to initiate wide-bodied service on Delta's system. Both of these types have now been disposed of and a fleet of Lockheed TriStar aircraft (for which Delta was one of three launch customers) has since been progressively introduced into

Eastern Air Lines

Eastern began life as Pitcairn Aviation which was formed in 1927 and initiated an air mail service between Brunswick (New Jersey) and Atlanta on 1 May 1928 using PA-5 Pitcairn Mailwings. North American Aviation Inc purchased the carrier in July 1929 and renamed it Eastern Air Transport in January 1930. Eastern initiated passenger service on 18 August 1930 between New York and Richmond, Virginia, using Ford Trimotors, and by the end of that year had acquired Curtiss Condors and extended services to Atlanta. The traffic rights of New York Airways between New York and Atlantic City were acquired in 1931 and Ludington Air Lines, operating between New York, Philadelphia and Washington DC, was taken over in 1933. The carrier assumed its present title in 1934 and subsequently introduced DC-2 aircraft into service.

By 1946 Eastern had expanded its network to St Louis, Detroit and San Juan, Puerto

Rico, and introduced the DC-4 into service. Lockheed Constellations joined Eastern's fleet in May 1947 and the Super Constellation entered service between New York and Miami on 17 December 1951, the same year as the Martin 404 commenced operations with the airline. On 1 June 1956 Eastern absorbed Colonial Airlines which gave the carrier routes to Canada, Bermuda, New York State and New England. Mexico City was included in the network from 1957, and the Lockheed Electra began a long career with Eastern when introduced on the New York-Miami route on 12 January 1959 (the last Electra was not retired from Eastern service until 1977). Jet services with DC-8-21 aircraft commenced on 24 January 1960. Eastern began its now famous air shuttle operation in April 1961, linking Washington D.C., New York and Boston. The carrier became the world's first operator of the Boeing 727 in 1964 and DC-9-14 aircraft began

service. On 1 August 1972 Delta merged with Northeast Airlines, and so obtained Northeast's former traffic rights between Montreal and Miami, and services to Nassau and Freeport in the Bahamas and Bermuda. Delta initiated transatlantic service from Atlanta to London in 1978 and to Frankfurt in 1979.

Delta, currently employing 37,835 personnel, has established itself as one of the world's most successful airlines. Delta's network covers a total of 68 domestic points servicing 81 cities and 6 international destinations. Some 36,743,214 passengers were carried by the airline in its 1980/81 fiscal year and Delta has placed large orders for the new Boeing 757 and 767 aircraft.

Fleet Data
2	Boeing 727-291
11	Boeing 727-295
116	Boeing 727-232 Advanced
33	Lockheed L-1011 TriStar 1
1	Lockheed L-1011 TriStar 200
3	Lockheed L-1011 TriStar 500
13	McDonnell Douglas DC-8-61 (to be re-engined and become DC-8-71)
35	McDonnell Douglas DC-9-32

On Order
60	Boeing 757-232
20	Boeing 767-232
7	Lockheed L-1011 TriStar 1

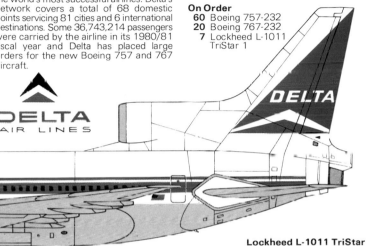

Lockheed L-1011 TriStar

---

operations with the carrier in 1966. The absorption of Mackey Airways in January 1967 gave Eastern access to Nassau and Freeport in the Bahamas. Eastern was one of the three launch customers for the Lockheed TriStar and was the first operator of the type with services being inaugurated on 26 April 1972. The 1973 acquisition of Caribbean-Atlantic Airlines (Caribair) greatly expanded Eastern's operations between the US and the West Indies.

A total of 121 cities in 17 countries are currently served through Eastern's route network. Eastern presently employs 36,500 personnel and carried 39,053,000 passengers in 1980.

Fleet Data
2	Airbus Industrie A300B2K-3C
7	Airbus Industrie A300B4-2C
16	Airbus Industrie A300B4-103
39	Boeing 727-25
25	Boeing 727-225
58	Boeing 727-225 Advanced
31	Lockheed L-1011-385 TriStar 1
58	McDonnell Douglas DC-9-31
18	McDonnell Douglas DC-9-51

On Order
15	Airbus Industrie A300B4-103
4	Boeing 727-225 Advanced
27	Boeing 757

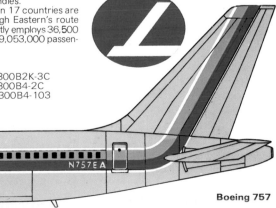

Boeing 757

Egyptair

Egyptair was originally formed as Misr Airwork in May 1932 by the Misr Bank and Airwork Limited, London. The company began domestic operations in July 1933 between Cairo, Alexandria and Mersa Matruh with D.H.84 Dragons. By the end of the year Asyut, Luxor and Aswan were also served and in 1934 the carrier's first international route, to Lydda and Haifa, was opened, followed by services to Baghdad and Cyprus in 1936. After the war Misrair entered a period of rapidly expanding operations with the emphasis on new Middle East destinations. In 1949 it became completely Egyptian-owned, and the title was changed to Misrair SAE. By 1951 Misrair's network covered approximately 11,930 unduplicated route miles (19,200km). Viscount 739 aircraft commenced operations in early 1956, and a London service was subsequently initiated.

On 1 January 1961 the carrier merged with Syrian Airways to form United Arab Airlines (UAA), following the union of Syria and Egypt in 1958. Syria withdrew during 1961, and the two carriers became independent once again, though the Egyptian carrier retained the UAA name.

Jet operations were started on 16 July 1960 with Comet 4C aircraft. UAA subsequently introduced Ilyushin Il-18D, Antonov An-24B and Tupolev Tu-154 aircraft into service. Ilyushin Il-62s were leased from Aeroflot in January 1971, but the Tu-154 and Il-62 aircraft were later returned to the Soviet Union and a fleet of Western aircraft procured. UAA's first Boeing 707-366C was delivered on 18 September 1968, and the first of seven Boeing 737-266 (Advanced) aircraft was delivered in March 1976 to replace the Tu-154s. The carrier adopted its present title on 10

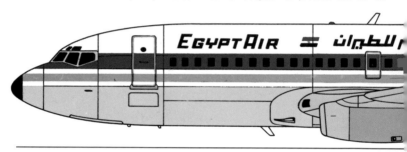

El Al Israel Airlines

El Al was founded in November 1948 as the country's national carrier. The carrier's inaugural flight took place between Geneva and Tel Aviv in September 1948, and scheduled commercial services commenced in July 1949 to Paris and Rome using DC-4 and Curtiss C-46 aircraft. Service to Johannesburg was started in 1950 and three Constellations were acquired in that year, initiating a Tel Aviv-London-New York route on 16 May 1951. El Al took delivery of the first of four Britannia 313 aircraft in 1957 and began service with the type between Tel Aviv and Munich in October of that year, followed by Britannia services on the New York route in December 1957. Jet operations commenced in 1961, initially with leased 707 equipment, and subsequently with El Al's own Boeing 707-458 aircraft which began direct New York-Tel Aviv service in June of that year and thereby set what at that time was the

record for the world's longest commercial flight: 5,727 miles (9,216km). El Al took delivery of its first Boeing 747-258B on 26 May 1971, and initiated wide-bodied services with it to New York in June of that year. The carrier's longest route, from Tel Aviv to Miami, was inaugurated in April 1979 and, entering a new era of Middle East detente, service to Cairo was started in April 1980. Leased 737 aircraft entered service in October of that year.

El Al's current route network covers passenger and cargo services to 24 destinations including services to New York, Miami, Montreal, Johannesburg, Nairobi, Istanbul and most European capitals. 1,179,350 passengers were carried in the 1980-81 fiscal year and 4,600 personnel are presently employed by the airline. Subsidiary companies of El Al include Teshet (responsible for the management of the carrier's non-opera-

October 1971 following the country's change of title to the Arab Republic of Egypt. Wide-bodied services were introduced with an Airbus Industrie A300B4-2C leased from TEA in April 1977, and the carrier has since acquired its own Airbus aircraft.

In addition to domestic operations, Egyptair currently undertakes a network of scheduled services to destinations in the Middle and Far East, Africa and Europe. The domestic services are operated under the name Misrair. Egyptair employs approximately 9,600 personnel.

Fleet Data
3 Airbus Industrie A300B4-203
7 Boeing 707-366C
7 Boeing 737-266 Advanced

On Order
5 Airbus Industrie A300B4-203

SU-AYH

Boeing 737

tional activities including hotel interests), El Al Charter Services (a wholly-owned charter subsidiary formed in October 1977 and operating flights to eight countries using El Al aircraft and crews) and Tamam (in-flight catering services).

Fleet Data
2 Boeing 707-458
3 Boeing 707-358B
2 Boeing 707-358C
2 Boeing 737-2M8 Advanced
  (leased from TEA)
4 Boeing 747-258B
1 Boeing 747-258C (SCD)
1 Boeing 747-258C
1 Boeing 747-258F
1 Boeing 747-124F

On Order
2 Boeing 737-258 Advanced
4 Boeing 767-258

Boeing 747

Finnair

Finnair, the Finnish national carrier, was founded on 1 November 1923 as Aero O/Y and operations began on 20 November 1924 with a Helsinki-Reval (Tallinn) service using Junkers F-13 aircraft. A Helsinki-Stockholm service via Turku with the seaplane commenced shortly afterwards. A new route to Berlin was later established and the building-up of a domestic route network got under way. 1936 saw the end of the seaplane era with the construction of airports at Helsinki and Turku and the acquisition of Dragon Rapide aircraft. By 1940 Aero was operating to nine domestic points and the carrier purchased two DC-2 aircraft. The ending of hostilities in 1944 resulted in a six month suspension of operations after which services recommenced from Hyvinkää (some 30 miles [48 km] from the capital). Services were resumed from Helsinki in 1947, and the first of nine DC-3 aircraft entered service with the carrier. Düsseldorf and Hamburg were served from April 1951 and the carrier now operated under its present title of Finnair, though this did not become the official name until July 1968. Finnair became the first European airline to purchase the Convair 340 and the type entered service with the carrier in 1953, later initiating a Helsinki-London service on 1 September 1954. An agreement was reached between Finnair and Aeroflot in 1955 as a result of which Finnair became the first non-communist airline to be granted traffic rights to Moscow after the war.

Jet operations with Caravelle III aircraft began on 1 April 1960 with services to Stockholm and Frankfurt. Finnair later became the first operator of the Super Caravelle when the first of eight of the type commenced operations in 1964. Transatlantic services began in January 1969 with the inauguration of a Helsinki-Copenhagen-Amsterdam-New York route using newly acquired DC-8-62CF aircraft. Finnair began services with the DC-9 in 1971 and wide-bodied long haul operations with DC-10-30 aircraft began in 1975.

Originally a private concern, Finnair is

Frontier Airlines

The Denver-based carrier has its roots in Monarch Airlines, which was formed early in 1946 and inaugurated local service from Denver on 27 November of that year. In December 1949 Monarch absorbed Challenger Airlines, and Arizona Airways, an intra-state operator, was taken over in April 1950. Monarch formally became Frontier Airlines on 1 June of that year. The effect of the mergers was to give Frontier an extensive north-south operation between Montana and Mexico, serving 40 points in 7 states. During the subsequent decade the carrier expanded its route system throughout the states between the Rocky Mountains and the midwest. DC-3 aircraft were supplemented by former United Convair 340s in 1959. Frontier undertook a re-engining programme involving the installation of Allison 501 turboprop engines in the Convair 340 aircraft, which were redesignated Convair 580s. The first of the Convair turboprops entered service on 1 June 1964, and eventually Frontier operated a total of 32 Convair 580s.

Jet operations were inaugurated with the first of 5 Boeing 727-191 aircraft in September 1966 and Boeing 727-291s were acquired in February 1968. These aircraft, however, did not entirely suit the carrier's route network and were replaced with Boeing 737 aircraft, the first of which (a 737-2CO) was acquired in May 1969. Another major phase of expansion was accomplished when Fort Worth-based Central Airlines merged with Frontier on 1 October 1967. Central had been formed in March 1944 and operated services in Texas and surrounding states with DC-3 and Convair 600 equipment. By 1974 Frontier was carrying in excess of 3 million passengers annually and serving some 100 destinations (more than United), though many of these were small communities.

Frontier Airlines currently provides flights

now a joint stock company, with the Finnish Government holding 76.1% of the share capital. Finnair currently operates to 26 countries with a scheduled route network that covers 20 domestic and 39 foreign destinations from newly-served Seattle and Los Angeles in the west, to Bangkok in the east. The carrier operates one of the world's densest domestic networks in relation to population. Finnair currently plans to initiate service to Tokyo in 1983 and has recently acquired DC-10-30ER capacity to cater for this projected route development. In the fiscal year ending 31 March 1981 a total of 2,991,638 passengers were carried by Finnair whose employment force presently numbers 4,923.

Fleet Data
- 3 Aérospatiale Caravelle 10D
- 2 Fokker F.27 Friendship 200
- 1 McDonnell Douglas DC-8-62
- 6 McDonnell Douglas DC-9-14
- 1 McDonnell Douglas DC-9-15
- 2 McDonnell Douglas DC-9-15MC
- 6 McDonnell Douglas DC-9-41
- 12 McDonnell Douglas DC-9-51
- 2 McDonnell Douglas DC-10-30
- 1 McDonnell Douglas DC-10-30ER

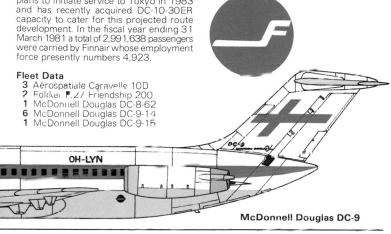

McDonnell Douglas DC-9

to 86 points in 27 US states, Canada and Mexico. RKO General (a subsidiary of the General Tyre and Rubber Company) took control of the carrier in 1964. Under the new designations laid down by the CAB, Frontier is now defined as a national carrier (ie a carrier with an annual revenue of 75-1,000 million US dollars). 5,893 personnel work for Frontier and over 5 million passengers are carried annually.

Fleet Data
- 4 Boeing 737-214
- 3 Boeing 737-222
- 2 Boeing 737-247
- 5 Boeing 737-291
- 5 Boeing 737-2CO
- 1 Boeing 737-2H4
- 1 Boeing 737-212 Advanced
- 22 Boeing 737-291 Advanced
- 2 Boeing 737-2A1 Advanced
- 16 Convair 580

On Order
- 6 Boeing 737-291 Advanced
- 3 McDonnell Douglas DC-9-82

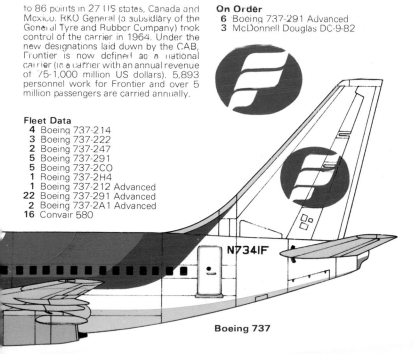

Boeing 737

Garuda Indonesian Airways

Garuda was established on 31 March 1950 as the national carrier; the Indonesian Government and KLM were equal shareholders. Garuda succeeded the post-war Inter-Island Division of KLM, which had been operating throughout the East Indies since August 1947, and the pre-war KNILM. The carrier's initial fleet comprised twenty DC-3s and eight Catalinas. Shortly afterwards Garuda acquired eight Convair 240 and fourteen De Havilland Heron aircraft. The carrier was nationalised in 1954 and eight Convair 340s were purchased. Garuda also commenced its first international service, to Singapore, in the same year. Lockheed Electra L-188C turboprops entered service at the beginning of 1961 and new routes were opened to Hong Kong later that year and to Tokyo in 1962. With the return of Irian Jaya (formerly Dutch New Guinea), the operations of the domestic airline De Kroonduif were absorbed by Garuda on 1 January 1963.

Jet operations were initiated following the introduction of Convair 990A aircraft in September 1963 on routes to Manila and Tokyo. Services to Rome, Prague, Frankfurt and Amsterdam through Bangkok, Bombay and Cairo were started in 1965 in association with KLM. Garuda took delivery of its first DC-8-55 in June 1966 and began services with the type to Sydney from Jakarta via Bali. DC-9-32 aircraft entered service on domestic and regional routes in 1969, followed by F.28 Fellowship 1000 aircraft in 1971. Garuda is currently the world's largest user of the F.28 Fellowship. Wide-bodied operations began to Amsterdam and Paris in April 1976 with DC-10-30s and the carrier's first Boeing 747-2U3B was received in August 1980. In October 1978 Garuda took over Merpati Nusantara Airlines which was formed by the Indonesian Government on 6 September 1962 and operated services in Borneo, Irian Jaya and a number of regional routes. Merpati continues to operate under its own name.

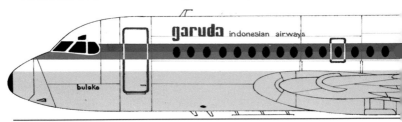

Gulf Air

Gulf Air was formed on 24 March 1950 as Gulf Aviation Company Limited by F. Bosworth, and from modest beginnings the carrier has grown rapidly to become a full international airline and the national carrier for the Gulf states of Bahrain, Qatar, Oman and the United Arab Emirates. Services connecting Bahrain, Doha, Dhahran and Sharjah began with a single Anson aircraft and, later, Dove aircraft. In October 1951 BOAC became a major shareholder; four De Havilland Herons were purchased the following year, at which time services to Abu Dhabi, Dubai, Kuwait and Muscat were started. Four DC-3s were acquired to meet the increasing traffic demand and also to operate charters on behalf of petroleum companies. Gulf Aviation took delivery of its first Fokker F.27 Friendship 400 on 6 January 1967, having earlier chartered Viscount capacity from Middle East Airlines.

Jet operations started with Trident 1E aircraft chartered from Kuwait Airways prior to the arrival of Gulf Aviation's first One-Eleven 432 in January 1970. That year saw the extension of services to Karachi, and the opening of a London route with VC-10 Type 1101 aircraft leased from BOAC. The carrier formally adopted its present title in late 1973, and on 1 April 1974 the Gulf States of Bahrain, Oman, Qatar and the UAE became sole owners of the carrier with equal shareholdings. "Golden Falcon" services from the Gulf to London were initiated that year with VC-10 Type 1101s purchased from British Airways. Wide-bodied operations on long haul services began in 1976 following delivery of the carrier's first Lockheed TriStar 100 on 16 January of that year. Boeing 737-2P6 (Advanced) aircraft entered service on regional routes in 1977 replacing the One-Elevens.

Gulf Air currently operates a network of scheduled passenger and cargo services

Garuda currently operates an extensive domestic network linking Jakarta with 31 destinations throughout the Indonesian archipelago. Scheduled passenger and cargo services are now operated to Amsterdam, London, Frankfurt, Paris, Rome, Zurich, Vienna, Athens, Abu Dhabi, Jeddah, Colombo, Karachi, Bombay, Bangkok, Kuala Lumpur, Singapore, Hong Kong, Tokyo, Sydney, Perth and Melbourne. Airbus A300B4-220 aircraft, the first to feature a forward-facing two-man cockpit, entered service during 1982. Garuda employs c.6,000 personnel.

Fleet Data
- 6 Airbus Industrie A300B4-220
- 4 Boeing 747-2U3B
- 21 Fokker F.28 Fellowship 1000
- 5 Fokker F.28 Fellowship 3000R
- 2 Fokker F.28 Fellowship 3000RC
- 7 Fokker F.28 Fellowship 4000
- 24 McDonnell Douglas DC-9-32
- 6 McDonnell Douglas DC-10-30

On Order
- 2 Boeing 747-200B
- 1 Fokker F.28 Fellowship 4000

Note: Garuda has ordered 6 Fokker F.27 Friendship 500 aircraft for operation by Merpati Nusantara.

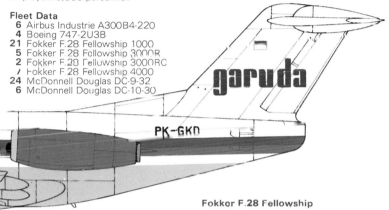

Fokker F.28 Fellowship

linking Bahrain with Abu Dhabi, Amman, Amsterdam, Baghdad, Beirut, Bangkok, Bombay, Cairo, Colombo, Dhahran, Delhi, Doha, Dubai, Hong Kong, Jeddah, Karachi, Kuwait, Larnaca, London, Muscat, Manila, Paris, Ras Al Khaimah, Salalah, Sharjah and Tehran. Gulf Air employs 4,100 personnel and carried 2,100,000 passengers in 1980. Gulf Air also undertakes charter services and subsidiaries of the carrier include Gulf Helicopters Limited and hotel and airport handling interests.

Fleet Data
- 9 Boeing 737-2P6 Advanced
- 4 Fokker F.27 Friendship 600
  (one leased from Danish Aero Lease)
- 5 Lockheed L-1011-385
  TriStar 100
- 3 Lockheed L-1011-385
  TriStar 200
- 2 Shorts Skyliner 100
- 3 Shorts Skyvan 3

Note: Gulf Air operates a VC-10 Type 1101 on behalf of the Qatar Government.

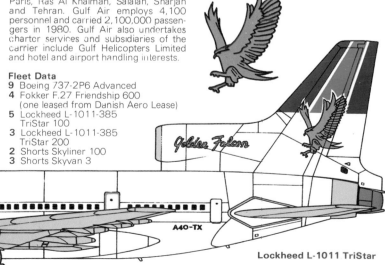

Lockheed L-1011 TriStar

Iberia

Iberia (Lineas Aéreas de Espana) was originally formed in 1927 with service commencing between Madrid and Barcelona on 14 December of that year. In 1928 Iberia merged with CETA and Unión Aérea Española to form CLASSA (Compañia de Lineas Aéreas Subvencionadas S.A.) which initiated operations on 27 May 1929 from Madrid to Seville with Junkers aircraft. International service commenced on the Madrid-Biarritz route on 19 August. In 1931 the carrier became Lineas Aéreas Postales Españolas and by 1933 had opened routes to Bordeaux, Paris, Casablanca and Las Palmas. DC-2 aircraft were purchased and in 1937 the carrier adopted the former name of Iberia once more. The carrier had been 51% owned by the Spanish Government with the balance owned by Deutsche Luft Hansa and private interests. In August 1943 the Instituto Nacional de Industria, a State organisation, purchased the Deutsche Luft Hansa and private holdings and acquired complete control of Iberia the following year. DC-3s were introduced into service in 1944 and

Madrid-London services commenced on 3 May 1946. Transatlantic services to Buenos Aires were initiated with DC-4 aircraft on 22 September 1946 in co-operation with FAMA, the Argentine airline. Service to Caracas was added to the network in April 1949, and Mexico City and Havana were served from March 1950. Three Super Constellations were acquired in 1954 and opened the New York route in September. Jet operations were started with the purchase of DC-8-52 aircraft which replaced the Lockheed Constellation on the New York route from July 1961. The first of many Caravelle VI-R aircraft entered service on 1 May 1962 between Madrid and Zurich. The Caravelles were initially supplemented and later replaced by progressive acquisition of DC-9-32 aircraft, the first of which was delivered in June 1967. Fokker F.27 Friendships were acquired in the same year for thin domestic routes. Following introduction of Boeing 747-156 aircraft into service at the end of 1970, Iberia became a member of the ATLAS Group

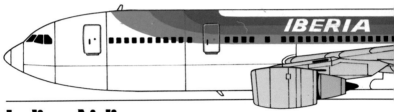

Indian Airlines

Indian Airlines came into being as a State corporation on 28 May 1953 as a consequence of India's 1953 Air Corporation Act, which was aimed at rationalising the fragmented domestic operations within the country. The assets and liabilities of eight major domestic operators (including Air India Limited, Airways (India) Limited, Air Services of India Limited, Deccan Aviation Limited, Indian National Airways and Kalinga Airways) were acquired by Indian Airlines and operations by the new carrier commenced on 1 August 1953. The fleet comprised ninety-nine piston-engined aircraft, including DC-3s, DC-4s and Vikings, and an equipment modernisation plan was formulated. Viscount 768 aircraft joined the fleet in 1957, with service inauguration on 10 October 1957, and the Fokker F.27 Friendship 100 began operations with Indian Airlines in May 1961. The carrier entered the jet era with the introduction of Caravelle VI-Ns on

services from February 1964. These aircraft provided the mainstay of Indian Airlines' fleet until the introduction of the HS-748 (assembled under licence by Hindustan Aeronautics Limited at Kanpur) with deliveries starting in June 1967. The carrier's first Boeing 737-2A8 was received on 9 November 1970, and the type eventually replaced the Caravelle aircraft. Wide-bodied service commenced in December 1976 with the acquisition of the carrier's first A300B2-1C Airbus.

Indian Airlines operates as an autonomous corporation under the administrative control of the Ministry of Tourism and Civil Aviation. Operations are organised into four regions controlled from Bombay, Calcutta, Delhi and Madras, and a 68 point domestic network is currently operated, as well as international services to 8 destinations in Afghanistan, Bangladesh, the Maldive Islands, Nepal, Pakistan and Sri Lanka. An average of 210 services are

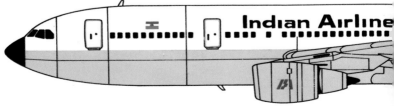

(which also consisted of Air France, Alitalia, Lufthansa and Sabena) involved with technical co-operation. Boeing 727-256 aircraft entered domestic trunk and European service following initial delivery in April 1972, and DC-10-30s were acquired from March 1973. The first A300B4-120 was delivered in March 1981 for introduction on European routes.

Iberia operates an extensive domestic and European route system as well as long haul services to North, Central and South America, Africa and the Middle East. Approximately 13·8 million passengers were carried in 1980 and over 23,500 personnel are employed. The carrier has interests in Aviaco and Transeuropa (60% owned), both being charter operators.

Fleet Data
- **4** Airbus Industrie A300B4-120
- **37** Boeing 727-256 Advanced
- **6** Boeing 747-256B
- **6** Fokker F.27 Friendship 000
- **1** McDonnell Douglas DC-8-63
- **2** McDonnell Douglas DC-8-63CF

- **27** McDonnell Douglas DC-9-32
- **4** McDonnell Douglas DC-9-33RC
- **8** McDonnell Douglas DC-10-30

On Order
- **5** Airbus Industrie A300B4-120

Airbus Industrie A300

---

provided daily over the carrier's 30,857 mile (49,657/km) system. Indian Airlines has developed into one of the world's largest regional carriers and currently handles over 17,000 passengers a day. In addition to scheduled and charter operations, Indian Airlines operates a night air mail system linking the country's four major cities. The carrier also provides leased 737 capacity, together with support for Maldive International Airlines, established jointly by Indian Airlines and the government of the Maldive Islands in 1977. Over 17,800 personnel are currently employed by Indian Airlines.

Fleet Data
- **8** Airbus Industrie A300B2-1C
- **5** Boeing 737-2A8
- **15** Boeing 737-2A8 Advanced
- **1** Boeing 737-2A8C Advanced
- **8** Fokker F.27 Friendship 100
- **12** HAL/BAe(HS) 748-224 Series 2

On Order
- **2** Airbus Industrie A300B2-1C
- **4** Boeing 737-2A8 Advanced

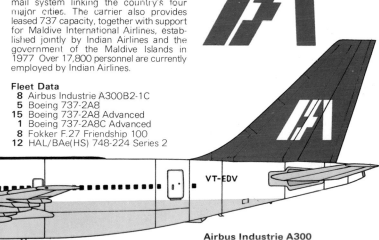

VT-EDV

Airbus Industrie A300

Interflug

Gesellschaft für Internationalen Flugverkehr GmbH (Interflug) is the national carrier of the German Democratic Republic and was formed as Deutsche Lufthansa in May 1954. Scheduled operations commenced on 4 February 1956 between Berlin and Warsaw using Ilyushin Il-14 aircraft, followed by services to Prague, Budapest and Sofia on 16 May, Bucharest on 19 May and Moscow on 7 October of that year. Domestic services were inaugurated on 16 June 1957 from Berlin to Barth, Dresden, Erfurt and Leipzig. On 18 September 1958 the carrier formed a subsidiary called Interflug GmbH to operate international services to the west. The subsidiary's title was determined by a ruling of the International Court of Justice at the Hague to avoid confusion with the West German Lufthansa. The subsidiary Interflug was run jointly by its parent airline and the Deutsche Reisebüro (German State Travel Agency), and operated its first service between Copenhagen and Leipzig on 27 February 1959 in association with the Leipzig Trade Fair.

Ilyushin Il-18 turboprops entered service on the Berlin–Moscow route in 1960 and the carrier adopted the title of Interflug for all operations in September 1963. Antonov An-24 aircraft were introduced on domestic services in 1966 and jet operations commenced following delivery of Tupolev Tu-134s ordered in 1967. Ilyushin Il-62 aircraft entered service with Interflug in 1970 and inaugurated a Berlin–Havana route via Gander in 1974. The international route network was progressively expanded to include services to Baghdad, Algiers, Cairo, Damascus, Istanbul, Larnaca, Amsterdam, Helsinki, Copenhagen, Stockholm and Milan in addition to further East

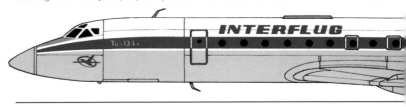

Iran Air

Iran Air (Iran National Airlines Corporation), also known as Homa (an acronym of its Persian name), was established in February 1962 through the merger of Iranian Airways and Persian Air Services to become the state-owned national carrier. Iranian Airways was formed as a private airline in December 1944 and began operations on 31 May 1945. The first scheduled service was inaugurated in May 1946 linking Teheran and Meshed, and a domestic network was subsequently developed using DC-3 aircraft. Regional services to Baghdad, Beirut and Cairo were initiated by the end of 1946, and a route to Paris was opened in April 1947. In 1949 Iranian absorbed Eagle Airlines, formed in 1948 and operating domestic services with one D.H. Dove aircraft. Transocean Airlines, a US supplemental carrier, provided technical assistance from 1954, and Iranian subsequently acquired DC-4 and Convair 240 aircraft. Viscount 782 services started in May 1958. Persian Air Services was formed in 1954 and commenced operations the following year with a cargo service between Teheran and Geneva using Avro Yorks operated under charter by Trans Mediterranean Airways. Regional and international services were developed, and in 1960 a DC-7C was leased from Sabena, followed by a Boeing 707 leased from the same source.

The state-owned carrier, Iran Air, commenced jet operations with Boeing 727-86 aircraft on 4 July 1965, and the route network was subsequently expanded to include London, Frankfurt and Moscow. In the meantime the carrier had signed a three year agreement with Pan American in 1964 covering the provision of management and technical assistance. Boeing 707-386C aircraft entered service in 1970 and were later used to inaugurate service to Tokyo in 1974. Boeing 737-286 (Advanced) aircraft were acquired in 1971 and commenced operations on domestic and regional services. Wide-bodied operations began with the introduction of Boeing 747SP-86 aircraft in March 1976 and services to New York with the type were subsequently initiated.

Scheduled passenger and cargo services are currently operated to 18 domestic points and to Abu Dhabi, Athens, Bahrain,

European destinations. Recent route developments include services to Hanoi, Luanda and Addis Ababa.

Interflug currently operates scheduled passenger and cargo services to 46 destinations in 36 countries covering 77,700 miles (125,000km) in unduplicated route distance. Approximately 1,200,000 passengers were carried in 1980. Charter Services are also undertaken and a separate division handles agricultural and aerial survey activities.

Fleet Data
14 Ilyushin Il-18D
5 Ilyushin Il-62
1 Ilyushin Il-62M
6 Tupolev Tu-134
12 Tupolev Tu-134A

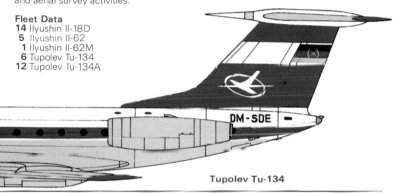

Tupolev Tu-134

Cairo, Bombay, Dhahran, Doha, Dubai, Frankfurt, Geneva, Istanbul, Kabul, Karachi, Kuwait, London, Moscow, Muscat, Paris, Rome, Vienna and Zurich. Charter operations are also undertaken. The change of government in 1979, and the current war with Iraq, are having their effect on Iran Air's operations and re-equipment programme. The carrier is nevertheless proceeding with the acquisition of a fleet of A300B2-203 aircraft, two of which are in service. Iran Air employs approximately 9,000 personnel.

Fleet Data
2 Airbus Industrie A300B2-203
1 Boeing 707-321B
1 Boeing 707-321C
3 Boeing 707-386C
3 Boeing 727-86
5 Boeing 727-286 Advanced
2 Boeing 737-286 Advanced
2 Boeing 737-286C Advanced
4 Boeing 747SP-86
2 Boeing 747-286B (SCD)
1 Boeing 747-186B
3 Boeing 747-2J9F (SCD)

On Order
4 Airbus Industrie A300B2-203

Boeing 747

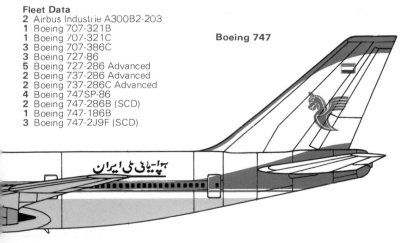

Iraqi Airways

Iraqi Airways was founded in December 1945 as a subsidiary of the government-owned Iraqi State Railways. Operations got under way on 29 January 1946 with a domestic service between Baghdad and Basra using D.H. Rapide aircraft, and a Baghdad-Mosul route was opened in the following May. By the end of that year Iraqi had started international services to Beirut, Damascus, Lydda (now Lod) and Cairo with DC-3s, and within two years the network had been expanded to include Teheran, Kuwait, Bahrain, Cyprus and Athens. Viscount 735 aircraft were acquired in 1955 and the type commenced operations on the Beirut service on 1 November of that year. Services to London which had been inaugurated in 1948 were restarted in April 1956 with Viscounts. On 1 April 1960 the carrier became financially independent of Iraqi State Railways. During Iraqi's formative years (until January 1960), BOAC provided the carrier with technical assistance and personnel.

Jet operations were initiated on London services in November 1965 following delivery of the first of three Trident 1E aircraft. A major re-equipment programme covering a fleet of Boeing 707-370C, 727-270 (Advanced) and 737-270C (Advanced) aircraft was completed during 1976 and wide-bodied services were introduced with Boeing 747-270C (SCD) aircraft in the same year. In addition to its domestic network, Iraqi Airways currently operates to a number of destinations in the Middle East, Europe, Asia and North Africa. Approximately 5,100 personnel are em-

Japan Air Lines

JAL (Nihon Koku Kabushiki Kaisha) was established in its original form on 1 August 1951 as a private company. The previous national carrier (Greater Japan Airways) had ceased operations in 1945. JAL commenced services on the Tokyo-Osaka route with a leased Martin 202 on 25 October 1951. The carrier took delivery of its own aircraft, DC-4s, in October 1952, and placed an order for five DC-6A/Bs for international services. The financial requirements of such expansion resulted in dissolution of JAL in August 1953, to be replaced by a national carrier of the same name, with 50% government financial participation. The carrier's first DC-6B was delivered on 15 September 1953 and commenced services between Tokyo and Sapporo on 2 October, the day after the new carrier was legally established. After flight trials over the Tokyo-San Francisco route via Wake Island and Honolulu had taken place, JAL's first regular international commercial service was inaugurated over the route on 2 February 1954. International services were subsequently expanded to Hong Kong, Bangkok and Singapore. DC-7C aircraft commenced JAL service in January 1958, and a Tokyo-Paris polar service was inaugurated with Boeing 707-328 equipment in association with Air France on 1 April 1960. Jet operations with the carrier's own equipment were started on the Tokyo-San Francisco route with DC-8-32 aircraft on 12 August 1960.

JAL introduced the Convair 880 into domestic service between Tokyo and Sapporo in September 1961, and the following month the type began serving JAL's south-east Asian routes. The Boeing 727-46 came into service between Tokyo and Fukuoka on 1 August 1965, and by the end of that year JAL's last DC-7C aircraft had been retired from service. The operation of a round-the-world service was finally realised on 6 March 1967 via Honolulu, San Francisco, New York, Europe and the Middle East. This service was terminated in 1972. Service from Tokyo to Moscow was inaugurated on 18 April 1967 in association with Aeroflot using Tupolev Tu-114s. Wide-bodied operations began on JAL's trans-Pacific routes from 1 July 1970 with Boeing 747-146 aircraft, and 747SR-46 (short range) aircraft began serving the Tokyo-Okinawa route in October

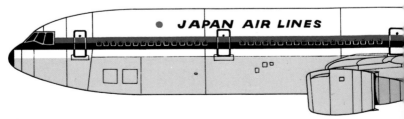

ployed. The continuing war with Iran is having an effect on the carrier's operations at present.

Fleet Data
5 Antonov An-12
(operated for the government)
2 Antonov An-24TV
2 Antonov An-24V
3 Boeing 707-370C
5 Boeing 727-270 Advanced
3 Boeing 737-270C Advanced
2 Boeing 747-270C (SCD)
5 Ilyushin Il-761
(operated for the government)
2 Tupolev Tu-124
(operated for the government)

On Order
1 Boeing 727-270 Advanced
2 Boeing 747-270C

Boeing 727

1973. The first DC-10-40 was delivered to the carrier in 1976 and on 7 March 1980 JAL became the first airline to operate scheduled wide bodied services to Beijing, using DC-10-40 aircraft. The carrier's 100 millionth domestic passenger was carried on 10 April 1981.

JAL currently operates an extensive network of scheduled passenger and cargo services linking 11 domestic points and over 40 international destinations in Japan, Australia, New Zealand, Asia, the Middle East, North, Central and South America, and Europe. Nearly 15 million passengers were carried by JAL in the 1980/81 fiscal year and over 22,000 employees work for the carrier. JAL operates the largest Boeing 747 fleet outside the USA having 41 in service. The carrier is also the biggest DC-10-40 operator in the world, using the type on both domestic and international routes.

Fleet Data
2 Boeing 727-46
7 Boeing 747-146
1 Boeing 747-146F
20 Boeing 747-246B
4 Boeing 747-246F
9 Boeing 747SR-40
1 McDonnell Douglas DC-8 55F
9 McDonnell Douglas DC 8-62
4 McDonnell Douglas DC-8-62AF
9 McDonnell Douglas DC 8-61
19 McDonnell Douglas DC-10-40

On Order
1 McDonnell Douglas DC-10-40

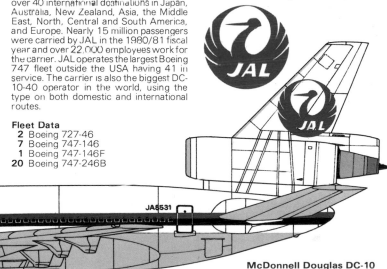

McDonnell Douglas DC-10

Jugoslovenski Aerotransport

Jugoslovenski Aerotransport (JAT-Yugoslav Airlines) was formed by the Yugoslav government in 1946 to replace air services temporarily provided by military aircraft. Domestic operations commenced in 1947 with Junkers Ju 52/3m aircraft. DC-3 aircraft were subsequently introduced into service, and by the end of 1947 JAT's network radiated from Belgrade to the main cities in the country and to several East European nations including Romania, Hungary and Czechoslovakia. Operations were suspended in 1948 following Yugoslavia's break with the Soviet Union. Domestic services began to be flown again in October of that year and some international services in 1949. The emphasis now switched to development of international routes to West European destinations and Convair 340 aircraft were acquired in 1953 to operate these services. Two DC-6B aircraft were purchased in 1958 to cater for the longer European routes and Convair 440s were added to supplement the Convair 340 aircraft. A number of Ilyushin Il-14s entered service in 1957, primarily on domestic and non-scheduled operations.

JAT commenced jet operations following delivery of the first Caravelle VI-N and new routes to Amsterdam, Berlin and Moscow were opened with it. Five DC-9-32 aircraft were acquired in 1970, JAT having leased a DC-9-32 from Alitalia in 1969, and these supplemented the Caravelles on European services. The carrier received its first Boeing 727-2H9 (Advanced) in June 1974, and wide-bodied operations were initiated following delivery of DC-10-30 aircraft at the end of 1978.

JAT currently operates a very extensive

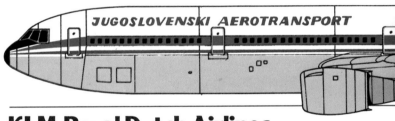

KLM-Royal Dutch Airlines

KLM (Koninklijke Luchvaart Maatschappij NV) was founded on 7 October 1919 and is the world's oldest airline still operating under its own name. The first and now oldest air route in the world was opened on 17 May 1920 between Amsterdam and London with a leased De Havilland D.H.16. In the subsequent years a European network was developed and various types of Fokker aircraft introduced into service. Initial services to the East Indies in 1929 led to the opening of a weekly service from Amsterdam to Batavia (now Jakarta) in October 1931. The DC-2 entered KLM service in 1935, and in 1937 the carrier became the first European operator of the DC-3 aircraft. Services in the West Indies based on Curacao were initiated in 1935 and were developed to serve Colombia, Venezuela, Barbados, Trinidad and the Guiana's. These services were continued throughout World War II, and subsequently extended to Cuba and Miami. On 21 May 1946 KLM started scheduled services to New York, making the carrier the first European airline to operate flights between the two continents after the war. South America and South Africa were added to the network in 1946 and 1947 respectively, and Australia was included in KLM's route network from 1951. DC6, DC-6B, Constellation and Super Constellation aircraft serviced the long haul routes at that time, while Convair 240 and 340 aircraft were employed on the European network. The DC-7C entered service in April 1957 and began a trans-polar Amsterdam-Tokyo route on 1 November 1958. Viscount 803 aircraft entered service on European routes in 1957, and the Electra began serving with the carrier in 1959, primarily on Middle and Far East routes. KLM became the first non-US airline to operate the DC-8 in April 1960. The DC-9 began to replace the Viscount and Electra aircraft from April 1966, and the 747B entered service with the carrier in January 1971, with the McDonnell Douglas DC-10-30 following by the end of 1972.

KLM currently flies to 117 points in 73 countries, providing a route network of scheduled passenger and cargo services from Amsterdam covering Europe, North and Latin America, Africa, the Near, Middle and Far East and Australia. The route system extends over some 224,947 miles

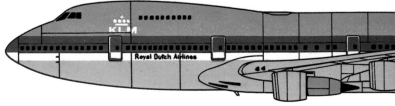

domestic system covering 16 points and scheduled passenger and cargo services are operated to 37 cities in Western and Eastern Europe, Scandinavia, North Africa, North America, and the Middle and Far East. Approximately 5,800 personnel are employed by JAT. Air Yugoslavia is a wholly-owned subsidiary formed in the late 1960s to operate charters mainly to countries such as Australia and the USA where large numbers of Yugoslav emigrants live. It charters aircraft from JAT when they are needed.

Fleet Data
- **2** Boeing 707-340C
- **2** Boeing 707-351C
- **9** Boeing 727-2H9 Advanced
- **13** McDonnell Douglas DC-9-32
- **2** McDonnell Douglas DC-10-30

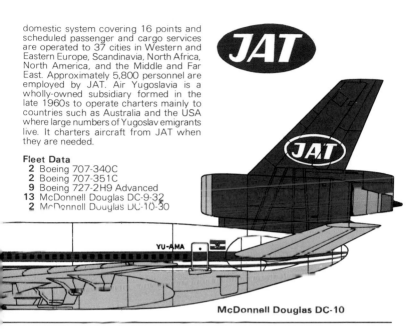

McDonnell Douglas DC-10

(362,300km) and the airline carried 4,293,000 passengers in the 1980-81 fiscal year. The Netherlands Government holds a 74.9% shareholding in KLM with the remainder of shares in private hands. The carrier currently employs 18,753 personnel, of whom some 15,050 are based in the Netherlands, and is a member of the KSSU Group (also including SAS, Swissair and UTA) which undertakes technical-operational co-operation on the 747 and DC-10.

KLM, which claims to be the sixth largest international air carrier, owns a number of subsidiaries which include NLM City Hopper, a domestic and regional operator founded in 1966, KLM Helicopters established in October 1965 and undertaking general offshore support duties and charters, and KLM Aerocarto which carries out survey work.

Fleet Data
- **9** Boeing 747-206B
- **7** Boeing 747-206B (SCD)
- **1** McDonnell Douglas DC-8-55F
- **11** McDonnell Douglas DC-8-63
- **2** McDonnell Douglas DC-9-15
- **12** McDonnell Douglas DC-9-32
- **6** McDonnell Douglas DC-9-33RC
- **8** McDonnell Douglas DC-10-30

On Order
- **10** Airbus Industrie A310-202
- **1** Boeing 747-206B (SCD)

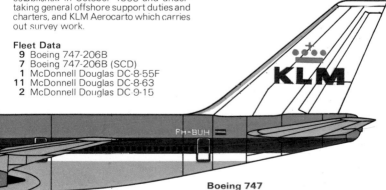

Boeing 747

243

Korean Air Lines

Korean Air Lines was formed as a government-owned carrier in June 1962 to succeed Korean National Airlines which was organised in 1945 by Captain Yong Wook Shinn, the country's first licensed pilot. Korean National was granted a permit in 1948 to establish scheduled domestic services, and operations from Seoul to Kusan, Kwanju, Pusan and Chunmunjin were started with Stinson aircraft. DC-3s were acquired in April 1950 and international services to Tokyo commenced in 1952, followed by services to Hong Kong in 1954.

Korean Air Lines, as it then was, introduced F.27 Friendship 200 aircraft in January 1964. Services to Fukuoka and Osaka were initiated and the Hong Kong route re-opened in 1966. Jet operations began following the delivery of a DC-9-32 aircraft in July 1967, and two former Eastern Air Lines Boeing 720-025s were added to the fleet in 1969. Wide-bodied operations with Boeing 747-2B5B aircraft began in

May 1973, and the first DC-10-30 was delivered in February 1978. Korean became one of the early operators of the Airbus when its first A300B4-2C aircraft was delivered on 31 August 1978.

Scheduled services are currently operated from Seoul, Pusan and Cheju to Tokyo, Nagoya, Osaka, Fukuoka, Kumamoto, Taipei, Manila, Hong Kong, Honolulu, New York, Los Angeles, Bangkok, Singapore, Bahrain, Dhahran, Jeddah, Zurich and Paris. The carrier was acquired by the Han Jin Transport Group in 1969. 9,859 personnel are employed by Korean Air lines, and a total of 3,600,589 passengers were carried in 1980.

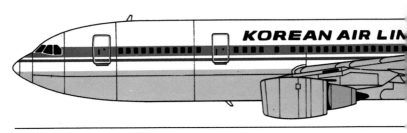

Kuwait Airways

The carrier was formed in late 1953 as Kuwait National Airways and began scheduled operations from Kuwait to Basra and Beirut in 1954 with DC-3 aircraft. Services to Bahrain and Cairo were introduced in 1956, and the carrier adopted the title of Kuwait Airways Corporation (KAC) in March of the following year. On 1 June 1958 BOAC took over management of the carrier under a five-year contract, and in March 1959 KAC absorbed British International Airlines, a BOAC subsidiary providing local charter services. Operations with Viscount 754 aircraft leased from MEA were inaugurated in 1958, replacing DC-4 equipment. By 1963 the carrier had become wholly-owned by the government of Kuwait and adopted its present title.

Kuwait Airways took delivery of its first Comet 4C on 18 January 1963, and a

London service with the type was inaugurated in March 1964. During the following month the carrier acquired Trans Arabia Airways, a major competitor since 1959. The latter operated a fleet of DC-6B aircraft on services throughout the Middle East and to London. The first of three Trident 1E aircraft for Kuwait Airways was delivered in March 1966, and the type subsequently operated on all regional services. An order for three One-Eleven 301 aircraft, however, was not taken up and the aircraft entered service with British Eagle. Boeing 707-369Cs entered service in 1968, and wide-bodied operations commenced in 1978 following delivery of the carrier's first Boeing 747-269B on 28 July. Routes to New York and Manila were opened in December 1980.

Kuwait Airways now operates scheduled

Fleet Data

 8 Airbus Industrie A300B4-2C
   (two leased to Saudia)
 1 Boeing 707-321B
 2 Boeing 707-321C
 2 Boeing 707-338C
 1 Boeing 707-373C
 1 Boeing 707-3B5C
 2 Boeing 727-22
 4 Boeing 727-281
 2 Boeing 747SP-B5
 3 Boeing 747-230B
   (one leased from ITEL)
 1 Boeing 747-230F
 5 Boeing 747-2B5B
 3 Boeing 747-2B5F (SCD)
   (one leased to Saudia)
 1 CASA 212-CB Aviocar
 4 McDonnell Douglas DC-10-30
 1 McDonnell Douglas DC-10-30CF

On Order

 1 Boeing 747-2B5B
 1 Boeing 747-2B5F (SCD)

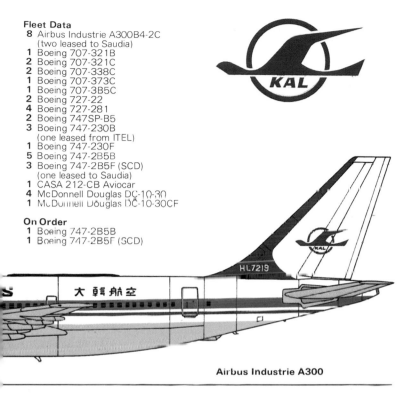

Airbus Industrie A300

passenger and cargo services to 39 destinations in 37 countries in the Middle and Far East, Europe, Africa and America. The carrier currently employs 6,198 personnel, and transported 1,076,214 passengers in 1980.

Fleet Data

 5 Boeing 707-369C
 1 Boeing 707-321C
 1 Boeing 707-311C
 4 Boeing 727-269 Advanced
 4 Boeing 747-269B (SCD)

On Order

11 Airbus Industrie A310

Boeing 727

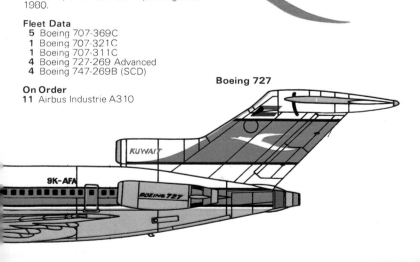

LanChile

LanChile (Lineas Aereas Chilenas) is the second oldest airline in South America and was founded on 5 March 1929 as a branch of the Chilean Air Force. The carrier, originally known as Linea Aeropostal Santiago-Arica, commenced operations between Santiago and Arica with D.H.60G Gipsy Moths. In 1932 the carrier became independent of the Air Force and adopted its present title, although LanChile remained a government-owned concern. Two Junkers Ju 86 aircraft were introduced during 1938 and the first of six Lockheed 10A Electras were delivered in 1941. Following the acquisition of Lodestars, LanChile used the type in 1946 to inaugurate international operations with a service from Santiago to Buenos Aires which was later extended to Montevideo. Procurement of Martin 2-0-2s and D.H. Doves from 1949 onwards facilitated an expansion of domestic services. Similar expansion of the international network, to Peru and Ecuador, followed the delivery of three DC-6B aircraft in 1955. Miami was added to the system in August 1958, and this route was later extended to New York. LanChile commenced jet operations following the delivery of the first of three Caravelle VI-R aircraft in March 1964, and the HS.748 turboprop entered service with the carrier in July 1967. In April of that year LanChile initiated service to New York with a Boeing 707-330B acquired from Lufthansa, and subsequently opened a European route with the type. Passenger services to Easter Island were started on 3 April 1967, and these were later extended to Papeete (Tahiti) thereby forming the first regular air link between South America and the South Pacific. In 1974 LanChile operated a Boeing 707 transpolar flight between Punta Arenas and Sydney and thus became the first airline to link South America with Australia via the South Pole. Wide-bodied operations began in December 1980 with a DC-10-30 aircraft leased initially from Laker Airways.

Libyan Arab Airlines

Libyan Arab Airlines was founded as Kingdom of Libya Airlines (KLA) in September 1964 and the carrier subsequently absorbed two existing Libyan operators, Libiavia and United Libyan Airlines. Libiavia started operations in July 1958 and provided services between Tripoli and Ankara using a DC-6B leased from UAT (now UTA). Services to Athens were added in May 1969 and Benghazi and Sebha were subsequently included in the network. KLA began operations with Caravelle VI-R aircraft and developed new international services while the domestic operations were contracted out to Aero Trasporti Italiani who used F.27 Friendship 200 aircraft based at Tripoli.

The carrier adopted its current title in September 1969 following the revolution, and subsequently acquired Boeing 727-224 aircraft in January 1971 to supplement and eventually replace the Caravelle fleet. Libyan Arab Airlines took over domestic operations, acquiring its own F.27 aircraft. The carrier currently operates a domestic system which links Tripoli with 6 other points in the country. Scheduled passenger and cargo services are also operated from Tripoli, Benghazi and Sebha to Rome, Paris, London, Athens, Casablanca, Zurich, Damascus, Jeddah, Tunis, Belgrade, Istanbul, Niamey, Frankfurt, Warsaw, Moscow, Sofia, Amman, Cotonou, Algiers and Malta. A number of flights are provided in support of oil operations in the country. Libyan Arab Airlines employs c. 2,500 personnel.

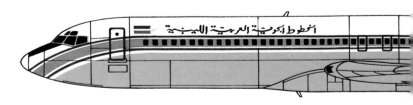

Following recent substantial rationalisation and re-organisation, LanChile has emerged as a successful carrier operating a five-point domestic system and international services from Santiago to Easter Island, Papeete, Buenos Aires, Montevideo, Rio de Janeiro, Madrid, Paris, Frankfurt, Caracas, La Paz, Lima, Panama, Miami and New York, representing a total unduplicated route distance of 26,926 miles (43,216km). A total of 449,400 passengers were carried in 1981, and LanChile currently employs approximately 1,600 personnel.

Fleet Data
- **2** Boeing 707-321B
- **2** Boeing 707-330B
- **1** Boeing 707-351C
- **1** Boeing 707-385C
- **1** Boeing 737-2A1 Advanced
- **1** Boeing 737-2S2C Advanced
- **1** McDonnell Douglas DC-10-30
  (leased from Pan Am)

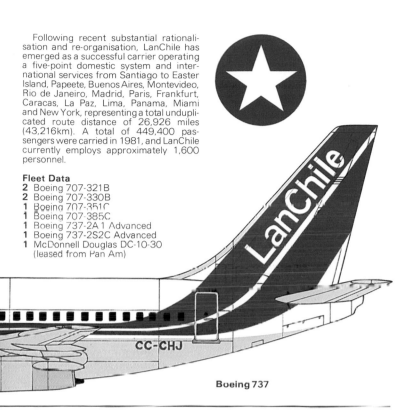

CC-CHJ

Boeing 737

Fleet Data
- **1** Boeing 707-3L5C
  (operated for the government)
- **1** Boeing 727-224
- **9** Boeing 727-2L5 Advanced
- **3** Fokker F.27 Friendship 400
- **7** Fokker F.27 Friendship 600
- **5** Ilyushin Il-76M
  (operated for the government)

On Order
- **6** Airbus Industrie A300B4-200
- **4** Airbus Industrie A310-200
- **8** Fokker F.27 Friendship 600

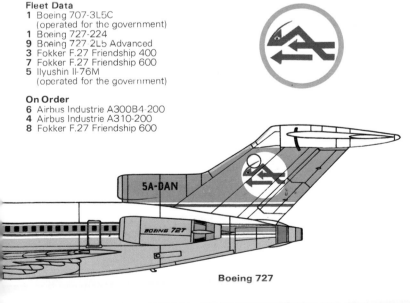

5A-DAN

BOEING 727

Boeing 727

LOT

LOT (Polskie Linie Lotnicze) was established as a state-owned carrier by the Polish government on 1 January 1929 to take over the two existing private operators, Aerotarg and Aerolot. Aerotarg was formed in May 1921 and operated domestic services from Warsaw. Aerolot was founded as Aerolloyd in 1922 and operated Junkers F.13 aircraft on domestic services and, in 1925, the country's first international routes to Austria and Czechoslovakia. LOT became a full member of IATA in 1931 and undertook a major expansion programme resulting in a network which covered thirteen countries by 1939, and a fleet of twenty-six aircraft including Lockheed 10A Electras, Lockheed 14s and Douglas DC-2s. The formidable task of re-establishing LOT after the adversities of war began early in 1945. Initially domestic services were restarted, and subsequently international routes to Berlin, Paris, Prague, Moscow and Stockholm were opened using Li-2 aircraft (Russian-built DC-3s). SE-161 Languedocs were used for a short while but were superseded by Ilyushin Il-12 aircraft in 1949. LOT subsequently introduced Ilyushin Il-14s and ex-Sabena Convair 240s, and in May 1961 the Il-18 turboprop commenced operations with the carrier, later inaugurating service to Cairo. Former BUA Viscount 804 aircraft were acquired in 1962, and the carrier's first Antonov An-24 entered service in April 1966.

Jet operations with the Tupolev Tu-134 started in November 1968, and from May 1972 the Ilyushin Il-62 began serving on the London, Paris and Moscow routes. Services to New York and Montreal were subsequently inaugurated, and in September 1977 LOT initiated scheduled operations to Bangkok via Baghdad and Bombay.

Lufthansa

The carrier was formed in 1953 as Luftag to succeed its pre-war forerunner, Deutsche Luft Hansa (DLH), which was established on 6 January 1926 through a merger of Deutscher Aero Lloyd AG and Junkers AG Luftverkehr. The roots of DLH stem back to February 1919 when Deutsche Luft-Reederei, a former company, commenced scheduled services between Berlin and Weimar. DLH undertook considerable expansion, so that by 1939 the carrier was the leading airline in Europe with a fleet of 150 various aircraft types, a worldwide route network of nearly 50,000 miles (80,000km)) and carrying an annual total of over 250,000 passengers. The carrier ceased operations in April 1945 and an Allied ban on German aviation was imposed. Luftag was formed on 6 January 1953. Four Super Constellation aircraft were ordered on 26 June 1953, followed by an order for four Convair 340s. The carrier adopted its present title—Lufthansa (Deutsche Lufthansa AG)—in August 1954, and scheduled operations began on 1 April 1955 with domestic services between Hamburg, Dusseldorf, Köln/Bonn, Frankfurt and Munich. Service to London, Paris and Madrid followed shortly afterwards, and on 8 June of that year Lufthansa inaugurated Super Constellation services between Hamburg and New York, via Dusseldorf and Shannon. Services to Chicago, Buenos Aires and points in the Middle East were started in 1956. Substantial development of the domestic and European route system followed the service introduction of Convair 440 aircraft in 1957 and Viscount turboprop aircraft in 1958. By the end of 1959 a 44 point network existed. Boeing 707-430 services between Frankfurt and New York from March 1960, and to San Francisco in May of that year, marked the beginning of jet operations for Lufthansa. Boeing 720-030B aircraft were acquired in 1961 to operate European, Middle East and South America services. Lufthansa became the first European customer for the 727 aircraft, and European services with the type commenced in 1964. The carrier subsequently launched the 737 airliner with an order for 21 of the type being placed in 1965. Wide-bodied services were inaugurated with 747 aircraft in April 1970 on routes to North America, while DC-10 operations were started in

LOT currently operates a 12 point domestic network and international services to 40 destinations in 32 countries in Europe, the Middle East, North Africa, North America and Asia. Over two million passengers are flown annually and 5,211 personnel are employed by the carrier. LOT also undertakes extensive charter operations.

Fleet Data
- **1** Antonov An-12V
- **14** Antonov An-24V
- **2** Antonov An-24RV
- **6** Ilyushin Il-18V
- **2** Ilyushin Il-18E
- **1** Ilyushin Il-18D
- **6** Ilyushin Il-62
- **5** Ilyushin Il-62M
- **1** Tupolev Tu-134
- **7** Tupolev Tu-134A

On Order
Ilyushin Il-86 (unspecified number)
Yakovlev Yak-42 (unspecified number)

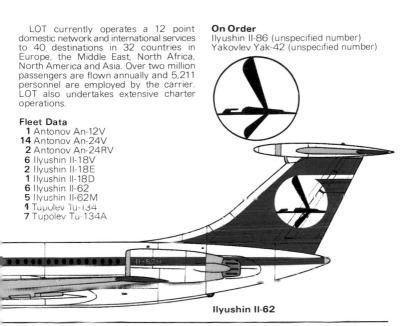

Ilyushin Il-62

1974 initially between Frankfurt and Rio de Janeiro. The Airbus A300 was introduced into service on European routes in April 1976, and three years later Lufthansa placed an order for 25 Airbus A310s, the first order for the model.

Lufthansa currently serves 120 points covering 69 countries in 6 continents through a network embracing Europe, Africa, the Near, Middle and Far East, Australia, North, Central and South America. The route system covers 251,761 miles (405,152km). Lufthansa employs 30,664 personnel and carried 13,943,853 passengers in 1980. The carrier is a member of the ATLAS consortium (also comprising Air France, Alitalia, Sabena and Iberia) established for technical co-operation on aircraft operation, and work is undertaken by Lufthansa on behalf of the ATLAS members.

Fleet Data
- **6** Airbus Industrie A300B2-1C
- **5** Airbus Industrie A300B4-2C (two leased to Air Algérie)
- **5** Boeing 707-330B
- **4** Boeing 707-330C
- **4** Boeing 727-230
- **30** Boeing 727-230 Advanced
- **36** Boeing 737-230 Advanced
- **3** Boeing 747-230B
- **8** Boeing 747-230B (SCD)
- **2** Boeing 747-230F (SCD)
- **14** McDonnell Douglas DC-10-30 (3 with Condor)

On Order
- **25** Airbus Industrie A310-201
- **2** Boeing 747-230B (SCD)

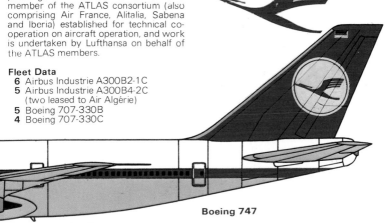

Boeing 747

Malaysian Airline System

MAS (Sistem Penerbangan Malaysia Berhard) was formed by the Government of Malaysia in April 1971 as the national carrier to succeed Malaysia-Singapore Airlines (MSA), following the decision by the respective governments to establish separate operations. The history of the carrier dates from 1937 with the registration of Malayan Airways Limited, a company formed by the Straits Steamship Company, the Ocean Steamship Company and Imperial Airways. During its first year of operation, in 1947, domestic services between Singapore, Kuala Lumpur, Ipoh, Penang, Kuantan and Kota Baru were inaugurated. Later in the year regional services to Jakarta, Palembang and Medan began when the airline took delivery of its first DC-3 aircraft. International services to Saigon were also initiated. In 1963 the carrier was renamed Malaysian Airways Limited and two years later the carrier

absorbed Borneo Airways. The title of Malaysia-Singapore Airlines was adopted following acquisition of a majority shareholding in the company by the Government of Malaysia and Singapore in 1966. The MSA fleet was steadily expanded to include F.27 Friendships, Boeing 737 and 707 aircraft.

Following the split-up of MSA, the new carrier, MAS, began operations on 1 October 1972, taking over the former MSA routes in the Malayan peninsula, Sabah and Sarawak. The initial route network comprised only 6 international destinations and 34 domestic points, operated by seven 737s, nine F.27 Friendships and three Britten-Norman Islander aircraft. Based at Subang International Airport, Kuala Lumpur, MAS has now expanded its network to serve 22 international destinations in Europe, Asia and Australia and 36 domestic points,

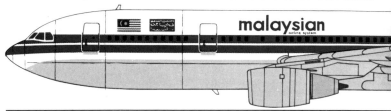

Mexicana

Mexicana (Compañia Mexicana de Aviacion) is the fourth oldest airline in the world and the second oldest in Latin America, having been originally founded as Compañia Mexicana de Transportes Aeros (CTMA) on 12 July 1921. Operations started from Mexico City to Tuxpan and Tampico with Lincoln Standards. The assets of CTMA were acquired in September 1924 by Compañia Mexicana de Aviacion (Mexicana) which was formed on 20 August 1924. Initial operations centred on payroll deliveries to remote oil fields (due to the vulnerability of ground routes to armed robbery). The carrier signed an air mail contract with the Mexican Government for the Mexico City-Tampico route on 16 August 1926, and passenger services were subsequently introduced on the route with Fairchild 71 aircraft on 15 April 1928. Pan American purchased Mexicana in January 1929 as part of its ambitious expansion plans in Latin America though Mexicana retained its separate identity. In 1931 the Ford Tri-Motor became standard equipment for Mexicana. In January 1936 Mexicana began services on its first

international trunk route from Mexico City to Los Angeles with Lockheed 10 Electra aircraft. Mexicana subsequently concentrated on the development of a trunk route network which included Guadalajara, Monterrey and Mérida. Boeing 247D aircraft were introduced into service in 1936 to be followed by the DC-2 in 1937 and the DC-3 a year later. Services to Havana, Mexicana's second international destination, were inaugurated on 25 October 1942. DC-6 aircraft were acquired in 1952, and on 7 December 1954 Mexicana took over Transportes Aereos de Jalisco (TAJ) giving the airline access to Puerto Vallarta.

In 1960 the carrier took delivery of its first Comet 4C jet aircraft which initiated service to Chicago on 4 July of that year. In the same year Mexicana acquired the routes of ATSA and TAMSA which gave access to the route structure in the Yucatán and additional services to Texas. The carrier overcame a series of setbacks and constraints during the 1960s and upgraded from Comet 4C (which proved uneconomical in Mexico's local environment) to the

representing 54,350 miles (87,467km) in total route distance. Long haul wide-bodied services commenced in 1976 with DC-10-30 aircraft and the subsequent introduction of the Airbus has brought wide-bodied service to domestic and regional sectors. In 1982 MAS becomes the sixth carrier to operate Rolls-Royce-powered 747 aircraft. MAS uplifted 4,151,000 passengers in its 1980-81 fiscal year compared with 1,902,000 in its first full year of operation and currently employs 9,327 personnel.

Fleet Data
4 Airbus Industrie A300B4-203
8 Boeing 737-2H6 Advanced
1 Boeing 737-2H6C Advanced
9 Fokker F.27 Friendship 500
2 Fokker F.27 Friendship 500F
3 McDonnell Douglas DC-10-30
4 Pilatus BN-2A-8 Islander

On Order
2 Boeing 747-200B
1 Boeing 737-2H6 Advanced

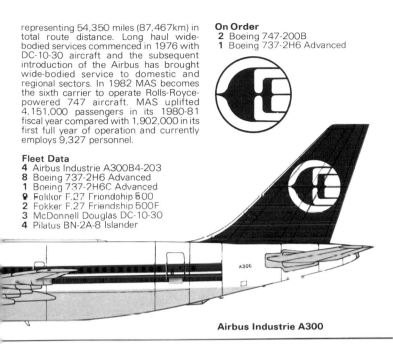

Airbus Industrie A300

Boeing 727. Pan American sold its remaining shares in the carrier in January 1968, and Mexicana gradually expanded its international route structure to include Dallas in 1972, St Louis in 1973, Kansas City in 1974, Costa Rica in 1977, San Francisco in 1978 and Seattle in 1979. Wide-bodied services with the high powered DC-10-15 aircraft followed delivery of the first of five such aircraft in June 1981. Mexicana currently operates an extensive route system which serves 39 points in Mexico, 10 points in the USA and also Havana, San Juan, Guatemala City and San Jose. The airline employs 10,560 personnel and carried 7,570,689 passengers in 1980. The Mexican Government holds 9% of the shares with the remainder in the hands of Board members and employees.

Fleet Data
1 Boeing 727-014
  (leased from Pacific Southwest)
2 Boeing 727-051 (leased from
  National Aircraft Leasing)
3 Boeing 727-264
33 Boeing 727-264 Advanced
3 McDonnell Douglas DC-10-15

On Order
10 Boeing 727-264 Advanced
2 McDonnell Douglas DC-10-15

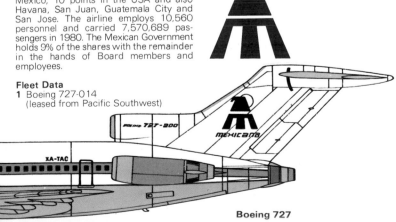

Boeing 727

Middle East Airlines

MEA (Middle East Airlines—Air Liban) was founded as a private company in May 1945. Middle East Airlines Company SA, as it was then known, began regular commercial services on regional routes from Beirut in January 1946 with three De Havilland Rapides. MEA employed 47 personnel at that time and 8,964 passengers were carried in its first year of operation. DC-3 aircraft were acquired and the network was expanded to include Ankara and Istanbul in 1947 and Kuwait, Bahrain and Dhahran in 1948. Following negotiations with Pan American in 1949, MEA became a joint-stock company, Pan American acquiring a 36% shareholding in the Lebanese carrier in return for which MEA received three additional DC-3s. In January 1955 the association with Pan American was terminated and in March of that year BOAC acquired a 38·74% holding as a result of which MEA was able to purchase a fleet of Viscount 754 aircraft, commencing services with the type on 2 October 1955. During the ensuing six years MEA's network was successfully expanded to include London, Rome, Geneva, Athens, Frankfurt and Vienna in Europe, as well as additional destinations in the Middle East. Four Comet 4C aircraft were ordered in 1960 and jet operations commenced with Comet 4s leased from BOAC prior to the introduction of MEA's own Comet 4Cs on 6 January 1961. The formal association with BOAC was terminated in August of that year and the British carrier sold its MEA stock to Lebanese shareholders.

On 7 June 1963 MEA merged with Air Liban, another major Lebanese carrier, which operated to Paris and to destinations in North and West Africa. Air France acquired a 30% holding in MEA through association with Air Liban. Caravelle VI-R aircraft were introduced by the close of the year which permitted MEA to introduce the Comet 4C on Air Liban's routes to Africa. By 1965 the two companies were fully integrated and the new carrier had adopted its current title. VC-10 and 707-365C capacity was leased during 1967 and the carrier's own Boeing 707-3B4C aircraft were introduced into service from

Nigeria Airways

Nigeria Airways began operations on 1 October 1958 as WAAC (Nigeria) Limited, taking over the domestic services of West African Airways Corporation (WAAC) in Nigeria. WAAC had operated in the former British colonies in West Africa. Services to Dakar and London were undertaken for WAAC by BOAC with Boeing Stratocruisers. Britannia 102, Comet 4, Boeing 707-436 and VC-10 Type 1101 aircraft were progressively introduced by BOAC on these international routes. The Nigerian carrier became wholly government-owned in March 1961, and Fokker F.27 Friendship 200 aircraft entered service in early 1963. The type was to remain in service with the carrier until 1981.

A former BOAC VC-10 Type 1101 was acquired in September 1969 and Boeing 707-3F9C aircraft entered service in May 1971. The carrier adopted its present title in the same year and introduced the F.28 Fellowship 2000 on domestic routes in 1973. Wide-bodied operations were initiated following delivery of Nigeria's first DC-10-30 on 14 October 1976. KLM provided management services and technical assistance under a two-year contract signed in September 1979.

Nigeria Airways currently operates a 13 point domestic network and scheduled passenger and cargo services link Lagos, Kano and Port Harcourt with New York, London, Amsterdam, Rome, Jeddah, as well as the African cities of Dakar, Banjul, Conakry, Freetown, Monrovia, Abidjan, Accra, Lome, Cotonou, Libreville, Douala, Niamey, and Nairobi. Nigeria Airways carried 924,000 passengers in 1980 of whom 800,000 flew on domestic services. A growth rate in excess of 20% per annum is currently being experienced making Nigeria Airways the fastest-growing carrier in Africa. It is undertaking an aircraft rationalisation programme which will result in a fleet consisting of Boeing 737 and

MEA

late 1968. The major part of MEA's fleet was destroyed by an armed attack on Beirut International Airport on 28 December of that year forcing the carrier to lease various aircraft. On 1 July 1969 MEA absorbed Lebanese International Airways (a scheduled carrier also serving Europe and the Middle East and whose fleet was totally lost in the 1968 raid on Beirut Airport) and acquired a fleet of Convair 990As from American Airlines. The Convair 990 aircraft were subsequently replaced with Boeing 720-023Bs, also purchased from American Airlines. Events in the Lebanon resulted in prolonged closures of Beirut Airport during 1975 and 1976, and this led to MEA's newly acquired 747-2B4B aircraft (along with other aircraft in the fleet) being temporarily leased out. MEA also established a temporary base at Paris-Orly Airport to develop its charter and leasing operations.

Despite the unsettled situation in the Lebanon, MEA has succeeded in maintaining viable operations and currently serves 34 destinations in Europe, the Middle East, North and West Africa. 1,042,265 passengers were carried in 1980 and MEA employs a total work force of 5,553.

Fleet Data
- **11** Boeing 720-023B
- **4** Boeing 720-047B
- **2** Boeing 707-347C
- **3** Boeing 707-3B4C
- **3** Boeing 747-2B4B (SCD)

On Order
- **5** Airbus Industrie A310

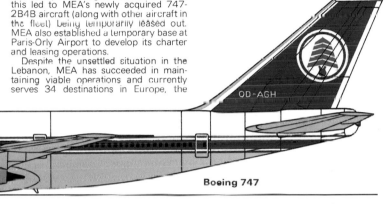

Boeing 747

747, DC-10-30 and Airbus A310 aircraft. 9,000 personnel are presently employed.

Fleet Data
- **3** Boeing 707-3F9C
- **2** Boeing 727-2F9 Advanced
- **2** Boeing 737-2F9 Advanced
- **1** Boeing 737-275
  (leased from Air Tara)
- **1** Boeing 737-275C
  (leased from Air Tara)
- **2** Boeing 737-281
  (leased from Air Tara)
- **1** Boeing 737-2H4
  (leased from Air Tara)
- **2** Boeing 737-2MB Advanced (leased from TEA)
- **6** Fokker F.28 Fellowship 2000
- **2** Fokker F.28 Fellowship 4000
- **2** McDonnell Douglas DC-10-30
- **8** Boeing 737-2F9 Advanced

On Order
- **4** Airbus Industrie A310

Note: Nigeria Airways plans to acquire Boeing 747 aircraft (model and quantity as yet unspecified).

McDonnell Douglas DC-10

Northwest Orient Airlines

Northwest Airlines (Northwest Orient Airlines) is the second oldest airline in the USA with a continuous identification and was formed on 1 August 1926 as Northwest Airways. The airline commenced operations on 1 October 1926 providing air mail service between Minneapolis/St Paul and Chicago, and passenger services were started in July of the following year. On 16 April 1933 the airline adopted its present title and acquired Northern Air Transport. Lockheed 10A Electras entered service in August 1934 and in March 1939 the DC-3 commenced operations with Northwest. On 1 June 1945 Northwest became the fourth US transcontinental airline when service was extended eastward from Minneapolis/St Paul to Newark and New York City via Milwaukee and Detroit. Northwest began to expand its routes through Canada, Alaska and the Aleutian Islands, and on 15 July 1947 a new Great Circle route through Anchorage to Tokyo, Seoul, Shanghai and Manila was inaugu-

rated with DC-4 aircraft. Services to Washington D.C. from Detroit via Cleveland and Pittsburgh began on 15 March 1948, and to Honolulu from Seattle/Tacoma and Portland on 2 December, making Northwest the first airline certified to link Hawaii with the Pacific North-West. The airline initiated service to Taiwan on 30 June 1950 and began operations with Boeing Stratocruisers. Northwest subsequently introduced DC-6A/B aircraft and by 1957 had also acquired Super Constellations and DC-7C aircraft. Services to Florida started in 1958 and Atlanta was added to the route system on 27 September 1959.

Lockheed Electra turboprop services began on 1 September 1959, and pure jet operations on 8 July 1960 on Far East routes with DC-8-32 aircraft, which were replaced by Boeing 707-351B aircraft from June 1963. Northwest also took delivery of Boeing 720-051Bs in May 1961 and the airline's first 727-51s were acquired in November 1964. Services to

Olympic Airways

Olympic was formed in January 1957 under the ownership of the Greek shipping magnate Aristotle Onassis to succeed the state-owned carrier TAE (Technical and Air Enterprises Company), which was placed into liquidation. TAE in its original form was established in 1935 to provide technical services, pilot training and air taxi charter services. At the end of the war TAE was re-established and began scheduled services from Athens to Thessaloniki, Heraclion and Hania in September 1946. By 1951 TAE had extended its operations to cover a twelve point domestic network and international services to Alexandria, Istanbul and Belgrade. However in an attempt to improve the economic performance of air transportation in Greece, TAE merged with two other Greek carriers, ELL.A.S. and A.M.E., at the behest of the Greek Government, to form the new TAE. The economic difficulties persisted and in 1955 the carrier was taken over by the Government. Subsequent agreement was reached with Aristotle Onassis as a result

of which the latter acquired the assets of the carrier together with a fifty year guarantee of sole designation as national airline and a monopoly of domestic routes. Olympic commenced operations on 6 April 1957 with a fleet of fourteen DC-3s and one DC-4 aircraft. In order to match stiff competition from other foreign operators, DC-6B aircraft were leased from UAT (now UTA) in advance of the carrier's own DC-6B fleet acquisition. The type inaugurated Olympic's first international flights on 2 June 1957 with services from Athens to Rome, Paris and London. Services to Zurich and Frankfurt were added to the network in August of the following year.

Comet jet services commenced on Middle East routes to Tel Aviv, Nicosia, Beirut and Cairo in May 1960 and two months' later replaced the DC-6B services to Rome, Paris and London. Olympic took delivery of its first 707-384C in May 1966 and inaugurated services with the type to New York via Rome and Paris in June. Boeing 727-284 aircraft progressively replaced

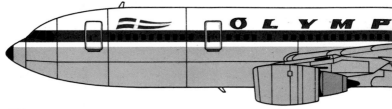

Hong Kong were inaugurated in October 1966 and to Osaka in April of the following year. Wide-bodied operations began following delivery of Boeing 747-151 aircraft in April 1970. The first DC-10-40 was delivered to Northwest at the end of 1972. Passenger operations to Europe began with the inauguration of transatlantic services on the New York-Copenhagen-Stockholm route in March 1979 and Northwest commenced services from Minneapolis/St Paul to London on 2 June 1980.

Based at Minneapolis/St Paul, Minnesota, Northwest Orient presently operates a 38,278 mile (61,600km) system encompassing 22 states in the USA and services to Canada, Japan, Korea, Taiwan, Hong Kong, the Philippines, Sweden, Denmark, Norway, the Netherlands, Ireland, Germany and the United Kingdom. Over 11,501,000 passengers were carried in 1980 and the airline currently employs 12,748 personnel.

Fleet Data
- **3** Boeing 727-51C
- **1** Boeing 727-151C
- **4** Boeing 727-51
- **23** Boeing 727-251
- **29** Boeing 727-251 Advanced
- **2** Boeing 747-135
- **10** Boeing 747-151
- **12** Boeing 747-251B
- **5** Boeing 747-251F (SCD)
- **22** McDonnell Douglas DC-10-40

Boeing 747

Comet 4Bs on the European routes from 1968, and the first NAMC YS-11A aircraft entered domestic and regional service in April 1970. On 4 March 1972 Olympic became a five continent operator with the inauguration of flights to Sydney via Bangkok and Singapore, and wide-bodied services with Boeing 747-284B aircraft began on the Athens-New York route on 27 June 1973. In December 1974 Onassis relinquished his rights to operate Olympic and the carrier resumed operations in January 1975 under the control of the Greek Government.

Olympic Airways currently serves an intensive domestic system and an international network covering some 27 cities in Europe, Africa, Asia and North America, representing a total route distance of nearly 38,500 miles (62,000km). The carrier's employment force has grown from 865 in 1957 to a present total of 8,794 employees. Swissair is currently providing management and operational assistance.

Fleet Data
- **6** Airbus Industrie A300B4-102
- **2** Boeing 707-304B
- **2** Boeing 707-384C
- **2** Boeing 707-351C
- **6** Boeing 727-284
- **11** Boeing 737-284 Advanced
- **2** Boeing 747-284B
- **3** NAMC YS-11A
- **4** Shorts 330

On Order
- **2** Airbus Industrie A300B4-102

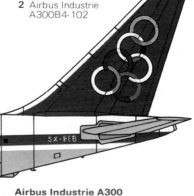

Airbus Industrie A300

Pakistan International Airlines

Pakistan International Airlines (PIA) was formally established as a scheduled carrier on 11 March 1955 with the takeover of Orient Airways. PIA had, however, initiated operations with Super Constellations on 7 June 1954 between Karachi and Dacca following its formation as a department of the Pakistan Ministry of Defence in 1951. Orient Airways became a registered company in 1947 and took over the routes of the pre-partition Indian operators in East and West Pakistan. In addition to its Super Constellations, PIA acquired Orient's Convair 240 and DC-3 aircraft. On 1 February 1955 PIA inaugurated its first international service on the Karachi-Cairo-London route. The first of an eventual fleet of five Viscount 815 aircraft entered service in January 1959.

Jet services were started on 7 March 1960 to London with a Boeing 707-121

leased from Pan American and operations were extended to New York on 5 May 1961. PIA then acquired its own Boeing 720-040B aircraft, and the first of these commenced operation in February 1962. In the meantime F.27 Friendship 200s had entered domestic service in February 1961, replacing DC-3 aircraft. Three Sikorsky S-61Ns acquired in 1963 formed the basis of an extensive helicopter network in East Pakistan. Services to Canton and Shanghai began on 29 April 1964. PIA's operations underwent substantial change following the 1971 war which resulted in East Pakistan becoming the independent state of Bangladesh, and services to and within the latter were terminated. New York services were resumed in 1972 and on 20 January 1973 PIA became the first foreign carrier to operate to Beijing. Wide-bodied operations were initiated with DC-10-30

Pan American World Airways

Pan Am was founded on 14 March 1927 and introduced air mail operations between Key West, Florida, and Havana on 28 October of that year with Fokker F.VII aircraft. Scheduled passenger services over the same route were started on 16 January 1928. Under the leadership of Juan Trippe, Pan Am was to develop into the world's most successful and important international carrier. Substantial private backing and government support aided the carrier to develop an extensive network throughout Central and South America and the Caribbean. During the 1930s and 1940s Pan Am acquired financial interests in many Latin American operators and pioneered services across the Pacific and Atlantic. Air mail service was inaugurated between San Francisco and Manila, followed by passenger services a year later. The Boeing 314 flying boat was used to initiate a scheduled transatlantic air mail service to Marseilles via Lisbon on 20 May 1939, with passenger services to Southampton and Marseilles commencing shortly afterwards.

Pan Am acquired American Overseas Airlines (AOA) from American Airlines on 25 September 1950. AOA was originally formed as American Export Airlines in 1936 and changed its title when American Airlines acquired a major holding in the company. AOA operated to West Germany, Scandinavia, Iceland and Finland, as well as scheduling services from West Berlin to points in West Germany. Pan Am progressively developed its route network to Europe, Africa and the Far East, and introduced DC-6B services in May 1952, followed by DC-7B and DC-7C aircraft. The carrier launched both the Boeing 707 and Douglas DC-8 aircraft in October 1955, and inaugurated jet services with the Boeing 707-121 on the New York-Paris route on 26 October 1958. Pan Am also placed the launch order for the Boeing 747 on 14 April 1966 and began operations with it to London on 22 January 1970. The carrier subsequently became the first operator of the 747SP and introduced the first non-stop services from Los Angeles and New York to Tokyo with it

aircraft in March 1974.

PIA currently serves a 19 point domestic network and operates scheduled passenger and cargo services to 33 international destinations in the Middle and Far East, North and East Africa, Europe and North America. The carrier employs approximately 22,800 personnel and carried 3,371,000 passengers in the 1980-81 fiscal year.

Fleet Data
4 Airbus Industrie A300B4-203
3 Boeing 707-340C
2 Boeing 707-351B
1 Boeing 707-373C
1 Boeing 720-040B
2 Boeing 720-047B
2 Boeing 747-282B
2 Boeing 747-240B (SCD)
7 Fokker F.27 Friendship 200
1 Fokker F.27 Friendship 400

2 Fokker F.27 Friendship 600
3 McDonnell Douglas DC-10-30

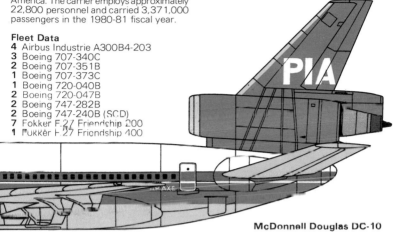

McDonnell Douglas DC-10

in April 1976. Pan Am formally acquired National Airlines on 7 January 1980 to become the second largest US carrier.

Pan Am currently operates a worldwide route network serving 78 cities in over 40 countries located in North and South America, Europe, Asia, Africa and Australia, and covering an unduplicated route distance of 85,400 miles (137,440km). 29,500 personnel are employed by Pan Am, and 15,216,700 passengers were transported in 1980.

Fleet Data
6 Boeing 727-21
2 Boeing 727-21C
8 Boeing 727-35
5 Boeing 727-51
24 Boeing 727-235
2 Boeing 727-2D4 Advanced
4 Boeing 727-221 Advanced
28 Boeing 747-121
3 Boeing 747-121 (F) (SCD)
1 Boeing 747-123 (F) (SCD)
1 Boeing 747-132
2 Boeing 747-221F (SCD)

10 Boeing 747 SP-21
12 Lockheed L-1011-385 TriStar 500
11 McDonnell Douglas DC-10-10
5 McDonnell Douglas DC-10-30

On Order
4 Boeing 727-221 Advanced

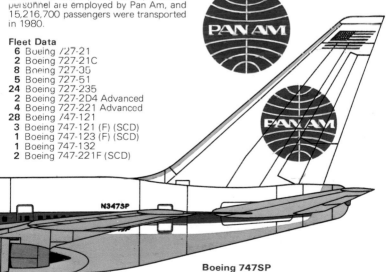

Boeing 747SP

Philippine Airlines

Philippine Airlines (PAL) was formed on 26 February 1941 by a group of industrialists, and inaugurated flights between Manila and Baguio on 15 March of that year with a Beech 18. PAL took over the franchise and routes of Philippine Aerial Taxi Company (PATCO) which had gone bankrupt in July 1940. PATCO had begun operations in March 1931 and initiated scheduled services from Manila in 1936. PAL resumed postwar operations with a Manila-Legaspi service on 14 February 1946, using newly acquired DC-3 aircraft. The carrier was designated the Philippine flag carrier to the US on 14 November 1946, and services to San Francisco with DC-4 aircraft began on 3 December. PAL's domestic system now covered 32 points. On 3 May 1947 the carrier purchased its main competitor, Far Eastern Air Transport, Inc (FEATI). DC-6 aircraft were acquired in May 1948, and in August of that year Commercial Air Lines, Inc (CALI) sold out to PAL making the latter the nation's only scheduled domestic airline at that time. By 1950 the carrier operated to 12 international destinations in Europe, the US, Asia and the Middle East. On 31 March 1954, however, all international routes were suspended (with the exception of Hong Kong) and emphasis was placed on development of the domestic network. On 1 June 1957 PAL introduced the Viscount 784 on the Manila-Hong Kong route. The type subsequently replaced Convair 340s on domestic trunk services, and F.27 Friendship 100 aircraft entered service on domestic routes in March 1960 replacing DC-3s.

Jet operations were inaugurated on the Hong Kong route with Boeing 707 aircraft chartered from Pan American on 11 December 1961. BAC One-Eleven 402 aircraft entered service on PAL's domestic and regional routes in May 1966, and HS 748-209s replaced the F.27s and DC-3s from November 1967. Wide-bodied services were introduced on the Pacific route following delivery of PAL's first DC-10-30 in

Qantas Airways

Qantas was registered by two ex-Flying Corps Lieutenants, W. Hudson Fysh and P.J. McGinness, as The Queensland and Northern Territory Aerial Services Limited (from which "Qantas" was derived) on 16 November 1920 with a paid-up capital of £6,037. For the first two years an Avro 504K and BE 2E were used to provide air taxi services and pleasure flights. The first scheduled service was inaugurated on 2 November 1922 from Charleville to Cloncurry in Queensland, via Longreach, using an Armstrong Whitworth FK8. A 1,475 mile (2,374km) route network in Queensland was established over the subsequent 12 years with flying doctor services forming part of the operations. On 18 January 1934 Qantas and Imperial Airways (forerunner of BOAC) formed Qantas Empire Airways Limited to operate the Brisbane-Singapore portion of the England-Australia route. An order was placed for Constellations in October 1946 and on 3 July 1947 the Australian Government purchased the remaining local shareholding in the carrier (having earlier purchased BOAC's holding) and became the sole owner of the airline, designating Qantas Empire Airways as the operator of Australia's international air services. The carrier commenced its own Sydney-London Constellation services on 1 December 1947, and subsequent overseas operations were rapidly developed. During this time Qantas participated as a shareholder in Tasman Empire Airways Limited (TEAL) of New Zealand to develop air links between the two countries. The San Francisco route (opened on 15 May 1947) was extended in 1958 to New York and London, making Qantas the first operator to provide regular round the world service by linking in London with the carrier's south-east Asia route to Sydney. By the end of that year the airline's network covered 72,306 miles (116,360km).

Jet operations were inaugurated on the North American services on 29 July 1959 following delivery of Boeing 707-138 aircraft. Lockheed Electras were also acquired in the same year and were used

July 1974, and the carrier now also operates a fleet of Boeing 747-2F6B and Airbus A300B4-103 aircraft.

PAL currently operates an extensive 41 point domestic network and 22 point international network. 3,306,274 passengers were carried in 1980 and the total network presently covers 66,325 unduplicated miles (106,743km). Some 10,081 personnel work for PAL, and the government currently maintains a 99.7% holding in the carrier.

Fleet Data

- **3** Airbus Industrie A300B4-103
- **1** BAe (BAC) One-Eleven 501EX
- **1** BAe (BAC) One-Eleven 516FP
- **2** BAe (BAC) One-Eleven 517FE
- **1** BAe (BAC) One-Eleven 518FG
- **1** BAe (BAC) One-Eleven 523FI
- **2** BAe (BAC) One-Eleven 524FF
- **4** BAe (BAC) One-Eleven 527FK
- **7** BAe (HS) 748-209 Series 2A
- **2** Boeing 727-134
- **4** Boeing 747-2F6B
- **4** McDonnell Douglas DC-10-30 (two leased from KLM)
- **5** NAMC YS-11
- **2** NAMC YS-11A

On Order

- **2** Airbus Industrie A300B4-103

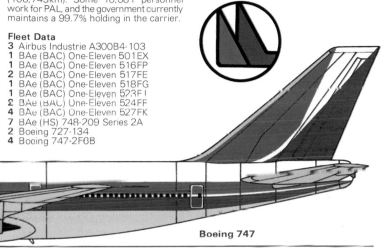

Boeing 747

to start the carrier's own services to New Zealand in 1961. Boeing 707-338C aircraft were introduced into service in 1965 and on 1 August 1967 the name of the carrier was changed to Qantas Airways Limited. Wide bodied services with the carrier's first 747-238B aircraft began in September 1971. On disposal of the carrier's last two 707-338C aircraft in March 1979, Qantas became the first airline in the world to operate an all-Boeing 747 fleet and was one of the first airlines to nominate Rolls-Royce RB.211 engines for its later 747B acquisitions.

Qantas currently operates a network of passenger and cargo services to Christchurch, Wellington, Auckland, Noumea, Fiji, Port Moresby, Honolulu, Los Angeles, San Francisco, Vancouver, Tokyo, Hong Kong, Manila, Bali, Jakarta, Singapore, Kuala Lumpur, Bangkok, Bombay, Bahrain, Damascus, Athens, Belgrade, Rome, Frankfurt, Amsterdam and London from Perth, Darwin, Melbourne, Sydney and Brisbane, representing 124,445 miles (200,266km)

in total unduplicated route distance. 1,887,451 passengers were carried in the 1980-81 fiscal year, and Qantas presently employs an average of 13,643 personnel

Fleet Data

- **19** Boeing 747-238B
- **3** Boeing 747-238B (SCD)
- **2** Boeing 747SP-38

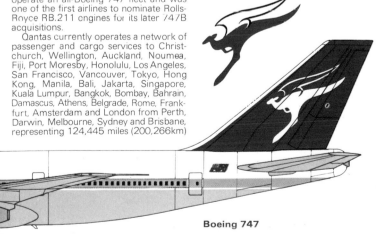

Boeing 747

Republic Airlines

Republic Airlines was formed in June 1979 as a result of a merger between North Central Airlines and Southern Airways. North Central, based at Minneapolis, was formed on 15 May 1944 as Wisconsin Central Airlines, and local service operations began on 24 February 1948 using Lockheed 10A Electras. Wisconsin Central introduced DC-3 aircraft in 1951, and during the following year the route network was expanded as far as the border with Canada and into North and South Dakota. The carrier adopted the title of North Central Airlines on 16 December 1952. Convair 340s entered service in 1959. In 1968 the first Convair 580 aircraft (turboprop conversion) entered service. North Central took delivery of its first McDonnell Douglas DC-9 jet in August 1967.

Southern Airways, based at Atlanta, was formed in July 1943, and commenced local service operations between Memphis and Atlanta with DC-3 aircraft on 10 June 1949. The first DC-9-15 was delivered to Southern on 8 May 1967 to supplement the carrier's Martin 404 and DC-3 equipment. Prior to the merger Southern operated to 67 points in 18 states with a network that extended north to Washington D.C. and New York, west to St Louis and south to Miami. A route from Miami to the Cayman Islands was also opened.

Republic Airlines initiated operations on 1 July 1979, and on 1 October 1980 the carrier acquired Hughes Airwest which was subsequently designated Republic Airlines West. Hughes Airwest had been formed in 1968 as a result of the merger of three operators—Bonanza Airlines, Pacific Airlines and West Coast Airlines—and had served a network of more than 40 destinations in western and midwestern states, as well as international services to Canada and Mexico.

The combined effect of the mergers and acquisitions has been to elevate Republic to the status of a major carrier. The amalgamated network of scheduled passenger and cargo services links 200 cities in 34 states, and also includes destinations

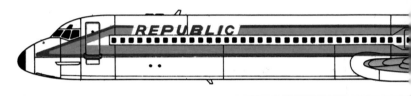

Royal Air Maroc

Royal Air Maroc (Compagnie Nationale de Transports Aériens) is the national carrier of the Kingdom of Morocco, and was formed on 28 June 1953 by the merger of Air Atlas and Air Maroc, brought about largely through the efforts of the Moroccan government. Air Atlas (Compagnie Cheri-fienne d'Aviation) was formed in 1946 to provide local services plus international links with Algiers and key cities in southern France. Operations commenced with Junkers Ju 52 aircraft which were replaced by DC-3s in the following year. Air Maroc (Société Avia Maroc Ligne Aérienne) was established in 1947 as a charter airline and operations with two DC-3s were introduced during the following year. Scheduled services began in 1949 to several European destinations including Paris and Geneva. Following the merger, Royal Air Maroc undertook development of both domestic and international services. Routes to Dakar, Gibraltar, Madrid and Frankfurt were opened, and Meknes, Oujda, Tetuan, Fez and Mellila-Nador were added to the domestic network.

The carrier introduced jet operations in 1960 with Caravelle III aircraft entering service on the Casablanca-Paris route on 20 May. Boeing 727-2B6 aircraft were acquired by Royal Air Maroc in May 1970, and the first 737-2B6 (Advanced) was delivered in February 1976. Wide-bodied services were initiated following delivery of a Boeing 747-2B6B aircraft on 29 September 1978.

Royal Air Maroc currently operates scheduled services from Casablanca and

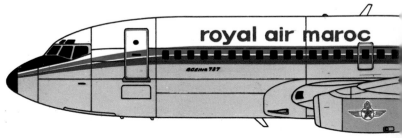

in Canada, Mexico and the Caribbean. Republic Airlines is publicly owned with approximately 42,000 stockholders and employs in the region of 15,000 personnel.

Fleet Data
- 10 Boeing 727-2M7 Advanced (two leased to PAL)
- 7 Boeing 727-2S7 Advanced
- 18 Convair 580
- 20 McDonnell Douglas DC-9-14
- 8 McDonnell Douglas DC-9-15
- 9 McDonnell Douglas DC-9-15F
- 52 McDonnell Douglas DC-9-31
- 12 McDonnell Douglas DC-9-32
- 1 McDonnell Douglas DC-9-32CF
- 28 McDonnell Douglas DC-9-51
- 3 McDonnell Douglas DC-9-82

On Order
- 11 McDonnell Douglas DC-9-82

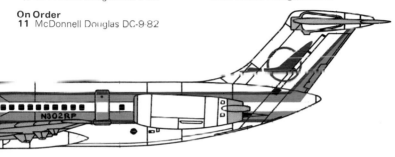

McDonnell Douglas DC-9

Tangier to domestic points and to destinations in North Africa, the Middle East, Europe, North and South America. Charter and inclusive-tour operations are also undertaken. The Moroccan government has an 89·84% holding in the carrier and other shareholders include Air France, Compagnie Générale Transatlantique and Aviuco. Royal Air Maroc employs approximately 3,600 personnel. Royal Air Inter was formed as an associate of the carrier in 1970 to operate domestic services from Casablanca.

Fleet Data
- 2 Boeing 707-351C
- 2 Boeing 727-2B6
- 6 Boeing 727-2B6 Advanced
- 4 Boeing 737-2B6 Advanced
- 1 Boeing 747-2B6B (SCD)

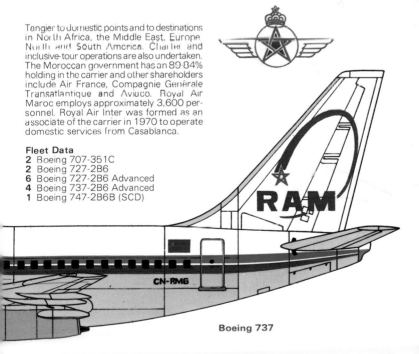

Boeing 737

Sabena-Belgian World Airlines

Sabena (Société Anonyme Belge d'Exploitation de la Navigation Aérienne) was established on 23 May 1923 with an initial capital of six million francs. Principal shareholders were the Syndicat National pour l'Etude des Transports Aériens (SNETA), the Belgian Government and the Belgian Congo. SNETA was Sabena's predecessor which had been formed to develop the necessary infrastructure for the establishment of air services within Europe and to the Belgian Congo (now Zaire). SNETA continued to represent the private capital in the new carrier until its liquidation in 1949. Sabena's initial route development focused on air links between the Low Countries and Switzerland, and on 1 April 1924 a cargo service was inaugurated on the Rotterdam-Brussels-Strasbourg route which was extended to Basle on 10 June. With the arrival of Handley Page W.8 aircraft, Sabena began passenger services on the route on 14 July 1924. In addition to building up European operations, Sabena proceeded to develop what became an extensive network of services in the Belgian Congo where the SNETA-formed company, LARA, had already pioneered air services. Delivery of DC-4 aircraft, ordered during the war while Sabena was temporarily headquartered in Leopoldville, facilitated the inauguration of services between Brussels and New York on 4 June 1947. DC-6, DC-6B and DC-7C aircraft were subsequently acquired for the carrier's long haul operations.

In 1949 Sabena was granted a monopoly of scheduled services in the Congo, and the carrier acquired two small local independent operators, Aeromas and the original Air Congo. Following independence for the Congo, Sabena assisted in the formation in June 1961 of the new Air Congo (now Air Zaire). Sabena introduced jet operations with the Boeing 707 starting

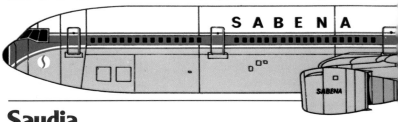

Saudia

Saudia (Saudi Arabian Airlines) was founded in 1945 by the Saudi Government as the national carrier, and domestic operations commenced with three DC-3 aircraft on 14 March 1947. The domestic network expanded rapidly and service was initiated between Jeddah and Cairo. A fleet of Bristol Freighter 21 and DC-4 aircraft was introduced into service from 1949, followed by ten Convair 340s from 1954. Three DC-6 aircraft were added in 1960 to enhance the route system within the Arab world and improve travel facilities for pilgrims. The acquisition of two Boeing 720-068B aircraft permitted jet services to be inaugurated in April 1962, progressively to cover Amman, Beirut, Cairo, Istanbul, Bombay and Karachi. In 1963 King Faisal decreed the corporate status of Saudia. 1967 marked the opening of Saudia's inaugural route to Europe, serving Geneva, Frankfurt and London, and later that year the carrier initiated services to Tripoli, Tunis and Casablanca. DC-9-15s were also introduced into service on domestic and regional routes in 1967 but by March 1972 these were being replaced by Saudia's first 737-268 (Advanced) aircraft. Acquisition of Boeing 707-368Cs enabled non-stop Jeddah-London operations to begin in 1968. Wide-bodied services were inaugurated with Lockheed TriStar 100 aircraft (later converted to the Series 200 standard) in 1975. Boeing 747 services were initiated on the Riyadh-London route and on services to Cairo in 1977 with capacity leased from MEA. Saudia took delivery of the first of its own 747-168B aircraft in 1981. A new and fully comprehensive flight training centre was opened in Jeddah in April 1979.

Saudia, the largest national airline in the Middle East, now operates a 21 point domestic network and scheduled international passenger and cargo services to a further 38 destinations in Europe, Asia, Africa, the Middle East and North America. The "Arabian Express" shuttle services on

Brussels-New York services in January 1960 and the Caravelle VI-R starting Brussels-Nice services in February 1961. 747 aircraft were acquired in late 1970 and the first DC-10-30CF was delivered in September 1973.

Sabena currently operates an extensive scheduled network of services within Europe and to Africa, the Middle East, Far East and North America, covering a total unduplicated route distance of approximately 132,000 miles (213,000km). Some 74 points are served in 51 countries. Sabena carried 1,974,455 passengers in its last full year and currently employs just over 10,000 personnel.

Fleet Data
- **4** Boeing 707-320C
- **11** Boeing 737-229 Advanced
- **4** Boeing 737-229C Advanced
- **2** Boeing 747-129 (SCD)
- **5** McDonnell Douglas DC-10-30CF

On Order
- **3** Airbus Industrie A310-220
- **1** McDonnell Douglas DC-10-30CF

McDonnell Douglas DC-10

---

the Riyadh-Jeddah and Riyadh-Dhahran routes, initiated in 1976, were providing 104 flights per week and 101 flights per week respectively by the end of 1980. The airline carried some 9,500,000 passengers during 1980 compared with 681,000 in 1971, and is expecting to handle 15,000,000 passengers by 1984. Saudia employs 19,800 personnel, of whom 10,200 are foreign nationals.

Fleet Data
- **6** Boeing 707-368C
- **17** Boeing 737-268 (Advanced)
- **2** Boeing 737-268C (Advanced)
- **5** Boeing 747-168B
- **1** Boeing 747SP-68
- **2** GA (Grumman) Gulfstream III
- **17** Lockheed L-1011-385 TriStar 200

A number of additional aircraft are leased from various carriers, and include Airbus, DC-8, 747 and F.28 Fellowships.

On Order
- **11** Airbus Industrie A300-600
- **3** Boeing 747-168B
- **1** Boeing 747SP-68

HZ-AIF

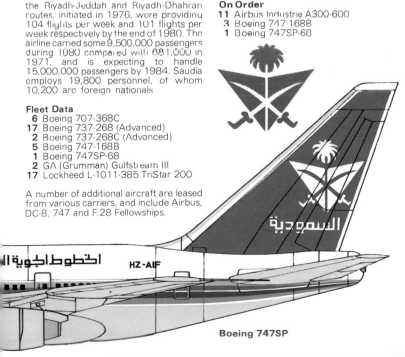

Boeing 747SP

Scandinavian Airlines System

SAS is the national carrier of Denmark, Norway and Sweden and was originally formed as a consortium of Det Danske Luftfartselskab (DDL), Det Norske Luftfartselskap (DNL) and AB Aerotransport (ABA), the leading pre-war airlines of those three nations respectively, on 1 August 1946 for intercontinental operations. Scheduled services were inaugurated on the Stockholm-Copenhagen-New York route on 17 September 1946 with DC-4 aircraft. On 18 April 1948 the three partner airlines formed the SAS European division and in July of that year Svensk Interkontinental Lufttrafik (SILA), another Swedish airline, merged with ABA. Agreement was reached on 8 February 1951 for unification of the whole SAS consortium under a centralised management and the three participating carriers became non-operating holding companies. The consortium is owned 28.5% by DDL, 28.5% by DNL and 43% by ABA, with each of the parent airlines being a private company owned 50-50 by private shareholders and the respective government of the three countries involved.

SAS initiated service to Buenos Aires on 29 December 1946 and opened a route to Bangkok in October 1949. The carrier inaugurated the world's first scheduled polar service between Copenhagen and Los Angeles on 15 November 1954 using DC-6B aircraft. DC-7C and Convair 440 aircraft were introduced in 1956 and a transpolar service to Tokyo via Anchorage was initiated from Copenhagen on 24 February 1957 with the DC-7C. Jet operations started with a Copenhagen-Beirut Caravelle service on 26 April 1959, making SAS the first airline to put the type into scheduled operation. DC-8-32 aircraft entered service on the New York route on 1 May 1960. The carrier introduced the DC-9-21 and DC-9-41 aircraft into domestic and European service in 1968 (both models having been developed to the carrier's specifications). On 13 January 1969 SAS signed a technical and operational agreement with KLM and Swissair (and later, UTA) to

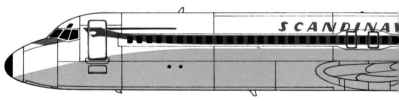

Singapore Airlines

Singapore Airlines (SIA) was formed on 24 January 1972 as the state-owned national carrier to succeed the jointly operated Malaysia-Singapore Airlines (MSA) following the decision in January of the preceding year by the Malaysian and Singapore Governments to set up separate national airlines (see pp 250-1). SIA commenced operations on 1 October 1972 serving the total MSA international network with former MSA Boeing 737 and 707 aircraft. Additional 707 capacity was soon acquired and in 1973 the network was extended to Amsterdam and Medan. On 2 April of that year SIA began daily services to London, and on 3 September 1973 the carrier's first two 747B aircraft were delivered. Boeing 727-212 aircraft entered SIA service on regional routes in September 1977 and the first of an eventual seven DC-10-30 aircraft was delivered to the carrier in November 1978. In May of that year SIA signed a record purchase deal with Boeing valued at nearly US $900 million for the supply of thirteen 747B and six 727-212 aircraft, and less than twelve months later SIA ordered six Airbus A300B4 aircraft, the first of which entered SIA service to Kuala Lumpur and Jakarta on 20 January 1981.

Meanwhile Concorde services between Singapore and London via Bahrain in conjunction with British Airways were inaugurated on 10 December 1977 but suspended shortly afterwards due to the Malaysian Government decision to ban supersonic operations over Malaysia. Although the service was allowed to resume in January 1979, it was finally terminated in November 1980.

Singapore Airlines' route network now covers services from Singapore to Auckland, Melbourne, Perth, Sydney, Honolulu, Los Angeles, San Francisco, Osaka, Tokyo, Seoul, Taipei, Hong Kong, Brunei, Manila, Jakarta, Medan, Kuala Lumpur, Penang,

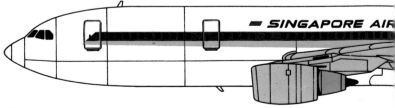

form the KSSU Group. Wide-bodied services commenced between Copenhagen and New York in April 1971 with Boeing 747-283B aircraft, and DC-10-30s were introduced on polar routes in 1975.

SAS currently operates to 100 destinations in 46 countries covering Europe, Africa, the Middle and Far East, and North, Central and South America. Total route distance amounts to 139,200 miles (224,000km). 8,413,000 passengers flew with SAS in the 1980-81 fiscal year and the airline employs 16,425 personnel.

Note: DHC-6 Twin Otters of Swedair and Lockheed L-188A Electras of Fred Olsen operate certain flights for SAS.

Fleet Data
4 Airbus Industrie A300B2-320
3 Boeing 747-283B
3 Boeing 747-283B (SCD)
3 McDonnell Douglas DC-8-62
4 McDonnell Douglas DC-8-63
(two leased out)
9 McDonnell Douglas DC-9-21
2 McDonnell Douglas DC-9-33AF
49 McDonnell Douglas DC-9-41
5 McDonnell Douglas DC-10-30

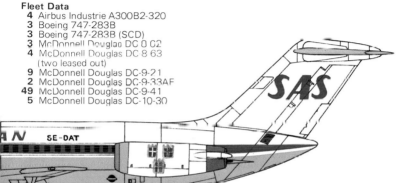

McDonnell Douglas DC-9

Bangkok, Colombo, Bombay, Madras, Dhahran, Dubai, Abu Dhabi, Bahrain, Athens, Amsterdam, Brussels, Copenhagen, Frankfurt, London, Paris, Rome and Zurich, representing 35 destinations in 27 countries. Approximately 10,316 personnel are employed by SIA, and the carrier's current fleet modernisation programme is aimed at eventual operation of the 747B and Airbus A300 types only. The DC-10-30 aircraft are being phased out and only a small residue of 727-212 aircraft will be retained for the time being.

Fleet Data
6 Airbus Industrie A300B4-203
4 Boeing 727-212 Advanced
16 Boeing 747-212B
4 McDonnell Douglas DC-10-30

On Order
6 Airbus Industrie A300B4-203
8 Boeing 747-212B (SUD)

Airbus Industrie A300

South African Airways

SAA is the national airline for the Republic of South Africa and was formed on 1 February 1934 when the Government (through the South African Railways Administration) took control of Union Airways which had been operating since 1929 as a private company with five Gipsy Moth aircraft, supplying air mail services from Port Elizabeth to Johannesburg, Cape Town and Durban. SAA inaugurated services with the three Junkers F13 and one Junkers W34 aircraft taken over from Union Airways but these were replaced in November 1934 by three Junkers Ju 52s which had previously been ordered by SAA's predecessor. On 1 February 1935 SAA acquired South West African Airways which had been operating a Windhoek-Kimberley air mail service since 1932. By the outbreak of war SAA had established a regional network of services which encompassed all adjacent territories. Operation between Johannesburg and London, known as the Springbok service, began in co-operation with BOAC on 10 November 1945 with Avro York aircraft and later

with DC-4s. By the end of 1947 a network of domestic, regional and international services was being operated with a fleet of 41 aircraft comprising DC-3, DC-4, Viking, Lodestar and Dove aircraft.

Early in the 1950s SAA took delivery of Constellation aircraft for use on the Springbok service, and in 1953 the carrier commenced jet operations with Comet I aircraft leased from BOAC. The Comet services were subsequently withdrawn due to the structural problems of the aircraft, and replaced once more by Constellations. In 1956 SAA became the first airline outside the United States to operate the DC-7B which commenced service for SAA on the London route, and subsequently inaugurated SAA service to Perth via Mauritius and the Cocos Islands on 25 November 1957. Viscount 813 aircraft entered major domestic and regional service with the carrier in November 1958 and were to remain with SAA until 1971. SAA recommenced jet operations on 1 October 1960 following delivery of Boeing 707-344 aircraft. The carrier acquired 727-44s in 1965 to

Swissair

Swissair was founded on 26 March 1931 through the merger of Ad Astra Aero and Balair. Swissair began operations over a network of 2,785 miles (4,480km). In April 1932 Europe's first regular services with the Lockheed Orion single-engine monoplane were initiated on the Zurich-Munich-Vienna route establishing new standards in fast air transportation. Swissair was the first European airline to employ air stewardesses with the introduction of the sixteen-seat Curtiss Condor. DC-2 aircraft were also acquired in 1932, and services to London began with it on the 1 April. By the outbreak of the war Swissair's fleet consisted of eleven aircraft which included five DC-3s. Services were resumed on 30 July 1945 and the airline was designated as the national carrier in February 1947. Swissair's first transatlantic service, from Geneva to New York, was operated by DC-4 on 2 May of that year, but a regular service did not begin until April 1949. Swissair began Convair 240 services in 1949, and acquired DC-6B aircraft from 1951 for long haul operations. On 27 May

1954 Swissair inaugurated DC-6B services to Rio de Janeiro and Sao Paulo, extended to Buenos Aires in April 1957 and Santiago in August 1962. In 1956 the carrier took delivery of its first DC-7C and Convair 440 aircraft, and in 1957 added Tokyo to its network. Jet operations began on 30 May 1960 with DC-8 services to New York. Caravelles were introduced on European routes in the same year and Convair 990s entered service in 1962 to the Far East and South America. The acquisition of DC-9-15 aircraft from July 1966 marked the beginning of a long association with the type and was followed by deliveries of DC-9-32s from 1967 and the DC-9-51 aircraft (for which the carrier was the launch customer) from 1975. Wide-bodied services to New York began in April 1971 following delivery of two 747B aircraft, and DC-10 operations to Montreal and Chicago commenced in December 1972. In October 1977 the carrier was again the launch customer for another DC-9 model, the series 81, which entered service on European routes on 5 October 1980.

supplement Viscount operations on the trunk domestic and regional services. Wide-bodied operations began on 10 December 1971 with the introduction of Boeing 747-244B "Springbok" services, and SAA's first Boeing 747SP-44 was delivered in 1976.

In addition to an 11 point domestic route system and regional operations to neighbouring African countries, SAA operates to more than 25 destinations in Australia, the Far East, Europe, North and South America. Total unduplicated route distance covers 145,150 miles (233,585km) and 4,003,955 passengers were carried in the fiscal year ending in March 1981. A total of 11,772 personnel are employed by SAA.

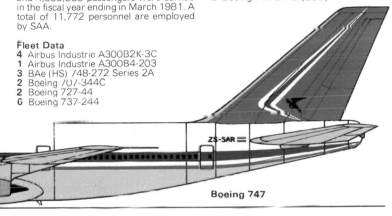

9 Boeing 737-244 Advanced
5 Boeing 747-244B
2 Boeing 747-244B (SCD)
6 Boeing 747SP-44

On Order
1 Airbus Industrie A300B4-203
4 Boeing 737-244 Advanced
2 Boeing 747-244B (SUD)

Fleet Data
4 Airbus Industrie A300B2K-3C
1 Airbus Industrie A300B4-203
3 BAe (HS) 748-272 Series 2A
2 Boeing 707-344C
2 Boeing 727-44
6 Boeing 737-244

ZS-SAR

Boeing 747

Swissair currently operates a world-wide network to points in Europe, North and South America, Africa, the Middle and Far East, comprising 93 destinations in 64 countries and covering a total route distance of 168,327 miles (270,884km). From 64 employees in 1931 Swissair's work force has grown to over 16,000. Some 6,953,593 passengers were carried in 1980. Swissair is a member of the KSSU consortium which was formed by the carrier along with KLM, SAS, and UTA to co-operate on technical and equipment activities. Approximately 76% of Swissair's share capital is held by private interests with the balance being held by government institutions and local authorities. Swissair was the first customer for the stretched upper deck (SUD) Boeing 747.

Fleet Data
2 Boeing 747-257B
4 McDonnell Douglas DC-8-62
4 McDonnell Douglas DC-9-32
1 McDonnell Douglas DC-9-33F
12 McDonnell Douglas DC-9-51

15 McDonnell Douglas DC-9-81
11 McDonnell Douglas DC-10-30

On Order
10 Airbus Industrie A310-220
2 Boeing 747-257B (SUD/SCD)
3 Boeing 747-257B (SUD)
2 McDonnell Douglas DC-10-30ER

SWISSAIR

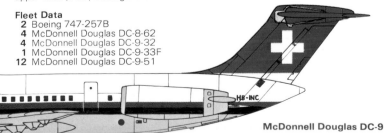

HB-INC

McDonnell Douglas DC-9

Tarom

Tarom (Transporturile Aeriene Romane) was originally formed in 1946 as Transporturi Aeriene Romana Sovietica (TARS) by the governments of Romania and the Soviet Union. TARS succeeded the pre-war state airline LARES, and provided domestic and international services radiating from Bucharest. Routes to Prague, Budapest and Warsaw were opened with Li-2 aircraft, and in 1954 TARS adopted its present title when Romania took over complete control of the carrier. Ilyushin Il-14 aircraft were acquired enabling Tarom to expand its international network, including new services to Moscow, Vienna, Zurich, Paris, Brussels and Copenhagen. Ilyushin Il-18 turboprops entered service in 1962 and further expansion took place with services to Belgrade, Sofia, Athens and Frankfurt. Antonov An-24s were introduced on domestic services in 1966, supplementing and eventually replacing the fleet of Ilyushin Il-14s previously operated.

Jet operations on European routes began after delivery of the first of an initial fleet of six One-Eleven 424 aircraft on 14 June 1968. Ilyushin Il-62s were acquired in 1973 primarily for holiday charter traffic, and the first of three Boeing 707-3K1C aircraft entered service in 1974. New routes to New York via Amsterdam and to Beijing via Karachi were inaugurated in April and May 1974 respectively, and in 1975 Tarom formed Liniile Aeriene Romane (LAR), a charter subsidiary which began operating in December of that year with former Tarom One-Eleven 424s. Tarom is now acquiring a number of One-Eleven 525 aircraft built under licence in Romania.

In addition to its domestic network, Tarom currently operates scheduled international passenger and cargo services within Europe and to Tripoli, Algiers, Casablanca, Amman, Baghdad, Beirut, Cairo, Damascus, Istanbul, Kuwait, Nicosia, Tehran, Tel Aviv, Karachi, Beijing and New York.

Thai Airways International

Thai Airways International Limited (Thai International) is the designated national flag carrier of Thailand for scheduled international services, and was formed in August 1959 by Scandinavian Airlines System (SAS) with a 30% shareholding, and Thai Airways Company Limited (the Government-owned domestic airline of Thailand) with a 70% shareholding. Operations commenced in May 1960 on regional services within Asia, utilising technical and managerial assistance provided by SAS, and three DC-6B aircraft leased from the airline. Rapid development of international routes led to the opening of "Royal Orchid" services to Kuala Lumpur, Singapore, Jakarta, Rangoon, Calcutta, Saigon (now Ho Chi Minh City), Hong Kong, Taipei and Tokyo.

Jet services were inaugurated in 1962 with two Convair 990A aircraft on lease from SAS. The type was replaced from January 1964 with SAS Caravelle IIIs which provided the backbone of Thai International's operations until the introduction of leased DC-9-41 aircraft in 1970, followed by DC-8-32s from SAS a year later. Wide-bodied operations with DC-10-30 aircraft leased from SAS and UTA were initiated prior to delivery of Thai's own DC-10-30s from March 1977. At this point, SAS's residual shareholding in the carrier was acquired by Thai Airways Company Limited. The A300B4-2C Airbus entered service in 1977, and Boeing 747-2D7B services were started in 1979 following delivery of Thai's first such aircraft.

Thai International's current route network of scheduled passenger and cargo services

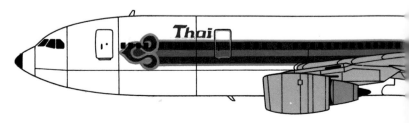

Fleet Data
25 Antonov An-24RV
2 Antonov An-24T
3 Antonov An-24RT
5 Antonov An-24V
4 Antonov An-26
2 BAe (BAC) One-Eleven 424EU
1 BAe (BAC) One-Eleven 401AK
1 BAe (BAC) One-Eleven 402AP
1 BAe (BAC) One-Eleven 487GK(F)
6 BAe (BAC) One-Eleven 525FT
1 BAe (BAC) One-Eleven 525RC
2 Boeing 707-3K1C
2 Boeing 707-321C
9 Ilyushin Il-18V
3 Ilyushin Il-18D
3 Ilyushin Il-62
2 Ilyushin Il-62M
6 Tupolev Tu-154B
1 Tupolev Tu-154B-1
4 Tupolev Tu-154B-2

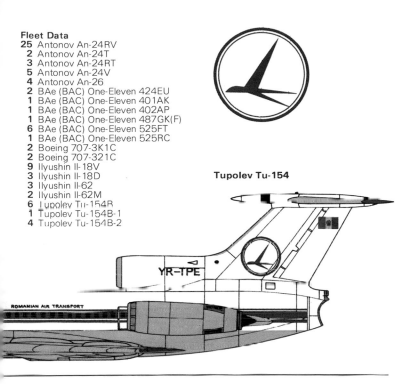

Tupolev Tu-154

YR-TPE

ROMANIAN AIR TRANSPORT

covers 34 cities in Australia, Bangladesh, Burma, Denmark, France, Germany, Greece, Hong Kong, India, Indonesia, Italy, Japan, Kuwait, Malaysia, Nepal, Netherlands, New Caledonia, Pakistan, Philippines, Saudi Arabia, Singapore, South Korea, Sri Lanka, Taiwan, Thailand, the United Kingdom and the USA. 1,845,000 passengers were carried by the carrier in 1980, and Thai International currently employs 7,350 personnel.

Fleet Data
10 Airbus Industrie A300B4-2C
6 Boeing 747-2D7B
1 McDonnell Douglas DC-8-62AF
3 McDonnell Douglas DC-8-63

On Order
2 Airbus Industrie A300-600

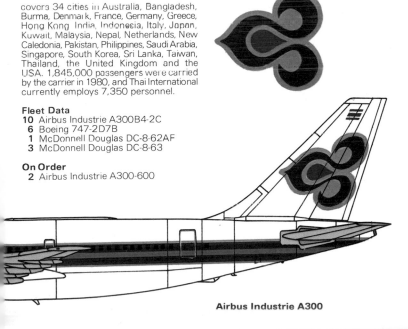

Airbus Industrie A300

Trans-Australia Airlines

The Australian National Airlines Commission was appointed by the Commonwealth government on 12 February 1946 under the National Airlines Act to operate a network of domestic services. The Commission's operations are conducted under the name Trans-Australia Airlines (TAA). Operations began on 9 September 1946 between Melbourne and Sydney with DC-3 aircraft. By December of that year all state capitals had been linked, and principal coastal routes were operated in competition with those operated by Australian National Airways (now part of Ansett). DC-4 aircraft entered service to supplement the DC-3s, and in 1949 TAA acquired and subsequently developed the Queensland interior routes pioneered by Qantas Empire Airways Limited (now Qantas), as well as their flying doctor services. Convair 240s were acquired in

1948, followed by Viscount 720 aircraft which entered service on 18 December 1954. A fleet of F.27 Friendships replaced DC-3s in 1959, and TAA's first Lockheed L-188A Electra went into service on 7 July of that year. In 1960, at the request of the government, TAA acquired the Papua-New Guinea route network previously served by Qantas, and also the six DC-3s and four De Havilland Otters operated by Qantas on these routes. DC-6B services were provided to Port Moresby and Lae, and DHC-6 Twin Otters were introduced on Papua-New Guinea routes in November 1966.

Jet services were inaugurated by TAA with Boeing 727-76 aircraft on 2 November 1964, simultaneously with its major competitor, Ansett-ANA. DC-9-31 aircraft commenced operations in April 1967. In

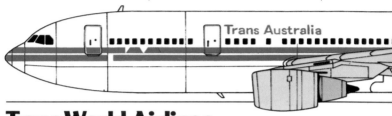

Trans World Airlines

TWA traces its history back to the formation of Western Air Express (WAE) which initiated mail services between Los Angeles and Salt Lake City in April 1926 and began passenger services on the same route in May of that year. In 1929 the carrier absorbed Standard Air Lines and in July 1930 WAE merged with Transcontinental Air Transport Inc (TAT) to form Transcontinental and Western Air (TWA). TAT had been founded in May 1928 and inaugurated a combined air-rail, coast-to-coast service in 1929. Prior to the merger, TAT had acquired Maddux Airlines which gave TAT access to San Francisco and San Diego. Following the merger, the rail connections were dispensed with and TWA inaugurated an all-air, coast-to-coast service on 25 October 1930. In 1934 the former WAE was bought out of TWA and subsequently became the current Western Airlines. TWA introduced the DC-2 aircraft into service between Columbus and New York in May 1934 and DC-3s entered service with the carrier in June 1937.

In association with Pan American, TWA sponsored development of the Boeing

307 Stratoliner which became the first pressurised airliner to enter service on US domestic routes in July 1940. Constellation services were inaugurated in February 1946 between New York and Paris via Gander and Shannon, representing TWA's first international route and also the first commercial link between the US and Paris. This route was further extended to Bombay via Rome in 1947. In 1950 the corporate name was changed to Trans World Airlines which reflected TWA's international route expansion. Introduction of the Constellation enabled TWA to initiate the first non-stop coast-to-coast service between Los Angeles and New York on 19 October 1953. Super Constellations commenced a transpolar Los Angeles to London service via San Francisco in October 1957. On 20 March 1959 TWA operated its first jet service with the service introduction of the Boeing 707 on domestic routes. International jet operations began on 23 November 1959. Convair 880 aircraft entered domestic service in January 1961 and were later supplemented from April 1964 by Boeing 727s. Short haul DC-9

association with Ansett, Qantas and the Australian government, TAA helped to form Air Niugini in 1973. TAA initiated wide-bodied services with the first of five Airbus A300B4-203 aircraft on 22 July 1981 between Melbourne and Sydney.

TAA's current network of scheduled passenger and cargo services links more than 50 points in Australia, including all state capitals and numerous provincial towns throughout the country. It currently employs approximately 8,500 personnel.

On Order
2 Airbus Industrie A300B4-203

Fleet Data
3 Airbus Industrie A300B4-203
12 Boeing 727-276 Advanced
2 Fokker F.27 Friendship 200
8 Fokker F.27 Friendship 600
12 McDonnell Douglas DC-9-31

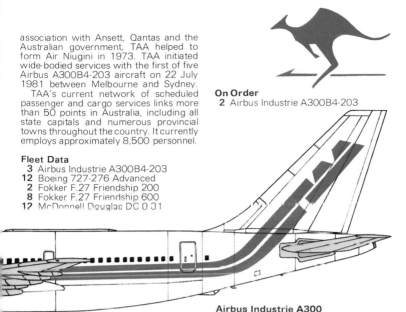

Airbus Industrie A300

operations commenced in February 1966. Wide-bodied services with 747 aircraft were initiated in 1970 and the TriStar, for which TWA was one of three launch customers, entered service in June 1972.

TWA currently operates an extensive domestic network and international routes to Europe and the Middle East, serving some 51 cities within the USA and 11 international destinations. Charter and inclusive tour operations are also undertaken by TWA. The carrier operates an all-jet fleet of over 200 aircraft and carried more than 20 million passengers in 1980. Some 34,000 personnel work for TWA.

3 Boeing 747SP-31
24 Lockheed L-1011 TriStar 1
8 Lockheed L-1011 TriStar 100

On Order
10 Boeing 767-231
3 Lockheed L-1011 TriStar 100

Fleet Data
72 Boeing 707-131B/331B
8 Boeing 707-331C
26 Boeing 727-31
6 Boeing 727-31C
2 Boeing 727-180C
36 Boeing 727-231
20 Boeing 727-231 Advanced
11 Boeing 747-131
2 Boeing 747-136
2 Boeing 747-156

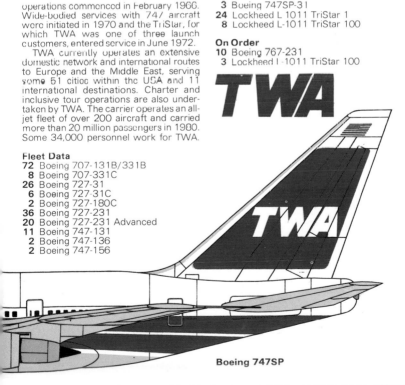

Boeing 747SP

Tunis Air

Tunis Air (Société Tunisienne de l'Air) was founded in 1948 as a co-operative venture between the Tunisian Government, Air France and various private investors who were later bought out. Operations started in 1949 with DC-3 aircraft initially serving the traditional markets between Tunisia, France and Algeria. The first DC-4 aircraft was delivered in 1954 in order to serve new destinations in France. The declaration of independence resulted in the Tunisian government taking a 51% (and later, 85%) controlling interest in the carrier in 1957, with Air France holding the balance. The fleet was then composed of three DC-3s and two DC-4 aircraft and the route network covered international services to Paris, Marseille, Lyon, Rome, Bonn and Algiers. The introduction of the airline's first Caravelle III in September 1961 represented a major advance for Tunis Air, and as additional Caravelles were added to the fleet, the route system was progressively expanded to include services to Amsterdam, Brussels and Frankfurt in 1966, Zurich in 1967, and Casablanca in 1968. Nord 262 aircraft were acquired for domestic operations in 1969 and the carrier's first Boeing 727-2H3 entered service in 1972, during which year Luxembourg and Jeddah were added to the system. London services were inaugurated in the following year.

Tunis Air currently operates scheduled passenger and cargo services from Tunis, Djerba, Monastir and Tozeur to 32 points in 20 countries within Africa, Europe and the Middle East. A total of 1,472,392 passengers were carried in 1980, 92% of

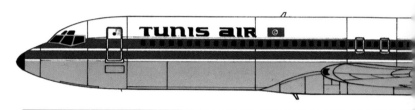

Turk Hava Yollari

THY AO, (THY-Turkish Airlines) Turkey's national airline, was founded on 20 May 1933 as Devlet Hava Yollari (State Airlines), and was part of the Ministry of National Defence. In 1935 the airline was transferred to the Ministry of Public Works. Operations commenced between Ankara and Istanbul with aircraft which included the De Havilland DH 86B Express and Rapide; other domestic routes were subsequently opened. On 3 June 1938 the airline became known as the General Directorate of State Airways, and the Ministry of Transportation assumed control. The airline operated only domestic services until 1947, when a route to Athens was opened. DC-3 aircraft were introduced, and the airline took delivery of the first of seven De Havilland Herons in February 1955. In May of that year the Turkish government established a Corporation to handle air transportation and on 1 March 1956 the new Corporation commenced operations under the present title of Turk Hava Yollari AO. The Turkish Government had a 51% holding in THY, and BOAC held 6.5% of the share capital, through which THY was able to order a fleet of five Viscount 794 aircraft. The airline's first Viscount entered service in May 1958 on domestic trunk routes. THY subsequently ordered ten F.27 Friendships and the first of these commenced operations in July 1960.

Jet services were introduced in August 1967 with a DC-9-15 leased from Douglas, and four Boeing 707-321 aircraft were purchased from Pan Am in 1971. Wide-bodied services commenced in December 1972 with DC-10-10 aircraft, and the airline's first F.28 Fellowship 1000 was delivered in the same month for domestic routes. THY acquired Boeing 727-2F2 (Advanced) aircraft from November 1974 to supplement the DC-9-32s, acquired earlier, on the European routes.

THY currently operates from Ankara, Istanbul, Antalya, Izmir and Adana to domestic points, and international services to Austria, Belgium, Cyprus, Denmark, Egypt, France, Germany, Greece, Italy,

whom travelled on international flights. Tunis Air currently employs 4,032 personnel and will commence wide-bodied operations in 1982 following delivery of its first Airbus aircraft.

Fleet Data
1 Boeing 727-2H3
9 Boeing 727-2H3 Advanced
3 Boeing 737-2H3 Advanced
1 Boeing 737-2H3C Advanced

On Order
1 Airbus Industrie A300B4-203

Boeing 727

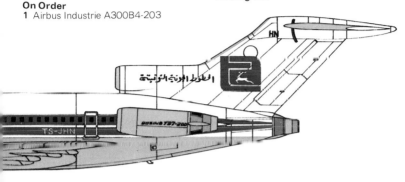

Ireland, Iraq, Libya, the Netherlands, Pakistan, Saudi Arabia, Switzerland, the United Kingdom and the United Arab Emirates. The route network covers a total unduplicated distance of 36,520 miles (58,772km), and THY expected to carry well over two million passengers in 1981, having carried a total of 1,450,384 passengers in the previous year. THY is 99.9% owned by the Turkish Government and employs 5,518 personnel. Kibris Turk Hava Yollari (Cyprus Turkish Airlines) is a subsidiary, formed on 4 December 1974 to provide scheduled services from Ercan, Cyprus, to Adana, Ankara and Istanbul.

Fleet Data
3 Boeing 707-321B
5 Boeing 727-2F2 Advanced
2 Fokker F.28 Fellowship 1000
9 McDonnell Douglas DC-9-32
2 McDonnell Douglas DC-10-10

On Order
4 Boeing 727-2F2 Advanced

Boeing 727

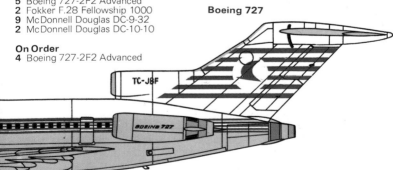

Union de Transports Aériens

UTA was created on 1 October 1963 through the merger of Union Aéromaritime de Transport (UAT) and Compagnie de Transports Aériens Intercontinentaux (TAI). UAT was formed in 1949 with the backing of Compagnie Maritimes des Chargeurs Reunis, a shipping company, to succeed Aeromaritime which had been founded by the same company in 1935 to operate services in French West Africa. UAT began DC-4 services in 1950 between Paris and Dakar, Pointe Noire and Saigon. Jet operations to Dakar with Comet 1A aircraft were inaugurated in 1953, and were subsequently extended to Brazzaville and Johannesburg. Following grounding of the Comet 1As in 1954, DC-6A/B aircraft were acquired. In 1955 UAT took over Société Aigle Azur which operated Boeing Stratoliners from Paris to Brazzaville, Madagascar, Saigon and Hanoi. Jet operations recommenced in September 1960 with the acquisition of DC-8-32 aircraft and UAT, in association with Air France,

subsequently helped to form Air Afrique which took over their extensive route network in French Africa.

TAI was formed on 1 June 1946 as a successor to Regie Air Afrique (founded in 1934), and began services to North Africa a month later with Junkers Ju 52/3m aircraft and later with Bristol 170 freighters. In 1947 routes from Paris to Tananarive and Saigon were opened using DC-3 aircraft. TAI acquired DC-6Bs in 1953 and its first DC-7C at the end of 1957. On 1 January 1956, as a result of a reallocation of routes, TAI was able to extend its Saigon services to Darwin and Noumea, followed by further extension to Auckland on 4 February 1957. The Paris-Tahiti-Honolulu-Los Angeles route was opened in 1960 using DC-7Cs: this represented the world's longest route, linking with Air France in Los Angeles for the continuation through Montreal to Paris. TAI introduced DC-8 services in 1960, starting non-stop service between Los Angeles and Papeete.

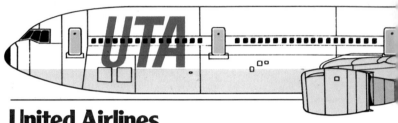

United Airlines

United traces its origin to Varney Air Lines which began air mail services between Paso, Washington and Elko, Nevada on 6 April 1926. Varney Air Lines was later merged with Pacific Air Transport and National Air Transport, both of whom were air mail carriers, into Boeing Air Transport which was part of a combine that included the Boeing Airplane Company and Pratt and Whitney, the engine manufacturer. United was organised on 1 July 1931 as the management company for the airline division. Three years later the combine broke up and the corporate divisions became separate entities. By this time United was operating the Boeing 247 which had entered service in March 1933 and established regular coast-to-coast operations. DC-3 operations began in 1937 and DC-4 aircraft entered United service on the New York-Chicago route in March 1946 with the DC-6 following in April 1947. By May 1947 the route network had been expanded to include Boston,

Denver, Washington D.C. and Hawaii. DC-6B services began in 1951 and the Convair 340 was introduced on short haul routes in 1952. Transcontinental services with the DC-7 began in April 1954 and jet operations with DC-8 aircraft were inaugurated on 18 September 1959. Boeing 720 aircraft were introduced in July 1960 initially between Chicago, Denver and Los Angeles. United made its first purchase of a foreign aircraft when a fleet of twenty Caravelle VI-R aircraft was ordered. The type commenced services between New York and Chicago on 14 July 1961.

United's size increased significantly on 1 June 1961 when the carrier took over Capital Airlines, founded in November 1936 as Pennsylvania Central Airlines. As a result of the merger United's route system was increased by 7,200 miles (11,600km) and the carrier became the world's largest privately-owned airline in terms of annual passengers carried and passenger miles flown. The Caravelles and

274

UTA

Since its creation in 1963 UTA has grown into one of Europe's most prominent independent airlines. In 1970 UTA signed an agreement with KLM, SAS and Swissair to become part of the KSSU group of airlines co-operating in the technical support and operation of DC-10 and 747 aircraft. Wide-bodied services commenced in 1973 with the DC-10-30 and the first Boeing 747-2B3F (SCD) aircraft was delivered in 1978. UTA operates an extensive passenger and freight network covering 45 cities in 40 countries in Europe, Africa, South East Asia, the Middle East, Australasia, the Pacific and North America, representing a total route distance of 163,515 miles (263,140km). 874,370 passengers were carried in 1980 and the airline has 7,105 employees.

3 McDonnell Douglas DC-8-62
2 McDonnell Douglas DC-8-63
1 McDonnell Douglas DC-8-63CF
6 McDonnell Douglas DC-10-30

On Order
2 Boeing 747-2B3B (SUD)

Fleet Data
2 Boeing 747-2B3B (SCD)
2 Boeing 747-2B3F (SCD)
3 McDonnell Douglas DC-8-55F

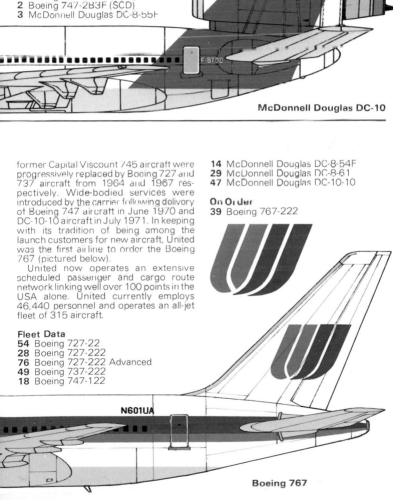

McDonnell Douglas DC-10

former Capital Viscount 745 aircraft were progressively replaced by Boeing 727 and 737 aircraft from 1964 and 1967 respectively. Wide-bodied services were introduced by the carrier following delivery of Boeing 747 aircraft in June 1970 and DC-10-10 aircraft in July 1971. In keeping with its tradition of being among the launch customers for new aircraft, United was the first airline to order the Boeing 767 (pictured below).

United now operates an extensive scheduled passenger and cargo route network linking well over 100 points in the USA alone. United currently employs 46,440 personnel and operates an all-jet fleet of 315 aircraft.

14 McDonnell Douglas DC-8-54F
29 McDonnell Douglas DC-8-61
47 McDonnell Douglas DC-10-10

On Order
39 Boeing 767-222

Fleet Data
54 Boeing 727-22
28 Boeing 727-222
76 Boeing 727-222 Advanced
49 Boeing 737-222
18 Boeing 747-122

Boeing 767

USAir

USAir was formed on 5 March 1937 under the name of All-American Aviation. The carrier was the first to be certificated by the former Civil Aeronautics Board following the passage of the Civil Aeronautics Act in 1938, and began a specialised "pick-up" air mail service to isolated communities without adequate airport facilities. By 1949 adequate airports had been constructed in a number of cities on the carrier's pick-up routes and on 7 March of that year passenger services were inaugurated from Pittsburgh to Washington D.C. and Atlantic City, and later to New York, Buffalo and Cincinnati, using DC-3 aircraft. With the introduction of passenger operations, the carrier changed its name to All-American Airways. The title was changed again in 1953 to Allegheny Airlines Inc. Route development in the eastern states continued and by 1959 Allegheny's system extended from Boston in the east to Cleveland and Detroit in the west. The DC-3 aircraft were initially replaced by Martin 202s and later by Convair 340 and 440 aircraft. In 1963 Allegheny relocated its principal operations and maintenance base from Washington D.C. to Pittsburgh.

After an initial operation with five Napier Eland-powered Convair 540s, the carrier undertook a programme from mid-1965 to late 1967 to convert its fleet to all turbine-powered aircraft using the Allison 501 turboprop. Fairchild F-27J aircraft were also added to the fleet from November 1965 and pure jet operations were inaugurated in July 1966 with a leased DC-9-31. In July 1968 Allegheny merged with Indianapolis-based Lake Central Airlines. Further rapid growth was enhanced by a merger with Mohawk Airlines of Utica in April 1972. Mohawk operated in the eastern seaboard states, and also to eastern Canada. By mid-1978 the carrier had become an all-jet operator. Former United 727-22 aircraft were acquired during 1978 and with the passage of the Airline Deregulation Act, Allegheny added routes

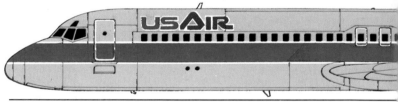

Varig

Varig (Viacao Aerea Rio Grandense), the national carrier of Brazil, was founded on 7 May 1927 with technical assistance provided by the German-backed Kondor Syndikat, and proceeded to develop domestic services within the Rio Grande do Sul. Service to Montevideo began in August 1942, and Lockheed 10A Electras were acquired in 1943 inaugurating service to Rio de Janeiro via Florianopolis, Curitiba and São Paulo. The acquisition of Aero Geral in late 1951 gave Varig access to routes north of Rio de Janeiro for the first time. Buenos Aires was added to the network in the following year, and on 2 August 1955 Varig's first Super Constellation inaugurated services to New York.

Convair 240 and Curtiss-Commander C-46 aircraft began operations on Varig's domestic routes and jet services were started with Caravelle IIIs on the New York route from 19 December 1959. Boeing 707-441 aircraft were delivered in 1960 and began services on the New York route on 2 July of that year. In August 1961 Varig obtained a controlling interest in the REAL Aerovias airline consortium. REAL was founded in February 1946 and had become the largest operator in South America through a series of mergers and take-overs, operating a very extensive domestic network as well as international services to a number of destinations. REAL's route system and aircraft fleet were progressively integrated with those of Varig, and in 1965 the route network and aircraft of the bankrupt Panair do Brasil were also acquired. Additional routes to Europe and to Johannesburg and Lagos were subsequently opened and wide-bodied services with DC-10-30s commenced in 1974. The Foundation of Employees (the owners of Varig, and nowadays known as the Ruben Berta Foundation) acquired control of Cruzeiro do Sul in May 1975. The two carriers maintain separate identities but have combined schedules to avoid duplication.

In addition to a 34 point network within Brazil, Varig currently serves 62 foreign

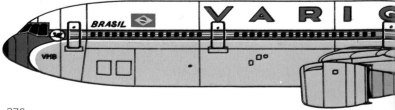

to Arizona, Florida, Louisiana, North Carolina and Alabama. The carrier adopted its new title, USAir Inc in 1979.

USAir currently operates a scheduled route network providing services to over 70 cities in 25 states situated in the north eastern and mid western regions of the United States. USAir employs approximately 10,400 people and operates a fleet of over 90 jet aircraft which carried 14,212,764 passengers in 1980. USAir has retained its responsibility to serve the smaller and intermediate-sized cities through the establishment in 1967 of the unique Allegheny Commuter programme. Allegheny Commuter service is provided under the terms of an agreement with USAir and is operated by eleven independent operators using a combined fleet of over 75 aircraft, ranging from the Beech 99 to the de Havilland Dash 7, to feed into major USAir hubs. Over 2·6 million passengers were carried by the commuters during 1980 of which over 30% interlined with USAir.

Fleet Data

- **10** BAe (BAC) One-Eleven 203AE
- **14** BAe (BAC) One-Eleven 204AF
- **3** BAe (BAC) One-Eleven 215AU
- **10** Boeing 727-22
- **1** Boeing 727-22C
- **5** Boeing 727-2B7 Advanced
- **66** McDonnell Douglas DC-9-31
- **2** McDonnell Douglas DC-9-32

On Order

- **15** Boeing 737-200
- **10** Boeing 737-300

McDonnell Douglas DC-9

---

destinations throughout Central and South America, and in the USA, Europe, Africa and Asia. A total of 4,442,469 passengers were carried by the airline in 1980 of whom 1,702,230 were flown on the Rio de Janeiro-São Paulo "Punta Aerea" air shuttle service. Varig currently employs 16,722 personnel.

Fleet Data

- **2** Airbus Industrie A300B4-203
- **1** Boeing 707-320C
- **1** Boeing 707-323C
- **5** Boeing 707-324C
- **1** Boeing 707-341C
- **2** Boeing 707-345C
- **1** Boeing 707-379C
- **1** Boeing 707-385C
- **1** Boeing 727-30C
- **4** Boeing 727-41
- **2** Boeing 727-95
- **1** Boeing 727-172C
- **2** Boeing 727-173C
- **10** Boeing 737-241 Advanced
- **3** Boeing 747-2L5B (SCD)

- **10** Lockheed L-188A Electra
- **2** Lockheed L-188CF Electra
- **12** McDonnell Douglas DC-10-30 (two leased from SIA)

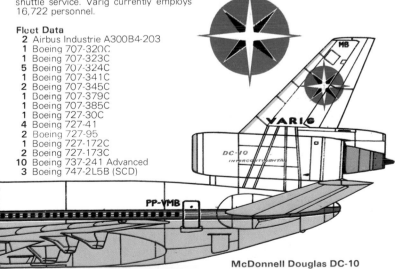

McDonnell Douglas DC-10

VIASA

VIASA (Venezolana Internacional de Aviacion SA) was created in January 1961 by Aerovias Venezolanas (Avensa) and Linea Aeropostal Venezolana (LAV) to take over the international routes operated by both Venezuelan carriers. Avensa was formed in 1943, and started domestic passenger services in 1944, followed by international services in June 1955. LAV was formed in 1933 when the government decided to nationalise the Venezuelan branch of the French Compagnie Générale Aéropostale which had been operating since 1929. Due to the financial requirements associated with the procurement of competitive jet equipment, the Venezuelan government encouraged Avensa and LAV to form VIASA to operate international services on their behalf, with Avensa holding 45% of the shares and LAV holding the balance.

VIASA commenced operations with Super Constellation and DC-6B aircraft acquired from its parent companies, and on 8 August 1961 the carrier began jet services to the USA with Convair 880 aircraft which had previously been on order for Avensa. Close co-operation was established with KLM, and DC-8 aircraft were leased from the Dutch airline which enabled VIASA to operate jet services from Caracas to Amsterdam via Paris and London from 6 April 1961.

VIASA acquired its own DC-8-53 aircraft in 1965, and in December 1971 an agreement was reached with KLM and Iberia for joint operation of the central Atlantic routes using Boeing 747 aircraft. VIASA currently operates scheduled passenger services from Caracas and Maracaibo across the Atlantic to Las Palmas, Lisbon,

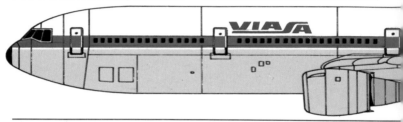

Western Airlines

Western Airlines (WAL) was incorporated on 13 July 1925 as Western Air Express (WAE) and is the oldest US carrier. Operations began with air mail services between Los Angeles and Salt Lake City via Las Vegas on 17 April 1926 using Douglas M-2 aircraft. Passenger services on the route began on 23 May of that year, and this represented the first scheduled passenger service in the USA. By early 1930 WAE had taken over Colorado Airways, Pacific Marine Airways, West Coast Air Transport and Standard Air Lines. On 16 July of that year, under pressure from the Postmaster General, WAE merged with Transcontinental Air Transport to form TWA in order to gain the mail contract for the Los Angeles-Kansas City section of the transcontinental route which had previously been flown by both airlines. In 1934 WAE was bought out from TWA and operated for a while as General Air Lines. On 17 April 1941 the carrier officially changed its title to Western Airlines. By this time Boeing 247-D and DC-3 aircraft had been acquired, and

National Parks Airways been absorbed. Services on the carrier's old Los Angeles-San Francisco route were restarted in 1944 and extended to Portland and Seattle in 1947. DC-4 aircraft entered service in January 1946 and Convair 240s commenced operations in September 1948. Western became the first operator of the DC-6B on 11 April 1951.

The first of twelve Lockheed Electra turboprops flew on the Los Angeles-Seattle route in August 1959, and jet services were inaugurated on 1 June 1960 with Boeing 707-139 aircraft leased from the manufacturer prior to delivery of the carrier's first Boeing 720-047Bs in April 1961. Western received its Boeing 727-247 aircraft from October 1969 to replace the Electras. On 1 July 1967 Seattle-based Pacific Northern Airlines (PNA) was merged into Western. Founded in 1932 as Woodley Airways, PNA operated services linking southern Alaska with Washington State and Oregon. Western commenced wide-bodied operations following delivery of its first DC-10-10 in April 1973. Service

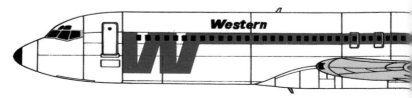

Madrid, Milan, Rome, Paris, Frankfurt, London and Amsterdam, and to New York, Miami, Washington, Mexico City, San José, Panama City, Bogota, Cali, Quito, Lima, Rio de Janeiro, Buenos Aires, Curacao, Santo Domingo, San Juan, Port of Spain and Barbados in North, Central and South America and the Caribbean. The Venezuelan Government has a 75% shareholding in the carrier with Avensa holding the remaining 25%. VIASA employs approximately 1,800 personnel.

Fleet Data
2 McDonnell Douglas DC-8-53
2 McDonnell Douglas DC-8-63
1 McDonnell Douglas DC-8-63CF
6 McDonnell Douglas DC-10-30

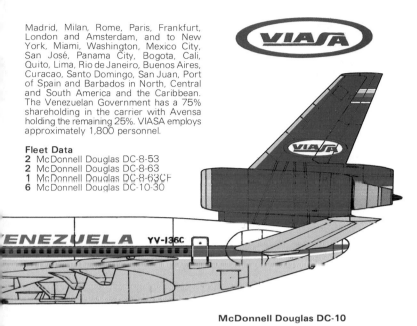

McDonnell Douglas DC-10

---

between London and Honolulu via Anchorage was inaugurated in October 1980 but was terminated a year later. However, Western inaugurated a Denver-London service on 24 April 1981 with a former Air New Zealand DC-10-30.

Western, headquartered in Los Angeles, currently operates scheduled passenger and cargo services to 33 destinations in the USA (including Honolulu and Anchorage), to several points in Canada, Mexico and to London. 9,130,000 passengers flew with Western in 1980 and the carrier employs 10,657 personnel.

Fleet Data
6 Boeing 727-247
40 Boeing 727-247 Advanced
1 Boeing 727-208 Advanced
(leased from Interlease)
11 Boeing 737-247
10 McDonnell Douglas DC-10-10
1 McDonnell Douglas DC-10-30
(leased from Interlease)

On Order
6 Boeing 767-247

Boeing 727

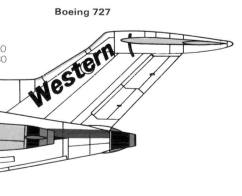

OTHER SUPER-VALUE AVIATION GUIDES IN THIS SERIES......

AN ILLUSTRATED GUIDE TO

ALLIED FIGHTERS OF WORLD WAR II

160 fact-packed pages in colour
Descriptions of over 40 aircraft types, plus many variants

Over 110 photographs, many in colour
More than 120 detailed line drawings
Over 60 colour drawings

Bill Gunston

AN ILLUSTRATED GUIDE TO

BOMBERS OF WORLD WAR II

160 fact-packed pages in colour
Descriptions of well over 50 aircraft types, plus many variants

More than 140 detailed line drawings
90 dramatic photographs, many in colour
Over 40 colour drawings

Bill Gunston

AN ILLUSTRATED GUIDE TO

GERMAN, ITALIAN AND JAPANESE FIGHTERS OF WORLD WAR II

Major Fighters and Attack Aircraft of the Axis Powers

160 fact-packed pages in colour
Descriptions of well over 50 aircraft types, plus many variants

120 dramatic photographs, many in colour
More than 180 detailed line drawings
Over 50 colour drawings

Bill Gunston

AN ILLUSTRATED GUIDE TO

MODERN FIGHTERS AND ATTACK AIRCRAFT

Fact-packed descriptions of 50 of the world's most exciting warplanes

120 action photographs most in full colour
160 line drawings
34 superb colour profiles

Bill Gunston

AN ILLUSTRATED GUIDE TO

MILITARY HELICOPTERS

Full-colour directory of combat rotorcraft

51 aircraft described in 160 fact-packed pages
More than 100 superb action photographs, most in colour
21 detailed colour profiles, 51 three-view drawings

Bill Gunston

AN ILLUSTRATED GUIDE TO

THE AIR WAR IN VIETNAM

Aircraft of the Southeast Asia Conflict

160 fact-packed, fully illustrated pages in colour
Descriptions of more than 80 aircraft types, plus many variants

More than 140 dramatic photographs, many in colour
Over 120 accurately detailed line drawings and 15 colour profiles

Bernard C. Nalty
George M. Watson Jacob Neufeld

OTHER ILLUSTRATED MILITARY GUIDES NOW AVAILABLE....

Modern Soviet Air Force
Modern Submarines
Modern Tanks
Modern US Air Force
Modern Warships
Pistols and Revolvers
Rifles and Sub-Machine Guns
World War II Tanks

* Each has 160 fact-filled pages
* Each is colourfully illustrated with hundreds of action photographs and technical drawings
* Each contains concisely presented data and accurate descriptions of major international weapons
* Each represents tremendous value

Further titles in this series are in preparation
Your military library will be incomplete without them.

PRINTED IN BELGIUM BY

proost
INTERNATIONAL BOOK PRODUCTION